The PAN and Democratic Change

David A. Shirk

BOULDER
LONDON

Published in the United States of America in 2005 by
Lynne Rienner Publishers, Inc.
1800 30th Street, Boulder, Colorado 80301
www.rienner.com

and in the United Kingdom by
Lynne Rienner Publishers, Inc.
3 Henrietta Street, Covent Garden, London WC2E 8LU

Library of Congress Cataloging-in-Publication Data
Shirk, David A., 1971–
Mexico's new politics : the PAN and democratic change / David A. Shirk.
p. cm.
Includes bibliographical references and index.
ISBN 1-58826-294-4 (hardcover : alk. paper) — ISBN 1-58826-270-7 (paperback : alk. paper) 1. Partido Acción Nacional (Mexico) 2. Mexico—Politics and government. I. Title.
JL1298.A23S55 2004
320.972—dc22

2004014910

British Cataloguing in Publication Data
A Cataloguing in Publication record for this book is available from the British Library.

Printed and bound in the United States of America

∞ The paper used in this publication meets the requirements of the American National Standard for Permanence of Paper for Printed Library Materials Z39.48-1992.

5 4 3 2 1

Contents

Tables and Figures

Tables

Figures

Preface

We remember, because the past has an irreplaceable value of experience that Mexico should not lose, because it is necessary to avoid the . . . false generosity of memory lapse, because the present is not understood without that past which penetrates and conditions it.

—Manuel Gómez Morin, PAN's founder, 1941

I will never forget a conversation I had with a few friends in Puebla, Mexico, nearly ten years prior to writing this book. The events of the 1994 presidential election unfolded before us in a cramped apartment room illuminated only by a television, candles, and the kind of earnest discussion so often fueled by the warmth of a bottle of wine. Naturally, the topic centered on Mexican politics and our respective predictions for its future. At that time I made the rather vague and unsubstantiated observation that the best hope for democracy in Mexico rested in the hands of the National Action Party (Partido Acción Nacional, PAN). I had just completed my first graduate classes at the University of California, San Diego, so I was speaking from the vantage of sheer ignorance. Yet, it seemed to me that out of all Mexico's parties, the PAN had the least number of strikes against it and was the best prepared to take on the ruling Revolutionary Institutional Party (Partido Revolucionario Institucional, PRI). Had I been hardened by a few more years of observing Mexican political reality, I would have believed otherwise. But then, the PRI had governed Mexico for more than sixty years, using a highly successful combination of patronage, corruption, graft, and electoral manipulation. It was, in effect, the world's largest and most prodigious political machine. Anyone who knew anything about Mexican politics knew that the PRI was unbeatable.

Back in the United States after the 1994 Mexican elections, I gradually cast aside my other scholarly interests in East Asia and Russia, and Mexico became my obsession. I fell under the influence of prominent Mexico scholars, such as Wayne Cornelius, Ann Craig, Peter Smith, Kevin Middlebrook, Eric Van Young, Van Whiting, and dozens of rising stars who passed through the doors of the Center for U.S.-Mexican Studies at the University of California in San Diego. One of them, a bright young undergrad named Cynthia Álvarez, had recently conducted field research in Baja California that sparked my interest in the changes occurring just a few miles south of San Diego. Later, in 1996, I initiated my own field research in Ensenada, the sleepy Baja California port city that launched the political career of Ernesto Ruffo, the PAN's first governor in 1988. There I began to understand the true potential of the PAN, and the reasons why it presented the best possible hope for bringing democracy to Mexico.

My first conversation with a real live Panista gave me some clues. Jesus "Chuy" del Palacio LaFontaine served as Ensenada's second PAN mayor (1988–1992). This conversation taught me three things about the PAN that piqued my curiosity. First, del Palacio impressed me with his own personal story. He was a successful local businessman, one of a handful in Ensenada who suddenly launched their political careers in the early 1980s after years of disinterest in politics. Second, his zeal for listing his administration's many concrete achievements—new lights, new streets—with a seemingly endless number of statistics showed me the kind of go-getter mentality that characterized this new generation of PAN activists. These were men of action who wanted to see measurable results. And with their help, PAN actually seemed to be accomplishing tangible benefits for its constituents. With his emphasis on classic themes of good governance, such as accountability and transparency in public administration, del Palacio revealed a commitment to a political ideology that sounded reminiscent of the progressive reform movement that transformed U.S. politics starting in the 1920s and 1930s.

Third, del Palacio—then the head of the local party organization—handed me a list of the PAN's registered members in Ensenada, complete with phone numbers and addresses. He told me to give anyone a call. This simply floored me. Earlier interviews with representatives from the local PRI had failed to yield the most mundane information; they even refused to tell me how many members they had, despite newspaper reports I had read about a recent party census. They rejected interviews without prior written authorization from higher-ups. In short, local PRI members showed me that studying a political machine would be much more difficult than studying their reform-minded opponents. The PAN promised to be a rich source of data and presented an intriguing dilemma. Could these modern-day progressive reformers truly transform Mexican politics?

Dozens of interviews later, my research took me deeper into Mexico. A few weeks in Mexico City conversing with national party leaders and knowledgeable PAN experts such as Yemile Mizrahi and Juan Molinar made it clear that the PAN would make a great subject for my research. However, I needed to expand my knowledge of the party's experience in its other political bastions. In early 1997, I headed to León, Guanajuato, in the heart of what I like to call Mexico's "Bible Belt." Five months of field research there gave me insights into the place where PAN's founder, Manuel Gómez Morin, spent his youth and gave me access to prominent PAN leaders such as then governor Vicente Fox and his predecessor, Carlos Medina Plascencia, the state's first PAN governor. Short trips from León to the state capitals of Guanajuato, Guadalajara, Puebla, and Mexico City gave me a chance to evaluate the PAN's efforts elsewhere in Central Mexico, both successful and unsuccessful.

Later, driving on to Yucatán, I spent five more months learning about the conservative party's efforts to make inroads in the impoverished south. The state capital of Mérida was home to such nationally prominent party leaders as former PAN president Carlos Castillo Peraza and Ana Rosa Payán. Governed by hard-line political boss Victor Cervera Pacheco, who ran the state as his personal fiefdom, Yucatán gave me a glimpse of the "old days," when a handful of *ilusos* (dreamers) struggled against the overwhelming might of the PRI. I spent the next two years on both sides of the U.S.-Mexican border, where I returned to study Baja California and the "most visited city in the world," Tijuana. The insights I gained there taught me not only about the PAN, but about life along the border and the complex relationship between Mexico and the United States.

In the end, these travels devoured two transmissions, a radiator, a bumper, a front corner panel, two sets of tires, and chalked up over 100,000 miles on my 1987 Dodge Omni. In 1999, I gave up on the Omni and traded up for a 1988 Nissan pickup truck. However, I continued to follow the PAN, which to me seemed poised to go the distance. At that point, Vicente Fox was widely recognized as the strongest opposition candidate in the race for Mexico's presidency, but few thought Fox could actually topple the PRI. Indeed, almost no one outside the PAN believed this enough to stake his or her professional reputation on the claim. Hence, Fox's victory took Mexico and the world by storm and left many unanswered questions about the candidate and the political party that managed to bring democracy to Mexico. How did the PAN come into being, and why was its candidate able to defeat the powerful PRI? Most important, what did the future hold for Mexico in the wake of the PAN and Fox's triumph? This book attempts to address these and related questions.

* * *

I would not have been able to write this book without the guidance and support of many people, including all of the individuals mentioned above. My research received the generous support of the UC-MEXUS Foundation; the National Science Foundation Fellowship for Minorities; the Office of the Dean of Social Sciences at the University of California, San Diego; and the University of California's Presidential Fellowship for Minorities. Much of the work on the book was made possible through a fellowship from the Center for U.S.-Mexican Studies at the University of California, San Diego. I am also deeply indebted to the Instituto Tecnológico Autónomo de México, California State University–San Marcos, the Center for U.S.-Mexican Studies, San Diego Dialogue, Soka University of America, and the University of California, San Diego, for financial assistance and opportunities to do research and teaching related to my work.

The guidance of colleagues at these and other institutions was both invaluable and inestimable, given the many conversations and interactions that shaped my understanding of Mexican politics in so many ways. I would especially like to acknowledge the direction, support, and encouragement of my dissertation committee cochairs, Ann Craig and Wayne Cornelius, and committee members Amy Bridges, Steven Erie, Steph Haggard, and Chris Woodruff. I thank them for suffering through wild tangents, multiple drafts, missing page numbers, and often inscrutable grammar to provide sage advice and constructive criticism. While each of these six people proved extraordinarily generous with their time and patience, I must express special appreciation and admiration for Ann Craig, an exceptionally conscientious adviser, mentor, and friend from the beginning of my graduate studies.

This is an exciting time in Mexican history, and my research included stimulating conversations and interactions with many interesting and exciting persons in Mexico and the United States. First, I must thank the staff, activists, and leaders of the Partido Acción Nacional who contributed so much to this project and to their cause. They are too numerous to mention here, but wherever possible their names, contributions, and stories are acknowledged in the text and notes. (As this book goes to print, I am somewhat saddened to report that two of my favorite PAN members, "Chuy" del Palacio and Karla de la Peña, have distanced themselves from the party that they inspired me to study.) Also, I thank the many political activists and government officials who made their perspectives available to me.

I am also heavily indebted to numerous colleagues and friends who have in some way contributed valuable input to my research at multiple stages of its development. In particular, my research and writing were greatly enriched by discussions, comments, criticisms, mentoring, and other assistance from John Bailey, Kathleen Bruhn, Enrique Cabrero, Roderic Camp, Lucila Casares, Esperanza Garcia, Alain and Claudia de Remes, Emily Edmonds, Victor Espinoza Valle, Federico Estevez, Richard Feinberg, John and Lisa Fletcher,

Carolina Gómez, Judy Harper, Tania Hernández, Jane Hindley, Alan Houston, Daniel Kaufman, Joe Klesner, Chappell Lawson, Mona Lyne, Eric Magar, Victor Magagna, Kevin Middlebrook, Yemile Mizrahi, Juan Molinar, Enrique Montalvo Ortega, Oscar Moya, Antonio Ortíz Mena, Charles Nathanson, Esperanza Reyes, Luis Miguel Rionda, Gaspar and Shannon Rivera, Victoria Rodríguez, Karina Romero, Marc Rosenblum and Katie Sellers, David Samuels, Matthew Shugart, Kaare Strom, Luis Tucker, Maria and Guadalupe Valencia, Eric Van Young, Flor Villegas, Peter Ward, Jeff Weldon, Tom and Olivia Webber, Jeff Wright, and Steve Wuhs.

Two colleagues in particular, Todd Eisenstadt and Kenneth Greene, provided special encouragement and access to contacts and data without which this project would not have been completed. My colleagues in the Political Science Department of the University of San Diego welcomed and accommodated me in many ways in the final stages of drafting, for which I am much indebted. I also thank two of my favorite students, Jacqueline Shiroma and Monica Ohtsuka, for valuable research assistance and transcription. I am very grateful to Lynne Rienner, Shena Redmond, Kathy Hamman, the editorial staff, and two anonymous reviewers for their patience, skillful editorial assistance, and useful recommendations on this book. Needless to say, any flaws, omissions, or misjudgments are purely my own responsibility.

Last, I thank my wonderful family and friends, whose support and understanding helped me to maintain perspective on life. I am especially grateful for my grandfather's gentle editorial guidance, my siblings' thoughtfulness and generosity, and the steadfast love and support of my parents, Tom and Carole Shirk. I also thank the many friends who hosted me, fed me, entertained me, gave me shelter, and in many other small ways shared their friendship and kindness. Appreciation is inevitably due to the ever faithful Tosca, my canine traveling companion from day one of the long drive to Mexico and back. Final recognition and gratitude are due to Alexandra Webber, the woman whose patience, caring, and encouragement enabled me to write this book and to whom I dedicate it with my love.

1

Introduction: Mexico's Democratization and the Rise of the PAN

The tyrants will tremble at hearing our call: A generous country and a life with honor! . . . May the disgrace end now! . . . It is the hour to fight! Our Mexico should be, with justice and liberty, a country for all and a protector of the ideal.

—Hymn of the National Action Party[1]

Mexico's July 2, 2000, presidential election was widely hailed as the triumph of democracy and the coming of a new era in Mexican politics. The victory of Vicente Fox, candidate of the National Action Party (Partido Acción Nacional, PAN) brought bountiful expectations of a new and better future. At that moment, Mexico seemed full of possibility and promise. Gone were decades of corrupt and authoritarian rule by the septuagenarian Institutional Revolutionary Party (Partido Revolucionario Institucional, PRI), a seemingly invincible party machine that one Mexico expert appropriately labeled Mexico's "Goliath."[2] Like the giant Philistine of biblical lore, the PRI was felled by an unlikely opponent who delivered Mexico into a new era of free and fair competition. Suddenly, or so it seemed, votes actually counted, and elections really mattered. For decades, observers had waited for such a milestone, but now it was obvious that things had changed in Mexico.

If not for this momentous event, however, the casual observer might have easily missed Mexico's democratization. Prior to Fox's victory, scholars had long debated whether Mexico's political system was a "perfect" authoritarian regime or an "imperfect" democracy. Gradually, by the 1990s, experts cautiously began to describe Mexico as a country "in transition" to democracy. While democracy was hardly a certain or proximate outcome, scholars looked anxiously for signs that Mexico was indeed progressing toward that end. In attempting to identify a clear "watershed" event for the Mexican transition, many scholars focused on the presidential elections of 1988, the first national election in which the PRI faced serious challenges from both the right and left of the ideological spectrum.[3] Subsequently, others focused on the 1995–1996 political reforms and the loss of the PRI majority in the lower house of the legislature in the midterm elections of 1997 as key episodes in Mexico's transition to democracy.[4] Since then, the 2000 elections have been widely heralded as the quintessential and definitive moment of Mexico's transition.

Yet, the foundations of Mexican authoritarianism began to erode well before these events. The synchronicity of decades of macroeconomic restructuring, hard-won political reforms, vigilant civic activism, and careful strategizing by the PRI's political rivals all helped to break the ruling party's lock on power. As a result of these efforts, candidates from opposition parties began to win more seats in state and national legislatures beginning in the 1960s and 1970s, gradually bringing greater legislative autonomy and allowing opposition legislators to impact the political process. Further gains were made at the subnational level in the 1980s and 1990s, as municipal and state governments became footholds for the opposition and began to obtain real fiscal and political independence from the federal government. The entire political system was strengthened in the 1990s, through reforms to the electoral process and the judiciary that brought more effective oversight and protections to promote the rule of law. All along, the courageous demonstration of political activism by ordinary citizens challenged PRI authoritarianism and kept the promise of democracy alive.

The protracted transition to democracy in Mexico proved more significant for the PAN than for any other opposition party. As Mexico's oldest surviving opposition party, the PAN was founded in 1939 by a small coalition of entrepreneurs, religious activists, and professionals who were opposed to growing state interventionism, anticlericism, and the semiauthoritarian practices of the ruling party.[5] The party struggled for decades without significant political gains, and was widely—if sometimes unfairly—perceived as a reactionary and even counter-revolutionary force in Mexican politics.[6] The PAN and other opposition parties made intermittent progress by wresting concessions from the PRI, fighting for additional political spaces and fairer electoral results. Still, while it was the largest and most prominent opposition party, the PAN remained a far distant second to the PRI well into the 1980s. Indeed, in 1987, the PAN controlled only 18 of the nation's roughly 2,400 local governments and governed fewer than 1 percent of the Mexican people. In presidential elections, the PAN had averaged just below 14 percent of the vote from its first formal presidential campaign in 1952 through the 1994 election. Even in 1994, when PAN presidential candidate Diego Fernández de Cevallos achieved an all-time high of 25.8 percent of the national vote, the PAN's share of the national vote was still barely more than half of the 50.3 percent officially claimed by the PRI in that same election.

However, the tide gradually began to turn for the PAN, as significant gains were made in the late 1980s and early 1990s. Thanks to significant political reforms and the party's own efforts, the number of directly elected PAN legislators in the Chamber of Deputies (Cámara de Diputados), the lower house of the Mexican legislature, doubled, from 9 to 18, while the number of PAN legislators elected to the same body through proportional representation nearly quadrupled, from 32 to 119. By 1997, the number of PAN mayors increased to 223, and the party had placed six state governors in office. Such seemingly minute state and local advances obscured the fact that the party was winning contests in several of the most populous and vibrant urban centers in Mexico. After just ten years, these PAN mayors and state governors increased the party's tiny fraction of political control eventually to govern over roughly one-third of Mexico's entire population. Though for several decades official figures deliberately obscured its actual electoral strength, the gradual accumulation of PAN victories during the 1980s and the explosion of such victories in the 1990s demonstrated the true political potential of Mexico's oldest surviving opposition party. This sweeping undercurrent of subnational successes laid the foundations for the party's success in 2000.

More important, the PAN's electoral success had begun to make a real difference in transforming Mexican politics. For the citizens who elected the PAN to power at the municipal and eventually the state level, the party's "opposition governments" brought innovative approaches to public administration, fierce advocacy of subnational governmental autonomy, improvements in the provision of public works and services that were long overdue, and created new expectations with regard to the conduct of both government officials and average citizens.[7] Meanwhile, for the activists and leaders of the party itself, the PAN's victories were accompanied by unprecedented growth and organizational development, an urgent demand to fill and effectively administer previously inaccessible government positions, as well as the challenge of cultivating (rather than criticizing) the relationships between party and government. Over the course of a decade, the most troublesome problems facing the PAN changed from those of winning and defending the party's electoral victories to those of learning to govern and to manage the party's own organizational development.

Understanding the Rise of the PAN

Studies typically compartmentalize the activities of political parties according to the distinction made by V. O. Key (1942), who described three separate spheres of party life: party as organization, party in the electorate, and party in government.[8] However, in most cases, scholars tend to focus primarily on only one of these categories or to give too little attention to the relationship among them. This has also been the case with respect to the PAN. As the PAN's candidates racked up successes in the 1980s and 1990s, scholars were much more preoccupied with the political entrepreneurs for whom the party became a vehicle and the challenges faced by the governments of the opposition than with the influence of the PAN as a party organization. Fresh faces were a novelty in the Mexican political system, long described as a "living museum." Hence, the new businesspeople who began to take center stage in the PAN and political observers focused intensely on the political and technical challenges they faced as electoral novices, serving at the helm of local governments. In short, few scholars focused on the PAN as an organization because there were more pressing questions to be asked.

Furthermore, relatively little work had been done to follow up on pioneering studies of the party from the 1970s, notably the outstanding work of U.S. scholars Mabry (1973a) and Von Sauer (1974). Hence, correspondingly little was known about what transpired in the PAN in the critical years following these studies, when the party suffered a significant internal breakdown in 1976 and was forced to restructure its priorities. Gradually, new studies emerged to analyze the PAN's newfound success from the inside out, particularly as the party's electoral fortunes improved over the course of the 1990s. At that time, inspired Mexican scholars—notably Carlos Arriola (1988, 1994), Soledad Loaeza (1999), and Yemile Mizrahi (2003)—began to fill the void.[9] U.S. scholars gradually joined the effort, as Vikram Chand (2001), Kevin Middlebrook (2001), and Victoria Rodríguez and Peter Ward (1994) provided useful case studies of the PAN's struggle for democracy in Mexico. These studies all greatly advanced scholarly understanding of the PAN and its evolution as a party.

This book similarly seeks to fill the long-standing, significant gaps in our empirical understanding of the PAN and also offers new perspectives on recent Mexican history and politics. It is important to note that this book is different from other contemporary studies of political parties—and even many other accounts of the PAN experience—in that it consistently focuses on the evolution of the party through competing groups, as well as philosophical currents, within the party and emphasizes the subnational challenges and opportunities of the party. Throughout the telling of this story, the book provides valuable insights for understanding the challenges of party-building in an authoritarian regime and lessons for those hoping to adjust to the realities of Mexico's new democratic politics, where internal party dynamics and subnational impulses will play an important role in shaping the future.

While several key questions are incumbent on this inquiry, foremost on most readers' minds will be two questions. Why was the PAN able to defeat the seemingly undefeatable PRI? And why were so few observers able to anticipate the PAN's victory? The answer to the second question is inherent in the first. Frankly, it was a fairly safe bet that the PRI would win in 2000. The PRI was the longest lasting and most effective political machine of the twentieth century, and, despite significant setbacks suffered in the 1990s, the ruling party presented a formidable electoral challenge to any aspiring rival. In brief, the PRI had ample human and financial resources, a larger share of the professed party identification among voters, and an experienced, popularly nominated candidate. Moreover, given a strong economy and relative satisfaction with its incumbent administration, it seemed probable that the PRI could win even without resorting to massive vote fraud or other electoral chicanery. Not surprisingly, few pundits or scholars dared to predict that the PRI would fall; hardly anyone was willing to stake his or her professional reputation on the claim. Indeed, previous research conducted by the few PAN scholars mentioned above gave little indication that a PAN victory was imminent in 2000. It was, therefore, perhaps youthful folly or sheer idealism that attracted me to the PAN and ultimately led to my belief that a PAN victory was possible, and indeed, probable.

The key question, of course, remains why? Why was the PAN able to do what many believed impossible and only a few dared to dream? Was the PAN's victory the result of a sudden electoral realignment in Mexico, a massive conservative shift to the right by Mexican voters? Or was this a triumph of a broad-based coalition of the opposition of the kind that brought victory to the "Solidarity" movement in Poland and an end to Augusto Pinochet's regime in Chile? At the time of the election, Fox's campaign rhetoric and supporters certainly tried to suggest the latter, though many PAN leaders and activists might have preferred to believe the former. In my view, any explanation for the rise of the PAN—from its birth in 1939 to its unexpected triumph in 2000—requires a thorough examination of the complexities of party organizational development, as well as some inquiry into the relationship between parties and their external political environment. Understanding this connection is the key to explaining how the PAN came to power in 2000, the obstacles the party faces in the aftermath of its success, and how Mexico's new political game will be played for the foreseeable future.

Children of Democracy: Party-Building and Mexico's New Political Context

Political parties are undoubtedly important, if not essential, to the functioning of democracy. Indeed, Max Weber, arguably the father of modern social science, once described parties as the "children of democracy." Democracies give birth to political parties, and they are fundamental to democratic politics because they serve as vehicles for electoral competition and mechanisms to promote collaboration within government. In the electorate, parties facilitate the coordination, expression, and representation of societal preferences. In government, they function as advocates of policy and provide a basis for cooperation among their members, all the while working to inform and mobilize the public. Yet parties, as political organizations, are frequently misunderstood creatures. Too often their behavior and performance are explained in terms of their external context. That is, political observers tend to focus more often on the rules and constraints that parties face and on the competition between and among them than on what happens inside political parties. Indeed, only rarely do we catch a glimpse of what goes on behind the scenes to understand the internal logic (or illogic) that makes parties behave as they do. This makes it difficult to answer the question of when and how some parties change their strategies and why others fail to do so.

Following the example of recent scholarship in the United States, I argue that these internal dynamics—particularly the competing coalitions and internal rules and regulations of a party—play a determining role in setting the ultimate course of party behavior and organizational development. Notably, I subscribe to John Aldrich's (1995) "new institutionalist" view that parties must be understood as institutions whose "endogenous" or internal characteristics provide salient insights into their behavior. That is, while changes in a party's "exogenous" environment certainly shape its incentives and opportunity structures, the actions and decisions of political actors operating *within* a party organization are equally critical to explaining party behavior. This view was not always considered relevant. In fact, while some of the earliest studies of political parties focused explicitly on internal party dynamics, most conventional approaches treat the political party as a "black box" that merely responds reflexively to the irresistible influences of external stimuli.[10]

Consider early explanations for the development of the permanent, professional, and mass-incorporating electoral organizations known as "mass" parties. Beginning in the nineteenth century, such organizations gradually displaced the more sporadic and relatively informal "clubs of notables" that represented elite interests in many European legislatures. Rather than relying on the political connections and assets of wealthy elites, mass parties engaged and mobilized newly enfranchised voters. Most explanations for this transformation focused on external contextual factors: the reshaping of socioeconomic cleavages over the course of the industrial revolution,[11] the expansion of participatory institutions that empowered common citizens by extending the franchise to previously excluded groups,[12] the emergence of democratic ideologies,[13] and the "contagious" spread of new, competitive strategies in the nineteenth and early twentieth centuries.[14]

Later, as observers tried to explain the post–World War II replacement of the "mass" party—the very icon of modern democratic politics for some scholars—by alternative forms of organization and electoral competition in the late twentieth century, the focus remained on external variables. In such explanations, observers emphasized the decline of class cleavages;[15] new institutional provisions for campaign finance and candidate selection;[16] the decline of class-based ideological divisions in the postwar era; the proliferation of media technologies—especially the rise of a new god, television—in popular culture;[17] and the competitive advantages of stylized, candidate-centered campaigns.[18] In other words, most explanations for party organizational development or decline have focused primarily on macro-level party system changes, with a highly deterministic emphasis on historical contexts and external variables. In short, parties have most often been seen by political scientists and other analysts essentially as creatures of their exogenous environment.

Whether the emphasis is on the role of socioeconomic factors, the role of political culture and ideology in shaping incentives for party-building, or the impact of competitive pressures, these explanations fail to explain when, how, and *whether* parties will develop strategies to take advantage of their historical and environmental contexts. In the conventional wisdom, a party organization is like a vessel whose course is determined by the currents, the weather, and other external forces; little attention is paid to the role of its captain or crew. In other words, conventional explanations of party behavior often fail to explain the endogenous collective choices made by party leaders and members about how their organization will respond to its external context and adapt to changing conditions.

Without an understanding of how such choices are made, it is difficult to explain how parties like the PAN can undergo such rapid and dramatic changes or what growing pains they suffer in the process. Whether or not a party takes advantage of (or acquiesces to) externally generated incentives and opportunity structures ultimately depends on the internal processes, strategies, and decisions of the organization. Indeed, some scholars have drawn attention to the role of endogenous factors that affect party development *as the parties react to* external incentive structures. As Wilson (1994) observes, "Given the manipulative and conscious nature of party reform, the perceptions, skills and actions of the leaders are crucial to understanding party transformation. In effect, then, party change is really an internal matter, with the key to change found in the attitudes and behavior of party leaders and reformers."[19]

The key difference between this approach and many conventional explanations is a focus on parties as bodies of collective choice, in which political actors cooperate and often *compete* with each other in order to achieve their respective goals. The strategies and actions of these political actors within the context of the organization itself constitute a "nested game"—a set of strategic considerations within another set—which affects the party's collective decisions and behavior with respect to its external environment.[20]

In the case of the PAN, internal dynamics are critical to explaining why and how the party organization responded to changing external opportunity structures in Mexico's political context. Such factors played a highly consequential role in setting the trajectory of the PAN's organizational development, in the strategies employed by Vicente Fox en route to the Mexican presidency, and on party-government relations under the Fox administration. The somewhat surprising point I make in subsequent chapters is that the PAN won the 2000 elections despite itself. That is, focusing on the importance of party leaders, competing coalitions, and internal institutions that shaped PAN decision-making, I argue that these factors ultimately led to Vicente Fox's circumvention of the party through a variety of measures. By targeting his political appeals outside the party, Fox secured the support of nonpartisans and supporters of other parties and successfully convinced the majority of Mexican voters that he was the candidate of "change"—the champion of Mexico's political liberation from the PRI and all that it symbolized—much more so than the candidate representing the PAN. The facts that Fox's rogue, candidate-centered appeals and skillful outsider approach are what toppled the PRI in 2000, instead of the capable stewardship of party leaders or the building of an effective party apparatus, had major consequences for his administration and for the PAN's prospects for organizational development and electoral success.

Here again is a fundamental point of difference—perhaps the key difference—between this book and other accounts: this study sees parties as institutions that resolve or are meant to resolve collective action problems for party activists, candidates, government officials, and voters. The institutions of a party and the ways that institutions resolve these collective action problems are shaped by the decisions and actions of individuals within the party who react to each other and to the political context in which the party operates. In this sense, parties are constantly evolving. While it is important that parties continue to resolve the essential problems of coordination among multiple interests, political parties will grow and adapt through strategic interactions and choices. Hence, Mexico's new political scenario is one in which the internal contests for power within political parties, while powerfully influenced by external incentives, will have a logic of their own. Whether or not parties resemble the old "strong" mass-incorporating organizations of the early twentieth century (like the PRI) is, therefore, probably of less concern than whether parties do indeed function to resolve the essential dilemmas of collective action of their day. Today, Mexico is experiencing a period of extraordinary, rapid change in the structural, institutional, cultural, and competitive environments of parties. This presents new and different challenges from those of the past. It is now more important than ever to focus on the choices made by actors within party organizations and on how they can be improved to enable the "children of democracy" to make a positive contribution to Mexico's new political future.

Case Studies and Methodological Approach

As emphasized throughout this book, the hegemony of the PRI at virtually all levels in the political system involved a system of loyalty and control that depended in large part on the high degree of political, administrative, economic, and even demographic centralization in Mexico during the twentieth century. Indeed, so engrained was the notion of Mexico City's supremacy and superiority that its inward-looking residents condescendingly referred to outlying states and regions as the "periphery" (*la periferia*). Hence, there was a general perception among Mexicans and Mexico observers that the events of regional, state, and local politics were of minor significance. My research methodology reflects a different point of view that relates to a second major thematic premise of this book: gaining an understanding of the importance of subnational political actors and processes is essential to understanding contemporary Mexican politics and has been so historically. This research asserts that, in part, disregard for the *periferia* contributed to the PRI's undoing and also helps explain the failure of observers to anticipate its fall.

Though I do indeed focus on issues confronting the PAN generally and at the national level, I draw on extensive research into the PAN's party-building experiences in three significant subnational cases: León (Guanajuato), Mérida (Yucatán), and Tijuana (Baja California). In each of these geographically and demographically differentiated urban centers, the PAN won multiple consecutive terms, beginning in the late 1980s. At the time of publication, five successive PAN administrations governed each of these cities without interruption. These cases, therefore, afforded a unique opportunity to study processes and experiences that would otherwise have been lost to the rapid rate of turnover in Mexican municipal government, which is subject to mandatory three-year term limits. Most of my research in these cases was conducted between 1997 and 1999, after which I continued to conduct interviews and collect evidence about the party in other cases and at the national level, particularly in Mexico City and the states of Baja California, Campeche, Jalisco, and Mexico.

State and especially local politics are a vital component of the PAN's story because this is where the party made the greatest electoral progress in the 1980s and 1990s. Also, thanks to ongoing trends toward greater administrative decentralization in Mexico, a municipal-level focus during my early research offered me an exciting view of an increasingly influential arena of political activity. As such, the case studies that inform this research are relevant to the party's development during the 1990s. I use their stories to expand from the party's experience at the state and municipal levels to help explain the larger national experience of the PAN. Though I draw primarily from these highly successful local cases, my research also evaluates the PAN's experience at the national and state levels. Additionally, I also observed and analyzed cases in which the PAN had little or mixed success, including Campeche (Campeche), Ensenada (Baja California), Guanajuato (Guanajuato), Mexicali (Baja California), and Tecate (Baja California).

Evaluating each of the primary case studies from a historical perspective enabled me to contrast the PAN's organizational, electoral, and governmental experience over time and against those of the PRI in earlier periods. In each case, I collected data on elections and electoral regulations from state and local officials, as well as experts in local and regional politics in these areas. While other PAN scholars eschew such methods, my research relied heavily on in-depth interviews with local and state party leaders, staff and elected officials, as well as individual and group interviews with party members at the subcommittee level.[21] I attended dozens of local PAN committee meetings, campaign rallies, and events to better understand and connect with the people I was studying. This approach was particularly necessary to a study of the PAN, which for many years lacked the institutional resources to maintain detailed and accurate records of its own experience. While more testimonies and historical records exist at the national level (particularly since the 2000 elections), this is less often the case for research oriented toward the regional and local levels. Thus, individual testimonies and direct observation often proved to be the only means of obtaining any information at all. My research is, therefore, bolstered by consultations with party activists who possess a wide range of experience and deep knowledge of the PAN, including former and current governors, state and national legislators, campaign managers, and local officeholders—from appointed bureaucrats to mayors and city council members.[22] These interviews provided key insights into the workings of the party, its electoral campaigns, and its governments.

The danger and appropriate criticisms of this approach, of course, are that the researcher "goes native" and exposes himself to the influence and bias of his subjects. This is certainly a fair criticism. The only answer is to explain the rationale for this methodology, recognize the potential biases up front and with due diligence, and document information obtained from interviews as much as possible with other sources. Hence, testimonials and participant observations are enhanced by data generously made available by local government archivists, former and current politicians, party activists, and academics encountered in the field. When available, I analyzed local party records and publications, collected and meticulously scrutinized rare publications on the PAN and the local political system, reviewed municipal and party archives, and inspected official government publications and documents. However, where local party records fell short, as they often did, it was frequently necessary to rely on media accounts (especially newspaper archives) and existing Spanish and English publications on these cases.

Organization of Remaining Chapters

This book tells the story of the PAN and its contributions to Mexico's political transformation. An overview of Mexico's transition from authoritarianism to democracy is presented in Chapter 2, which explains both the sources of

PRI support and its gradual decline. This discussion provides those unfamiliar with Mexican politics a broad overview of the features of this political system, as well as insights into the challenges and opportunities that opposition parties such as the PAN faced in Mexico. Chapter 3 examines the emergence of the PAN, its original goals, statutes, ideology, and traditional bases of support and examines the divisive internal debates that nearly ruptured the party in the 1970s. The 1970s was a lost decade for the PAN, both in terms of its political progress and scholarly understanding of the party. Chapter 4 details the dramatic resurgence of the PAN in the 1980s and explains how it became the party best positioned to defeat the PRI in 2000. Again, special attention is given to the roles of leaders and competing coalitions within the PAN and their impacts on the party's organizational transformation in the 1980s and 1990s, particularly regarding its professionalization, membership growth, and electoral prospects.

This sets the stage for a discussion of Fox's successful campaign for the presidency, discussed in detail in Chapter 5, which also provides insights into the competitive dynamics among the three major parties in the 2000 presidential election. Illustrated in this chapter is one of the book's central arguments: the intensification of conflicts between competing coalitions within the PAN contributed to Fox's circumvention of the party itself in his pursuit of the presidency, thereby undermining PAN Party leaders' traditional control of the organization. The implications of this contest between the candidate and his party proved extremely significant for his government.

Hence, Chapter 6 explores the challenges faced historically by opposition governments in Mexico and the early problems faced by the Fox administration. Special attention is given to the challenges facing Fox when he was governor and since his election as Mexico's first "opposition" president. Also relevant to this discussion are the relations between Mexico's executive branch and the legislature, which have begun to perpetuate the patterns of divided government found in the United States.

Throughout this book, there is a deliberate effort to demonstrate that the story of the PAN and the triumph of Vicente Fox hold valuable lessons about the institutional challenges of party-building, as well as key insights on democratization and democratic consolidation. In Chapter 7, the concluding chapter, particular attention is given to the implications of the 2003 midterm elections, the way that would-bc candidates may follow Fox's example in future elections, and the significant dilemmas and opportunities this may pose for parties, politicians, and voters alike. In general, several interesting comparisons are made across areas that have been heavily studied in U.S. politics and elsewhere, including electoral behavior, strategic voting, campaign tactics (for example, negative campaigning), media effects, and the role of parties in government. Above all, the story of the PAN, including the triumph of Vicente Fox, provides valuable insights into this new era of political opportunities for

Mexico, as well as a useful case study with noteworthy implications for comparative analysis.

Two consistent observations arise as central themes throughout the text. First, as a political party, the PAN was, above all, a "team" of individuals acting collectively to place and coordinate its members in elected office for the purpose of effecting political change. As in all political parties, the collective choices of these individuals resulted in the positions and decisions ultimately taken by the organization. Second, while power in the Mexican political system was traditionally highly centralized, at both the national level and in the executive branch, the role of actors at the subnational level was critical in Mexico's democratization and the rise of the PAN. Actors and events at the state and local levels, arenas traditionally excluded from political analyses of the Mexican system, were influential in shaping political outcomes at the national level and provided purchase for the seeds of opposition in Mexico's many and diverse subnational contexts. The increased relevance of the internal dynamics of political parties and growing influence of subnational actors will shape national-level electoral contests and governmental policies for the foreseeable future. The story of the PAN sheds light on why and how this new political context emerged and holds important lessons in anticipation of Mexico's intermediate and long-term political development.

Notes

1. Author's translation. This song is played at virtually all formal PAN ceremonies and events, including the weekly meetings of local committees. In Spanish, the full verse of the hymn reads as follows: "*Levantada convicción de justicia y de verdad varonil resolución, nuestra lucha inspirarán. Los tiranos temblarán al oir nuestro pregón: ¡Una Patria generosa y una vida con honor! ¡LIBERTAD! ¡EXIGID! ¡LA NACIÓN! ¡PROCLAMAD! ¡Que el oprobio cese ya! ¡LIBERTAD! ¡CONQUISTAD! ¡CON ACCIÓN! ¡NACIONAL! ¡Es la hora de luchar! Nuestro México ha de ser con justicia y libertad una Patria para todos y un baluarte del ideal.*" www.pan.org.mx.
2. Bruhn, 1997.
3. Cornelius et al., 1989.
4. Bailey and Valenzuela, 1997; Lawson, 1998.
5. Arriola, 1998; Arriola, 1994; Gómez Morin, 1939; Gómez Morin and Partido Acción Nacional, 1996; Mabry, 1973a; Moctezuma Barragán, 1997.
6. Brandenburg, 1956; Moctezuma Barragán, 1997; Montalvo Ortega, 1996.
7. Arriola, 1998; Rodríguez and Ward, 1994; Rodríguez and Ward, 1995; Rodríguez and Ward, 1992.
8. Key, 1942.
9. Espinoza Valle, 1998; Hernández Vicencio, 2001; Reveles Vázquez, 1996; Reveles Vázquez, 1993.
10. For early studies of political parties that looked into their internal structures to explain their development and behavior, see Michels, 1959; Ostrogorski and Clarke, 1902.

11. Beer, 1997; Epstein, 1980; Lipset and Rokkan, 1967; Ostrogorski and Clarke, 1902; Sartori, 1976.

12. Duverger, 1966; Weber, 1958.

13. Kirchheimer, 1966; LaPalombara and Weiner, 1966.

14. Epstein, 1980.

15. Kirchheimer, 1966.

16. Agranoff, 1972; Lawson, 1968.

17. Blondel, 1978; Kirchheimer, 1966; Sundquist, 1990; Wattenberg, 1990.

18. Cain, et al., 1987; DiClerico, 2000; Fletcher, 1991; Levine, 1992; Maisel, 1998; Swanson and Mancini, 1996.

19. Wilson, 1994: 264. Many contemporary scholars provide similar justifications for attention to parties' internal dynamics; see Aldrich, 1995; Katz and Mair, 1994; Kirchheimer, 1966; Lawson, 1994; Müller and Strom, 1999; Panebianco, 1988; Wilson, 1994.

20. Tsebelis, 1990.

21. Loaeza (1999) rightly points out the problems of obtaining reliable data (especially historical data) from human subjects, who may deliberately or unintentionally provide misleading information. However, in my experience, interviews and participant observation have been useful in a variety of ways, as they provided access to perspectives that often escape the annals of history and even contemporary record (which are sometimes no more reliable).

22. Interviews conducted for this study included prominent members of the PAN, such as Ernesto Ruffo, Alejandro González Alcocer, Héctor Osuna Jaime, Carlos Castillo Peraza, Vicente Fox, Carlos Medina Plascencia, Ana Rosa Payán Cervera, Luis Correa Mena, and Luis H. Alvarez. In total, more than ninety formal interviews were conducted in the course of the initial research project, though this does not account for numerous informal interviews and repeated contacts with subjects.

2

The Democratization of Mexican Politics

I believe that when discontent with a government takes root, it gradually acquires so irresistible a strength that nothing is able to restrain it.

—President Porfirio Díaz, 1891[1]

Today we have been able to prove that ours is now a mature democracy, with solid and reliable institutions, and with a population of great conscience and civic responsibility.

—President Ernesto Zedillo, 2000[2]

In the past, the nature of the Mexican political system elicited ample scholarly debate. Resistant to neat classifications, Mexico appeared neither fully authoritarian nor fully democratic.[3] Government actors only rarely applied the threat or use of force. The regime tolerated and even openly encouraged political contestation. Yet, Mexican politics regularly included practices of coercion and co-optation, and political opposition against the regime typically resulted in alienation and ignominy. On paper, Mexicans possessed electoral freedom of choice but, in fact, had only one real political option at the polls, the Revolutionary Institutional Party (Partido Revolucionario Institucional, PRI). In the context of Latin America, where nondemocratic rule typically involved strident militarism and blatant oppression, Mexico stood out as a "mild" and even questionable case of authoritarianism. For some, Mexico was an authoritarian regime on the verge of democracy; for others, it was a democracy on the verge of authoritarianism. In either case, Mexican politics was always qualified with modifiers: an authoritarian regime "in transition" or a "restricted democracy." Proponents of the regime and even many outside observers, including numerous U.S. officials and experts, tended to regard Mexico in the more positive light of an "emerging democracy." Meanwhile, those excluded from power and their sympathizers saw the PRI regime as repressive, illegitimate, and at best, "semiauthoritarian."

Over the course of the twentieth century, evidence supported either view, as government reforms simultaneously allowed contestation while otherwise constraining political opposition. Today, looking back on history from the comfortable vantage of the present, most are likely to agree that the political system that developed after the 1910 Revolution was one of the most stable and long-lasting authoritarian regimes in the twentieth century. That there was any question in the first place about the nature of the Mexican political organization is one of the greatest achievements of its architects, as their highly efficient system perpetuated Mexico's long period of authoritarianism. Understanding the making and unmaking of Mexican authoritarianism requires careful attention to the socioeconomic, institutional, cultural, and strategic factors confronting those who advocated democracy.

The Making of PRI Authoritarianism

The irony of modern Mexican authoritarianism is that it grew out of a violent social revolution against a history of dictatorship and repression. Three hundred years of Spanish colonial rule ended with the War of Independence in 1821, a destructive, eleven-year struggle that broke Mexico's ties to Spain and severed its only established lines of trade. After the war came a prolonged administrative and economic withdrawal, characterized by political instability and financial turmoil for the next half-century. In the next five decades, the fledgling nation experienced more than fifty different governments—including a French-imposed, Austrian-born emperor—and lost nearly half its territory to the United States. The primary domestic cleavage during the nineteenth century was between conservative throwbacks to the colonial period and liberal reformers most notable for their attempts to promote "republican" governance, assimilate native peoples, and diminish the influence of the Catholic Church. Stability finally came about during the thirty-four-year dictatorship of General Porfirio Díaz (1876–1910), a period commonly known as the Porfiriato.[4] The Díaz regime's slogan of "Order and Progress" aptly characterized the successful combination of authoritarianism with international capitalism, through which Díaz repressed potentially destabilizing elements while foreign capital fueled Mexican development.[5]

By the turn of the century, however, the Díaz regime faced a crisis of multiple dimensions. First, middle-level elites grew dissatisfied with the ossification and lack of upward mobility of the Porfirian political system.[6] Second, frustration with the hierarchy, cronyism, and centralization of the Porfiriato created a yearning for greater regional and local autonomy.[7] Third, the regime was rocked by severe losses of foreign capital during the worldwide panic of 1907, which exposed Mexico's dependency on the international economy and intensified nationalist resentment of foreign economic intrusion.[8] Similarly, issues of land tenure that had plagued Mexico since its independence were exacerbated by the turn of the century commercialization of agriculture.[9] While these factors, many of them interrelated, combined to make Mexico a powder keg, it was a crisis of presidential succession that sparked the Revolution in 1910. That year an aspiring politician from the north of Mexico, Francisco I. Madero, urged Díaz not to seek reelection and launched an independent campaign for the presidency. Madero was jailed until after the election, when he denounced Díaz's victory and led a northern rebellion against the dictator. The catalyst of Mexico's Revolution, Madero was "the right man at the right time" to unleash the pent up social forces brewing for several years, according to David La France.[10]

Given the intensity of discontent Madero's rebellion exposed, the Porfiriato was toppled relatively quickly; the dictator negotiated his surrender and went into exile within a year. Likewise, the depth of these underlying currents caused the struggle to consolidate a new regime that lasted for over a decade. Indeed, as Díaz set sail for permanent retirement in Europe, he remarked that Madero had unwittingly unleashed a tiger. This observation was confirmed, as Madero and other revolutionary figures—notably, Francisco "Pancho" Villa and Emiliano Zapata—struggled to promote democratic virtues and social justice and perished in the fight to stave off counter-revolutionary forces. Hence, while the Revolution ultimately succeeded, the roots of authoritarianism remained deep.

From at least 1929, Mexico was governed by a political monopoly that used state resources for co-optation, fraud, and occasional coercion in order to maintain the hegemony of the "revolutionary family." This family was embodied by the diverse coalition of middle-class, labor, agrarian, and military interests that coalesced under the umbrella of the ruling party eventually known as the PRI.[11] The party's institutional apparatus directly benefited the victors and heirs of the Revolution in ways that merely reconfigured preexisting inequalities and power arrangements and perpetuated conditions of social, economic, and political injustice.

This system of PRI-authoritarianism was relatively consolidated by 1939—the year that the National Action Party (Partido Acción Nacional, PAN) emerged—and persisted over the next two decades without major alterations. Indeed, the features of the PRI regime were so stable and well defined that observers often described Mexico as a "living museum," in which spectators could marvel at the unchanging wonders of post–Revolutionary authoritarianism.[12] However, during the 1970s, the high degree of stability characteristic of PRI-authoritarianism began to erode in the wake of a major political crisis in 1968, caused by the harsh repression of student-led political protests. During the subsequent thirty years, a series of political and economic crises projected Mexico into a period of transition away from authoritarianism and toward a more liberalized set of political arrangements.

Understanding the PRI regime and its ultimate undoing requires careful attention to the key features of the regime and their implications for the PAN and other opposition parties. Four key factors or "pillars" undergirded PRI authoritarianism, and it was the gradual dissolution of those four pillars that made Fox's victory possible in 2000. The first pillar of the PRI regime was found in the inherent characteristics of the ruling party itself, which provided certain strategic advantages to members, preventing competition and encouraging authoritarian practices. The broad coalition of interests incorporated into the party ensured its predominance in the electorate, and its lock on power solidified these advantages through the manipulation of public policy. The second pillar comprised the formal rules and institutional mechanisms that regulated contestation and political decisionmaking under successive PRI regimes; these were deliberately designed to lock in the ruling party's inherent advantages and concentrate political power in ways that ensured regime continuity. While difficult and, even now, controversial to discuss, a third pillar of PRI support included the norms, attitudes, and beliefs that created disincentives for genuine political participation and open contestation in the context of Mexico's overall political culture. The fourth pillar was based on Mexico's long period of economic prosperity throughout the mid-twentieth century, which provided "performance legitimacy" for the PRI and contributed to the regime's relative stability until the late 1960s.

The Competitive Context: Birth of a Ruling Party

The competitive context of the Mexican system after 1929 was characterized by one overwhelming reality: the absolute dominance of a single party affiliated with the Revolution. The creation of this party resulted from elite actors' efforts to promote regime consolidation and secure a legitimate or at least a continuous power base. During the latter part of the Revolution and in the early stages of post–Revolutionary regime consolidation, the establishment of central authority proved a precarious task, due to recurrent plots (*cuartelazos*), coups, and military insurrections. In 1929, outgoing Mexican president, Plutarco Calles (1924–1928), resolved to limit this problem through the establishment of an all-encompassing "Revolutionary" Party in 1929.[13] His creation of the National Revolutionary Party (Partido Nacional Revolucionario, PNR), the first incarnation of the PRI, created a forum for the mediation of disputes and succession by providing a formal structure to allow for dialogue and distribution of political benefits through institutionalized channels of clientelism. In particular, the organizational structure of the ruling party helped to incorporate the sectors most active in the Revolution—and, therefore, the most potentially destabilizing to the government—through formal incorporated group or "corporatist" representation. With the presidency of Lázaro Cárdenas (1934–1940) and the rebirth of the PNR as the Mexican Revolutionary Party (Partido Revolucionario Mexicano, PRM), the ruling party developed distinct sectors for laborers (*obreros*), agrarian workers (*campesinos*), members of the military (*militares*) and the middle class (*clase popular*).

Thanks to President Cárdenas's efforts, the ruling party developed a labor sector that included officially sanctioned worker organizations, such as the Confederation of Mexican Workers (Confederación de Trabajadores Mexicanos, CTM) and the National Agrarian Confederation (Confederación Nacional Campesina, CNC).[14] The so-called popular sector consisted primarily of the National Confederation of Popular Organizations (Confederación Nacional de Organizaciones Populares, CNOP), which allowed for representation of the middle class. As the regime became more consolidated, the military was phased out as a formal sector of the ruling party when President Manuel Ávila Camacho (1946–1952) restructured and renamed the party as the Institutional Revolutionary Party (Partido Revolucionario Institucional, PRI).[15]

Through the above-mentioned corporate associations, the party helped mobilize support for the regime and acted as a broker between organized interests and the state. At the former, the party was extremely successful. The PRI consistently generated mass demonstrations of support, enormous margins of victory at all levels, and near total hegemony in virtually all electoral contests. This capacity to manufacture such widespread support and permanent political control resulted from the "official" party's relationship with the government and media and its unscrupulous electoral tactics. The explicit connection between the party and government provided the PRI with access to government resources and services, a means of obtaining political support, and public endorsements for its candidates by government officials. This party-government connection also granted the party an unfair advantage in its relationship with media outlets, which either favored the government and its party or prevented opposition parties from obtaining the permits and resources they needed to survive.

Also contributing to the antidemocratic character of post–Revolutionary Mexico was the PRI's utilization of classic machine-style politics. Political machines are so called because of their mechanical ability to deliver guaranteed results at the polls and in government. The results delivered by political machines, often through fraud or corruption, create a system of rewards and punishments for the organization's supporters and opponents, respectively. Networks of exchange between machine politicians and their beneficiaries are often described as patron-client, patronage, or clientelistic networks. PRI clientelistic networks often provided jobs for cronies, special favors in government, and minor rewards for common people, like food or money on the day of an election. Meanwhile, in addition to the exclusionary use of public resources to maintain political control, the PRI frequently resorted to fixing electoral contests through a variety of fraudulent techniques, from multiple-voting and ballot-stuffing to the incorporation of deceased citizens onto voter rolls and unabashed manipulation of official figures. At its worst, the PRI maintained its dominance through the use of intimidation and coercion. Punishments might include extortion, intimidation, fraud, or other abuses of power. Though such tactics were typically only a last resort when co-optation and patronage failed, physical coercion was a real and credible threat that prevented the expression of alternative viewpoints and freedom of political choice. Indeed, the fact that violence was so rarely employed illustrates the true power and effectiveness of the PRI machine.

Additionally, the PRI had the advantage of a relatively pragmatic ideology that allowed it to shift its political positions in order to draw support away from the opposition. Indeed, many scholars described the PRI as a political pendulum that gravitated from right to left from one presidential administration to the next in order to maintain support across the ideological spectrum.[16]

The PRI's advantages were unique and constrained the available political avenues for its political opponents. The practical alternative to fight fire with fire did not exist, since there were few societal bases available to mobilize against the PRI. Nor was it feasible to stake a permanent claim on alienated elements of the political spectrum, as the PRI's pragmatic flexibility allowed it to draw "lost sheep" back into the fold. The PRI was the antithesis of what *panistas* wanted from a political party and, therefore, shaped the PAN's formation and development not as a role model but as a villainous illustration to be avoided at all costs. The PAN, as the primary voice of the political opposition (at least until the late 1980s) provided the antithesis to the PRI in its ideology and organizational approach.

Mexico's Post-Revolutionary Institutions

The Mexican political system found its institutional beginnings in the writing of the 1917 Constitution in Querétaro; its authors drew heavily from the anticlerical, liberal Constitution of 1857. Despite its point of origin, several innovations derived from the revolutionary experience made the 1917 Constitution unique. In particular, two key innovations significantly impacted the post-Revolutionary political system and definitively shaped its primary features, most notably the nature of executive power and the formation of a perpetual ruling party. One came in the form of single term limits for all elected officials, both legislative and executive. This was the result of revolutionary cries for "effective suffrage, no re-election" in response to the uninterrupted continuity of the *Porfiriato*. The second innovative aspect was the progressivism of the 1917 Constitution, a document born from the twentieth century's first great social revolution. In it were elaborate promises of education, health care, social equality, labor rights, land redistribution, and social welfare for the masses.[17] Hence, the 1917 Constitution was quite distinct from the laissez-faire Constitution of 1857, in that it advocated much greater state intervention in the economy and set a new agenda for modern Mexico. Though these aspects of the Constitution were not consistently observed in actual practice, they sometimes provided a basis for fulfilling revolutionary promises and preserving the PRI's legitimacy.

Setting single-term limits proved to be a defining characteristic of the 1917 Constitution and contributed to significant problems of accountability at all levels of government. The constitutional provision to prevent re-election created a system that helped make Porfirian personalism untenable. That is, the "no re-election" clause helped to separate the presidency from the personalities that would occupy the office.[18] At the same time, "no re-election" eventually helped to strengthen the ruling party as an institution in at least two ways. First, as just mentioned, the ban on reelection decreased the ability of individuals to establish permanent personal bases of power via executive positions; this increased the significance of the ruling party as an institutional mechanism. Second, the extension of "no re-election" to legislative positions in 1929 helped to strengthen the executive power and the ruling party by limiting legislative experience and increasing the dependence of legislators on the executive and party leadership for future appointments and candidacies.[19]

In addition to these key constitutional provisions, the ruling party was afforded sizable institutional advantages by the legal democratic procedures employed within the system. Most significantly, the ruling party derived numerous benefits provided by the electoral system. The establishment of the first electoral regulations of the new regime in 1918 allowed for the decentralized regulation of federal, state, and local elections. However, a general pattern of restrictive voting requirements and loose regulation over electoral competition and associations prevailed, with the latter tendency encouraging independent candidacies for the presidency, such as those of José Vasconcelos and Juan Andreu Almazán. However, throughout this period, instances of "competitive" electoral contests between two or among more candidates proved rare and occurred primarily in large cities.[20]

The formation of the Federal Electoral Law of 1946 restructured existing arrangements to place federal elections under the control of the Mexican government's Ministry of the Interior (Gobernación). The Interior Ministry's control over the electoral process, as well as its ability to regulate the formal registration of candidates and political parties, reinforced PRI hegemony until political reforms were enacted in the early 1990s. Executive control of the electoral process through the Interior Ministry further enhanced these powers by giving the president complete control over the election of his party's candidate, who, in practice, was handpicked by the president for the nomination.[21] For all these reasons, Mexico's electoral process did not operate autonomously and transparently; instead, it was frequently manipulated to the benefit of the ruling party. At the same time, the restructured 1946 system also benefited the ruling party through its strict regulation of political parties in order to minimize and monitor challenges to the newly reborn PRI.[22] Because the Interior Ministry decided whether the legal requirements for participation were fulfilled, access to formal political recognition was ultimately determined by the executive power.

Several significant modifications of the electoral system did occur between 1946 and the eventual formation of a new regulatory framework in the early 1990s. First, in 1963, President Adolfo López Mateos proclaimed the need for greater plurality and added so-called party deputies to the national legislature. The 1963 reforms allowed for the addition of a limited number of seats to the federal legislature, which comprised two houses, the Senate (Senado) and the lower house or Chamber of Deputies (Cámara de Diputados). While the Senate remained unchanged by the 1963 reforms, additional seats were allocated to the Chamber of Deputies, to be distributed to minority parties on the basis of their electoral performance. This provided a limited form of proportional representation (PR), by which seats were allocated to minority parties on the basis of their electoral performance. To obtain party-deputy seats, a political party had to obtain between 2.5 percent and 20 percent of the nationwide vote for federal deputies. Any party within this range would receive a base of five party-deputy seats plus an additional seat for each additional .5 percent of the nationwide vote obtained, to a maximum of twenty seats.[23] The distribution of party-deputy seats depended on opposition performance, and, therefore, the number of party deputies was subject to fluctuation at each three-year election cycle.

The introduction of party deputies produced an immediate and significant impact on the ability of opposition parties to find representation within the system. The presence of minority parties in the legislature increased dramatically from 1960 to 1963 as a direct result of these reforms. At the same time, the introduction of party deputies provided seats that did not reduce the PRI's share of the legislature but merely tacked on new and temporary spaces for the opposition. Furthermore, maximum limits on the qualifications for party-deputy seats created disincentives for opposition parties to grow beyond 20 percent of the vote. Only the PAN came within remote proximity to the 20 percent threshold during this period, with its share of the national vote in federal elections growing from 11.5 percent in 1964 to 14.7 percent in 1973. Hence, the PAN never lost party-deputy seats due to its strong electoral performance. However, the dilemma remained that the PAN's total number of deputyships would actually decrease if its percentage of the national vote increased by five to ten points in a given election. The only way to overcome this situation would have been to achieve officially recognized victories in more than twenty districts. However, as illustrated in Figure 2.1, the PAN rarely scored more than a handful of recognized victories in individual districts prior to 1976. In that election, the PAN was not assigned party-deputy seats because it did not run a presidential candidate, but ironically the PAN succeeded in capturing more district seats than ever before.

Figure 2.1 PAN Federal Deputies, 1940–1976

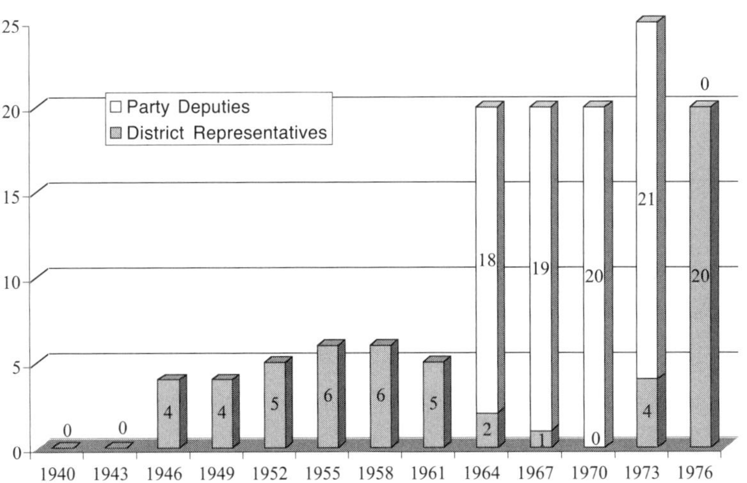

Sources: Mabry, 1973a, p. 69; Cervantes Varela, 2002, p. 369.

Furthermore, the party-deputy system fractionalized the electorate by creating "a minor industry of small parties whose only base of support was and still is financing from the dominant party."[24] Between 1964 and 1972, small parties such as the Popular Socialist Party (Partido Popular Socialista, PPS) and the Authentic Party of the Mexican Revolution (Partido Auténtico de la Revolución Mexicana, PARM) frequently failed to meet the threshold set by the 1963 reform; nonetheless, they received party-deputy seats in the legislature. Thus, party deputies brought both new opportunities and new limitations to "opposition" parties of the Mexican political system. In 1972, the minimum threshold to obtain party-deputy seats was lowered from 2.5 to 1.5 percent of the national legislative vote, thereby increasing opposition access to the legislature without creating incentives for parties to grow. Shrewdly, the 1972 reforms facilitated the proliferation of small parties and created disincentives, preventing larger opposition parties from growing *too* large.[25] Once again, the regime's strategy of political accommodation was a double-edged sword for opposition parties, because it both served to avert and even control political opposition and to enhance the illusion of plural democratic competition.

This illusion of democracy was nearly shattered in 1976, when no opposition party launched a presidential candidate against the PRI candidate, José López Portillo, due primarily to internal problems faced by the PAN. On December 28, 1977, in light of this politically embarrassing situation, President López Portillo revised seventeen separate articles of the Constitution to implement the most significant set of reforms since the formation of the 1946 electoral system. One of the most important features of López Portillo's sweeping political reform initiative was the Federal Law of Political Organizations and Electoral Processes (Ley Federal de Organizaciones Políticas y Procesos Electorales, LFOPPE), which (1) added 100 proportional representation seats to the 300-member Chamber of Deputies to allow for permanent minority representation, (2) eliminated the role of the Interior Ministry in determining party registration, and (3) made registration dependent on a party's share of the national vote.[26] Under this new "mixed" system, Mexico now elected deputies both by majority rule in single-member districts *and* by lists of candidates selected by the parties and assigned in proportion to their share of the vote.[27] As in the case of past reforms, there were important drawbacks to the new reform package, as well as some token benefits for the opposition.

On the one hand, the apparent intention, or at least the effect, of the LFOPPE was not to create a stronger political opposition that could viably compete against the PRI. Rather, the 1977 reforms ensured an increase in the level of diversity in the party system by making the electoral process more accessible to smaller opposition parties, thereby bolstering PRI legitimacy without directly challenging its hegemony. For example, while the introduction of true proportional representation had noticeable effects, resulting in the immediate recognition of three new parties within the first year of the reforms, the limited number of seats granted to the opposition could never threaten the PRI's majority or its ability to govern. Furthermore, because the size of the legislature was expanded, the LFOPPE did not reduce the absolute number of seats the PRI could expect for its own candidates to the Chamber of Deputies. Thus, like previous alterations to the federal electoral system, the 1977 reforms helped to protect the advantages of the PRI, while placating the opposition with token representation. At the same time, the 1977 reforms again perpetuated a perverse incentive structure by creating a "protective" threshold that gave only relatively small parties access to proportional representation, while discouraging larger opposition parties—more specifically, the PAN—from trying to grow too large. Indeed, explaining the PAN's reasons for opposing the LFOPPE, PAN President Manuel González Hinojosa observed that the new reforms sought "to force [opposition] political parties to accept their status as a permanent minority."[28]

On the other hand, the political spaces created for access to representation and governmental experience expanded the opportunities, however marginal, for the opposition to parry against the regime. While such initiatives benefited a host of Lilliputian parties that were ultimately linked to and supported by the PRI, the PAN still managed to come out of the 1970s as the primary beneficiary of these reforms. Indeed, the pace of systemic change appeared to slip out of the PRI's control during the 1980s and 1990s, when the

PAN achieved major electoral successes at the municipal and state levels and when internal divisions within the ruling party led to major defections away from the PRI to form the PRD. Though significantly more attention was given by many political observers to the birth of a new and viable source of electoral competition on the left, the PAN's rapid expansion—and internal transformation—over these two decades would ultimately prove much more significant in laying the groundwork for Mexico's transition to democracy in 2000.

In short, a complex institutional structure helped to shape and support post-Revolutionary authoritarianism in Mexico. The circumstances of the Revolution and the particular features of the 1917 Constitution helped to produce the conditions for the establishment of a tremendous political machine that coordinated the elements of the "Revolutionary Family." A set of electoral institutions bolstered that mammoth party organization, undergirding and protecting its hegemony. The intricate crafting of these institutions skillfully produced the illusion of political pluralism in an authoritarian regime. Through reforms that incorporated and co-opted political opposition, the regime maintained a veneer of tolerance that helped pacify both domestic and international advocates of democracy. Though much would change toward the end of the twentieth century, understanding this institutional mix helps to explain the persistence of authoritarianism in Mexico and is essential to understanding the constraints faced by the PAN.

The Political Culture of Post-Revolutionary Mexico

While institutions can explain a great deal about the nature and persistence of authoritarianism in Mexico, no discussion of this problem would be complete without reference to the controversial topic of political culture. The analysis of Mexican political culture is nested within a larger set of scholarly efforts to tackle the same subject throughout the Latin American region, where clientelism, corporatism, and the limits of civic attitudes are especially controversial topics. The key question that emerges in most debates on these topics is whether people's cultural attitudes, beliefs, and norms have any causal relevance to political outcomes or whether they are merely symptoms of other problems. Restated as a chicken-and-egg conundrum, do the political cultural features of a society lead to certain outcomes (like authoritarianism), or do political circumstances lead to certain attitudes, values, and beliefs? As intriguing as this question may be, it is less relevant than whether or not attitudinal orientations toward politics play some role in shaping strategies and preferences of entrepreneurial actors within a given political context.

Hence, even if studying a particular political culture tells us little about the causal question of why a country suffers from authoritarianism or enjoys democratic government—that is, even if political culture is merely the outcome of some other causal factor—it *does*, in and of itself, present challenges and opportunities that ultimately affect the decisions and actions of political actors and organizations. For example, if people have an attitude of distrust toward politicians or political institutions, it has an impact on their behavior toward those actors and institutions (whether or not their distrust is well founded). Likewise, if beliefs about politics help to determine an understanding of individual rights, justice, the definition of "the good," and the role of the state, then at the very least they shape the objectives and rationalizations of political actions. Thus, if political norms feature the predominance of material exchange as a mechanism for determining political decisions and distribution, this naturally affects calculations of those actors and organizations that are materially constrained. The prevalence of certain attitudes, beliefs, and norms in a particular electorate's orientations toward politics is, therefore, of great relevance to understanding how political parties can mobilize supporters, motivate activists, and perform other basic functions in a given political context.

In reference to the persistent hegemony of the PRI and the authoritarian features of the Mexican political system, it is not necessary to retrace the course of decades of analysis into this subject in order to capture the key cultural features of post-Revolutionary Mexican politics.[29] Rather, below I outline three main features of Mexican political culture that prevailed during this period: (1) negative attitudes toward politics, (2) belief structures that helped to legitimize authoritarianism, and (3) norms of political interaction that channeled interests within that system. Each of these factors contributed in some way to the emergence, consolidation, and permanence of the Revolutionary Family manifested in the dominant party, as well as to the difficulties faced by political entrepreneurs interested in mobilizing support against the hegemonic system.

Early research on political culture focused heavily on the nature of citizens' attitudes toward politics. Examination of political attitudes in Mexico drew special attention in the classic and much criticized 1963 study by Gabriel Almond and Sidney Verba, *The Civic Culture*.[30] Mexican political culture was characterized, they claimed, by justifiably negative attitudes about politics and civic participation and by symbolic nationalism, attributing "revolutionary" legitimacy to the ruling party.[31]

To illustrate the second point, the 1910 Revolution powerfully impacted the character of Mexico's political arrangements, providing the regime's "creation myth," a source of legendary heroes championing ideals of social justice, democracy, and national sovereignty.[32] Almond and Verba noted that Mexicans viewed the Revolution "as an instrument of ultimate democratization and economic and social modernization."[33] The reality of the Revolution, however, was that despite the widespread popular mobilization that accompanied it, the goals of its most legendary protagonists—Francisco I. Madero, Emiliano Zapata, Pascual Orozco, Francisco Villa, and others—were (at least initially) set aside by men of ruthless ambition with ties to strong domestic and international interests and few sympathies for revolutionary causes.[34] Nonetheless, the Revolution served as the symbol of Mexico's solidarity and unity of purpose and became an effective source of legitimacy within the system.

The identification of the dominant party with the Revolution helped convert appeals to revolutionary themes and ideals into explicit approval of the PRI-government amalgam. The dominant party thus held a monopoly on politically popular concepts that capitalized on deeply instilled beliefs about the "good" derived from the Revolution. This naturally posed a limitation on political groups unaffiliated with or disapproving of the Revolution. Certainly, the fact that the dominant party used the symbols of the Revolution was not "improper" or illegal. However, the PRI's adept use of revolutionary imagery provided some significant advantages. For example, the PRI's use of the colors of the Mexican flag conflated the party with the nation and subtly suggested that a vote for the opposition was a vote against Mexico.

Third, attitudes and beliefs such as those described above helped to validate norms of political and social interaction that further consolidated the ruling party's hegemony. Some of these norms were simply extensions of practices initiated in the colonial and independent periods of Mexican history. Most notably, the practice of both clientelism and corporatism after the Revolution contributed greatly to the functioning of authoritarian Mexico and drew from traditions shared throughout the Americas, thanks to the legacy of Spanish conquest and administration.

What was perhaps most significant about the practice of clientelism and corporatism in post-Revolutionary Mexico was their institutionalization through the channels of the ruling party. The institutional mechanisms of the ruling party helped to depersonalize the traditional practice of clientelism in ways that assured greater structure than seen elsewhere. Similarly, the ruling party provided an institutional mechanism for coordinating corporate interests—industrial and agricultural labor as well as business interests—in their relationship with the state. Though the institutionalization of such practices distinguished Mexico from other parts of Latin America, it nonetheless reflected a continuation of cultural norms traditionally associated with the region. These practices influenced individual calculations of what appeared politically possible and acceptable in the Mexican system.

In this sense, the establishment of patron-client relationships involving the exchange of materialistic benefits for political support proved to be as important to the PRI's long-term hegemony as it was to the political machines of Chicago and New York. The benefits provided by the clientelistic norms of political machines were a form of excludable good that could be delivered to loyal supporters and withheld from opponents. This system of patron-client exchange enabled the PRI to generate massive support, often with minimal compensation; for example, the PRI's importunate *acarreados* (individuals bused or trucked from rural areas to political rallies and polling places) often received only very minor benefits, such as free sandwiches or hats. As in U.S. machine politics, the PRI machine provided very limited access to more significant material benefits, such as property, jobs, and money, as well as nonmaterial alternatives that were less costly to provide: special government attention and services, intervention and assistance in nonpolitical spheres, and status-enhancing activities on the part of party leaders and public officials (e.g., participation in social functions, such as weddings and funerals). It is also important to note that, like other political machines, the PRI was able to use the negative application of selective benefits as a form of punishment. That is, withholding certain benefits or even causing harm were persuasive forms of coercion, and the ruling party strategically applied the use of such selective penalties against its enemies.

As the third pillar of PRI authoritarianism, Mexico's post-Revolutionary political culture created an equilibrium that consolidated the status quo and presented substantial collective action problems for would-be opponents of the regime. The features of Mexican political culture described above—apathetic and negative attitudes toward politics, widespread acceptance of the regime's creation mythology, and practices that structured political interactions and payoffs within the regime—helped both to consolidate the ruling party and to limit the prospects of political entrepreneurs seeking to establish political alternatives to the PRI. Furthermore, the perpetuation of clientelistic norms of exchange and the application of selective benefits (and punishments) in this process contributed to undemocratic practices, also historically used in the United States and other developing democracies. Most important, this combination of factors created a post-Revolutionary political culture that served to strengthen the regime and to produce significant obstacles for would-be opposition parties.

Post-Revolutionary Economic Prosperity and Stability

A final pillar of PRI hegemony was the remarkably successful performance of Mexico's economy from the early post–World War II era through the beginning of the 1980s. Though the long-term consequences of Mexico's economic arrangements may have proved unstable, the PRI-government amalgam played an essential role by providing the political stability and policies of state-led growth that allowed for the impressive performance of the economy throughout this period. As a result, economic factors helped to bolster the PRI's performance legitimacy. Still, during the immediate aftermath of the Revolution, Mexico's economic policy looked distinctly unrevolutionary. The policies of early post-Revolutionary presidents did little to follow through with the bold visions of land redistribution, nationalism, and social welfare provisions set forth in the 1917 Constitution. Rather, the vested interests of large landholders and international and domestic capital still held sway during the reigns of Presidents Venustiano Carranza, Alvaro Obregón, and Plutarco Calles. In the 1930s, however, the sweeping economic reforms of President Lázaro Cárdenas initiated a dramatic transformation.

Cárdenas came to the presidency in 1934, after a trio of Calles's stooges who served as interim-presidents: Emilio Portes Gil (1928–1930), Pascual Ortiz Rubio (1930–1932), and Abelardo Rodríguez (1932–1934). This period was known as the Maximato, because Calles remained the consistent strong man behind all three men.[35] Unlike these predecessors, President Cárdenas was ultimately successful in breaking with Calles and, in the process, established the autonomy of the executive power in Mexico. In the vein of Argentina's Juan Perón, the United States' Franklin Roosevelt, and Brazil's Juan Vargas, Cárdenas attained mythic status as the great uncle (el Tata) of Mexico's underprivileged and working-class groups in an age of populism and welfare state-building. Indeed, Cárdenas helped fulfill the seemingly forgotten promises of the Revolution.[36]

During his term (1934–1940), Cárdenas completely transformed the nature of Mexico's economy. Like the rest of the world, Mexico was then suffering from the Great Depression, which caused its export sectors and foreign capital investment to dry up. As economic conditions worsened, so did the relations between labor and capital, both foreign and domestic. Labor had been systematically ignored since the Revolution and grew increasingly dissatisfied under Calles and his lackeys. Thus, when Cárdenas entered the presidency and sought to establish his autonomy from Calles (by eliminating Callista governors, military men, and cabinet officials), labor was a natural ally and proved decisive in forcing Calles to back down from further attempts at intervention. Cárdenas encouraged the development of a labor union structure that fortified the ruling party for the remainder of the century, most notably the two main labor unions for industrial labor and agrarian workers, the Confederation of Mexican Workers (Confederación de Trabajadores de México, CTM) and the National Agrarian Worker Confederation (Confederación Nacional Campesina, CNC).

Free from ties to foreign and domestic investors who had supported previous post-Revolutionary governments, Cárdenas established himself as a veritable revolutionary president by following through on long neglected promises of the 1917 Constitution. As a result, Cárdenas elicited strong reactions during his presidency, both from the masses, who adored him, and conservatives, who despised him. Among his most notable accomplishments, Cárdenas initiated the largest redistribution of land since the Revolution; promoted the development of state-owned communal farms (*ejidos*), ostensibly modeled on indigenous customs and traditions; expropriated foreign-owned land and enterprises; nationalized the petroleum industry; and promoted a massive educational reform in Mexico. In short, Cárdenas established himself as the great red hope of Mexican socialism and the true champion of the Revolution in which he fought.

This was a critical juncture for Mexico's economy. During the Great Depression and World War II, Mexico experienced a natural shift in production toward a model known as import substitution industrialization (ISI). Both global economic disruptions created a natural opportunity for Mexico to develop domestic production not only of the primary goods it traditionally exported (raw materials like sisal), but also of higher value-added manufactured and consumer goods (such as refrigerators and footwear). For Mexico in the 1930s and 1940s, ISI was the result of natural market forces and did not reflect deliberate government policies or strategies. Later, however, Mexican economic policy was tailored to perpetuate the phenomenon of ISI through increased governmental expenditures in infrastructure; import restrictions such as tariffs and quotas on finished consumer goods; and reduced import restrictions on capital goods.[37] Significant currency devaluations in the late 1940s and early 1950s combined with this strategy of state-led growth to produce a period of stabilizing development, also known as the Mexican miracle, in which exchange rates remained extremely stable due to sound fiscal and monetary policies, economic growth, low inflation, and high confidence from business and financial sectors. Stabilizing development took its toll, however, as a dramatic shift in Mexico's demographics produced an underrepresented middle class and a rapidly growing number of urban poor, drawn from marginalized rural areas. It was the middle class, educated and articulate, that later produced the heterogeneous mix of leftist intellectuals and other opponents who contributed to the student movement of 1968.

Police intervention in 1968 in a fight between two rival Mexico City high schools escalated into a major political phenomenon, as gatherings by students to discuss their grievances brought repeated attacks by police. University students, especially those of the Autonomous National University of Mexico (Universidad Nacional Autónoma de México, UNAM) and the National Politechnical Institute (Instituto Politécnico Nacional), organized demonstrations to protest police brutality and the occupation of academic facilities by the military. In addition to issues of repression, students were concerned about their general lack of influence and limited prospects for upward mobility in the Mexican system. Ongoing mobilization and protests by students drew large segments of labor, the middle class, merchants, and professionals to join or support the demonstrators. State actors and supporters responded with increasingly violent and coercive measures. The culmination of the conflict came on October 2, 1968, as nearly ten thousand demonstrators prepared to meet at a middle- and working-class Mexico City housing development in Tlatelolco. Protesters found themselves infiltrated by hundreds of plainclothes police and surrounded by a force of five thousand soldiers and dozens of tanks. Nearly an hour after the meeting began, soldiers opened fire on the speakers and the crowd with machine guns and heavy artillery. At least thirty individuals were killed in a half hour of shooting (though some sources put the death toll in the hundreds), hundreds were injured, and over fifteen hundred more were arrested. Eight government soldiers died from their cohorts' fire in the skirmish. Student organizers were arrested, stripped naked, and taken into custody.[38]

The violent suppression of the 1968 student movement was a tragedy and a political earthquake, with shockwaves that reverberated for the remainder of the century. While the blow to the student movement was severe, it did not quell protests against the PRI regime. In the months and years that followed, the government's systematic efforts to track and intimidate leaders of the movement became Mexico's closest equivalent to Argentina's "dirty war." In the medium term, the incident proved to be a serious strategic error by leaders of the regime, who suffered a dramatic decrease in political legitimacy. Over the course of the next three decades, their efforts to buy back support brought forth a new era of political and economic instability that ultimately undermined the PRI regime and gave rise to increasingly potent sources of opposition.

The Unmaking of Mexican Authoritarianism

Each aspect of the PAN's external political environment explored in the previous section—the unfavorable competitive conditions, institutional arrangements, cultural matrix, and economic foundations of the PRI regime—created significant barriers to the organizational development of opposition parties. Yet, the gradual erosion of Mexico's authoritarian foundations, beginning in the aftermath of the 1968 massacre, facilitated the growing strength and determination of the political opposition over the next thirty years. Given the dependence of Mexican authoritarianism on a confluence of structural, institutional, cultural, and strategic pillars, understanding Mexico's democratization requires reference to the gradual deterioration of those supports.

With the exhaustion of Mexico's miraculous model of economic development, a pillar whose cracks first became apparent with the social unrest of the 1960s, the country experienced nearly thirty years of economic tremors, resulting from a combination of genuine misfortune and often counterproductive macroeconomic policies that caused many Mexicans to experience ever worsening income distribution, wage deterioration, price distortions, and currency devaluations. Unsurprisingly, the deterioration of the ruling party's "performance legitimacy" played an important role in the regime's undoing. At the same time, the continued redrawing of Mexico's institutional structures in order to sustain an image of popular support and democratic pluralism gradually began to provide opposition parties with a real foothold for contestation. In this context, the PAN and other parties suddenly found themselves able to capitalize on the dissatisfaction of key sectors of the Mexican electorate. All of these factors coincided to create a changing competitive context within the PRI regime that created opportunities for credible contestation and real democratic action. Throughout the transformation of the Mexican political system, the legacies of authoritarianism and gradual processes of democratization shaped the opportunity structures for the PRI's political opponents and dramatically affected their prospects.

The Political Economy of Mexico's Democratization

As discussed in the previous section, a strong economy fortified PRI-authoritarianism during the period of sustained development, which lasted from the late 1940s until the 1960s. The political crisis of 1968 was a partial result of the exhaustion of Mexico's miraculous economic growth. The growing demands of frustrated students and an increasingly underrepresented middle class were themselves a sign of the regime's inability to satisfy rising expectations. More important, as in most applications of force, the regime's unexpectedly harsh reprisals were more a sign of political weakness than of strength. Thus, when President Luis Echeverría Alvarez began his term in 1970, he adopted new strategies intended to buy back regime support and legitimacy. This was a difficult challenge for Echeverría, because he had served as secretary of the Interior in the previous administration. Many people believed that Echeverría had participated in high-level decisions that led to the 1968 massacre. Echeverría, therefore, went to great lengths to distinguish himself from his predecessor, Díaz Ordaz. Most notably, Echeverría adopted rhetoric extolling the virtues of President Salvador Allende of Chile and the new Latin American left; he also advocated state intervention on behalf of the people.

Echeverría's advocacy of state intervention went beyond the model of ISI protectionism and infrastructure investments, which had sustained nearly three decades of continuous economic development, albeit poorly distributed. Rather, his populist model included direct government involvement in the private sector through the creation of state-run enterprises, expanded agricultural subsidies, and increased funding for social programs to reduce social inequality.[39] In the process, total public spending began to exceed government revenues by significant margins (see Figure 2.2), due to the combination of Echeverría's inability to secure support for tax increases and subsequent economic difficulties created by the worldwide 1973 oil crisis.

Hence, under Echeverría, Mexico's government began to experience major fiscal deficits for the first time in decades. In the latter half of his administration, private sector confidence plummeted and worried domestic

Figure 2.2 Total Mexican Federal Government Revenues and Expenditures, 1965–1976

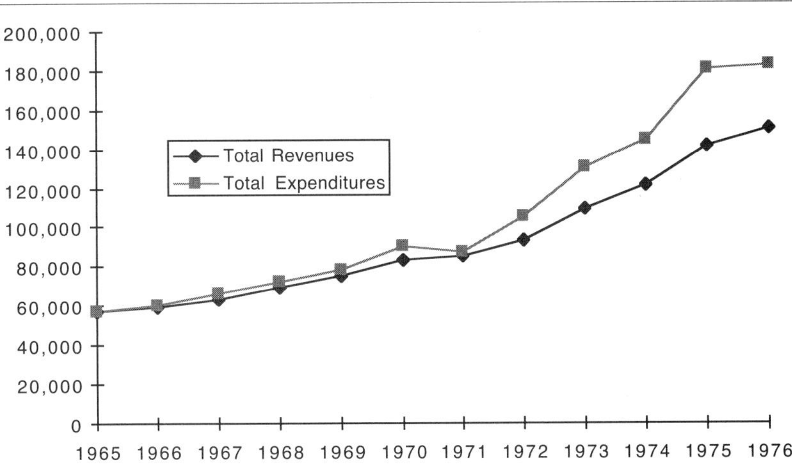

Source: Adapted from Carlos Bazdresch and Santiago Levy's Table 8.3 "Indicators for Public Finance" in "Populism and Economic Policy in Mexico, 1970–1982," in *The Macro-economics of Populism in Latin America*, ed. Rudiger Dornbusch and Sebastian Edwards (Chicago: University of Chicago Press, 1991).

and international investors began to pull their capital out of Mexico. Of immediate concern were a looming monetary crisis that resulted from dwindling capital reserves, Mexico's Central Bank could no longer maintain the long stable 1954 exchange rate, and in 1976 was forced to float the peso against the foreign exchange market for the first time in a generation. The result was a 40 percent devaluation and an economic crisis of accelerated inflation and output decline. Echeverría was forced to seek assistance from the International Monetary Fund (IMF).[40]

This seemingly impossible situation changed dramatically with the discovery of vast oil deposits immediately after President José López Portillo (1976–1982) took office. Government control of Mexico's national resources—a legacy of the 1917 Constitution and the nationalization of the petroleum industry by President Lázaro Cárdenas in 1938—promised to bring unprecedented levels of growth through the state-owned oil company, PEMEX (Petróleos de México). Mexico's deus ex machina salvation from IMF-imposed austerity measures and massive economic restructuring also spelled political deliverance for the PRI. An ample supply of credit, made possible by premium oil prices and the low international interest rates of the late 1970s, allowed López Portillo to exercise continued co-optation and populist state intervention in order to sustain regime support and performance legitimacy for the PRI.

As fortune smiled on Mexico, López Portillo optimistically described his term as one of "administering abundance." The prospect of higher revenues led to excessive investments from both the public and private sectors, which, in turn, produced impressive increases in both output and employment during the boom. In the process, the peso soon became overvalued and deficit spending (based on expected future revenues and expected decreases in external interest rates) produced an increasing balance of payments problem. Mexico's already substantial foreign public debt more than tripled from U.S.$29.45 billion in 1976 to U.S.$92.41 billion in 1982.[41] Furthermore, the appreciation of the peso's exchange rate on the dollar damaged nonresource-based exports, resulting in a flood of imports and a reversal of the ISI Mexico had long cultivated.[42] The stage was set for disaster. In just over a decade, the Mexican economy had slipped from relative stability and growth to instability, uncertainty, and a looming debt crisis. The catalyst that brought down this precarious house of cards was the near simultaneous worldwide drop of oil prices and rise of interest rates in 1981–1982. López Portillo infamously condemned himself to a lifetime of hounding when he allowed the peso to plummet, just days after dramatic claims that he would defend the peso "like a dog."

The ensuing crisis was met by tentative and partial efforts to restructure the economy by López Portillo's successor, President Miguel de la Madrid. De la Madrid's most important contributions included international agreements to renegotiate foreign debt and Mexico's 1986 entry into the General Agreement on Tariffs and Trade (GATT), which evolved into the World Trade Organization (WTO) in 1995. However, despite these tentative steps toward liberalization, recurrent deficits and soaring rates of inflation continued until the end of the decade (see Figure 2.3). The IMF and a new generation of foreign-educated technocrats in Mexico began to call for continued trade liberalization and a major restructuring of the domestic economy, by which state intervention would be greatly reduced through the privatization of government-owned enterprises and parastatals. De la Madrid's successor, President Carlos Salinas de Gortari (1988–1994), heeded these calls by implementing wholesale privatization and by further opening the Mexican economy to global competition through the North American Free Trade Agreement (NAFTA). Salinas, educated at Harvard, represented a new generation of technocrats, ambitious young men who worked their way to positions of power in the bureaucracy, rather than through the ruling party apparatus, and were quite different from past PRI leaders. However, Salinas's administration remained focused on sustaining the political status quo. Indeed, under Salinas, whose six years of neoliberal economic reforms were tempered by "neopopulist" programs, such as the National Solidarity Program (Programa Nacional de Solidaridad, PRONASOL), the PRI recovered a significant degree of "performance legitimacy."[43]

However, certain flaws became apparent in Mexico's implementation of the neoliberal model, notably high levels of corruption in the bidding process of privatization and negative trends in Mexican living standards throughout the 1980s and 1990s. Soon, these problems were accompanied by, if not contributors to, a bizarre level of political turmoil that struck the nation in 1994. Armed rebellion in the state of Chiapas and guerrilla activity in other states, high-level political assassinations, national corruption scandals, and Mexico's worst currency devaluation since the early 1980s combined to make that year a chaotic parade of tragedies.[44] In short, the long journey from crisis to crisis and devaluation to devaluation set the scene for Mexico's accelerated political transition in the latter part of the 1990s. Despite several important recoveries, the gradual destruction of the economic pillar of the PRI's legitimacy and support was a decisive factor in the regime's undoing.

Democratization and Political Institutions in Mexico

Like its long period of sustained economic growth prior to the 1970s, Mexico's institutional arrangements also served as a pillar of PRI hegemony for decades. However, here again, gradual but consequential changes spanning

Figure 2.3 Total Mexican Federal Government Revenues and Expenditures, 1976–1988

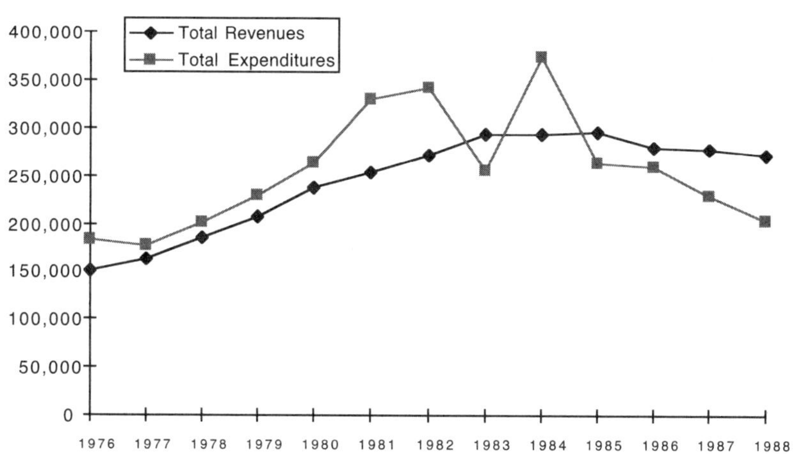

Source: Adapted from Carlos Bazdresch and Santiago Levy's Table 8.3 "Indicators for Public Finance" in "Populism and Economic Policy in Mexico, 1970–1982," in *The Macro-economics of Populism in Latin America*, ed. Rudiger Dornbusch and Sebastian Edwards (Chicago: University of Chicago Press, 1991).

four decades helped to increase the political spaces for opposition and benefited the PAN directly by increasing its political representation at all levels. Taking advantage of these new spaces, PAN candidates gained greater political experience, as well as opportunities to monitor and criticize the regime; these successes laid the groundwork for future gains at the municipal and state levels. Also, as a result, the PAN was able to press for further opening; when the PRI gave an inch, the PAN pushed for a yard, incrementally increasing the literal geographic base of the party. Over time, alterations to the regime's electoral institutions were most significant to improving the PAN's opportunity structure, though other reforms empowering local and state governments also deserve mention.

The gradual opening of the electoral system can be reduced to three major periods: the 1963 Party Deputies system, the 1977 LFOPPE system, and the Federal Code of Electoral Institutions and Procedures (Código Federal de Instituciones y Procedimientos Electorales, COFIPE) system of the 1990s. The first two periods, described in the previous section in greater detail, were primarily oriented toward increasing the pluralistic representation of the regime without ceding the PRI's lock on elected office. First, because party-deputy seats provided temporary spaces for the opposition without reducing the PRI's access to the legislature, they have been cited frequently as part of a strategy to legitimize and reinforce PRI hegemony, to create disincentives for opposition parties to grow, and to fragment the electorate by rewarding relatively small parties.[45] Second, the LFOPPE reforms of 1977 again provided limited improvement of proportionality in the Chamber of Deputies. The most notable effect of these reforms was the replacement of the old party-deputy system, expanding the Chamber of Deputies by 100 permanent seats that were allocated by proportional representation.[46] Both the 1963 and 1977 reforms focused on altering the degree of plurality in the political system and were primarily designed by the PRI, despite pressures from the opposition. Both did offer the PAN and other opposition parties greater access to public office, valuable professional political experience in the legislature, and opportunities to showcase their ideas and criticisms of the regime.[47] Positions in elected office enabled the PAN to reward its activists with candidacies of real value and, despite disincentives to "overperform," presented a major incentive for the PAN to field legislative candidates.

In the period from 1989–1990, the PAN and the PRI collaborated to end more than four decades of direct executive control of electoral processes by creating two new, relatively independent authorities, the Federal Electoral Institute (Instituto Federal Electoral, IFE) and the Federal Electoral Tribunal (Tribunal Federal Electoral, TRIFE), to manage federal electoral processes and the adjudication of disputes, respectively.[48] The new electoral laws, known as the COFIPE, brought an emphasis on electoral transparency—free and fair elections, not just greater proportional representation—through independent monitoring of the electoral process and multiparty negotiation of the terms of electoral competition.[49] In the short run, these reforms initially maintained a significant role for the Ministry of the Interior; introduced electoral formulas for proportional representation that initially overrepresented the PRI; and, for good measure, included a clause that automatically assured a simple majority in the Congress to the largest minority party.

In the long run, these and subsequent reforms in 1994 and 1996 strengthened the Federal Electoral Institute, increasing outside representation on its Council; ended the system by which the Congress approved electoral results; introduced proportional representation to the Senate, a long-standing PAN demand; provided new penalties for electoral fraud; placed the electoral tribunals under the control of the Supreme Court; and tightened IFE control of the parties' use of public funds. These changes spelled real and major improvements in the credibility of Mexican federal elections and served as a model for electoral reforms at the subnational level.[50] The cumulative result of these institutional changes was a slow but steady decline in the PRI's share of the vote in Mexican federal elections (see Figure 2.4).

Figure 2.4 Declining PRI Hegemony: Vote Percentages in Mexican Federal Elections, by Party, 1952–1997

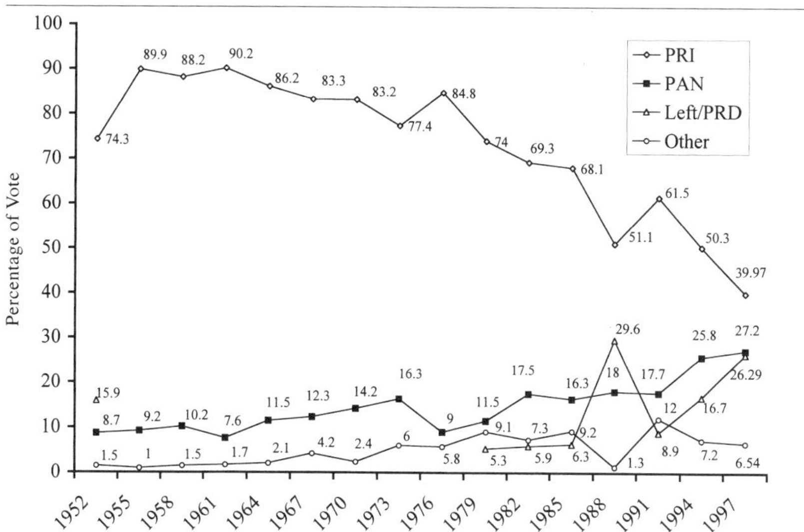

Sources: Adapted from Silvia Gómez Tagle, *La Frágil Democracia Mexicana: Partidos Políticos y Elecciones* (Mexico City: García y Valadés Editors, 1993); Juan Molinar Horcasitas, "The 1985 Federal Elections in Mexico: The Product of a System," in *Electoral Patterns and Perspectives in Mexico*, ed. Arturo Alvarado. Monograph Series, 20 (La Jolla, Calif.: Center for U.S.-Mexican Studies, 1987); Carlos Sirvent, "Las Elecciones de 1997: El Voto por la Alternancia," in *Estudios Políticos*, Cuarta Época, no. 16 (September–December, 1997), pp. 67–89.

In addition to these federal electoral reforms, President De la Madrid introduced amendments to Article 115 of the Mexican Constitution in 1983 with the express intention of revitalizing local government and helping to fuel the nation's social and economic development. In theory, municipal governments were given greater responsibilities and autonomy; in practice, there were several problems with these decentralization initiatives.[51] First was the fact that the 1983 municipal reforms granted local governments the responsibility to operate in policy arenas that they were not equipped to manage because of their limited financial and administrative capacity, often leading to "the *de facto* performance of many of these functions by state governments."[52] In fact, as the opposition began to win spaces at the municipal level over the course of the decade, non-PRI mayors frequently found themselves politically and financially marginalized—even harassed—in their relationships with state and federal governments.[53] A second problem with decentralization initiatives under de la Madrid was that, despite the central government's formally stated agenda of devolution of power to municipalities, many federal agencies and their activities were merely "deconcentrated" to local areas.[54] That is, many federal agencies simply created additional field offices to provide more direct links between local constituents and the federal government. In this sense, the central government once again restructured institutional arrangements as a means of regaining the regime's eroding legitimacy and reinvigorating the center's control.

Still, the 1983 constitutional reform's introduction of proportional representation to the municipal level offered new political spaces to the opposition. While municipal governments were relatively weak and the ability of opposition city council members (*regidores*) to influence policy was extremely limited, they did provide parties a more prominent vantage from which to observe and criticize the regime. By gaining firsthand experience in local government, PAN city council members learned about the workings of local government, which would prove valuable as the party accumulated municipal and state victories over the course of the 1980s and 1990s.

Then, the PRI's declining hegemony spelled significant gains for the PAN. The PAN was especially well prepared to take advantage of these institutional reforms and other circumstances for three reasons. First, as discussed in the previous chapter, unlike the majority of opposition parties that proliferated from the 1940s until 1988, the PAN was one of a handful that was fully autonomous from the PRI. It was, therefore, able to present itself as a real alternative to the ruling party rather than as a token opposition force.[55] Second, because the PAN came into existence under relatively strict federal regulations, unlike other genuine opposition parties like the Mexican Democratic Party (Partido Demócrata Mexicano, PDM), for example, which emerged in the 1970s, the party had established a national brand name and organizational presence. Thus, the party was consistently able to generate the high levels of representation under the proportional formulas. Third, as discussed in Chapter 3, the PAN's organizational development in key regional strongholds established a local tradition that allowed it to seize new spaces created for political contestation at the subnational level in the 1980s. In short, the institutional changes presented the PAN with opportunities for which it was particularly well suited in comparison with other opposition parties.[56]

Political Culture and Democratization in Mexico

The transformation of patterns of behavior, political beliefs, and attitudes demonstrated in the 1980s and 1990s was very significant for the PAN. In discussing the political culture of authoritarianism in Mexico, I noted that PRI hegemony was made possible in part by norms of clientelism and corporatism, revolutionary nationalism, and justifiably negative attitudes about politics and civic participation. The public's positive perception of the PRI—and negative perceptions of the opposition—together with a complex network of entrenched interests based on traditional practices of paternalism and interest-aggregation, ensured PRI support over several decades. Again, this is not to suggest that Mexicans have a preference for or are inherently predisposed to authoritarianism. To the contrary, as discussed below, political culture in Mexico underwent a considerable shift correlated with the process of democratization; this shift was relevant to the ability of the opposition to mobilize support against the regime.

First, the PRI's reduced capacity to rely on clientelism and corporatism as a means of generating political support came in tandem with the exhaustion of the long successful Mexican economic model. The 1980s shrank the pie that fed the PRI's patron-client networks, severely straining the state's relationship with its corporatist organizations and client groups and having significant cultural implications. That is, if there ever was an Iberian tradition that helped to perpetuate corporatism and clientelism in Mexico and the rest of Latin America, that tradition was seriously undermined when the state's resources for patronage shrank during the economic crises of the 1980s. Patterns of acceptable behavior that once obstructed political participation gave way, circumscribing the PRI's capacity for hegemony and providing new opportunities for the PAN and other parties of the opposition to mobilize support against the regime. In short, under these circumstances, the PRI—the world's largest, oldest, and most successful political machine—could not afford to sustain itself through its traditional practices.

An important illustration came in the 1980s, with the rise of new grassroots and urban popular movements that represented a significant change in Mexican political behavior.[57] This change evolved over two decades of activity by poor and middle-class groups, who were forced to act on their own behalf by the inadequacy of the government's response to Mexican urbanization since the 1930s. The effectiveness of these activist groups was bolstered by the 1968 student movement's impact on the national culture as well as its leaders' skills, according to Vivienne Bennett.[58] Such popular mobilization represented an important innovation in Mexican political culture because the groups presented alternatives to traditional norms of behavior, emphasizing civic awareness and the autonomy and responsibility of the community.[59]

Others have linked the proliferation of urban popular movements in the 1980s to the improved electoral performance of the left. Yet, new "civic" attitudes generated by outrage over recurring economic crises and the inadequacy of government services were hardly limited to a particular ideology or class.[60] Vivienne Bennett (1992) notes that while the economic crises of the 1980s aggravated and extended existing poverty, economic constraints had more of an impact on the lifestyles of middle income groups, as the poor could often rely on their already developed survival strategies to cope with poverty. Verily, many of the concerns raised by PAN militants in cities like Tijuana, León, Mérida, and elsewhere simply reflected demands for basic urban services like trash collection, a safe and reliable water supply, adequate housing, and public safety. These activists often employed similar strategies of popular mobilization, including public demonstrations, marches, occupation of public buildings, and the like. Nor were *all* of the urban poor necessarily associated with the ideological left, as seen in the previous chapter.

Second, many Mexicans were quickly disillusioned by the regime's failure to address the multiple crises of the 1980s. The failure of the De la Madrid government to respond to these crises clearly had an important impact on civic beliefs about the nature of the state and its mythology. The crises of the 1980s revealed the limitations of "the man behind the curtain," and many Mexicans—like Dorothy in the *Wizard of Oz*—soon learned that they had much more control over their own destinies than the overbearing Wizard. For example, at the national level, the limited capacity of the state was made painfully clear in 1985 by the aftermath of the disastrous Mexico City earthquake, which immobilized the city for several days. The government's slow response prompted many citizens to pool their own resources to deal with the damage, while disaster relief given to the Mexican government by international sources mysteriously disappeared in some cases.[61] The example of Mexico City was symptomatic of the regime's failure to address basic concerns at the local level in urban areas throughout the nation, which offered significant opportunities to the PAN in other important cases, such as Chihuahua (Chihuahua), León (Guanajuato), Mérida (Yucatán), and Tijuana (Baja California).[62]

It is especially worth noting that the media came to play a very significant role in pulling back the curtain to reveal the character and limitations of the PRI regime, just as it had once played a part in perpetuating the PRI's power and mythology.[63] Under the old regime, the news and entertainment media was dominated by the PRI government and functioned essentially as its lackey. Those few independent media voices that survived in the wilderness frequently suffered significant instances of discrimination, harassment, and abuse.[64] However, over the 1980s and 1990s, the emergence of new, independent media sources was both a reflection of and a contributing factor in the changing political culture of the late twentieth century. Traditional sources of PRI support in the media, such as Televisa, now faced competition from new television media outlets, such as TV Azteca, and increasingly emboldened print media sources, such as *Zeta*, *Frontera*, *A.M.*, *La Crónica*, and the *Diario de Yucatán*. Above all, television and the instantaneous transmission of powerful images and ideas was a powerful force that affected people's attitudes toward the regime; the ability of the regime effectively to monopolize the use of the media declined as the media itself changed and as various opposition groups became more adept at using it to transmit their points of view. In this sense, video not only killed the radio star but also became a battleground in the struggle against Mexican authoritarianism.

A third major shift in Mexican political culture can be seen in people's improved attitudes toward politics. In their study of democratization and public opinion in Mexico, Jorge I. Domínguez and James A. McCann argue that, since the late 1950s, attitudes have changed dramatically and in ways that have been favorable for the prospects of Mexican democracy.

> As time has passed, Mexicans have . . . become less likely to prefer reliance on strong leaders over reliance on the rule of law; they do not favor the participation of nondemocratic institutions in political life; and they strongly favor the internal democratization of the ruling party's presidential nomination practices. . . . The point is that Mexico has changed, and its citizens are ready for a more democratic polity.[65]

One important aspect of this attitude adjustment is that the opposition was seen as a *real* alternative. In this sense, attitudes about what *can be* in Mexican politics have changed dramatically. For the PAN, this new optimism about the prospects of the opposition came with slogans like Baja California's "Yes, it can be done!" (*¡Sí, se puede*!), which became a national battle cry for political change. The overt message of optimism is that anything is possible; the underlying implications are that collectively Mexicans can work toward their goals together. In short, the notion that political action can positively affect peoples' lives was a major revelation for many Mexicans in the 1980s and 1990s and helped to mobilize support for the opposition.

Democratization and Mexico's Changing Competitive Environment

Additional key factors that directly contributed to the PAN's political opportunities over the 1990s were the changing competitive circumstances created by internal divisions within the ruling party and by the emergence of a new major opposition party. Cleavages within the regime had developed as early as the 1970s, when Mexico faced financial troubles prior to the discovery of oil. However, it was not until the crisis finally set in during the 1980s that PRI divisions over economic policy reached the boiling point. In the midst of spiraling inflation and massive discontent, a new faction of the PRI called the Democratic Current (Corriente Democrático) emerged, favoring internal party reforms and a return to state-led growth. The selection of technocrat Carlos Salinas as the PRI's next presidential candidate drove such elements to bolt the ruling party and form an electoral alliance of leftist parties, united under Cuauhtémoc Cárdenas, son of former President Lázaro Cárdenas. Cárdenas generated massive support and ranked closely with both the PRI and PAN candidate in polls preceding the election. Yet on election day major irregularities placed Cárdenas second and PAN candidate Manuel Clouthier third behind Salinas. Nevertheless, Cárdenas continued to press for a new leftist alternative to the PRI and helped to found the Party of the Democratic Revolution (Partido de la Revolución Democrática, PRD), which brought former elements of the PRI together with elements of Mexico's long fragmented left.

While the recurrent political and economic crises of the 1970s and 1980s are commonly associated with rising support for the "new left" in Mexico, the PRD was not the only beneficiary of dissatisfaction with the PRI. The PAN was also a beneficiary of the PRI's troubles and registered strong increases in support in the mid-1980s and also fared very well in the 1988 elections, despite being overshadowed by Cárdenas's defection from the PRI. The PAN had particularly strong appeal to elements of the middle class and urban poor demanding basic services at the local level.[66] Furthermore, as discussed in subsequent chapters, the 1981–1982 devaluations and bank nationalizations brought a significant number of small- and medium-sized businesspeople into the PAN, who provided important elements of leadership and innovation within the organization.

In addition, the emergence of the PRD contributed in significant ways to the regime's apparent tolerance for PAN victories, viewed by many scholars as a necessary concession by the Salinas administration.[67] Salinas was faced with a severe legitimacy crisis at the beginning of his term, and the PAN provided crucial political and legislative support. In particular, the PAN was instrumental in recognizing Salinas's questionable victory, providing support for the president's neoliberal package and passing constitutional amendments that required approval by a two-thirds majority in Congress. Hence, many believe that the PAN sold out by negotiating a surreptitious pact or "concertation" (*concertación*) with the PRI in exchange for political favors, including recognition of PAN victories and the passage of many of the political reforms generated during the Salinas administration.[68] Yet, this explanation tends to overlook the tremendous activism of the PAN to earn its victories and protest local and state fraud.[69] Furthermore, many Panistas resolutely deny the existence of such a pact. PAN President Carlos Castillo Peraza (1993–1996), for example, argued that such allegations were completely false "because no one has won more against the PRI than the PAN. . . . It is absurd that the PRI [would] make some agreement to lose; that is stupid."[70] The fact that the PAN did engage in private meetings with Salinas was long cited as evidence of such collaboration, though in 1999 it was revealed that Cárdenas had also engaged in similar meetings soon after the 1988 election.[71] It is, therefore, difficult to be certain that a formal PAN-PRI pact was established.

What is clear is that, *concertación* or not, the PRI obtained short-term benefits from PAN support. First of all, the PAN's de facto recognition of Carlos Salinas's questionable victory in the 1988 presidential elections lent the party's "good name" to the legitimacy-starved regime. Furthermore, PAN's acceptance of measures designed to protect PRI hegemony in the legislature helped to ensure a PRI sweep of the Chamber of Deputies in 1991.[72] At the same time, whether or not the PAN benefited from the PRI's increased tolerance for its electoral victories, PAN advocacy of these reform packages helped to satisfy some of its long-standing demands and yielded long-term advances for the political system, including the establishment of an independent electoral authority, the restructuring of the Senate, and the reform of public funding for political parties. Furthermore, the internal divisions within the PRI, the split with Cárdenas and other members of the Democratic Current, and their eventual formation of the PRD were very disorienting for the PRI and strengthened the PAN's relative position in the party system, as the PRI and PRD battled over similar elements in the electorate. In short, the shift in Mexico's competitive context, resulting from the PRI's significant internal crisis, presented the PAN with important opportunities to mobilize and integrate new elements into the organization.

Challenges and Opportunities for the PAN

For decades, the socioeconomic, institutional, cultural, and competitive dynamics of Mexican authoritarianism constrained the PAN and other opposition parties from developing as effective political organizations. The PRI's particular brand of authoritarianism was successful because competition from different political alternatives was tolerated and even encouraged, while obstacles within the system ensured that only the PRI could hold power. As explored in Chapter 3, during this early period, the PAN functioned more as a club than as an effective mechanism for placing candidates in office. Hence, PAN activists were most commonly quixotic activists dedicated to the party, its ideological principles, and the ultimate goal of transforming the PRI regime. Beginning in the 1960s and much more notably in the 1980s and 1990s, democratization and new opportunities for electoral success provided the PAN with important opportunities to develop from a club-like cadre into a larger, more professional, and more mass-oriented organization. Increasing electoral success in this period was accompanied by unprecedented growth in membership, organizational development, and sharp growing pains, all of which would dramatically shape the course of Mexico's political future.

Notes

1. Quoted in Krauze, 1997, p. 235.
2. Televised concession by Ernesto Zedillo at 11:05 P.M. on July 2, 2000.
3. Reyna and Weinert, 1977.
4. Díaz governed Mexico directly as president throughout this period, except from 1880–1984, when he ruled through a puppet president, Manuel Gonzales.
5. Naturally, the formula was somewhat more complex than portrayed here. For example, as Hansen (1974) notes, the Díaz regime provided protective tariffs that benefited both foreign and domestic producers, provided tax incentives for various types of investment, and pegged the peso to silver in order to make foreign imports less domestically competitive.
6. Krauze, 1997.
7. Benjamin and Wasserman, 1990; Knight, 1986; Womack, 1968.
8. Hart, 1987.
9. Womack, 1968.
10. La France, 1990.
11. To avoid confusion, I give preference to the ruling party's better-known acronym, PRI, even though the party existed in two previous incarnations as the Partido Nacional Revolucionario (PNR) and the Partido Revolucionario Mexicano (PRM).
12. Cornelius, et al., 1989.
13. At the same time, Calles faced a tremendous political crisis in the wake of the assassination of president-elect Gen. Alvaro Obregón. Obregón had been the strongman behind Calles, who oversaw the elimination of the clause preventing re-election in order to pave Obregón's way back into the presidency. The creation of the ruling party was thus partly an attempt by Calles to consolidate his own power.
14. Both the CTM and CNC were creations of Lázaro Cárdenas and intended to bolster the representation of these neglected groups within the official party vis-à-vis the military and the popular sectors.
15. Garrido, 1995.
16. Cornelius and Craig, 1984.
17. Hellman, 1988.
18. It should be noted that initially the practice of personalistic politics prevailed despite the no re-election clause. Both the "shadow" of Gen. Alvaro Obregón (1920–1924) and the "Maximato" of Plutarco Calles (1924–1928) demonstrated the weakness of the early post-Revolutionary Mexican presidency as an institution. It was not until the presidency of Lázaro Cárdenas (1934–1940) that the institution achieved an autonomous and continuous base of authority that outlasted and overcame personalities. Aguilar Camín and Meyer, 1993.
19. Taylor's (1997) discussion of this and other problems resulting from the extension of the ban on re-election to legislative positions is excellent.

20. Molinar Horcasitas, 1991.

21. Castañeda, 2000; Garrido, 1989.

22. In particular, the Federal Electoral Law established new requirements for party registration, requiring a base of thirty thousand nationwide members, dispersed in groups of at least one thousand persons in twenty-one (two-thirds) of Mexico's thirty-two federal districts.

23. Taylor, 1997, p. 312.

24. Ibid., p. 312.

25. Interestingly, many of the smaller parties were still unable to reach the 1.5 percent threshold despite the reforms but were granted party-deputy seats because it was in the PRI's self-interest to perpetuate the illusion of pluralism.

26. Parties that failed to meet this minimum threshold were still granted the right to participate in national elections in order to seek registration.

27. These deputyships were allocated to parties on a regional and proportional basis and were only distributed to parties that captured fewer than sixty single-member district seats. An additional requirement was that to obtain proportional representation (*plurinominal*) seats, a party had to run candidates in at least one hundred districts. Plurinominal seats were distributed by a formula of proportional representation that some suggest left room for tampering. See Taylor, 1997.

28. Vives Segl, 2002, p. 50.

29. Almond and Verba, 1963.

30. Paired against the United States, the United Kingdom, Germany, and Italy, Mexico was an unusual case selection that brought particular and controversial findings to the study.

31. While *The Civic Culture* was methodologically flawed, the study unleashed a wave of research that sought to identify the nature and significance of political attitudes in Mexico. In a critical revisiting of Almond and Verba's work, Ann Craig and Wayne Cornelius note three broad types of flaws in the 1963 study: methodological problems, problems of validity and conceptual equivalence, and substantive problems. Craig and Cornelius, 1989, pp. 325–383.

32. Kevin Middlebrook (1995) cogently argues that authoritarianism was the outcome in many countries in the twentieth century—beginning with Mexico in 1910, followed by the Soviet Union, China, Cuba, and a host of others—in large part because of the high degree of mass mobilization that accompanies social revolution, which requires newly empowered elites to establish mechanisms to channel and control highly mobilized actors without compromising elite political control.

33. Craig and Cornelius, 1989.

34. These protagonists were the faces of the slogans of effective suffrage and political alternation, land distribution, local autonomy, and social justice, among others. Two leading antagonists in the struggle for power in the course and aftermath of the Revolution, Alvaro Obregón and Plutarco Calles, often worked in direct opposition to the achievement of such goals. For example, Obregón—the *caudillo* whose shadow loomed over Mexico in the 1920s—went so far as to breach the regime's solemn commitment to "no reelection" by having then President Calles amend the Constitution to pave Obregón's way for a return to the presidential palace. Obregón was only prevented from such a return when, as president-elect, he was assassinated in one of several attempts on his life.

35. Calles first appointed Portes Gil as interim president; Portes Gil replaced president-elect Alvaro Obregón, who was assassinated after making the first and last attempt at reelection to the presidency after the Revolution. It may be unfair to refer to Ortiz Rubio as a "Callista stooge." Ortiz Rubio, who was shot in the face on the day

of his inauguration, spent two years trying to resist the influence of Calles before finally resigning. Abelardo Rodríguez, on the other hand, was clearly one of Calles's longtime cronies. Calles had appointed him governor of Baja California, where he grew rich from graft taken from liquor, gambling, and prostitution businesses serving the San Diego–Tijuana border region during the era of U.S. prohibition.

36. Cárdenas fought in the Revolution; at the age of 16, he walked halfway across Mexico to join the forces of Plutarcho Calles. He quickly advanced to lieutenant colonel by the age of 20 and ultimately achieved the rank of general by the age of 27. He fought as a Carrancista, Obregonista, and Callista against revolutionary legends Villa and Zapata, as well as the Yaqui Indians of Sonora. Through his affiliation with Calles, Cárdenas was awarded the post of governor of Michoacán. Governor Cárdenas developed a strong local base of supporters by establishing broad labor confederations and redistributing land to agrarian workers. Cárdenas was later able to advance in the PNR, thanks to this support and Calles's perception of his loyalty.

37. This policy was beneficial to and strongly supported by the Mexican private sector, which then President Miguel Alemán saw as the primary agent of change in his program for national development. Bazdresch and Levy, 1991, pp. 88–89.

38. See Donald J. Mabry, *The Mexican University and the State: Students Conflicts, 1910–1971* (College Station: Texas A&M University Press, 1982); Elena Poniatowski, *La noche de Tlatelolco* (New York: Viking, 1975).

39. Hierro and Sanginés Krause, 1990, p. 143.

40. Lustig, 1992, pp. 19–24.

41. By 1976, Mexico's debt levels had already risen to more than three times the 1970 rate of U.S.$8.63 billion. Bazdresch and Levy, 1991.

42. Lustig, 1992, pp. 19–24.

43. Salinas's use of the National Solidarity Program (Programa Nacional de Solidaridad, PRONASOL) is frequently cited as one of the most successful measures to offset the costs of economic restructuring and trade liberalization. Cornelius, et al., 1994; Dresser, 1991.

44. This strange year of chaos culminated in both the sudden eruption of the volcano Popocateptl and public hysteria over claims about the emergence of a supernatural goat-sucker or *chupacabras*.

45. Taylor (1997) suggests that the introduction of party deputyships was a response by the regime to the PAN's protests against fraud, violence, and repression in the legislative elections of 1958 and subsequent state elections in Baja California and Yucatán. In contrast, Mabry (1973a) suggests that the very concept of party deputyships might well have been suggested to future President Díaz Ordáz by future PAN President Christlieb during their tenure as representatives to the Federal Electoral Commission. Furthermore, argues Mabry, the PAN's relatively cordial relationship with the government under Christlieb probably facilitated López Mateos's support for the party-deputy system. See also Prud'homme, 1997.

46. The 1976 reforms also introduced public funding for political parties, though the PAN refused the bulk of this funding for more than a decade.

47. In fact, a number of PAN proposals were actually adopted by the PRI majority, albeit with the ruling party claiming credit for the legislation.

48. Under the COFIPE, the IFE was headed by representatives from the executive and legislative branches, registered political parties, and the citizenry.

49. An extension of the 1977 reforms came in the late 1980s as a new Federal Electoral Code (Código Federal Electoral, CFE), effective from 1986–1988, increased the number of proportional representation seats from one hundred to two hundred. Another important effect of the new system of proportional representation was to

regionalize the selection of listed candidates. See Alcocer V., 1995; Molinar Horcasitas, 1991; Molinar Horcasitas, 1993.

50. Eisenstadt, 2004.

51. The reforms identified the following as areas of municipal responsibility: water supply and sewage, sanitation, urban roads and transportation, parks and cemeteries, slaughterhouses and markets, public lighting, local police and traffic, land use planning, and environmental protection.

52. Nickson, 1995.

53. Cornelius, et al., 1999; Espinoza Valle, 2000; Espinoza Valle, 1998; Hernández Vicencio, 2001; Rodríguez and Ward, 1994; Rodríguez and Ward, 1995; Rodríguez and Ward, 1992; Shirk, 1999.

54. Rodríguez, 1997.

55. Many of the PRI-affiliated or parastatal parties were insignificant, phantom parties that had little real organizational basis and whose representatives closely followed the PRI party line.

56. Eisenstadt, 2004.

57. For an interesting discussion of the evolution of urban popular movements and popular resistance from the left, see Vivienne Bennett, 1992; Hodges and Gandy, 2002.

58. Many of these groups found their roots in the 1968 student movement, which produced a generation of experienced activists who were able to contribute their organizational and leadership skills. This "cohort of militant students . . . responded to the violent repression of 1968 and 1971 by looking for direct links with the masses." Vivienne Bennett, 1992, pp. 240–242.

59. Vivienne. Bennett (1992) argues that such movements helped to construct new channels for poor urban residents to express their needs, and demonstrated the inability of corporatist organizations such as the CTM and the CNOP to co-opt the urban poor because of their shrinking resource base.

60. Indeed, some activists from these movements actually became involved in the PAN. Interview with Cuauhtémoc Cárdona (March 4, 1999) in Mexico City.

61. One *panista* recounted working at an abandoned Red Cross facility; since the regular employees never arrived, the respondent and a group of concerned citizens began to provide voluntary relief. While this voluntary operation was functioning, the Mexican first lady and her entourage made a visit to the shelter, where she borrowed an apron from one of the volunteers, posed for several photographs, immediately removed the apron, and left the shelter without providing any further "assistance." Also, on more than one occasion, supplies being delivered to this shelter were commandeered by police officers at gunpoint. Informal interview in Mexico City (July 14, 1998).

62. For decades, the "curtain" was maintained in part by the "great and all-powerful" regime's capacity to isolate the periphery by limiting communication of discontent from region to region. Thus, what is particularly significant about the 1985 earthquake is that it was an experience shared by millions of Mexicans that could not be ignored or covered up.

63. Lawson, 2002.

64. Interview with Carlos Menéndez, owner of the *Diario de Yucatán* (August 4, 1997).

65. For Domínguez and McCann (1996: 47–48), these attitudinal changes have resulted primarily from a more educated population, the limited impact and/or reform of the Catholic Church since the 1960s, "international influences," and the very increases in political competitiveness experienced in the institutional arena.

66. See Arriola, 1994; Middlebrook, 2001; Mizrahi, 2003.

67. For the most comprehensive analyses of the political circumstances following Salinas's election, see Cornelius, et al., 1989.

68. Alcocer V. (1995) argues that these reforms were "the principal expression of an unspoken alliance between the ruling party and the PAN, facilitating a political transition not to a multiparty system but to a bipartisan (PRI–PAN) system, particularly in the Congress and local governments" (p. 62). Likewise, long-standing PAN demands for institutional reform—such as a restructuring of the Senate to allow for limited proportional representation—were met during the Salinas administration. See also Eisenstadt, 2004; Klesner, 1993.

69. This includes filing legal complaints, holding demonstrations, marching, occupying government buildings, staging hunger strikes, as well as persistent and skillful political maneuvering at both the national and subnational levels.

70. Interview with Carlos Castillo Peraza (July 16, 1998) in Mexico City. Interestingly, in the same interview, Castillo accused the PRI and PRD of a tacit alliance against the PAN in the 1997 elections, arguing that the PRI now perceived the PAN as a significant threat.

71. In response to revelations about this meeting in Jorge Castañeda's book, *La herencia*, Cárdenas admitted that he met with Salinas soon after the July 6, 1988, presidential elections. "Admite Cárdenas haberse reunido con CSG," *La Jornada*, April 15, 1999.

72. The PAN's representation in the lower house dropped from 101 to 90 seats after the 1991 elections. The PRD fared much worse, partly due to problems of its own, the possible targeting of government resources through PRONASOL, and as a result of the reconfiguration of the institutional context to its disadvantage. At the same time, the PRI surged ahead. The PRI's average rise in PRD strongholds was 142 percent, compared with the PRI's 43 percent rise in PAN strongholds. Stansfield, 1996.

3

The Origins and Development of the PAN

We had confidence, we had faith . . . in the rationality of politics; in that, by the strength of rational argument, one day the Party would some day convince the people.

—Manuel Gómez Morin, c1964[1]

The hard path for Mexico, but at the same time, the undeniably obligatory path for Catholics, is to promote the political rehabilitation of the country through the installation of a representative regime.

—Efraín González Luna, 1954[2]

Characterizing any political party requires an understanding that parties are not unitary actors but groups of individuals cooperating and sometimes competing to achieve their objectives. The standard metaphor used to characterize political parties portrays them as "teams" of men and women working toward shared political objectives by placing their teammates in government. In a country like Mexico, where access to power was available only to a single party, competition for governmental representation by opposition parties seemed futile and even irrational. Yet, beginning in 1939, teams of men and women came together to form the National Action Party and succeeded in making it the primary political force opposed to the hegemonic PRI for most of the next sixty years. Why did these individuals embark on this seemingly irrational endeavor? How did they sustain the PAN in a tormenting political context that was at once open to contestation but ultimately hostile to credible opposition challenges against the PRI? Was the PAN simply a manifestation of reactionary, counter-revolutionary tendencies: a legacy of the Porfiriato? Or was it a pawn or tool of the PRI system? In short, what were the motives of those who became involved in the PAN, how did they sustain their organization over so many years, and, ultimately, how did they begin to challenge the PRI successfully in the late twentieth century?

The answers to these questions are not simple or clear-cut. Many characterizations of the PAN's ideology and programmatic agenda too frequently fall into the trap of conceptualizing the party as a unitary actor or focusing solely on a single aspect of the organization. Like blind men grabbing different parts of an elephant, explanations of the essential character of the PAN have been quite varied: alternately describing the party as a counter-revolutionary force, a religious movement, or a reaction to the Mexican left. However, a party is at least the sum of its parts, if not more than that. Thus, it is important to note how the objectives and motivations of individuals involved in the PAN varied and changed over time, depending on the political context and opportunity structures both inside and outside the organization. These subtleties help to explain how the PAN itself developed different tendencies at various periods in its history. In fact, continually shifting internal cleavages are one of the most important and enduring features of the PAN and are essential to understanding the party's developmental trajectory in the context of Mexico's unique brand of authoritarianism.

The Impossible Dream: Birth and Organizational Formation of the PAN

The PAN was founded in Mexico City in September 1939, after the wrenching period of national political consolidation that resulted in the hegemony of the so-called revolutionary family that was institutionalized in the form of the PRI. The birth of the PAN reflected a diverse set of concerns brought about by the Revolution and its aftermath. Some concerns resulted from the betrayal of the original liberal democratic principles that inspired the Revolution itself. Many of these concerns paralleled those of post–Revolutionary militant Catholic groups angered by secular reforms. Still others reflected the anti-despotism of the late 1920s and the concerns of private-sector interests alarmed by the leftism of the 1930s. Thus, among the PAN's earliest supporters were professionals, intellectuals, entrepreneurs, and ardent Catholics who reacted to growing anticlericism.

Manuel Gómez Morin was the visionary and chief architect of this new opposition party. Gómez Morin was a lawyer, economist, educator, and intellectual who personified Mexico's professional and entrepreneurial traditions. In 1918, Gómez Morin graduated with a law degree from the National Autonomous University of Mexico (Universidad Nacional Autónoma de México, UNAM), a unique vantage for observing the regime's early constitutional formation. During his studies at UNAM, Gómez Morin was among a select group of students teasingly nicknamed the "seven sages" of Mexico, a cohort that indeed included some of the most notable intellectuals of their generation.[3] After graduation, Gómez Morin served as undersecretary of finance and financial adviser to Presidents Alvaro Obregón and Plutarco

Calles, respectively, and in the process became one of the foremost architects of the Mexican financial system. Gómez Morin authored the laws that helped establish the basis of taxation and credit in post–Revolutionary Mexico, including those that created the Bank of Mexico in 1925 (which he directed during its first four years). Gómez Morin spent some time working as an international financial consultant in New York at the height of its progressive reform movement. Throughout his career, Gómez Morin also served periodically on the law faculty of his alma mater, UNAM, and was appointed rector of the university during a short but decisive period, from 1933 through 1934.[4]

Soon after the PRI, the "official" party, was founded in 1929, Gómez Morin became convinced that Mexico needed an alternative as a counterbalance to the regime. Gómez Morin strongly believed that an opposition force must rely on institutions rather than on individual personalities or occasional manifestations of societal discontent. Although the PAN's birth and early development depended heavily on Gómez Morin's own leadership, connections, and charisma, he did not take advantage of this influence and worked instead to institutionalize his vision of an opposition party. Meanwhile, Gómez Morin's background as a law student and professor likely contributed to his conviction that antisystem tactics were ineffective, undesirable means of producing political change.[5]

Gómez Morin's commitment to institutionalized opposition through legal channels was contrasted by one of Gómez Morin's close associates, José Vasconcelos, who became the first candidate to lose an election by fraud to the ruling party soon after its founding in 1929. Like Gómez Morin, Vasconcelos initially supported the Revolution and its governments. After finishing his law degree in 1905, Vasconcelos became active in the Anti–Reelectionist movement against Porfirio Díaz; Vasconcelos is believed to have originated Francisco I. Madero's slogan of "Effective Suffrage, No Reelection."[6] Later, after Madero's assassination, Vasconcelos served in various positions related to education, serving as minister of education under provisional President Eulalio Gutiérrez, rector of UNAM (1920–1921), and the first secretary of Public Education (1921–1924).

Vasconcelos's educational philosophy emphasized outreach to the masses, particularly Mexico's native peoples and those who were illiterate. For this reason, Vasconcelos encouraged the production of inexpensive, accessible textbooks, as well as the use of the arts as a form of education. Under Vasconcelos's supervision, Mexico's Secretariat of Public Education fostered the creation of many of Mexico's great murals—the works of José Clemente Orozco, Diego Rivera, and David Alfaro Siqueros—which helped both to celebrate and educate Mexicans about their own history on the very walls of government buildings. Vasconcelos was also well known for his somewhat controversial pronouncements on the virtues of the "Cosmic Race."[7]

Vasconcelos's first bid for public office, a 1924 opposition candidacy for the governorship of Oaxaca, was unsuccessful and led him to flee Mexico in exile. He returned to run an independent presidential campaign against the newly created ruling party in the 1929 presidential elections. According to Gómez Morin, who served as campaign treasurer for Vasconcelos, this opposition movement harked back to the 1910 Revolution:

> Above all the movement was political and [Vasconcelos] did not want to think about the possibility of the organization of a permanent party. . . . [Vasconcelos] wanted to put an end to the military dictators, to the "barbarous" dictators, as he used to say; he wanted to establish a civilian government, of political, not military, leaders, and subject to the norms of the Constitution.[8]

During the campaign, Gómez Morin tried but failed to convince Vasconcelos to found a more permanent organization to carry on his political movement. In 1928, Gómez Morin posed the question to Vasconcelos in a prophetic manner: "Is it better to start a fight that can lead opposition groups to extermination, in order to achieve an intermediate triumph or none at all? Or is it better to sacrifice the intermediate triumph to acquire the strength that can only come from a well oriented organization with the capacity to survive?"[9] A cautious adherent to practical and legal solutions, Gómez Morin advocated the institutionalization of opposition over sporadic, populist appeals. Yet, despite Gómez Morin's counsel, Vasconcelos refused to focus his efforts on developing a parallel political organization to support his campaign for the presidency. While his campaign achieved enormous popularity, Vasconcelos ultimately lost to the revolutionary party's candidate, Pascual Ortíz Rubio, and was forced to flee Mexico in exile. From the United States, Vasconcelos issued his *Plan de Guaymas*, which advocated a violent uprising against the fraud, but ultimately his movement failed.[10]

Vasconcelos's experience convinced Gómez Morin even more that legality and institutionalization were the keys to establishing effective opposition. As Gómez Morin began to lay the foundations for his vision in 1938, he expended tremendous energy making contact with friends and colleagues throughout Mexico, forging a network of committed individuals to develop a lasting base of organized support. Gómez Morin's recruitment strategies drew his colleagues and allies from multiple professions and explicitly encouraged these individuals to plant seeds for the organization in their respective states.[11] A memo written by Gómez Morin in 1939, directed to doctors, lawyers, architects, and other professionals, illustrated his view that a change in government personnel through the ruling party would not be sufficient to achieve the "deeper renovation of the orientation, methods, [and] spirit of national life." Instead, what

Mexico required was the creation of a new political party, which he described as follows:

> Its name is National Action. Action, because it is not about a new discussion, but rather the decided affirmation that things need to be certain for those who are frustrated with the current situation in society and in the Nation, and because those who have a definite conviction should seek to achieve its realization. National, because it should not be limited to a single group or region, but rather should extend throughout Mexico and to all aspects of Mexican society . . . [to achieve] the effective realization of a better life, spiritually and materially, for all Mexicans.[12]

By 1939, with help from a diverse group of supporters, Gómez Morin felt sufficiently confident to initiate formal procedures for constituting a new political party. An organizing committee was created in early 1939 to handle basic logistical and organizational matters and to define the party's general principles and objectives. In September 1939, the organizing committee called hundreds of party supporters together for the party's Constitutive Assembly (Asamblea Constitutiva) to witness the signing of the PAN's founding documents.

Gómez Morin's targeted recruitment strategy initially produced a "party of notables," with fewer than three hundred individuals signing the PAN's founding document. PAN organization developed at essentially two levels, both national and regional. Substantial decision-making authority and discretion resided in the hands of the party's national leadership, embodied by the National Executive Committee (Comité Ejecutivo Nacional, CEN). The concentration of authority in the CEN largely resulted from the limitations facing the regional committees; decentralization of responsibility was neither practical nor in great demand because the party's organizational capacity in the regions was still inchoate or sporadic at best. Also, considering that the party extended from the center to the periphery of the country, largely via Gómez Morin's informal contacts, the party's links to its regional committee were somewhat random and selective. Moreover, the party's selective formula for recruitment and its ideological aversion to aggregated interest representation limited its impetus to develop a mass base at the subnational level. Consequently, the resulting party resembled more of a social club with political tendencies than a mass-oriented party organization. Weak and sporadic subnational organization meant significant limitations for the party's candidates for national office, as the success of such candidates clearly depended on the PAN's regional organizations' capacities to mobilize voters and defend their victories from electoral fraud. In most cases, however, the party lacked a permanent paid staff, basic supplies and equipment, and even the physical space with which to conduct party business. The party's lack of resources meant that party leaders and candidates typically shouldered most of the expenses and activities of campaigning. Hence, one of the most noticeable implications of the party's limited resources at the subnational level was the inability to attract full-time, professional leaders who could attend to party business on a regular basis and recruit viable candidates for public office.[13]

Despite labels that long portrayed the PAN as the party of the rich, affiliation with the PAN was neither a sign of prestige nor elite social status, because those who actually participated regularly did not possess great wealth. Baja California PAN leader Salvador Rosas Magallón rejected assertions that the PAN was a party of bankers by asking why PAN campaigns featured journalists, workers, and carpenters as candidates for elected office.[14] Indeed, for most of the party's existence, the PAN was rarely able to attract notable or wealthy candidates. As PAN Senator Norberto Corella noted in a 1998 interview, "Formerly, the people who were in the party were very, very . . . good people, good citizens; but not sufficiently prominent or successful in their businesses or their professions, so their image in the community was not the best of images. They might have been the best of people, but they were not perceived so by the citizens."[15]

The PAN's lack of resources and effective candidates for elected office were mutually reinforcing problems that contributed to the party's dim prospects for victory. At the same time, the fact that activism in the PAN involved significant material and personal sacrifices speaks volumes about those who joined in the organization. If we simplify the three types of motivations often associated with participation in political parties—policy-seeking incentives, office-seeking incentives, and social gratification—the PAN lacked the kind of selective benefits that might serve as a motive for collective action, and the prospect of achieving public office through the PAN was slim. Thus, for many who chose to join the organization, the emotive aspect and social rewards derived from participation in a community of like-minded individuals, which provided their essential motivation. The PAN was, in the words of poet and party activist Roger Cicero, a party of quixotic "dreamers" (*ilusos*).

The PAN Paradox: Liberal, Democratic Conservatives

Outside the party, portrayals of the PAN were far less romantic. Almost immediately, the PAN acquired a reputation as a party with "a very high level of economic and human resources, [whose] . . . movement had influence far beyond its numbers . . . representing the interests of the Church, big business, and upper- and middle-class professional people . . . meriting its popular designation as *club bancario*, 'the bankers' club.'"[16] At best, this characterization, a widely accepted view of the party and its historical origins even today, greatly oversimplifies the various interests and actors that came together to form the party in 1939. At worst, this description was the product of decades of anti-PAN propaganda perpetuated by the PRI regime. However, the true political orientation and ideological underpinnings of the PAN are more complex than this and require a more substantial discussion.

Given widespread popular conceptions of the PAN as a menacing party of the right, it is important to examine the notion that the party emerged as a reactionary or counter-revolutionary force against the Revolution of 1910. This view can be found prominently in scholarly interpretations of the PAN and its origins. According to Brandenburg (1956), for example, the PAN was the direct ideological successor of traditional conservatives from the nineteenth century. Echoing the general sense of relief in the United States that Mexico had finally found stability and was making progress after the revolutionary turmoil and its aftermath, Brandenburg overgenerously praised the "visionaries of the Revolutionary Family" to whom he dedicates his book, *Mexico: An Experiment in One-Party Democracy*.[17] "Traditional conservatives," on the other hand, represented a more sinister element and were definitely not part of that family, according to Brandenburg. He described traditional conservatism as

> a concoction of Spanish colonial values intermixed with corporate state designs. Its elite . . . view society as founded on caste-like racial distinctions and composed of inferiors and superiors, with the latter (themselves)—selected from among large landowners, wealthy bankers and industrialists, the upper hierarchy of the Catholic clergy, and the "educated" foreigners, particularly from pro-Franco constituents within the long-resident Spanish colony—filling the role of overlords.[18]

The elite of traditional conservatism, Brandenburg claimed, comprised "old families of wealth antedating the Revolution, whose offspring are prominent in agriculture, banking, commerce, insurance, and real estate, as well as elements of the proclerical *nouveau riche*, foreign interests, professional men, and Franco enthusiasts in the Spanish colony."[19] The PAN was, for Brandenburg, traditional conservatism incarnate: "The political embodiment of Traditional Conservatism is the National Action Party. . . . Originally established as a pro-Axis political movement, the PAN even today espouses a pseudo-McCarthyism."[20] Within Mexico, Brandenburg's essential argument was frequently perpetuated by regime propaganda and other critical accounts portraying the PAN as a reactionary, anti–Revolutionary organization. In these often partisan accounts, the PAN is the party of the ultraconservative and extremely wealthy.

At the same time, it seems reasonable to interpret PAN conservatism as a reaction against Cárdenismo, the leftist policies of President Lázaro Cardenas during the 1930s. Indeed, Loaeza (1989, 1999) explicitly identifies the leftist populism of Cárdenas as the catalyst for PAN formation:

> Contrary to conventional wisdom, the PAN was not born as the lay appendage (*brazo laico*) of Church political action. The original project, marked by the *anticardenista* reaction, conceived of the party more as a pressure group that would unify and channel the political demands of private enterprise: businessmen of any level, liberal professionals, small property-owners, and in the end all those whose income did not depend on the State.[21]

Indeed, Gómez Morin's experience in government and as a leader in the financial community helped him to establish connections with businesspeople and industrialists. However, at least some of these individuals traced their dissatisfaction with the regime back to the 1920s and the Vasconcelos movement. José Ayala Frausto, an industrialist and founder of the PAN's regional committee in León, Guanajuato, provides a useful example. In 1941, Gómez Morin invited Ayala Frausto and a handful of close friends to join the newborn political party: "First he asked, 'Have you had any experience in politics?' to which I responded that I had only participated in the meeting to support Vasconcelos when he came to León and spoke at San Juan de Dios, when the authorities forced us to disperse with the butts of their rifles."[22]

Still, the PAN's emergence likely reflected at least a partial reaction from those opposed to Cárdenas's policies. Gómez Morin's brief but eventful stint as rector of UNAM gave him the support of many professionals and intellectuals from among his colleagues and students, particularly as he defended the institution against Cárdenas's efforts to revise Article 3 of the Mexican Constitution to impose "socialist education." His university battles also won Gómez Morin the sympathies of Catholic activists who saw the post–Revolutionary government as a vehicle for anticlericism, and some would have viewed the Cárdenas administration as the rise of creeping, godless communism. However, reducing the PAN to an instrument of contemporary, probusiness conservatism is problematic. PAN doctrine and rhetoric is hardly steeped in neoconservative values of less government and low taxation. Rather, the PAN's emphasis on a reduced role for government must be understood as a reaction to a context of Mexican authoritarianism in which the state had a demonstrated record of inefficiency, fiscal mismanagement, and abuse. Gómez Morin claimed that in Mexico:

> The people do not need more taxes when they don't get anything out of those taxes; or when they are spent on 'whistles and flutes' or on lavish things and trips abroad, and on propaganda and the deification of the people in power. . . . Besides, it is not true that the PAN has asked for a decrease in taxes. . . . On the contrary, we have always sustained that taxes should be sufficient to attend to the extraordinary necessities, as are education, health-care and economic substructures in all under-developed countries. Generally, the people of the official party and their international allies make National Action

> into a wax monkey to which they attribute the characteristics that they can make stick most easily, presenting it unfavorably.[23]

Such criticisms of the state and its abuses hardly established the PAN as the kind of reactionary, antirevolutionary movement portrayed by its critics. In fact, PAN doctrine holds more important similarities to the initial goals of the Revolution than to those of traditional Mexican conservatism. Rather than the visceral reactionary conservatism of the counter-revolutionary forces that emerged in the early years of the armed conflict, the PAN actually embraced the primary goals of the Revolution, as espoused by Francisco I. Madero, the father of the Mexican Revolution, its first president, and its first great martyr. Madero's most fundamental contribution to the Revolution was his advocacy of effective suffrage and an end to the political monopoly of the Díaz regime. Von Sauer (1974) cites nine key aspects of the PAN's "Declaration of Principles," which coincided with fundamental revolutionary goals: effective, competitive multiparty system, with all parties organized on a permanent basis; respect for state and local autonomy; effective separation of powers and an independent legislature; respect for political pluralism; free and fair elections; freedom of labor; freedom of religion and religious choice; liberty to select one's education; private property rights; and social and economic freedom.[24]

In short, at the core of its political and social agenda, the PAN advocated the practical application of liberal democratic principles to political organization, participation, and governance. The PAN, in many ways the flagbearer of Madero's original principles, was indeed a legitimate member of Mexico's revolutionary family, albeit a far distant cousin from the PRI and its various permutations.[25] Indeed, one U.S. observer went so far as to suggest PAN doctrine makes it Mexico's "True Revolutionary Party," an organization that is "Mexican to its core, a Mexican political party working to solve Mexican problems."[26]

It bears emphasis that the PAN's advocacy of liberal democratic principles places it distinctly outside the nefariously illiberal brand of "right-wing conservatism" that many of its Latin American contemporaries have adopted in Chile, Argentina, Bolivia, Ecuador, Uruguay, and a number of Central American countries. In a region where conservative parties have been the detractors of democracy and the purveyors of brutal violence, the PAN is the exception among Latin American political parties of the right. This is largely because PAN conservatism is uniquely defined by the context of the Mexican political condition. In no other Latin American country have political parties of the right been forced to struggle for decades against left-leaning authoritarianism.[27] Hence, rather than a classic conservatism oriented toward preservation of the traditional social order and hierarchy, the PAN's doctrine is better characterized as conservative in the sense that it promotes values of special importance to all Mexicans, such as the preservation of private property, low taxation, reduced government intervention in the economy and in labor relations, and the protection of practices, beliefs, and institutions commonly associated with elites.

Catholic Humanism: The Religiosity and "Mystique" of the PAN

The linkages of the PAN to traditionally conservative beliefs and institutions are most notable in its connection to the Catholic Church. This connection is closely related to the deterioration of Church-State relations in the decades preceding the PAN's emergence.[28] However, it is important to note that the Revolution brought significant changes in this relationship, as certain hopeful Catholic groups saw new opportunities to develop a positive relationship with the state, after a century of liberal-conservative division over the place of religion in Mexican society.[29] In other words, the Revolution—despite its radical, anticlerical legacy—was not immediately perceived as a threat to Church interests.[30] Indeed, Catholic organizations initially thrived under Madero's tolerance and what seemed to be an almost excessively conciliatory attitude toward the opposition.[31] Most notably, the National Catholic Party (Partido Católico Nacional, PCN), a conservative party predating the PAN, did moderately well in Mexico's 1912 federal elections (winning four Senate seats and twenty-nine deputyships) and capturing four governorships (Querétaro, Jalisco, México, and Zacatecas) and twenty-six city governments (in Guanajuato, Aguascalientes, Oaxaca, Puebla, Querétaro, and Veracruz). Moreover, the PCN's new brand of Mexican Catholicism embraced key revolutionary ideals, such as political pluralism, local autonomy, individual freedom, and a new concern for social change.[32] Nonetheless, religious conservatives ultimately brought about their own undoing when they opted to support the counter-revolutionary efforts of General Victoriano Huerta in his short-lived coup in 1913.[33]

Indeed, the Church's support of Huerta was a major factor contributing to its later exclusion from politics when anti–Huerta forces returned to power and produced the 1917 Constitution, which featured harsh anticlerical provisions. This, in turn, facilitated the later alienation and even persecution of Catholics under post–Revolutionary governments. The vociferous anti–Catholicism of President Plutarco Calles (1924–1928), a strident atheist,[34] sparked three years of bloody conflict, by restricting the activities of the Church and submitting the clergy to the regulatory authority of the government. The violent reaction of Catholics became known as the Cristero Movement and brought the death and exodus of thousands of people in Central Mexico from 1926 to 1929.[35] Later, in the 1930s, religious conservatives were further agitated by President Lázaro Cárdenas (1934–1940), who was viewed by many conservatives as the person who brought godless socialism to Mexico. His efforts to socialize education placed him in direct conflict with UNAM rector and future PAN founder Manuel Gómez Morin.

This mood of anticlericism led Catholic leaders—guided by international trends in the Church to establish lay appendages to promote the spread of Catholic doctrine and the ideas of social reform—to promote the formation of student, political, and other conservative lay organizations to further their religious agenda.[36] The church-associated lay associations that resulted—the National Union of Catholic Students (Unión Nacional de Estudiantes Católicos, UNEC) and its predecessor, the National Confederation of Student Catholics of Mexico (Confederación Nacional de Estudiantes Católicos de México, CNECM); the Base; the National Sinarquist Union (Unión Nacional de Sinarquístas, UNS); and other church-associated organizations—provided formative political experiences for many activists who later joined the PAN and, in some cases, were feeder organizations whose militants were channeled directly into the PAN.[37] From these organizations came an entire generation of future PAN leaders.[38]

Given these historical antecedents, it is not surprising that a second line of PAN doctrine, separate from the liberal democratic ideologies linked to Gómez Morin, speaks to a set of normative, spiritual, and social welfare concerns derived from Catholic thought.[39] This line of thought, political humanism (*humanismo político*), was developed by another major figure within the PAN, Efraín González Luna. Born in the state of Jalisco, González Luna was, like Gómez Morin, a lawyer and a committed Catholic. González Luna's primary contribution to the PAN was providing its philosophical links to Catholic thought. This doctrine of political humanism, developed in González Luna's numerous speeches and writings, became known as the mystique (*mística*) of the PAN.[40] As political humanism is less precisely defined in conventional rhetoric than Gómez Morin's clear-cut agenda for good government and liberal democracy, it requires careful examination and clarification.

Political humanism, commonly used in contemporary PAN rhetoric to refer to a general notion of respect and sympathy for fellow human beings, was actually derived from a more sophisticated set of ideas with a long historical tradition closely linked to Catholic thought. At different periods in history, the notion of humanism was employed to espouse the celebration of humanity, human accomplishments, and the individual and collective potential of human beings as a species. In its earliest manifestation, the humanist perspective reflected Renaissance admiration for the accomplishments of the ancient Greeks and Romans, who appeared (for those emerging from the Dark Ages) to have reached the greatest heights of human civilization.[41] Humanists ultimately sought to accomplish a perfectly engineered society—such as that reflected in Thomas More's magnum opus, *Utopia*—whose basis would be a citizenry capable of improving its quality of life by learning how to govern itself and provide for the community. More and other Catholic thinkers, like Thomas Aquinas, embraced the humanist ideal that human beings could construct a better, if not a perfect, society in this world by maximizing their innate human potential. It is likely the integration of these concepts into classic Catholic philosophies that especially captivated González Luna and other early founders of the PAN.

Hence, González Luna laid out a vision of the PAN that was much more numinous than that of the practical, secular blueprint of Gómez Morin. That is, González Luna focused on the notion of perfecting man as a spiritual entity (as well as the implicit connection of man and God). According to González Luna:

> Man requires the emphatic accentuation of spiritual values as the essence of his ontological affirmation. He is not made a man by his greater capacity or intensity for material gain, by his greater, purely biological perfection. All of this does not transcend the zoological level. The satisfaction of the beast is not enough for the fulfillment of man. . . . We need that which makes us, that which, joined to the organic fact, transforms us into something infinitely higher than just an organism, that which makes us men: the spirit, the soul and its essence, its faculties and operation.[42]

Contemporary critics of the PAN view this humanistic philosophy as a thin veil for what they see as the fundamentally religious core of *panismo*. To be sure, González Luna made no secret of his religious beliefs. For many PAN activists, humanism provides the political justification for otherwise purely religious positions on such issues as the "right to life" (with regard to the prohibition of both abortion and the death penalty). Thus, in this sense, humanism facilitates the complicity of Catholic ideals with the PAN's political mission. Yet, the legitimacy of humanism as a political philosophy is not to be so easily discounted. González Luna also grounded his version of humanist philosophy in Mexican political reality, using it to focus the doctrine of the PAN on combining man's material and spiritual needs and on realizing the "common good."[43] From this perspective, the authoritarian character of PRI hegemony was detestable because of the limits that it set on human potential, freedom of expression, competition of ideas, individual choice, and, above all, the entrepreneurial spirit of the individual.

Hence, classical humanism is also a perspective that can easily be related to the interests and philosophies that promote free market ideals in the philosophical tradition of nineteenth-century classical liberalism. In this sense, political humanism as applied in Mexico can be seen as a philosophy whose ultimate objective is to help others to help themselves. One of the primary prescriptions derived from this interpretation of humanism is decreasing dependence on the state, particularly because of the long-standing patterns of state abuse in Mexico. Indeed, González Luna's doctrine provides an antithesis to the regime's paternalism, emphasizing the importance of encouraging individual development rather than merely catering to the needs of the flesh, and favoring individual capacity and self-reliance over dependence on handouts from the state. In this fashion, González Luna was able to use humanism to address a variety of political issues: property rights, family rights, liberty in education, free practice of religion, and the economic elevation of workers in both the fields and the factories.

In short, González Luna's humanism emerges as a Mexican genuine compassionate conservatism, which balanced the technically oriented and legalistic PAN of Manuel Gómez Morin.[44] The blending of these two lines of thought produced sophisticated theoretical ideals for the achievement of their collective vision through government institutions and political action. Through the ideals of its principal architects, the PAN accumulated a well-developed doctrine on the role of the state in the economy, the role of the municipality, the value of knowledge and learning, the importance of free expression, the need for community responsibility and collaboration, and the urgent need for free, individual (rather than corporate) political participation. Frequently, this doctrine has formed the basis for the party's political positions with regard to a variety of issues, including Mexico's economic development, federalism and the role of the municipality, education, public-private partnerships in community development, and political organization—all essential aspects of democracy.

Confronting the PRI: Political Participation and Regional Repression

In addition to the complexities of the party's political orientation, the PAN faced another kind of identity crisis from the time of its founding in 1939 until well into the 1970s. The party's principal problem during this period was how it should relate to the ruling party. The PAN's rhetoric and vision stood in clear opposition to that of the PRI. Yet, less clear was how the PAN should relate politically to a party and a system that it viewed as fundamentally corrupt and illegitimate. What should be the role and strategy of an opposition party in such a system? And how could the PAN pursue its programmatic goals without becoming tainted through complicity with the PRI?

The first debate on the issue of political participation came during the 1939 Constitutive Assembly, which immediately moved to consider the possibility of PAN participation in 1940 elections. A majority of the party's founding members (89 out of 129) advocated indirect participation, through the endorsement of an independent candidate, General Juan Manuel Almazán. Almazán broke from the ruling party to form the National Unification Revolutionary Party (Partido Revolucionario de Unificación Nacional, PRUN) due to his political disagreements with Cárdenas administration. It is notable that the PAN supported Almazán's candidacy, contrary to the inclinations of both Gómez Morin, who was not personally impressed by the candidate, and González Luna, who opposed any participation at this stage, on the principle that it would merely legitimate the regime.[45] In this sense, the party was anything but an instrument of demagoguery for its two most prominent founding fathers.

Ultimately, supporting Almazán's candidacy proved unsuccessful in defeating PRI candidate Manuel Avila Camacho and of little direct benefit for the PAN. Significant tensions developed during the campaign and brought violent clashes between Almazán and Avila supporters. After the election, Almazán fled the country, and federal troops intervened to prevent all-out rebellion, especially in the North. The descent into violence during the 1940 election was at odds with the legalistic approach and ultimate objectives of Gómez Morin and vindicated his intuition about Almazán's candidacy. The PAN's affiliation with the Almazán movement had placed it in the company of more radical, antisystem elements and led the PAN to be viewed as a potentially disloyal force.[46] The next ten years, therefore, became a critical period for the PAN to define its relationship to the ruling party more carefully and to develop its reputation as a responsible, if not "loyal," opposition movement.

For this first decade, at the national level the PAN remained somewhat conflicted on the issue of how to relate to the ruling party. The PAN wrestled over the decision to participate in national elections in the 1943 legislative contest, ultimately opting to participate but running very few candidates. During the debates over participation, Gómez Morin consciously refrained from efforts to influence the party's decision directly. González Luna, in contrast, emerged as a more vociferous advocate of nonparticipation. Ultimately, however, the party's national assembly consistently proved willing to participate in federal electoral contests in 1943 and 1946, with delegates supporting participation by margins of 49 to 31 and 115 to 13, respectively.[47] However, given the PAN's limited membership base and organizational development, it was difficult to muster candidates in both elections; only 21 candidates ran in 1943, garnering approximately 21,000 votes.

The vote to participate in the 1946 presidential elections illustrated that sometimes the party's desire to participate was greater than its capacity. The lack of a viable PAN candidate led the party to nominate an individual, Luis Cabrera, who had not actually consented to run. Cabrera briefly flirted with the idea but ultimately declined. Still, in 1946, the success of four PAN legislative candidates—Antonio L. Rodríguez (Monterrey), Aquiles Elorduy (Aguascalientes), Miguel Ramírez (Tacambaro, Mich.), and Juan Gutiérrez Lascuráin (D.F.)—and the PAN's first municipal victories (Quiroga, Michoacán; Llano Hondo, Oaxaca) helped provide incentives for continued electoral participation at the national level.[48] By the legislative elections of 1949, the PAN mustered sixty-nine candidates, again electing four of them successfully with six hundred thousand votes nationwide. Thus, the PAN's willingness to participate in elections, its relative tolerance for the clearly fraudulent and uneven nature of electoral competition, and, more important, its resistance to adopting a rabidly antiregime stance was conducive, if not essential, to its survival. Had the party followed its moral inclination to boycott the electoral process consistently, that decision might have led to its ultimate dissolution or, at least, irrelevance.

By 1949, when Gómez Morin stepped down as the party's president, the PAN had successfully distanced itself from the disastrous Almazán campaign and thereby reduced its image as a radical, antisystem party.[49] The limited success of the party at the national level during the 1940s also taught the PAN's leadership to focus its participation mainly on elections where its prospects were strong and led the party to concentrate its efforts on legislative and municipal contests rather than wasting its efforts on the impossible challenge of defeating the ruling party in presidential contests. Thus, the 1950s brought PAN to a second phase of organizational development, when the party opted for a subnational strategy to strengthen its local and regional bases of support.

As Lesley Byrd Simpson (1967) famously observed in his book, *Many Mexicos*, Mexico is a place of tremendous diversity, a place of many places.[50] The PAN's regional and local experiences during this period provide particularly helpful examples for illuminating the practical difficulties of electoral competition against the ruling party. Certain very rare cases also illustrate the circumstances under which the PAN was able to present significant competition. Below I discuss two regional experiences of the PAN—centered in the municipalities of León, Guanajuato, and Tijuana, Baja California—that provide additional insights to the PAN's experience across Mexico's diverse center and north, respectively (incidents in Mérida, Yucatán, are considered in reference to the 1960s). Despite their geographic and cultural diversity, these case studies share notable commonalities that provide insights into the PAN's history and Mexico's overall political context at that time. These and other experiences endowed longtime PAN activists with a sense of martyrdom, righteousness, and ultimate vindication in the party's later triumphs.

1946: Massacre in León, Guanajuato

One of the first major incidents of violent repression against the PAN occurred early in 1946 in the city of León, Guanajuato. León is located in the agricultural corridor known as the Bajío, which once supplied produce to the highly productive mining towns stretching between Mexico City and Guadalajara.[51] The strongest and northernmost link in Guanajuato's industrial corridor, León is also the heart of Mexico's modern footwear (*calzado*) industry. Historically, the small- and medium-sized tanning and piecework operations that provided inputs for this industry facilitated generations of independent and family-owned businesses, many of which could remain autonomous from PRI-controlled unions and corporatist organizations. In addition to a certain level of labor independence, León's political development also reflected the intensely religious context of the Bajío, the region that essentially can be considered Mexico's Bible Belt.

Illustrative of the region's religiosity, León was the birthplace of Sinarquísmo, a Catholic social movement that emerged from the Cristero Rebellion. The Cristero Rebellion ensued when President Calles enforced articles 3, 5, 27, and 130 of the revolutionary Constitution, which circumscribed religious practice and required government regulation of the clergy. Calles's antagonism toward the Church led to the formation of the National Defense League for Religious Liberty (Liga Nacional Defensora de la Libertad Religiosa), which initiated the rebellion in Pénjamo, Guanajuato, on September 28, 1926. While Guanajuato did not see the bloodiest of the conflict, like almost all areas involved in the rebellion, this state was witness to extreme brutality on both sides of the conflict. Church leaders reached a compromise agreement with the Calles government and brought an end to the Cristero Rebellion in 1929.[52] As a result of continued hostilities among some supporters of the Cristero movement, a new organization, the National Sinarquist Union (Unión Nacional Sinarquísta, UNS) was formed to formalize their political dissent in León on May 23, 1937.[53]

Prior to the PAN's emergence in León in 1941, the field of electoral opposition was already occupied by the UNS and other conservative antiregime groups, most of which had links to the Cristero movement. This fact initially caused the PAN to operate as part of a coalition of parties and groups opposed to the PRI.[54] The first and most significant incident of early cooperation came in 1945, when the PAN and other organizations jointly supported opposition mayoral candidate Carlos A. Obregón.[55] Obregón's candidacy was fueled partly by dissatisfaction among business elites, as well as by many merchants and landowners, all of whom were incensed by local tax increases and a freeze on rents earlier that year. Running against the PRI government, Obregón's platform also advocated cleaning up elections, imposing standards of good government, citizen participation in decisionmaking, open and transparent planning of public works, support for education, and respect for human rights.[56]

Meanwhile, the Party of the Mexican Revolution (Partido de la Revolución Mexicana, PRM) launched Dr. Ignacio Quiróz as its candidate for mayor. Quiróz was, unsurprisingly, a devotee of Governor Hidalgo, though a local faction of the ruling party fiercely opposed him and appeared to have sympathized to some degree with the *sinarquístas*.[57] Historically, such internal PRI divisions occasionally resulted from local resistance to a candidate imposed by the ruling party's governor by fiat (*dedazo*). Factional tensions within the ruling party typically occurred in instances where the anointed candidate was an outsider or a member of a minority faction in the party. In some cases, individuals or entire groups felt scorned by the top-down selection process and bolted from the party or refrained from supporting the outsider candidate. When severe, internal factionalism of this sort occurred, opposition movements in Mexico often had their best chances for success.[58]

Internal divisions in the ruling party did not spare Obregón's campaign from intimidation and harassment by prosystem elements. Though Obregón's campaign was contentious from the beginning, the most significant tensions began the night of the mayoral elections on December 16, 1945. That evening, Obregón and key supporters of the campaign spoke to a sizable crowd in León's main plaza, urging respect for the vote and repudiation of any attempted fraud. Early rumors of an attempt to cover up Obregón's triumph eventually caused the crowd to storm city hall, though they were repelled by police and troops who were imported from the nearby city of Irapuato. The results were not announced until two weeks later, on December 30, when Quiróz was declared the victor. The opposition coalition countered with the audacious claim that Quiróz had received only 58 votes compared with Obregón's 22,173 votes, and people began to demonstrate in favor of Obregón in the city's central plaza. Opposition claims notwithstanding, Governor Hidalgo ordered Quiróz to take office on New Year's Day, 1946, in secret and under heavy guard.[59]

Outraged, the opposition staged an "unofficial" swearing-in ceremony the next day, drawing an animated crowd of nearly five thousand people. Burning effigies of Quiróz and other ruling party propaganda, the crowd soon raged out of control and began to hurl stones at city hall, drawing fire from troops guarding the building. The massacre that followed resulted in at least fifty deaths and dozens more wounded. In the aftermath of the violence, authorities claimed the incident was provoked by a fascist alliance of the right, downplaying the number of casualties and deaths and denying the use of automatic weapons. Physical evidence suggests otherwise. Many of those injured or killed in the skirmish received blows or bullet wounds from behind, and bullet holes still visible today in nearby buildings suggest that fleeing crowds were gunned down a significant distance from the main plaza. The eyewitness testimony of many survivors of the massacre reported puddles of blood near and beyond the plaza.[60]

The massacre in what is today known as the Plaza of the Martyrs of the 2nd of January (Plaza de los Mártires del 2 de Enero) was an embarrassment for the regime. So egregious was the situation that the national Senate eventually intervened, and Governor Hidalgo was obliged to appoint a citizen's council with Obregón at its head. However, the January 2, 1946, massacre resulted in at least a decade of political dormancy for many of León's citizens, as many understandably feared that political activity would cost them their lives.[61] Those few who remained politically active in the local PAN did so mainly out of conviction yet had considerable difficulty attracting others to the cause.[62] Hence, in subsequent years, the PAN had difficulty rallying voters and defending its rare electoral successes.[63]

1959 and 1968: Dual Incidents of Repression in Tijuana, Baja California

Another major instance of repression occurred in Baja California during the 1959 gubernatorial elections to replace Governor Braulio Maldonado Sánchez. Because the remote northern territory was not given statehood until 1953, this was only the second major electoral contest for the PAN in Baja California. The PAN had attracted supporters in the region long before then, sending a handful of the territory's representatives to the PAN's foundation in Mexico City in 1939 and establishing its first regional committee in Baja California in 1945. The party participated in the state's first elections, with PAN candidate Francisco Cañedo losing by a wide margin to Maldonado.

Maldonado quickly established a reputation for corruption and vice. The governor profited directly from the Los Kilómetros section of Tijuana, an enormous zone of tolerance for prostitution that provided revenues to Maldonado and contributed to a secondary "industry" for the governor's wife, Carlota Sosa y Silva de Maldonado, who used an orphanage as a front to sell the illegitimate children of the prostitutes.[64] Revelation of Maldonado's corruption by local media resulted in the first of a long line of assassinations of journalists in Baja California, as Maldonado and his family conspired to murder Manuel Acosta Meza, a reporter from *El Imparcial* and an active critic of the governor's Los Kilometros connections.[65] Maldonado was particularly reviled in Tijuana, where he allowed his cronies in Muebles y Maquinaria, S.A. to lay claim to two million square acres of land occupied by thousands of residents of the city's Río Zone.

Salvador Rosas Magallón, a lawyer active in the state party leadership of the PAN, stepped up to help these residents take their case to court. Though his legal defense was unsuccessful, Rosas Magallón's efforts helped to build a strong base of support for the party in Tijuana, especially among the low-income residents whom he championed. In the nominations for the 1959 gubernatorial elections, Rosas Magallón easily won his party's nomination, capturing over 80 percent of the primary vote against candidates Rafael Rosas and Tijuana's local PAN president, Professor Zeferino Sánchez Hidalgo.[66] Through tireless campaigning across Baja's rugged landscape to address the state's electorate, Rosas Magallón soon generated significant support outside as well as within his party.

Rosas Magallón also benefited from significant divisions within the state's PRI organization that developed when Governor Maldonado selected

Eligio Esquivel Méndez as the PRI's gubernatorial nominee, to the frustration of other potential candidates.[67] Spurned candidates represented a persistent dilemma for the PRI, which needed to balance orderly political succession and internal party loyalty with hierarchical party structures and decisions made by fiat. In Baja California, Maldonado and the PRI party leadership had made matters worse initially by encouraging internal competition for the nomination and later unveiling Esquivel as the party's "uncontested" candidate. To make matters worse, Esquivel originated from Yucatán and evidently lacked the local political base needed to unify the PRI.

As the campaign unfolded, the PRI apparatus maneuvered against the PAN's efforts to hold rallies in Mexicali and Tijuana in December 1958. Despite warnings by Governor Maldonado that these rallies would be treated as premature campaign activities, the PAN went forward with its first meeting on Sunday December 14, drawing hundreds of supporters. Units of the state police and fire departments, as well as armed henchmen hired by Governor Maldonado, surrounded the meeting place and turned hoses and tear-gas grenades on the crowd, speakers, and sound equipment. The crowd retaliated by throwing rocks from a nearby railroad, leading police to fire their weapons into the air. In the panic and chaos, large portions of the crowd began to disperse, though several individuals were captured and jailed by the governor's forces.[68] Undaunted, PAN leaders prepared for a December 27 meeting in Tijuana, where municipal authorities were instructed by Mayor Manuel Quirós to maintain order. When PAN supporters began to assemble, they were initially able to thwart police harassment and cause the authorities to retreat; however, police eventually returned with approximately four hundred officers armed with pistols, rifles, and tear-gas launchers.[69] Accompanying police on this occasion was the Tijuana fire department, whose units connected their hoses to portable tanks of sewage water just outside of range of the rally. Tear gas was launched at the speakers' platform and into the crowd. Some among the crowd started throwing stones and tear-gas canisters back at the police, driving them back. The firemen began to fire sewage water on the fleeing crowd but soon withdrew to avoid retribution. Though most of the crowd escaped, over two hundred people were detained by the authorities, and the PAN's offices were sacked.[70]

Harassment continued throughout the PAN campaign. For example, at a meeting of eighteen thousand people in Mexicali on Saturday, July 20, 1959, police armed with machine guns and other weaponry committed acts of violence against the assembled citizens, several of whom were wounded. In the wake of this event, eighty people were incarcerated in Mexicali, with seventy more detained in Tijuana. According to Rosas Magallón, "The government responded to our campaign with more violence: arrests of candidates and campaigners, many of whom landed in jail."[71] Despite the authorities' efforts,

Rosas Magallón continued to attract support throughout the state.[72] According to the candidate's own account, by the day of the election, the PAN was able to place an average of eighteen observers, compared with an average of six PRI observers, in each of the state's 6,318 polling places (*casillas*).[73]

Meanwhile, the PAN estimated that 6,700 soldiers under the command of General Hermenegildo Cuenca Díaz (2nd Military Zone) as well as state police and hired gunmen were present throughout the state during voting on Sunday, August 2, 1959. In spite of this, election day turnout was massive.[74] When polls closed, election officials in Mexicali refused to open the ballots when the polls closed. The next day the newspaper *Noticias* quoted PRI leader Roberto Martínez Ochoa as stating, "It isn't possible, where we thought we'd win they beat us. We need to report to our superiors. We won't do the counting until we receive orders from the Party." Meanwhile, the PAN's official newspaper, *La Nación*, claimed that in Tijuana the following took place:

> The victory of National Action was so apparent that government forces decided to make the ballot boxes disappear under the protection of soldiers and police. Only the results of 26 polling places were known (of 103 total) and 18 of them were won amply by the PAN. . . . In Tijuana, the thefts began at seven in the evening: one after another ballot boxes were taken by Federal Highway police, the local police and state troopers.[75]

PAN mayoral candidate and CDM president Professor Zeferino Sánchez Hidalgo was arrested under the charge of "social disruption" for being present when the people tried to prevent the theft of ballot boxes by the PRI. Others who attempted to prevent the theft found themselves at the wrong end of a weapon, and many were wounded (including one little girl who caught a policeman's bullet in the throat).[76] The military took Tijuana's ballot boxes to its headquarters, and *priístas* later privately confided to members of the PAN that Rosas Magallón had defeated Esquivel by 120 thousand to 10 thousand votes.[77] In the days following the election, the regime continued its crackdown on PAN leaders, jailing or kidnapping them. Rosas Magallón eventually sought refuge across the U.S. border in adjacent San Ysidro.[78] Photographic evidence and independent media sources, including reporters from San Diego and Los Angeles, all appear to substantiate that the repression and violence were real and pervasive.[79]

In short, a rare demonstration of civic activism was met with an equally rare show of outright repression by the PRI regime. As Ortega (1961) notes, regarding the aftermath of the events of 1959, "Baja California's cowards (*pusilánimes*) almost disappeared, those citizens that hide their pusillanimousness under the disguise of *gentes decentes* (decent folk) who refuse to participate in politics as if it were a lowly activity to fight for the cleaning of the nation's public life."[80] Despite this newfound courage among the citizens of Baja California, however, the PAN was unable to manage a strong presence in the 1964 state and 1965 midterm elections.[81]

* * *

There is an inferred bias in telling the story of the PAN's regional experiences by only focusing on a handful of the most egregious instances of PRI authoritarianism. Focusing on this negative political conduct by the PRI, it should be noted, fails to illustrate the numerous positive achievements of good PRI leaders and administrations. However, the reason for attention to these dramatic examples of PRI authoritarianism is to demonstrate the extremely limited prospects of organized, widely popular political opposition during the height of PRI dominance. For all the subtleties of PRI authoritarianism, Mexico was much more (or, rather, much less) than just an "imperfect" democracy. In Mexico, elections that could not be won by the ruling party through effective leadership and competent public administration were instead stolen by the threat or use of coercion. This fact is central to understanding the limited prospects for political opposition and the PAN's obstacles to developing its party structure.

However, from a more optimistic perspective, while the above instances of repression emphasize the limits imposed on PAN by PRI authoritarianism, they likewise point to some of PAN's early successes and growing bases of support. Over the course of the 1940s and 1950s, PAN scored several legislative and local victories but experienced repression similar to the events of 1959 in cases where the PAN's grasp exceeded the regime's level of tolerance. Nonetheless, the PAN's varied regional experiences in state and local contests fueled internal party debates at the national level over whether and how to press the regime for further concessions and policy reforms. During the 1960s and 1970s, the PAN experienced a growing internal division on these questions, which ultimately resulted in a major schism between its pragmatic and business-oriented party builders and its more ideological and religious elements.

Paladins and Clerics: A Divided "Loyal" Opposition

In the words of the great PAN scholar Donald Mabry, at its core the PAN was "a coalition of secular men and religious activists."[82] Over the course of the 1950s and 1960s, however, the PAN experienced a gradual internal transformation, in which the party's Catholic elements began to play a more prominent role in defining the party's political direction. What caused the rise of the party's Catholic elements in the wake of Gómez Morin's mostly secular leadership? Typical explanations for this shift suggest that the regime began to woo once-alienated business elites away from the PAN, leaving behind a dominant Catholic coalition. To be sure, beginning with the 1946 election of President Miguel Alemán, the regime began to cater much more to private-sector interests, who now found themselves no longer the victims but the beneficiaries of government intervention in the economy, thanks to protective tariffs and generous subsidies to foster domestic industry.

While eminently plausible, this hypothesis lacks substantial evidence on several accounts, especially as many of the party's private-sector activists stayed with the party throughout the 1950s and 1960s. Thus, I advance an alternative explanation that focuses more specifically on the competition among elites within the PAN, which I have heretofore argued is central to understanding internal party life. That is, I propose that withdrawal from the PAN—to the extent that business elements and other groups did indeed exit the party during this time—resulted not only simply from "pull factors" outside the organization, but also from internal "push factors" as the party's religious-oriented factions became more assertive in advancing their agenda.

The example of Aquiles Elorduy, a longtime, very active PAN member from Baja California, is particularly useful in consideration of this argument. Elorduy perfectly embodied the PAN's connection to Madero and the Revolution. He joined Madero in founding the Anti–Reelectionist Party, which opposed a continuation of Porfirio Díaz's rule, and later ran for and won a place in the federal legislature on Madero's ticket. Active in the PAN from its beginning in 1939, Elorduy was one of the few to achieve electoral success for the PAN in its early years, winning one of four legislative seats obtained by the party in 1946 in Aguascalientes. Both his success as a PAN deputy and his later reincarnation as a PRI senator may have illustrated his close ties to elements inside the PRI (most notably, President Miguel Alemán), dating to his earlier career as an academic.

Other key examples of party founders who exited during this period include Manuel Herrera y Lasso and Agustín Aragón, who left the PAN to become presidential advisers in 1947 and 1954, respectively. Teófilo Olea y Leyva left the party in 1941 to serve on the Supreme Court. Horacio Sobarzo left to serve as lieutenant governor (Secretario de Gobierno) of Sonora in 1946 and later served as interim governor of that state.[83] However, it would be only partially accurate at best to suggest that the above individuals were representative of the PAN's business sector; while some were indeed prominent businesspeople or professionals (as Herrera y Lasso), others were more closely affiliated with different tendencies within the PAN. What each of the above individuals share, however, is that none were closely identified with religious associations prior to entering the PAN. Thus, the argument advanced here is that the increasingly religious climate within the party and the tensions this generated were actually more central to the exit of certain *panistas* than the lures created outside the party by the more business-friendly posture of the regime. The dominance of the party's Catholic elements was, therefore, less the passive result of business "exit" than the active result of a concerted effort to redirect the party's secular agenda toward a more religious one.

Beginning in 1949, a shift in the balance of power began to develop within the party that virtually ensured that the PAN would be less attractive to primarily secular activists drawn from the private sector. The alienation of these groups *within* the party certainly seems to have been likely as this trend progressed. Indeed, one of the first indications of the internal assertiveness and increased clout of the party's Catholic elements could be seen in new variations in PAN rhetoric and ideology, which moved noticeably to the left.[84] This seemingly counterintuitive shift was actually a logical result of the emergent new directions in Catholicism in Latin America, as the forces moving the Church toward a more socially responsible position led to a greater emphasis on resolving problems of economic inequality. This ultimately culminated in Vatican II and the emergence of liberation theology in the 1960s. In this context, the PAN's religious elements began to engage in outright criticism of unbridled capitalism and its negative implications. Such rhetoric was no doubt of little attraction to business elites who otherwise might have expressed interest in joining the PAN.

Another indication of the party's growing religious bent was its closer association with the National Sinarquist Union (UNS), the León-based movement that grew out of the Cristero Rebellion. For a brief time, the PAN and the UNS considered a formal electoral alliance between the two organizations, but the Sinarquist Union ultimately declined due to concern that its membership base might be usurped by the PAN.[85] However, an informal PAN–UNS alliance was implemented in state elections in Baja California and Jalisco in 1952 and 1953, respectively. The UNS also supported González Luna when he ran as the PAN's candidate in 1952 and again supported the party in the 1955 midterm elections for federal deputies. Indeed, González Luna's victory over representatives of the party's business elements, Roberto Cossío y Cossío and Antonio Rodríguez, was itself a demonstration of the growing strength of the party's Catholic elements. González Luna—who was the party's and Mexico's first presidential candidate formally nominated through a competitive primary—took his campaign in a predictably erudite direction, emphasizing the virtues of PAN doctrine and ideological principles. Less predictable was his impressive effort to wage a national grassroots campaign, tirelessly visiting nearly every federal district and holding hundreds of rallies. Ultimately, however, González Luna lost the election to the PRI's Adolfo Ruíz Cortines by a 10 to 1 margin that, despite certain instances of fraud, clearly demonstrated massive electoral support for the ruling party at this time.[86]

In 1956, the PAN's clerical side was briefly displaced from the party leadership when the National Assembly selected Alfonso Ituarte Servín to replace Gutiérrez Lascuráin. Ituarte Servín was an accountant and Mexico City native; a founding member of the PAN, Ituarte Servín had recently been initiated as a federal deputy. Ituarte Servín's victory as PAN party leader appeared to illustrate frustration on the part of certain sectors of the party with the limited electoral gains in the previous six years, and, perhaps more important, the party leadership's failure to take a more active stance in protesting instances of fraud. Whatever the case, while a member of Catholic lay associations, connections as a businessman were more important in facilitating his relationships with other PAN leaders from outlying regions, particularly those from Mexico's secular and entrepreneurial north.

One of the most notable of Ituarte Servín's contacts was Luis H. Álvarez, a young, charismatic candidate from Chihuahua, who clearly represented the elements of the PAN that began to flourish under Ituarte Servín's leadership. In contrast to the more reticent posture of many Mexico City–based and religiously oriented party activists, Álvarez, who drew from firsthand experiences of political repression "in the provinces" (*provincia*), tended to assume a more aggressive posture toward the PRI and advocated more assertive measures to gain recognition for the PAN's state and local victories. Álvarez ran for governor in his home state of Chihuahua in 1952 and decided to seek the party's presidential nomination in 1957. Álvarez ran against several stalwart, founding party members in the primary, including José González Torres, Luis Castañeda Guzmán, Juan Gutiérrez Lascuráin, and Rafael Preciado Hernández. After two rounds of voting, Álvarez emerged the favorite and gained unanimous support through the concession of other candidates. Turning to his presidential campaign, Álvarez took a significantly more militant stance in opposing the regime, the ruling party, and its systemic abuses. His campaign mimicked U.S.-style presidential campaigns of the day, with a nationwide tour of every state in Mexico, drawing large crowds in 510 cities and towns. Dubbed by some as "reckless," Álvarez's campaign was certainly a shock to the system and presented bold criticisms of the regime, *caciquismo*, and Mexico's overall political situation.[87] The PAN's preliminary results suggested that Álvarez made a strong showing against PRI candidate Adolfo López Mateos, more than doubling the total number of votes for the PAN when it ran González Luna in 1952. However, official returns unsurprisingly favored the PRI only by a slightly smaller margin than in 1952, with the PAN's relative performance increasing only from 7.9 percent to 9.5 percent of the vote in 1958 (see Appendix 3).

Álvarez immediately pushed the PAN to follow through on its militant stance by refusing to accept the token victories—six federal deputyships in the states of Yucatán, Puebla, Baja California, Chiapas, and Zacatecas—that were recognized by the government in that same election. Subsequent admissions by key PAN leaders suggest that even these "victories" were fraudulent, and offered merely as a bribe to induce PAN's complicity with the regime.[88] After debates within the National Council, the party decided to protest through nonparticipation, by withdrawing its candidates from those six federal deputyships. Only two of the six candidates obediently rejected their positions, while the remaining four PAN candidates accepted their seats against the will of the National Council and were expelled from the party.[89] The response to the PAN's refusal to accept the token victories was swift and brutal. Indeed, President López Mateos showed little tolerance for the party that had so fiercely opposed his victory. As noted in the case studies discussed above, over the course of 1958 and 1959, PAN candidates and activists were blocked from alleged victories, harassed by PRI activists, jailed by government authorities, and even murdered during electoral contests and party conventions in Baja California, Chihuahua, Veracruz, Yucatán, and Zacatecas.[90]

During this time, PAN activists grew frustrated by the limits of electoral success and began to consider new strategies and directions. More specifically, some leaders within the PAN began to advocate emulation of the much more successful Christian Democratic parties of Europe and Latin America (notably, those in Venezuela and Chile). The popularity of this direction led to the selection of National Executive Committee (CEN) President José González Torres (1959–1962) at the party's 1959 convention; as secretary general of the party, he was already the de facto party leader going into the convention since Ituarte Servín had stepped down months before. In addition to being an adamant anticommunist, González Torres was closely affiliated with several Catholic associations, such as the Catholic Association of Mexican Youth (Asociación Católica de la Juventud Mexicana, ACJM) and Mexican Catholic Action. He benefited from direct personal ties to the international Christian Democratic movement and encouraged the PAN to follow the highly successful example of such parties elsewhere in Latin America, especially those in Venezuela and Chile. Most significantly, González Torres invited Rafael Caldera to address the party's National Convention in 1962. A prominent member of the International Christian Democratic movement and the founder of Venezuela's Independent Electoral Political Organizing Committee (Comité de Organización Política Electoral Independiente, COPEI), Caldera later became president of Venezuela (1969–1974).[91] While the more secular side of the PAN ruled the day during the 1950s, Caldera's appearance marked a shift in the balance of power, as the party moved toward a greater religious orientation in the 1960s.[92]

This trend continued, albeit in a significantly different fashion, under the direction of CEN President Adolfo Christlieb Ibarrola (1962–1968), a UNAM-educated lawyer, a devout Catholic, and a native of Mexico City. Christlieb Ibarrola's candidacy for the party presidency benefited from the open support of key party founders, including Efraín González Luna, the party's spiritual founder.[93] Still, Christlieb Ibarrola's religiousity was not part of his outward political profile, as his prior activism in politics and Catholic associations was relatively limited; instead, he focused on his law practice and his family. Christlieb Ibarrola declined to join the PAN in 1939, but he collected signatures to help the young party get its start and was personally connected to many of its founding members, including Manuel Gómez Morin, Efraín González Luna, Agustín Aragón, and Gustavo Molina Font. In 1958, having joined the party, Christlieb Ibarrola became actively involved in the party's postelectoral crisis and later served as the PAN's representative to the Federal Electoral Commission.[94] Thus, despite the strength of his own personal religious convictions, Christlieb Ibarrola did not wish for the PAN to fully embrace the Christian Democratic identity. This decision appears to reflect Christlieb Ibarrola's pragmatic ability to separate the spiritual from the political, as well as his concerns about the potential negative implications of the Christian Democratic approach. Though rarely inclined to assert his influence in the party, for example, even Gómez Morin clearly articulated his view that the "deep-seated anti-clericism" of the regime and its history of violent clashes over secular-religious issues created unfavorable conditions in Mexico for such a movement.[95] Moreover, Christlieb Ibarrola's wariness of the Christian Democratic approach reflected the realistic limits of Mexican electoral statutes at the time, which formally prevented registered political parties from expounding a religious agenda.[96]

Still, Christlieb Ibarrola's brilliant compromise was to follow the Christian Democratic model without taking the PAN over the edge to become a fully clerical party, while guiding the party toward a constructive dialogue with the regime. During his leadership, the party clearly embraced the postulations of Vatican II by revising the party's principles to address social justice concerns, such as increased economic distribution and the protection of human rights.[97] The PAN's campaign platforms and principles promoted equality of women in the workplace, egalitarian labor-management relations and profit sharing, credits for small and medium businesses, labor training, universal social security, as well as urban political reforms to increase local government accountability.[98] This emphasis on social justice and equality and the promotion of democratic participation directly followed the contemporary Catholic thought of the day.

Yet, at the same time, under Christlieb Ibarrola's leadership, the PAN also took a decidedly different posture toward the regime by opting to cooperate to obtain pragmatic objectives, rather than pursuing aggressive electoral competition in the vein of other Christian Democratic parties. The practical realism of Christlieb Ibarrola's compromise brought significant rewards. In recognition of the PAN's cooperative attitude, for example, in 1963, President López Mateos (1958–1964) supported introduction of a form of proportional representation through the party deputy system. The Chamber of Deputies also produced legislation previously advocated by the PAN, including modifications regarding federal electoral law, government regulation, foreign investment, and labor laws. In return, under Christlieb Ibarrola, the PAN broke the long established practice of rejecting presidential electoral results as fraudulent by formally recognizing PRI candidate Gustavo Díaz Ordaz's victory over PAN candidate José González Torres in 1964. Christlieb Ibarrola established a close, even friendly relationship with the Díaz Ordaz administration, drawing on his experience and connections as a former Federal Electoral Commissioner (1960–1961) during the tense period following 1958 elections. A federal deputy from 1964 to 1967, Christlieb Ibarrola regularly met with PRI leaders and achieved the appointment of PAN deputies to key committees.[99] During this time, the PAN even cooperated with the ruling party to the detriment of other opposition parties; under pressure from the PAN, the government revoked the Mexican Nationalist Party's registration to prevent the UNS from competing against the PAN in the 1964 federal elections.[100] By 1967, the PAN counted numerous successes following Christlieb Ibarrola's approach, with the party gaining control of the state capitals of Hermosillo and Mérida and other local governments in the states of Michoacán (Uruapan), Sonora (Santa Ana, Opodepe, San Miguel Horcasitas), Jalisco (Teocaltiche), and Puebla (San Juan Xiutetelco).[101]

The Limits of Tolerance for PAN Success

In effect, Christlieb Ibarrola successfully pulled the PAN back from the aggressive posture toward the regime, which was contributing to PRI backlash at the state and local levels during the 1950s, and helped the party reap the benefits of being the "loyal" opposition. However, this strategy also had its limits. While the cooperative relationship with the PRI government yielded the opening of new political spaces in the 1960s, the PAN's electoral progress and appetite for success quickly outpaced these opportunities. In 1967, the PAN increased its absolute number of votes in the federal midterm election and again reached the maximum limit of twenty party-deputy seats. Also, several incidents in 1968 and 1969 brought new difficulties for the PAN at the state and local levels in electoral contests in Baja California, Chihuahua, Sonora, and Yucatán. In Baja California, for example, the PAN again registered an especially strong electoral performance in state and local elections held on July 2, 1968, probably winning the mayoral races of both Mexicali and Tijuana.[102] In both races, the PAN opted for a strategy of positive campaigning rather than disparaging the PRI, as the party had long been accustomed to doing.[103] In Tijuana, the PAN's exit polls showed a marked advantage over the PRI, and the PAN finally proclaimed its victory by 30,269 votes to 24,272. Likewise, in Mexicali, with the PAN ahead in at least 176 of 179 polling places, PAN-friendly local newspapers began to print results proclaiming the party's victory. Nonetheless, the PRI claimed victory in both mayoral elections and attempted to turn the tables with charges of electoral irregularities against the PAN.[104] In a 1998 interview, PAN Senator Corella recalled, "We won the election[s] in Mexicali and Tijuana. And of course, being unable to pull their fraud, the PRI [ordered] the state legislature to decree that the elections were annulled. Why? Well, because there had been many irregularities."[105] The procedure should have allowed for new elections, but student demonstrations; hunger strikes; and appeals to the press, the Chamber of Deputies, and the Supreme Court by the CEN proved futile. Instead, joint PRI–PAN citizens' councils were appointed.[106]

Meanwhile, other major instances of fraud against the PAN occurred in the state of Yucatán. In Mérida, the PAN had actually won control of the city government. PAN candidate Victor Manuel Correa Racho, a respected lawyer, civic leader, and columnist, defeated PRI candidate Nicolás López Rivas by 38,074 votes to 13,200.[107] A devout Catholic and supporter of the Sinarquísta movement, Correa had been a vocal critic of the PRI government since the 1950s. He wrote 616 newspaper articles criticizing the PRI government from 1958 to 1970 and mobilized large sectors of the middle class. Correa Racho's victory came with the unprecedented wave of municipal victories elsewhere in Mexico that coincided with Christlieb's new posture toward the regime in 1967; in addition to Mérida, the PAN won 14 other victories at the municipal level that same year.[108] In government, Correa achieved a relatively transparent administration, a minimum wage for municipal employees, professional criteria for the municipal police, and improvements to those few areas where the city government had direct control, such as parks, gardens, and sporting facilities.[109] Still, the good will achieved by Christlieb to enable the PAN to govern in Mérida in 1967 was short-lived. After enduring harassment by the state government, Correa Racho took a leave of absence to run for governor in 1969 against PRI candidate Carlos Loret de Mola, a one-time journalist and former PAN activist who had left the opposition to take a position as a PRI senator.[110]

In previous gubernatorial elections, the PRI had faced hardly any challenges from the PAN and seems to have been unprepared for the sudden surge of support generated by Correa Racho's candidacy.[111] The number of local committees throughout the state increased from 75 to 98, and the candidate drew an impressive turnout at his numerous campaign stops throughout the state.[112] PAN accounts suggest that their rallies began to draw the crowds away from the ruling party, even in PRI strongholds like Tixcocob, Valladolid, and Motul.[113] Meanwhile, all through the campaign, elements of the PRI worked to undermine the PAN by threatening and harassing the party's candidates and supporters and inciting skirmishes as a means of arresting PAN activists.[114] The most significant violations and clashes came on election day, November 23, 1969. The PRI's list of electoral violations included hiding polling locations from the public, manipulation of electoral identification, and other efforts to enable fraud through the use of "vote tacos," "merry-go-round voting," pre-stuffed ballot boxes, and urn theft.[115] The official vote gave the PRI 203,163 votes to the PAN's 55,921 and 816 for the PPS.[116] As a security measure, Governor Luis Torres Mesías surrendered the city to military control at 7:00 P.M.

In response to the PRI's fraud, state and national representatives of the PAN encouraged their supporters to turn over their electoral credentials to the party to demonstrate the strength of the PAN vote, collecting over one hundred forty thousand electoral credentials. However, two weeks after the election, the PAN's offices were broken into and sacked, with archives and equipment destroyed and the electoral credentials stolen.[117] Meanwhile, for days after the election, the PAN protested the fact that more than one hundred people were being held without legal basis—and in some cases were tortured.[118] Yet, formal electoral protests (filed with the state legislature by PAN CDE President Tomás Vargas Sabido and General Secretary Carmen Robleda de Solís) and to the state and federal law enforcement authorities were not acknowledged. Meanwhile, Correa Racho refused to incite potentially violent mass mobilizations as a means of asserting his victory; on announcement of the PRI victory, Correa Racho spoke to a crowd of over one thousand people at the regional offices in Mérida and called on the people to move on and prepare for future battles.[119]

PAN Disarray and Political Turbulence in the 1970s

At the age of fifty, Adolfo Christlieb Ibarrola died just two weeks after the fraudulent gubernatorial elections in Yucatán. Christlieb Ibarrola had actually stepped down from the PAN presidency a year before, his health failing from the onset of cancer.[120] In the last year of his life, Christlieb Ibarrola's disappointment grew with the diminishing returns brought to the party by his strategy of pragmatic collaboration with the regime and culminated with the unfortunate events in Yucatán that preceded his death. The premature departure of Christlieb Ibarrola from the party leadership came at a particularly inopportune moment for the PAN, occurring just a few weeks before the Tlatelolco massacre of students on October 2, 1968. In the aftermath of Christlieb Ibarrola's departure, the party fell into disarray; leaders were frustrated with the conciliatory model, which was no longer effective. The CEN passed through two party presidents in quick succession, first under Ignacio Limón Maurer (1968) and next under Manuel González Hinojosa (1969–1971). In 1971, José Angel Conchello Dávila (1971–1975) took over as party president, followed by interim periods for both Efraín González Morfín and Raúl González Schmall in 1975. In 1975, Manuel González Hinojosa (1975–1978) finally took over the organization for a full three-year term (see Appendix 1).

Thus, Christlieb Ibarolla's withdrawal from the party leadership brought the PAN six different CEN presidents in as many years and left the party less prepared to respond effectively to the 1968 political crisis and the turmoil that followed. This was especially unfortunate because many aspects of the PAN's modified social doctrine of the 1960s might otherwise have appealed greatly to the supporters and activists of the student movement. Appeals for job creation, greater economic equality, and increased political access were all central to the PAN's new program, but the party was virtually paralyzed by its internal disorder. In this context, the party once again struggled with the issue of electoral participation, the primordial question of PAN opposition to an authoritarian regime. The party narrowly approved participation in the 1970 presidential elections, offering its candidacy to González Morfín, and again in the 1973 midterms. Despite the party's uncertainty over the issue of participation, the party did relatively well. However, internal disagreement over the party's direction and strategy grew with each contest.

To make matters worse, party founder Manuel Gómez Morin died in 1972. In his absence, the PAN's internal factions appeared to revert to their classic positions, which had divided the party from the beginning, struggling over the issue of political participation and the ideological direction of the party. On the one hand, Efraín González Morfín, son of the party's moral forefather, Efraín González Luna, represented the classic religious elements of the PAN and sought to continue the party's orientation toward the 1960s model of social activism linked to the progressive Catholic Church, which González Morfín now branded with the label "solidaritism" (*solidaridismo*). González Morfín's vision was markedly more leftist than any prior president of the party; he advocated such radical ideals as redistribution of property, business reforms, social justice, and other goals reflected in the PAN's platforms during the height of his period of influence in the mid-1970s.[121]

González Morfín initially backed José Ángel Conchello Dávila to become PAN president in 1972, though he would later greatly regret this decision. Conchello was a highly unusual choice for González Morfín to support, given that the latter was the first PAN party president since Gómez Morin without any prior experience in Catholic lay associations. Indeed, Conchello was practically a replica of the party's recently departed founder. Conchello was, like Gómez Morin, the son of a Spanish immigrant (his father), and, similarly, he came from Monterrey, the industrial state capital of Nuevo León. Conchello's connections to the PAN developed initially when he studied law at UNAM and later served as a personal assistant to one of the PAN's first federal deputies, Antonio L. Rodríguez. During the 1950s and 1960s, Conchello developed a career as a prominent businessman, starting out in his father's paper factory, traveling as a trade representative to Switzerland and Canada, directing publications for the Moctezuma beer distributor, and serving in various chambers of commerce (the Monterrey Chamber of Commerce, Confederation of Industrial Chambers, Confederación de Cámaras Industriales, and the Council of Nacional Chambers of Commerce).

Throughout the development of his business career, Conchello maintained his connections to the PAN, first running for Congress in 1952 and later heading the party's Propaganda Commission (1955–1960). He also wrote numerous articles for the PAN's official magazine, *La Nación*, though he did so under various pseudonyms.[122] As a federal deputy, Conchello spoke out with sharp criticism against business sectors (even though he was affiliated with several through his many contacts) that applauded the government's harsh response to the student movement: "In Mexico, not to our pride, but for shame, those who have applauded the government's actions most strongly have been the [official chambers of commerce] CONCANACO, CONCAMIN, and the Knights of Columbus."[123]

After his failed bid for the Mexican Senate in 1970, Luis H. Álvarez urged Conchello to run for the PAN party presidency. In the internal elections held on February 12, 1972, Efraín González Morfín offered key support and referred (perhaps mistakenly) to Conchello as "doctrine in action." Conchello won with 75 percent of the vote (114 of 152 total), handily defeating Guillermo Ruiz Vázquez (who received 32 votes) and a young Diego Fernández de Cevallos (with 4 votes).[124] As PAN president, Conchello immediately began to seek support for the PAN by lashing out at the most unpopular man in México: President Luis Echeverría. Though believed by many to have ordered the student massacre in 1968 (as secretary of the Interior under President Díaz Ordaz), Echeverría spent the first three years of his term trying to co-opt the support of the left. To do so, Echeverría took up the mantle of the left by calling for greater economic redistribution, aiding the leftist media, and praising the triumph of Salvador Allende in Chile. Echeverría's leftist appeals drew harsh attacks from Conchello, who condemned the regime's repressive one-party statism and new state-led economic policies:

> inspired certainly by Hitler's National Socialist Party: Nothing against the party! Nothing outside of the party! Everything within the party! And in the same fashion, [the PRI's] campaign slogans are written on all the walls: "Who vaccinates your children? The PRI," "Who builds your roads? The PRI," "Communal farm worker: Who gave you your land? The PRI," "Student: Who gives you your schools? The PRI."[125]

Conchello's caustic antileftist attacks drew equally biting responses from the PRI, which accused him of fascism and likened him to Chile's Augusto Pinochet.[126] Indeed, Conchello's rhetoric frequently bordered on anticommunism of the kind not heard in the PAN since the party presidency of José González Torres. This tack was strategically sound, perhaps, given the posture and unpopularity of the regime during the Echeverría era, but it also reflected Conchello's close connection to the business sector, his background in finance, and his personal ties to Monterrey. Moreover, Conchello's efforts to capitalize on dissatisfaction with the regime not only targeted powerful elite interests, but also appealed to the middle classes. He sought to open the organization to the masses by reducing and simplifying membership criteria and to educate the public about the party's ideological beliefs. Drawing on his own personal charisma and flair for public speaking, Conchello attempted to eliminate the image of the PAN as a stuffy, aristocratic entity that was out of reach of the general public. His goal, in the end, was to build the mass support necessary for the party to fulfill Gómez Morin's vision and one day to defeat the PRI.

This was a vision not shared by a majority of the party's upper ranks. Indeed, Conchello's leadership of the PAN reflected a sharp departure from the anticapitalist bent of the PAN during the previous decade. Most notably, this tendency directly challenged the leftist philosophical leanings of González Morfín, who very quickly grew to regret his prior support for the party president and began to speak out against Conchello's "pragmatic opportunism."[127] Perhaps even more significant was the fact that Conchello's vision threatened fundamentally to alter the very organizational nature of the PAN itself. That is, by modifying the PAN's message and target audience, Conchello intended to transform the PAN from a politically irrelevant club of notables into a competitive mass party. This threatened not only what the PAN stood for, but also an entire way of life for a significant number of party members—especially cerebral and devout Catholics—who had few political options in Mexican society. As the 1975 contest for the PAN party presidency drew near, the feud between González Morfín and Conchello, a conflict over the party's organization and ideology, became a struggle for the body and soul of the PAN.

González Morfín went to battle with two goals in mind, to oust Conchello from the PAN presidency and, in so doing, to preserve the socially responsible direction and organizational composition championed in the party a generation before by his father, Efrain González Luna. González Morfín succeeded in the former but ultimately failed in the latter. Though two of the four candidates nominated for the party presidency in 1975, Luis H. Álvarez and José González Torres, dropped from the race before the first round of voting, victory did not come easily for González Morfín. Five rounds of voting took place, during which González Morfín consistently bested Conchello but failed to achieve the qualified majority of 65 percent required to win outright. In contrast with common practice in the PAN's internal electoral process, Conchello refused to concede the election to González Morfín until the sixth round (see Table 3.1).[128]

González Morfín's victory in the contest for the party presidency did not resolve the two competing visions of the PAN, however. This battle raged on into the next significant internal contest, the nomination for the PAN's candidate for the 1976 presidential elections. This was the party's first presidential

Table 3.1 1975 PAN Internal Election for Party President

	González Torres	Conchello	Abstentions
First Round	110	77	—
Second Round	108	79	—
Third Round	109	66	1
Fourth Round	108	75	4
Fifth Round	109	70	8

Sources: Adapted from Arriola (1994), p. 33; Cervantes Varela (2000), p. 27.

contest since the death of PAN founder Manuel Gómez Morin. According to Vikram Chand (2001), the PAN had a long tradition of ceding the first pronouncement of support for the presidential nominee to its esteemed founder. This tradition differed substantially from the unveiling (*destape*) in the ruling party in that Gómez Morin's preferences were in no way binding to PAN members, and conventions often chose to disregard his favored candidate.[129] Chand submits, "González Morfín believed that as PAN president he had inherited this right from Gómez Morin and was infuriated when Conchello and his supporters preempted him by launching Pablo Emilio Madero."[130] Madero, the nephew of the revolutionary icon with whom part of the PAN's ideology can be identified, was also representative of the Monterrey business interests that Conchello courted during his leadership of the party. Meanwhile, González Morfín backed another popular candidate: Salvador Rosas Magallón, the legal activist, former federal deputy, and defrauded Baja California gubernatorial candidate.

However, before the party's Twenty-Fifth National Convention, held October 17–19, 1975, where the PAN's presidential candidate was to be selected, González Morfín appealed to the party's National Council for a formal censure of Conchello for his undisciplined behavior. The National Council stopped short of a formal censure, thus allowing the Conchello faction to proceed with its support of Madero in the PAN primary. The PAN primary went ahead as planned in the Mexico City Opera House, bringing hundreds of party delegates and three main contenders for the party nomination: Madero, Rosas Magallón, and David Alarcón Zaragoza. The first round of voting produced a clear majority of 495 votes (57.5 percent) for Madero, with Rosas Magallón receiving 252 votes (30.03 percent) and Alarcón Zaragoza receiving only 93 votes (10.96 percent) (see Table 3.2). Madero's support fell well short of the 80 percent threshold required by internal statutes to win the nomination in a given round of balloting. After Alarcón Zaragosa withdrew before the second round, the support of his followers for Rosas Magallón and a slight decrease in turnout reduced Madero's majority to 483 votes (57.5 percent) and increased Rosas Magallón's support to 357 votes (42.5 percent) of the vote.

Table 3.2 1976 PAN Internal Nomination for President of Mexico

	Pablo Emilio Madero	Salvador Rosas Magallón
First Round	499 (57.88%)	363 (42.12%)
Second Round	546 (63.3%)	316 (36.6%)
Third Round	557 (64.6%)	304 (35.3%)
Fourth Round	601 (69.7%)	260 (30.2%)
Fifth Round	609 (70.7%)	249 (28.9%)
Sixth Round	610 (70.7%)	242 (28.8%)
Seventh Round	629 (72.9%)	228 (24.4%)

Source: Adapted from Arriola (1994), p. 40.

Rosas Magallón made further gains in the third round, with 390 votes (46 percent) to Madero's 449 (53 percent), though the unwillingness of either side to concede defeat—for years the gentlemanly alternative to internal infighting—made it clear that neither candidate would meet the necessary threshold. González Morfín used his authority as party president to terminate the process, postponing a decision until a new convention could be called.

The next month, in November 1975, now bearing evidence of the potential damage inflicted by Conchello, González Morfín reiterated his appeals to the party hierarchy to censure and expel Conchello. In this instance, González Morfín condemned Conchello for attempting to create a shadow organization within the PAN, specifically alleging "the creation and maintenance, including financial maintenance, of another National Action Party, with an ideology, organization, hierarchy, loyalties, and communications at the margins and in opposition of the legal and legitimate National Action Party."[131] Conchello's undisciplined behavior and practices, he argued, were contributing to the disorientation and "poisoning" of the party and required immediate censure. In response, Conchello criticized González Morfín's fear of mass-oriented politics (*masificación*) and his desire to maintain the party in control of a "divine caste" of snobbish intellectual elites who considered themselves the custodial "true family" of the PAN.[132] However, the 179 members of the National Council that met to address the charges against Conchello reflected the internal divisions manifested in the party and ultimately failed to produce a formal censure of him in 1975. In utter frustration, González Morfín declared his own resignation as party president on December 13, 1975, followed by several other high-ranking party leaders of the CEN. This unexpected move led to the brief leadership of Raúl González Schmall as interim CEN president, followed by the National Council's selection of Manuel González Hinojosa, former CEN president (1969–1972) to fill the vacuum as party leader again from 1975 to 1978.

However, González Morfín's withdrawal did not solve the party's dilemma over its 1976 presidential nomination. On January 25, 1976, CEN President González Hinojosa called an extraordinary convention for the nomination of the party's presidential candidate, again pitting Madero against Rosas Magallón. The first round of votes brought results similar to those produced in the preceding October convention, with Madero obtaining 499 votes (58 percent) and Rosas Magallón obtaining 363 (42 percent); both candidates failed to achieve the 690 votes (80 percent) required of the total 862 delegates at the convention. Three subsequent rounds of voting failed to produce sufficient votes for either candidate, though Madero maintained his majority in each instance. González Hinojosa urged Rosas Magallón to consider his withdrawal, but at the same time admonished Conchello and Madero, warning: "You are wrong if you think that you can take over the Party."[133] Rosas Magallón refused to budge, viewing his stance as one of necessity to protect the moral integrity of the PAN. The voting continued late into the night through three more unsuccessful rounds, whereupon González Hinojosa attempted to persuade both candidates to step down in favor of a neutrally determined candidate. Failing to resolve the impasse, González Hinojosa declared an end to the process at 11:15 P.M., formally recognizing that the PAN would not produce a presidential candidate in 1976 for the first time in nearly twenty-five years.

Following the convention, a series of bitter and highly public exchanges occurred between Conchello and the party leadership. Conchello and Madero subsequently called on the state committees to force the CEN to call a third convention. The two had success in ten states but fell short of the number necessary to force action by the CEN and brought sharp public rebuke from the national leadership.[134] In February 1976, the CEN issued a public warning that unless Conchello, Madero, and two of their close collaborators (Bernardo Bátiz and Alejandro Cañedo) resigned voluntarily, they would be expelled from the party. To resolve the issue, the National Council appointed a special commission, headed by Martín Torres and including José González Torres, Juan Landerreche Obregón, José Minondo Garfias, Rafael Preciado Hernández, and Antonio Rosillo Pacheco.[135]

Meanwhile, an unrepentant Conchello sharply criticized the party leadership in a public interview with *Excélsior* a few months later, declaring that the PAN was losing its will to act in politics due to a "class of select intellectuals" who saw a broad popular base as a threat to their control of the party. From Conchello's perspective, the challenge was to "return the PAN to the people and allow the party to return to the path . . . of becoming a party with a large popular base."[136] CEN President González Torres rejected Conchello's remarks as absurd and declared that the party "was not born with Conchello, nor will it end without him."[137] Still, PAN's disastrous performance in the July 1976 election provided support for Conchello's criticisms. The absence of a PAN presidential candidate and the intraparty tensions that reverberated down to the state and local levels contributed to a dramatic decline in the party's national vote and provided no coattails for the party's candidates for federal deputyships and other state and local offices. Indeed, the PAN obtained a total of just 1.4 million votes or barely half the 2.3 million votes it won under Conchello's leadership in the 1973 midterm elections (see Figure 3.1).

The very public nature of this internal feud was unprecedented in the characteristically disciplined internal life of the PAN. The conflict was finally resolved when the Torres commission issued its report before 144 members of the PAN's National Council on September 18, 1976. The ten-member commission sought a delicate balance, as the party remained sharply divided: too great a penalty would incense Conchello supporters, while too small a penalty would insult the offended members of the party leadership and their supporters. The commission, therefore, recommended a mixed solution, exonerating Madero by a 6 to 4 margin, while placing partial responsibility on both

Figure 3.1 PAN Electoral Performance, by Percentage of National Vote, 1961–1976

Sources: Figures for 1961 are from Silvia Gómez Tagle, *La Frágil Democracia Mexicana: Partidos Políticos y Elecciones* (Mexico City: García y Valadés Editors, 1993). The figures for 1964 to 1976 are from Juan Molinar Horcasitas, "The 1985 Federal Elections in Mexico: The Product of a System," in *Electoral Patterns and Perspectives in Mexico*, ed. Arturo Alvarado, Monograph Series 20 (La Jolla, Calif.: Center for U.S.-Mexican Studies, 1987).

Conchello and Bátiz.[138] In the end, the commission worked to resolve the tension by requiring Madero, Conchello, and Bátiz to sign a conciliatory letter of apology, recognizing the error of their ways. At the same time, Conchello agreed to step down as a member of the National Council, to take a one-year leave of absence from the PAN for the sake of party unity, and to refuse nomination for elected office during that period. As a final action, at the request of González Hinojosa, a special commission was formed to promote internal unity within the party, bringing together both action-oriented "pragmatists," like Luis H. Álvarez and Norberto Corella, as well as ideologically oriented party loyalists, like Manuel Gómez Morin and José Lozano Padilla.[139] Madero, Conchello, and Bátiz were also invited to join the deliberations of this special commission on October 8 and 9, 1976, to provide their perspectives and to promote the party's healing.

On the Brink of Disaster

The divisions in the PAN during the 1970s reflected tensions in the competing ideological and strategic visions of party elites. As a team of men and women working within a single political organization, the PAN's leadership was severely divided over the goals of the organization and the proper approaches for achieving the party's objectives. Indeed, from its early beginnings, the PAN's fundamental strategic dilemma boiled down to decisions about how to manage political participation and how to determine its relationship to the ruling party in a fundamentally authoritarian regime. Competing successfully in Mexican politics involved a devil's bargain of accepting token rewards for slavish, prosystem opposition or suffering the penalties and indignities meted out for even moderate antisystem opposition. Had the PAN not negotiated a careful balance between pragmatism and principle, it is doubtful that the party would have survived or remained sufficiently distinct from the PRI to avoid co-optation. In other words, the choices made by the PAN about how to relate to the PRI and to the Mexican political context are central to explaining the PAN's capacity to survive and ultimately influence the regime itself.

Founded with the explicit purpose of establishing an institutionalized alternative to the PRI, the PAN was by far the most institutionalized of all the opposition political movements that emerged in Mexico from the 1930s through the 1960s. The PAN was a party rigorously devoted to procedure, statutes, and programmatic agendas. Party rules and procedures were, for the most part, strictly adhered to and provided a sense of order and stability not found in the PAN's external political context. For members of the PAN, then, party life provided a sanctuary and a source of fellowship that separated them from the cult of institutionalized revolution perpetuated by the PRI. Yet, like any other political party, the PAN was still an organization made up of and driven by powerful personalities and factions with specific political orientations and objectives. As a result, at the heart of its long-term survival is a story about internal leadership and coalitions competing strategically for organizational control.

The PAN's survival was, therefore, by no means predestined or pre-engineered by either its political context or its genetic blueprint. A political party is made up of potentially shifting coalitions of interests and individuals; while influenced by the original design of the party and changes in its external context, the interactions among these different and potentially competing interests is what drives party behavior and development. Indeed, it was the intensification of competition among the party's divergent coalitions—each struggling to assert its respective vision of the party in order to respond to challenges and opportunities identified in the external competitive context—that ultimately led to the fracture of the PAN in the mid-1970s. Conchello's biographer, Cervantes Varela (2002), accurately portrays the internal feud of the 1970s as a battle between the party's thinkers and doers, between its "intellectuals" and "pragmatists," its old and young, and between its elite "divine castes" and its mass-oriented innovators.[140] Moreover, this contest took place in highly ideological terms, with each side advancing an opposing philosophical and political orientation, with Conchello strongly opposing state intervention and González Morfín defending a more leftist political vision favoring communal "solidarity."

Yet, in the end, the battle for the PAN in the 1970s was a struggle over party strategy and organizational development, as party oligarchs sought to preserve the existing hierarchy against contamination by the unaffiliated masses, to whom Conchello consciously appealed. In short, the PAN's internal conflict was a manifestation of the dilemma posed by early party observer Robert Michels (1959), whose "iron law of oligarchy" keenly anticipated the tendency of party elites to employ organizational hierarchy to protect their power from the party rank-and-file and from the knuckle-dragging masses. For the PAN, the 1970s represented, therefore, a critical juncture in determining the party's orientation and future survival. Had the party fully rejected Conchello's vision in favor of González Morfín's, the PAN ultimately might have shriveled and disappeared or at least faded into utter irrelevance in the vein of other purely ideological movements like the UNS or the Mexican Communist Party. Alternatively, had Conchello and his followers opted for exit, the PAN certainly would have been ripped apart and would have lost all inclination toward mass politics. Thus, it was hardly an exaggeration that, in the midst of this internal crisis, state-sponsored media proclaimed that the PAN was on the verge of extinction.

Notes

1. Wilkie and Monzon de Wilkie, 1978, p. 56.
2. González Luna, 1988, p. 75.
3. The others included Alfonso Caso, Antonio Castro Leal, Vicente Lombardo Toledano, Jesús Moreno Baca, Teófilo Olea y Leyva, and Alberto Vásquez de Mercado. Calderón Vega, 1997.
4. Mabry, 1973a; Mabry, 1973b; Wilkie and Monzon de Wilkie, 1978.
5. Even González Luna, despite his deeply religious convictions and participation in church-affiliated associations, opted not to participate in the violent Cristero outbreaks against the Calles regime.
6. Vera Cuspinera, 1979.
7. This was Vasconcelos's (1997) term for the multiracial nations created by the Spanish conquest; in his view, this new hybrid race would one day overcome Anglo imperialism. While intended as an inspiration and celebration of Latin American multiculturalism, his own arguments about the fifth race, the Cosmic Race, tended to draw on and perpetuate stereotypes of the other "four" races: Blacks (passionate), Indians (soulful), Mongols (mysterious), and Whites (assertive).
8. Gómez Morin, 1939.
9. Letter from Manuel Gómez Morin to José Vasconcelos, in Luis Bernal, *Historia del PAN en La Nación,* Supplemental no. 1 (Mexico City: Partido Acción Nacional, 1991), p. 14.
10. Vera Cuspinera, 1979.
11. Even in Baja California, though still only a territory, it was through Gómez Morin's associates that the organization was founded there in 1949, establishing an important nucleus for the party when Baja California finally became a state in 1953.
12. Gómez Morin, 1939.
13. From a research standpoint, one of the most frustrating aspects of the PAN's early resource limitations was the fact that in most cases record keeping was extremely poor or irregularly maintained over time. For this reason, it was very difficult to get precise details on many aspects of the party's internal organization at the subnational level.
14. Medina Valdés, "Entrevista," *La Nación*, 1959: 2–3.
15. Interview with Norberto Corella (July 8, 1998) in Mexico City.
16. Scott, 1964, pp. 182–185.
17. Brandenburg, 1956.
18. Ibid., p. 127.
19. Ibid.
20. Ibid., p. 126.
21. Loaeza, 1989, p. 232.
22. "Quería mucho esta ciudad," *A.M.*, March 4, 1997.
23. Wilkie and Monzon de Wilkie, 1978.
24. Respectful references citing the very principles noted by Von Sauer (1974) can be found in early editions of the party's official publication, *La Nación*. For example, praise of Madero's support of antiabsolutism, political liberty, educational freedom, fortification of small and large farming, improvement of conditions for workers and farmers, and *libertad de conciencias* (particularly, from the PAN's perspective, with respect to religion) can be found in "Del Propósito de Francisco I. Madero A. . ." *La Nación*, November 12, 1942: 11–12.
25. Loaeza also notes a tendency to lump "the right" together without distinction, defining the right only in terms of opposition to the "positive qualities of the regime."

As a result, by portraying the PAN solely as a party of the church and business, "values are attributed to it that go against its parliamentary and liberal tradition." Loaeza, 1989, pp. 229–230.

26. Lux, 1967, pp. 267, 285.

27. If token political competition had been permitted in Cuba after 1959, there might be other exceptions.

28. Contemporary scholars, notably both Arriola (1994) and Prud'homme (1997), describe Mabry's treatment of the PAN's origins and formative years in his 1973 book, *Mexico's Acción Nacional: A Catholic Alternative to Revolution*, as the best scholarly work on the subject.

29. Von Sauer, 1974, p. 13.

30. Others contradict this view. Notably, Mabry portrays the PAN as fundamentally opposed to the revolutionary enterprise, as Mexico's "Catholic Alternative to Revolution," but he still views the PAN as part of a "Mexican response to the twentieth-century Catholic reform impulse in Latin America." Mabry, 1973a, p. xii.

31. Krauze (1997) asserts that Madero's excessive tolerance for opposition was his downfall, because his government quickly fell victim to a hostile press, a chaotic legislature, and, ultimately, the assassin's bullet.

32. Loaeza (1989, p. 232) suggests that the Vasconcelista movement served as an intermediate step between Maderismo and the PAN, because it constituted an attempt to revive Madero's ideals of democratic individualism, antiauthoritarianism, moral political criticism, rejection of professional politicians, reinvigoration of parliamentary procedure, nonviolence, and antimilitarism. Thus, for Loaeza, the foundation of the PAN was, in part, "an attempt to recuperate the civic enthusiasm that Vasconcelos knew how to arouse within the urban middle class in the face of the closing of the revolutionary elite."

33. Mabry, 1973a, p. 18.

34. According to Mabry, Calles "believed the Church to be reactionary and, therefore, a threat to Revolutionary rule." Mabry, 1973a, p. 6. Conflicts with the Church, beginning in Calles's presidential administration in 1926, should also take into account Krauze's (1997, pp. 319–356) views on the roots of his particular anticlericism.

35. Bailey, 1974; Meyer, 1976.

36. Mabry (1973a, pp. 18–28) provides an excellent summary of these events and the religious-based organizations of major importance during this period, including the National Defense League for Religious Liberty (Liga Nacional Defensora de la Libertad Religiosa) and the National Confederation of Students (Confederación Nacional de Estudiantes, CNECM). He suggests that the lay strategies of the Catholic Church sought "to recoup the losses created by the growing secularization of society, the rise of anticlericism, and the scarcity of ordained clergy."

37. The Base was a secret society that emerged from the National Defense League for Religious Freedom (Liga Nacional Defensora de la Libertad Religiosa), which had been instrumental in implementing Church policy against anticlericism and in organizing the Cristeros against government troops. According to Mabry (1973a, pp. 20–27), the Base emerged to pursue Church goals through other means, namely, by infiltrating organizations to recruit their members and spread the Church's philosophy. Mabry notes that the Base, Sinarquismo, and Opus Dei—"a secret association of wealthy Catholic men who seek to extend Church influence by using their occupations and aiding one another"—have important similarities. However, according to Mabry, "the Base's politicized progressives joined Acción Nacional while the conservatives went into UNS. . . . This split was apparently common in Catholic elite circles in the

1930s and explains why UNS and Acción Nacional have some doctrinal similarities but oppose each other."

38. From these organizations, for example, came such PAN activists as Manuel Ulloa Ortiz, Luis Calderón Vega, Jesús Hernández Díaz, and Luis Hinojosa.

39. Some scholars (e.g., Moctezuma Barragán, 1997) mistakenly place responsibility for the party's religious roots on the PAN's primary architect, Manuel Gómez Morin, though the real guiding force in this regard was González Luna.

40. González Luna, 1991.

41. Among the first to embrace this point of view, beginning in the thirteenth and fourteenth centuries, were Italian philosophers like Francesco Petrarch (1304–1374), and later Marsilio Ficino (1433–1499). It was Leonardo Bruni (1370–1444), however, who applied the term *humanitas* (humanism) to the so-called new learning being rediscovered in classic texts and philosophies. The Italians were followed by French thinkers like Lefevre d'Etaples (1455–1536) and Guillaume Budé (1468–1540). Over the fifteenth and early sixteenth centuries, this school of thought gradually spread to other parts of Europe, embraced by Dutch thinkers such as Desiderius Erasmus (1466–1536) and British thinkers like William Grocy (1446–1519) and Sir Thomas More (1478–1535).

42. González Luna, 1940, pp. 36–37.

43. Even here, González Luna (c. 1940, pp. 43–44, 50) waxed religious, pointing to man's need to follow the example of Christ's incarnation to recognize the connection between the needs of the material being and the spiritual self. It is the former, the flesh, that pulls humans down and the latter, the spirit, that raises them up.

44. Gómez Morin was not totally averse to spiritual rhetoric. One comment by Gómez Morin in particular has stuck in the collective minds of *panistas* as a battle cry for political change in Mexico: "We must move souls" (*Hay que mover las almas*).

45. Mabry, 1973a.

46. Ibid.

47. Ibid., pp. 41–42. See also Von Sauer, 1974, p. 112.

48. In 1947, the PAN also picked up another municipal victory in Zamora, Michoacán. Mabry (1973a) suggests that the PAN's first municipal victories were in Acámbaro, Guanajuato, though official party records indicate that Quiroga, Michoacán, was the location of the first victory. According to data provided by the PAN's Office of Elections, victories in the state of Guanajuato were not officially recognized until the party's 1986 victory in the municipality of San Francisco del Rincón.

49. Mabry, 1973a.

50. Simpson, 1967, p. 11.

51. Valencia García, 1998.

52. "Guanajuato," *unomásuno*, September 15, 1990: 1.

53. The UNS initially created a separate organization called the Popular Force (Fuerza Popular), later known as the Party of National Unity (Partido de Unidad Nacional), though this organization failed to obtain official registration. Another attempt to obtain registration as the Mexican Nationalist Party (Partido Nacionalista Mexicano) also failed. In 1990, the Partido Democrático de México (PDM) considered changing its name to the Democratic Christian Party (Partido Demócrata Cristiano), due to its strong social *cristiano* ideology, but opted not to because the Mexican Constitution discourages denominational parties. Early on, the party suffered a splintering in León, which led to the creation of the León Civic Union (Unión Cívica Leonesa, UCL) by José Trueba Olivares, the founder of Sinarquísmo in Guanajuato. Alemán Alemán, 1993, pp. 18–19.

54. In fact, the Sinarquist movement was unable to achieve formal government recognition to compete as a political party until the recognition of the Democratic Party of Mexico in 1976.

55. The UNS evidently agreed to support Obregón as long as that support was not made public, though the PAN openly supported the UCL candidate. Alemán Alemán, 1993, pp. 21–22.

56. Ibid., p. 19.

57. Ibid., p. 20.

58. Langston, 1993b; Ward and Rodríguez, 1999.

59. Alemán Alemán, 1993, p. 22.

60. Ibid., pp. 22–26. Also, informal interview (March 28, 1997).

61. Interview with Professor José Luis Lozano Padilla (May 13, 1997).

62. Fear of persecution, violence to themselves and their loved ones, electoral injustice, and the despair of constant defeat in the face of corruption and fraud were feelings expressed by nearly all the old guard *panistas* interviewed. I specifically cite those of Eulalio López Muñoz (April 30, 1997), José Luis Lozano Padilla (May 21, 1997), and Ernesto Dávila (May 16, 1997).

63. For example, López Sanabria ran as PAN candidate for mayor in 1976. Despite the party's problems at the national level (the party did not run a candidate in that year because of internal problems), López did very well in the election and appeared to have won. His victory was not recognized, though he headed a citizen's council that was granted as a concession. Ramírez Carrillo, 1993.

64. Mrs. Maldonado's activities reached such scandalous proportions that her Orphan's Committee was investigated and shut down by the federal attorney general, who reported that the chief pimp (*lenón*) of Los Kilómetros was Governor Maldonado himself. Meanwhile, Maldonado's brothers, Salomón, Loreto, and Melquiades Sández, also "happily exploited" prostitution and drug-trafficking by forming the Pimps' Union (*Unión de Lenocinio*) that was eventually found responsible for the assassination of journalist Manuel Acosta Meza. The Union established dozens of houses of prostitution and reportedly received weekly dues that amounted to U.S.$500 from each. Ortega, 1961, p. 10.

65. Ibid. No one was charged in Acosta's murder, but the assassination seemed to trigger a subsequent series of unpunished murders of journalists over the next few years.

66. The next day, Sanchéz also competed for the nomination for Tijuana's mayoral candidacy. Sanchez lost in a 34 to 12 vote to Octaviano "Güero" Flores. "El Partido Oficial Esta Derrotada de Antemano en Baja California," *La Nación*, May 3, 1959: 14–15.

67. Prominent PRI party members alienated by Maldonado's decision included former Senator Leopoldo Verdugo, Gen. José María Tapia, former Tecate Mayor Eufrosio Santana, former Tijuana Mayor Gustavo Aubanel, acting Mayor Manuel Quirós, State Attorney General Guilebaldo Silva Cota, Wulfrano Ruiz, and others. Medina Valdés, "Entrevista," *La Nación*, 1959: 2–3; Valderrábano, 1990.

68. Ortega, 1961, pp. 14–19.

69. Ibid. Police Chief José Moncayo arrived at the scene with eighty armed agents and demanded to see the meeting permit. When a young man rebuked the police chief for interrupting the rally, Moncayo began to beat him violently while the agents turned on the crowd. Moncayo and two of his men were struck down by rocks. Outnumbered, the chief and his forces were quickly forced to retreat, and many left their weapons behind.

70. Ortega (1961, p. 22) acknowledges that official reports claimed that only twenty-one were detained. Nine were given formal prison sentences: Juan Manuel García Montenegro, Roberto Mariscal Díaz, Virginia Díaz de Curiel, Alfonso Madrigal Cuevas, Agustín Quimi Flores, Sabino Téllez Durán, José Antonio Favela, Ignacio Zamora, and Gregorio Pérez Trejo.

71. Just days before the election, in fact, the PAN protested the harassment of its electoral representatives and the kidnappings of Victor González Rodríguez, Eleuterio Flores (candidate for deputy in the fourth electoral district), Luis Valdés (part of the Mexicali PAN municipal slate [*planilla*] of proposed city council members), and Lic. Carlos Pineda (CEN PAN delegate) by the governor's henchmen. "Cómo Responde el Pueblo a la Agresión," *La Nación*, June 28, 1959: 13–16; "Rosas Magallón, Gobernador Electo," *La Nación,* August 9, 1959: 13–15.

72. Rosas Magallón's candidacy apparently achieved a broad coalition from throughout the state's social spectrum, as "rich and poor, men and women, young and old, turned themselves over with fervor to the completion of their civic duty" (Ortega, 1961, p. 7). Rosas Magallón's popularity stemmed directly from his role in standing up to Maldonado in representation of oppressed citizens. Throughout the campaign, Rosas Magallón continued to pursue legal avenues to counter Maldonado, presenting a demand to the Supreme Court to remove the governor due to police brutality against residents of the Tijuana River zone at the end of 1958. Medina Valdés, "Sr. Presidente: su propio honor exige . . . la desaparación de poderes en Baja California," *La Nación*, May 31, 1959: 16–17.

73. Medina Valdés, "Entrevista," *La Nación*, 1959: 2–3.

74. Prior to the election, PAN had actually already complained about irregularities, such as the manipulation of voter lists. Though the federal list of electors had 150,000 electors, the local government claimed that, due to the increase in citizens of voting age and the number of new residents, the figure was up to 221,000 eligible voters. Ibid.

75. "Rosas Magallón, Gobernador Electo," *La Nación*, August 9, 1959: 13–15.

76. PAN accounts also note that Enrique Silva of Baja California's state party organization was tortured in an attempt to provoke a confession of conspiracy. Sarmiento, "Lo Principal en el Caso de Baja California," *La Nación*, August 9, 1959: 13–15.

77. Valderrábano, 1990, p. 25.

78. Interview with Alejandro González Alcocer and Rosalva Magallón de González (June 22, 1998) in Tijuana. The PAN state leader fled first to San Ysidro and later to Guerrero, taking with him his wife Rosalva and their six children, Sergio, Salvador, Alejandro, Efraín, Rosalva, and Belén. Other PAN leaders were also harassed. When PAN leaders attempted a reunion to decide their plan of action at a meeting—attended by PAN CDE President from Chihuahua, Dr. Octavio Corral; PAN CDE President from Baja California, Enrique Silva; Lic. Manuel Rodríguez Lapuente; and journalist Javier Blanco Sánchez—they were temporarily abducted from the Hotel del Norte. "Rosas Magallón, Gobernador Electo," *La Nación,* August 9, 1959: 13–15.

79. Even official papers found it difficult to ignore the repression. Pictures appeared on the front page of the *Baja California Press*, *Noticias*, and *El Heraldo* with headlines such as, "Lluvia de Amparos por Detención de Panistas Efectuada el Domingo Ppdo.," "Orden Aprehensión contra Luis Alvarez y Rosas Magallón," "Magallón Ratafica Sus Cargos: Acusa Directamente al Gral. Cuenca Díaz," "Declaran Testigos en el Caso de Zeferino Sanchez Hidalgo," "Ley Marcial contra Panistas y Ojedistas Aqui," and "Perdidos Secuestrados o Muertos, los tres Panistas." Nonetheless, the

governor's installation of Esquivel was successful, at least in the short term. "Verdad y Testimonio de Baja California," *La Nación*, August 16, 1959: 11–17.

80. Ortega, 1961, p. 7.

81. Ibid. In 1964, PRI candidate Raúl Sánchez Díaz defeated PAN candidate Norberto Corella, with 102,719 votes to 37,373. Corella conceded the victory without protest, reflecting a new direction in PAN strategy in its relationship to the regime under the leadership of Christlieb Ibarrola. Though the PAN was successful in winning a federal deputyship (with Salvador Rosas Magallón as its candidate), its successes were limited in other cases, primarily because of a lack of organization, particularly in Tijuana and Ensenada.

82. Mabry, 1973a, p. 72.

83. The term "Secretaría de Gobernación" is translated here as "Lieutenant Governor," given the second-in-command status and similar functions of both positions. However, there are important distinctions between the two positions, most notably that in Mexico, state constitutions generally do not have an automatic provision that the Secretaría de Gobernación will succeed the governor.

84. Interview with Mauricio Gómez Morin, Mexico City (2001).

85. The formal alliance was actually proposed in 1956, after the success of UNS-PAN collaboration in state-level competition.

86. Mabry, 1973a.

87. Ibid., p. 57.

88. Von Sauer, 1974, p. 122.

89. The historical record is unclear here. According to Donald Mabry (1973a), two PAN candidates—Felipe Gómez Mont and Jaime Haro Rodríguez—were expelled from the party for accepting their posts against the will of the party leadership. However, García Orosa (1991) provides a different account, claiming that Gómez Mont and Haro Rodríguez were the only two to obey the party leadership while four others (Eduardo José Molino Castillo, Germán Brambila, Antonio López y López, and José Humberto Zabadúa Luévano) were expelled. Here, García Orosa's account, from an official PAN publication, is given preference. Christlieb Ibarrola, 1968; García Orosa, 1991.

90. Mabry, 1973a, p. 60.

91. Caldera had initially named the COPEI after the PAN (Acción Nacional) at its founding in 1947, and his presence at the PAN's 1962 convention greatly inspired many party activists, especially the young and religiously devout.

92. González Torres especially encouraged participation from the party's young adults, who supported his bid for the party presidency, and women as well, by formally incorporating the Action Youth Sector (Acción Juvenil) and Women of Action (Acción Feminil) into the party's organizational structure.

93. Rafael Preciado Hernández, a founding member, a former teacher at the UNAM, and a mentor to Christlieb Ibarrola, also spoke on his behalf. García Orosa, 1991, p. 11.

94. Mabry, 1973a, p. 72.

95. Von Sauer, 1974, p. 124.

96. Ibid., p. 124.

97. In occasional instances when groups did so in violation of electoral law, such as the Christian Democratic Social Movement and the UNS, the PRI appeared to tolerate the religious rhetoric only to the extent that it drew support away from PAN and not from the regime.

98. Mabry, 1973a, p. 75.

99. Ibid., p. 76.

100. Ibid., pp. 76–77. Competition from the Mexican Nationalist Party, which now enjoyed the support of the UNS, would have potentially reduced the PAN's access to party deputyships. In both 1964 and 1967, the PAN obtained the full twenty party deputy seats available (in these elections the PAN won two and one single-member district plurality [SMDP] seats, respectively).

101. García Orosa, 1991, p. 57.

102. Prior to these elections, tensions had risen in the state because of a scandal involving former President Miguel Alemán, whose company, Inmuebles Californianos, S.A., claimed ownership of all nonpublic property in the city. Outraged *panistas* organized the Committee for the Defense of the Community of Tijuana under the leadership of former PRI leader Luis Enrique Enciso Clark, who defected to the PAN to run as mayor of Tijuana against PRI candidate Mario Santana. Meanwhile, in Mexicali, Norberto Corella ran against Gilberto Rodríguez for the mayorship.

103. The PRI responded with accusations that the PAN was being backed by the rich and the Church, that it too was involved in the Alemán scandal (see previous endnote), and in Mexicali charged that PAN candidate Norberto Corella was a member of the PRI and not a Mexican citizen.

104. Federal Minister of Government Luis Echeverría declared that irregularities had occurred, due to stolen ballot boxes in Tijuana (both U.S. and Mexican news sources had photographic evidence of urn theft) and challenges about Corella's citizenship. Though he was born in Douglas, Arizona, in 1928, Norberto Corella, at the age of eighteen, declared his Mexican citizenship to the U.S. consul in Agua Prieta, Sonora. Interview with Norberto Corella (July 8, 1998).

105. Ibid.

106. Preciado Hernández, 1969.

107. Interviews with Roger Cicero (August 7–8, 1997). Ramírez Carrillo, 1993, p. 84. The only book on the PAN's early experiences in Mérida is the firsthand account written by PAN militant Roger Cicero MacKinney (1987), which provides few details on the circumstances leading to the election.

108. Former Governor Carlos Loret de Mola offers a significantly more complex explanation of internal intrigue, arguing that then secretary of the Interior Luis Echeverría caused the party to lose the mayoral contest in order to embarrass Governor Torres Mesías, thereby preventing him from being a viable competitor to run against Echeverría for the PRI's presidential nomination. This sounds somewhat far-fetched, given Torres Mesías's apparent decision to remove himself from politics after completing his term. However, Loret de Mola's interpretation may derive from the fact that he was himself a pawn of Echeverría, who imposed Loret de Mola as the PRI's gubernatorial candidate in 1969.

109. Cicero MacKinney, 1987; Montalvo Ortega, 1996.

110. Correa also gained the sympathy of the population due to unfair treatment by the state government; the state's governor withheld funds from the municipality, encouraged taxi and bus strikes, and granted all local law enforcement authority to the state government against the will of the city council. Correa's candidacy and the external imposition of Loret de Mola by the president brought significant tensions to the PRI and even a number of defections to the PAN. The PAN used Loret de Mola's past affiliations against him, republishing articles that he wrote in criticism of the regime during his days as a member of the PAN. "Yucatán, un Rebaño Sumiso," *La Nación*, August 16, 1969: 16–18.

111. In the 1960s, the abuses made possible by the PRI's monopoly—including diversions of Inter-American Development Bank funds from a public water system

project that was never built and corruption in the *ejido* sector—generated substantial dissatisfaction with the PRI. Mabry, 1973a, p. 83.

112. Cicero MacKinney (1987) recalls that there were 103 campaign events in the state's interior (including Izamal, Temax, Akil, Yaxcabá, Timucuy, Suma, Temax, Mama, and other municipalities) and 49 in and around Mérida. Loret de Mola (1978, p. 42), however, asserts that the PAN conducted few events outside of its base in the capital.

113. By the end of Racho's campaign, the PAN was able to assemble thirty-five thousand to forty thousand people to march from the historic boulevard of Paseo Montejo to the Plaza Grande, the town's central square. PRI leaders responded by proclaiming their newfound preference for smaller, more intimate meetings. García Orosa, "Por Encima de la Violencia Oficial, Venceremos," *La Nación*, August 16, 1969: 16–18.

114. Cicero MacKinney (1987) records 24 wounded, one killed, and several incidents of shooting and stone throwing between attackers and PAN supporters.

115. Vote tacos were wads of folded ballots used to pad the PRI's poll results. Montalvo Ortega, 1996, p. 89. García Orosa, "Todo Yucatán Lo Grita: ¡Ganó Correa Rachó!" *La Nación*, December 1, 1969: 5–15.

116. Preliminary PAN estimates, based on the tabulations of PAN representatives who were allowed access to only 259 of 743 polling stations, gave Correa Racho 44,992 votes to 30,553 for Loret de Mola. Yet, even with figures in hand from areas where Correa Racho had already triumphed, Senator Loret de Mola announced his victory at 4:30 P.M., thirty minutes before the polls closed. According to his list, there were many cases where there was not a single vote for the PAN; when asked by a reporter how it was possible that not even the PAN representatives at the polls voted for their own candidate, Loret de Mola replied, "Perhaps there was some error." García Orosa, "Todo Yucatán Lo Grita: ¡Ganó Correa Rachó!" *La Nación*, December 1, 1969: 5–15.

117. Prior to the break-in, three *panistas* guarding the offices—Nelso Avilés, W. Chi, and Dolores Oy—were "bestially" beaten, robbed, sequestered, and dropped "half-nude" along the highway to Sisal. "Facinerosos del Gobierno-Partido Asaltan al PAN en Mérida," *La Nación*, December 15, 1969: 2–3.

118. García Orosa, "Todo Yucatán Lo Grita: ¡Ganó Correa Rachó!" *La Nación*, December 1, 1969: 5–15.

119. A few years later, Correa Racho shared the tragic fate of a curious number of opposition politicians when he was killed in an automobile accident, on September 16, 1977. Ultimately, the PAN's defeat was devastating, and Correa Racho's withdrawal was devastating to the local PAN, which saw its committees rapidly dry up and disappear. In the 1970 elections, the PAN lost Mérida to a young, ambitious PRI candidate named Victor Cervera Pacheco, who eventually emerged as the veritable kingpin of Yucatán over the next two decades. García Orosa, "El Pueblo Está Indignado; Orgulloso y Decidido, Vencerá," *La Nación*, December 15, 1969: 18–20.

120. Christlieb Ibarra stepped down as president of the PAN on September 10, 1968, four months before the end of his term. He died in Mexico City, on December 6, 1969; different accounts suggest that he suffered from either leukemia (Von Sauer, 1974) or stomach cancer (Mabry, 1973a).

121. Arriola, 1994.

122. Cervantes Varela (2000) offers the best account of Conchello's life.

123. Ibid., p. 18.

124. Ibid. Note that Arriola (1994) cites *La Nación* with a different figure (94 percent) for Conchello's victory, p. 31.

125. Ibid., p. 23.

126. Ibid., pp. 23–24. A series of conflicts developed between Conchello and his detractors when he publicly confused the names of Benito Juarez and Benito Mussolini, by stating, "You are all for the State, everything for the State, and nothing outside of the State. Just like that great fascist Benito Juárez . . . pardon me, Benito Mussolini."

127. Loaeza, 1999, p. 307.

128. Cervantes Varela, 2000, p. 27.

129. Chand, 2001, p. 96.

130. Ibid., p. 96.

131. Cervantes Varela, 2000, pp. 28–29.

132. Ibid., p. 29.

133. Ibid., p. 31.

134. State committees siding with Conchello and his collaborators included Campeche, Colima, Chiapas, Durango, Oaxaca, Puebla, San Luis Potosí, Taumalipas, and Yucatán.

135. Cervantes Varela, 2000.

136. Ibid., p. 33.

137. Ibid., p. 34.

138. Ibid. Five commissioners blamed Conchello solely, while five blamed both Conchello and Bátiz. At this point, Alejandro Cañedo had resigned from the party, though Bernardo Bátiz was still being considered for expulsion.

139. The commission was headed by Manuel González Hinojosa and included the following: Luis H. Álvarez, Norberto Corella, Miguel Estrada Iturbide, Juan Manuel Gómez Morin, and José Lozano Padilla.

140. Cervantes Varela, 2000.

4

The Rise of the PAN

In these years, the electoral growth of the Party has been one of the most relevant political phenomena in the life of the country. The Party grows and transforms: it confronts new and intense internal processes. . . . To continue growing we must fortify our identity, strengthen the confidence and credibility that people have in us, and at the same time promote the Party's vigorous growth with quality.

—PAN President Felipe Calderón, 1996[1]

It is clear that in the PAN there are two visible poles . . . one that tends toward dogma and doctrine, toward the origin of the party itself, toward conserving that essence, that tradition . . . that club or group of people that drink in the original doctrine . . . and there is another group of citizens that in recent times have become concerned about what is happening with the country . . . our philosophy is pragmatic and that we must resolve the country's problems quickly.

—Vicente Fox, 1997[2]

In the mid-1990s, the PAN would have been virtually unrecognizable to its founding fathers and early activists, especially those who came to dominate the party at the height of its Christian Democratic phase in the 1960s and early 1970s. Ideological principles and political objectives painstakingly developed and nurtured by members of the party's founding generation had been supplanted by new rhetoric and priorities, albeit derived from the same roots. No longer did the party agonize over the decision of whether to participate in elections; rather, by the 1990s, the PAN participated in elections as a matter of course and hungrily accepted public funds, once deemed to be tainted inducements for collaboration with the PRI. More significantly, despite the emergence of a second major competitor on the left, Democratic Current (Corriente Democrática, CD), in 1988, the PAN remained the opposition party governing the largest share of Mexico's population and actually continued to expand its holdings dramatically in the 1990s. In short, over the course of one generation, the PAN was transformed from a party without serious electoral prospects in the vast majority of local elections to the opposition party best poised to unseat the PRI in the 2000 presidential elections.

The PAN's success was, in part, a result of its past failures. That is, as traumatic and potentially destructive as the PAN's internecine struggles were during the mid-1970s, its failure to produce a presidential candidate in 1976 had even more significant reverberations outside the party. Without an opposition candidate to legitimate the regime's "democratic" processes, the unopposed victory of PRI presidential candidate José López Portillo simply revealed the charade of Mexican democracy. López Portillo became the first politically unopposed presidential candidate in Mexico since dictator Porfirio Díaz. This embarrassing situation led President López Portillo to pursue a series of political reforms, notably the 1977 Federal Law of Political Organizations and Electoral Processes (Ley Federal de Organizaciones Políticas y Procesos Electorales, LFOPPE). With Mexico still reeling from the regime's disastrous reaction to the 1968 political crisis and undergoing economic strain, these and later reforms provided the PAN with newly enhanced electoral opportunities.

Still, despite these contextual changes, the PAN's responses and ultimate success cannot be understood without attention to its changing *internal* circumstances. The most important shift within the PAN was the development of a new internal consensus—after nearly a decade of division—and an influx of activists recruited from the private sector and the middle classes. The PAN's new activists were driven to the party by their dissatisfaction with the PRI's economic mismanagement and frustration over the lack of accountability inherent in the system, particularly with the 1982 devaluation of the peso and subsequent nationalization of the banking system. From this generation emerged a new brand of candidates and party leaders who embraced political strategies and promoted mass appeals that greatly enhanced the PAN's electoral prospects and organizational capacity. Such newcomers were in many ways the inheritors of ideas and strategies advanced by José Angel Conchello, the upstart PAN leader who moved away from the more religious orientation that had emerged in the party in the 1960s and adopted an aggressively antiregime stance in the 1970s. Like Conchello, these "new Panistas" (*neopanistas*) hailed primarily from Mexico's northern regions and entered the party after virtually apolitical careers in the private sector. This reentry of middle-class businesspeople, who had been driven away from the party by more religious and leftist elements in the 1960s and 1970s, was ultimately the triumph of Conchello's vision.

The conventional wisdom among PAN experts in Mexico suggests that the entry of these *neopanistas*—individuals with new skill sets and resources but without strong ideological attachments to the PAN, referred to by one PAN observer as "rebels without a cause"—transformed the party's internal coalitions and enabled the unprecedented electoral progress of the 1980s and 1990s.[3] The main problem with this view is that, in focusing on the role of new entrants to the PAN as the drivers of its transformation, most scholarly accounts tend to gloss over the events that took place from 1976 to 1982. Thus, while this interpretation may correctly capture the general trends that accompanied the PAN's membership growth and electoral successes in the 1980s and 1990s, it fails to examine how the party moved on from the debilitating crisis of 1975–1976 to its acceptance and even recruitment of outsiders in subsequent years. Most important, this omission creates the impression that the triumph of Conchello's vision was the result of the injection of new blood into the party, rather than the facilitator of change. Yet, the careful negotiations that helped to heal the PAN in the late 1970s made this possible and, consistent with the general argument made throughout this book, illustrated how the interplay of interests within the party proved a determinant of party behavior and development.

The Triumph of Conchello's Vision

There is no doubt that the return of the PAN's prodigal sons and daughters from the private sector and middle classes had significant, positive impacts on the PAN's electoral fortunes over the course of the 1980s and 1990s. Their political mobilization was a direct result of Mexico's deteriorating economic situation, which began in the mid-1970s. The exhaustion of Mexico's traditional economic model and the regime's attempts to sustain political support, through massive public-sector spending at a time of worldwide economic turmoil, steered the country on a dangerous course. The discovery of Mexico's vast petroleum reserves in 1976 enabled Echeverría's successor, President López Portillo, to achieve substantial economic growth through continued public sector spending, thanks to loans and foreign investments based on (ultimately incorrect) projections of Mexico's oil revenues and future interest rates. The oil boom temporarily extended the regime's performance legitimacy and thereby prevented strong opposition to the political hegemony of the PRI. However, Mexico's dramatic reversal of fortunes in 1982, which included a steep drop in oil prices and a simultaneous increase in international interest rates, burst the economic bubble. The subsequent devaluation of the peso and the federal government's desperate and poorly managed efforts to rescue Mexico's spiraling economy by nationalizing the banking sector contributed to extreme dissatisfaction. Over the decade of the 1980s, average Mexican citizens would lose nearly 30 percent of their purchasing power, while Mexico rose to rank as the world's second most indebted nation, after Brazil.

The political reaction to these developments included severe rebukes from the middle classes and private sector, including official business associations. Still, it is important to note that most businesspeople, especially Mexico's super rich class of entrepreneurs, such as media mogul Carlos Slim and Televisa owner Emilio Azcarraga, instead opted to support the regime through traditional channels or simply abstained from political intervention. This is an important point because the PAN has long been labeled as the party of "the rich" and of "business." This was a counterintuitive accusation of a regime where business-people had long left politics to the politicians, while lending their tacit—and often explicit—support to the official party in return for political favors. However, a handful of well-known entrepreneurs and representatives of the middle class—especially those most disadvantaged by the evaporation of profits and personal savings resulting from the 1982 devaluation—became highly politicized by the Mexican economic roller coaster in the 1970s and 1980s. This was especially true in the northern regions, where industrial development depended on close ties to the United States, and business operations and commerce were, therefore, particularly sensitive to capital flight and fluctuations in the value of the peso. For example, one Baja California businessman traced his dissatisfaction with the regime's economic policies back to the mid-1970s but noted that the 1982 bank nationalization was the crystallizing event that led to the politicization of his generation:

> Around . . . maybe 1975 or 1976, a group of young business professionals began to get together. Inevitably, our discussion would fall on the topic of the government . . . that things were bad . . . weren't being done right. . . . There was a devaluation in 1975 or 1976 and it was after that. It was just after the administration of Echeverría. . . . In this group were Mr. Ruffo and a few others . . . we were about 6 or 7 total. Also around that time was the famous expropriation of the banks, right? That disturbed us a great deal . . . [though] we had spent many years in which we did little else apart from criticizing among ourselves . . . and, well, when it was decided by the group that we were going to participate in politics, some members of the group entered the PAN.[4]

This and similar stories told to the author in dozens of interviews with businessmen who entered the party in the 1980s tended to emphasize their role as pragmatists who embraced the PAN rather than the other way around. However, it is important to recognize the profound shift that occurred in the PAN from 1976 to 1982 that enabled the party to overcome its earlier resistance to such elements (witnessed by the severe reactions to José Angel Conchello's efforts as party leader in 1975–1976) and welcome a new breed of *panistas,* however warily, into the organization.

In other words, the entry of the Neopanistas would not have been acceptable within the PAN without the careful negotiation of a new consensus within the party in the aftermath of the 1975–1976 crisis. To his credit, Conchello's ultimate decision to adopt a disciplined and conciliatory approach and to accept censure contributed greatly to the achievement of this consensus. In return for this self-discipline, Conchello ally Pablo Emilio Madero was nominated as the PAN's presidential candidate in 1982. The decision to accept and even invite the participation of the private sector was a strategic choice made by PAN's leadership in an effort to move the party in a new, more progressive direction as part of this new consensus.[5]

New Blood and the Limits of Opposition

Manuel J. Clouthier, a prominent businessman known affectionately among *panistas* as el Maquío, was instrumental in renewing Conchello's vision within the PAN by drawing new members into the party. A former president of the Sponsorship Confederation of the Mexican Republic (Confederación Patronal de la República Mexicana, COPARMEX) and the Business Coordination Council (Consejo Coordinador Empresarial), Clouthier became involved in the PAN in the early 1980s after he was rejected for the PRI mayoral nomination in Culiacán, in his home state of Sinaloa. Like Clouthier, members of the National Federation of Chambers of Commerce (Confederación Nacional de Cámaras de Comercio, CONCANACO), COPARMEX, and other business associations were severely dissatisfied with the regime's economic policies, and these organizations became important recruiting grounds for bringing new supporters into the PAN. Clouthier actively mined his connections to recruit owners of small- and medium-sized businesses throughout the country to delve into politics. Indeed, thanks to Clouthier's ability to attract such actors to the PAN, the party succeeded in presenting increasingly intense competition against the PRI at the municipal and state levels over the course of the 1980s, especially in northern states such as Baja California, Chihuahua, Durango, and Sinaloa.

Two state-level electoral contests, notably the races for governor in Chihuahua and Sinaloa (in which Clouthier himself ran as the PAN's candidate), provide useful illustrations of both the surge in PAN support and the reluctance of the PRI regime to cede political space to the long marginalized opposition party. In Chihuahua, the PAN saw significant municipal victories in 1983. That year, former PAN presidential candidate Luis H. Álvarez took the mayorship of the state capital, Chihuahua. At the same time, Francisco Barrio won the mayorship of Ciudad Júarez, and the first city to fall in the 1910 Revolution against Porfirio Díaz became one of the first major cities to be lost by the PRI in the 1980s. These victories were a startling indication of the dissatisfaction of Mexico's business classes (as well as internal squabbles that undermined the PRI candidate) and signaled the beginning of the PAN's northern renaissance. The party had roots in Chihuahua, dating back to the birth of Manuel Gómez Morin in the town of Batopilas, and saw a period of intense party activism during the 1950s. Still, the PAN's organizational apparatus and electoral base had "all but vanished" in Chihuahua by the 1970s.[6] The 1982 financial crisis and nationalization of the private banking system dramatically changed the equation. Angry businessmen drawn from the powerful "Chihuahua Group," consisting of the local chapters of national business associations, demanded political alternation and, importantly, respect for the vote in the state's local elections.[7]

While the PRI conceded these municipal victories, there were limits to the regime's tolerance for the opposition. In 1986, the PAN's very popular gubernatorial candidate, Francisco Barrio, was foiled by blatant fraud by the PRI machine. In that election, the PAN attempted to defend the vote through acts of civil disobedience, a strategy not employed by the PAN since the 1950s. Once again led by Luis H. Álvarez, this more activist stance adapted new forms of civil disobedience to protest the regime's fraud, including "repeated blockades of the Pan American Highway linking Chihuahua to the rest of Mexico, consumer boycotts of businesses collaborating with the PRI, the seizure of international bridges connecting Ciudad Juárez and El Paso, plebiscites on whether the elections were fraudulent, silent marches, and the deliberate obstruction of major traffic intersections."[8] Most notably, Álvarez and the PAN's national leaders staged a hunger strike in Chihuahua that succeeded in bringing international attention to their plight. While the PAN was ultimately unsuccessful defending its victory in the 1986 gubernatorial election, the assertiveness and conviction of leaders like Barrio and Álvarez helped inspire a resurgence of party support and activism in the state and contributed to Álvarez's selection as PAN party president in 1987. Likewise, this provided a basis for Barrio's victory at the state level on his second attempt in 1992.

Meanwhile, like Barrio in Chihuahua, Clouthier's bid for the governorship of Sinaloa was fraught with fraud and chicanery by the PRI, provoking similarly unsuccessful acts of civil disobedience in the aftermath of the election. Though Clouthier had no prior political experience to build on, his campaign achieved widespread popular appeal and may very well have legitimately won the election, thanks to his national prominence as a business figure and his upbringing in the state. In this sense, Clouthier's candidacy was in sharp contrast to the PRI's "sky-diver" (*paracaidista*) candidate appointed from outside of Sinaloa, Francisco Labastida, the former secretary of Energy, Mining and Industrial Development, who lacked significant private-sector expertise and showed a poor record as an administrator of parastatal enterprises in the 1970s.[9] Nonetheless, the official result of that fraudulent election gave Labastida nearly 70 percent of the vote and left Clouthier with the paltry remainder.

Nevertheless, Clouthier introduced Mexico to a different kind of PAN candidate at the very least and perhaps a different kind of campaign. Observers of Clouthier's 1986 campaign for the Sinaloan governorship took note of his singularly personalized campaign style, his use of negative campaigning, and his lack of ideological connection to the PAN.[10] Clouthier's use of highly personalized campaign rhetoric, primarily focused on contrasting his personal qualities and strengths as a candidate against Labastida's mendaciousness and ineptitude, was likely due to the fact that Clouthier did not have well-established ties to the PAN. Accounts of Clouthier's campaign made particular note of his lack of familiarity with party precepts, his tendency to misconstrue or misstate the facts, his joviality and sense of humor (including often self-deprecating references to his enormous girth), and his generally low-brow appeals to the masses differentiated Clouthier from traditional PAN candidates.[11]

Clouthier demonstrated somewhat more sophistication in his 1988 presidential campaign than he did in his Sinaloan gubernatorial campaign. Clouthier inaugurated his 255-day campaign in November 1987 with homage to the icons of the PAN, including its founders and current party leadership and addressed themes central to PAN doctrine. His speeches and "dialogues with the people" included references drawn directly from the classic texts of the party, party founders' speeches, and the party hymn. Clouthier frequently inserted into his speeches elements from the party hymn (played at all the party's formal committee meetings), including key phrases, such as "it is the hour to fight" (*es la hora de luchar*) for "a bountiful and ordered fatherland" (*una patria ordenada and generosa*).[12] Clouthier promoted the PAN as an alternative that promoted longtime party ideals, such as humanism, social justice, human rights, education, agricultural reform, decentralization, freedom of expression, and social democracy.

Still, by the accounts of both party leaders and critics, Clouthier's presidential campaign brought out internal rifts within the PAN and remained characterized by a noticeable lack of familiarity with PAN doctrine.[13] For example, while Clouthier's nomination was overwhelmingly supported by the PAN's National Council, with a vote of 870 to 235, some within the PAN grumbled about the party's growing legions of "Northern Barbarians."[14] Clouthier brushed aside these criticisms, attributing them to excessive centralism and negative attitudes toward Mexico's outlying regions: "These expressions of 'barbarism from the north,' I think are nothing more than . . . a cry of desperation from many parts of the periphery that would like to see less centralization."[15] Meanwhile, Clouthier made little defense of his limited familiarity with PAN doctrine, noting its density and expansiveness: the party platform had "227 pages, ten chapters, and five sub-chapters."[16] Moreover, in recognition that the PAN did not have sufficient human resources to take over the presidency, Clouthier deliberately sought to develop broad, cross-party support: "I would choose the best people willing and available, independently of what party they belong to and even more: I would permit the Federal Attorney General to be named by our political opposition, so that they could make sure that the PAN's hands are clean. . . . Because I believe that democracy is the balance of power, [and that] every human being makes mistakes."[17]

Thus, in many ways, Clouthier ran a campaign that was uniquely his own, without detailed elucidations from the PAN party platform, its Christian Democratic doctrine, or other elements of contemporary conservative philosophy. To be sure, Clouthier tended to make strategic references to religion and "religious liberty," though these were typically targeted to Mexico's more devout regions.[18] Meanwhile, Clouthier's rhetoric drew somewhat inconsistently from the doctrine of free market-oriented conservatism, made popular in the 1980s by England's Margaret Thatcher and the United States' Ronald Reagan. For example, while Clouthier's concept of social democracy, emphasized the need for "more society and less government," and greater "simplification of the laws and regulation of economic development," Clouthier simultaneously criticized the limits of neoliberalism and the inequities of the free market.[19] However, despite, or perhaps because of, his infidelity to PAN doctrine, Clouthier's campaign appears to have opened new doors for the party by bringing substantial mass support. For example, Clouthier helped to draw significant support from women through "Clouthier's Ladies" (Damas de Clouthier), an organization that helped to organize fund-raising activities and rallies for the PAN.[20] In addition, the support of the middle class was manifested, at Clouthier's urging, by demonstrations and acts of civil disobedience that followed the Chihuahua model, including boycotts, marches, and caravans of automobiles. Most significantly, perhaps, Clouthier expressly sought to develop mass appeal, by portraying his campaign as one supported not solely by one party, but as part of a broader coalition between the PAN and the people that he called "PAN-Pueblo."[21]

Above all, Clouthier's campaign focused on attacking the PRI regime and lamenting Mexico's sunken economic fortunes. Harking back to the dictatorship of Porfirio Díaz known as the Porfiriato, Clouthier made sharp attacks against the excessive centralism, presidential absolutism, corruption, and abuses of the neo–Porfirian "PRIato."[22] To a lesser extent, Clouthier also attacked his little-known PRI opponent, Carlos Salinas de Gortari, whom he accused of being a liar and a technocrat with little political experience. In his attacks against the PRI, Clouthier emphasized Mexico's stagnant economy, triple-digit inflation, capital flight, and soaring national debt.[23] Moreover, Clouthier raised eyebrows when he urged the United States to cease economic aid to Mexico because it merely expanded the country's debt and helped finance PRI authoritarianism.[24]

Despite his antics and genuine popularity as a candidate, Clouthier drew less attention in the 1988 elections than the breakaway candidacy of Cuauhtémoc Cárdenas, who split from the PRI after President de la Madrid's designation of Carlos Salinas as the PRI's presidential candidate. The split reflected a gulf within the ruling party over the appropriate response to the nation's economic troubles: in contrast to Salinas, a technocrat espousing economic restructuring and trade liberalization, Cárdenas advocated a brand of economic nationalism harking back to the days of his left-leaning father, former President Lázaro Cárdenas. Cuauhtémoc Cárdenas initially tried to form a protest movement within the PRI, known as the Democratic Current, but later exited the party to run under a coalition of leftist parties dubbed the National Democratic Front (Frente Democrática Nacional, FDN). Given the dramatic nature of his candidacy and the substantial support drawn from sectors of society most disadvantaged by the economic crisis of the 1980s, Cárdenas was both a more notable and more serious challenge for the PRI. It is not surprising, therefore, that the PRI resorted to widespread and diverse forms of electoral fraud, from burned opposition ballots to a strange "system crash" (*caída del sistema*) during the vote count under the watch of President Miguel de la Madrid and Interior Secretary Manuel Bartlett.[25]

Despite these efforts at electoral manipulation, the PRI still did relatively poorly even by exaggerated "official" figures. Beginning in the 1960s, the PRI gradually lost approximately 10 percentage points per decade, as electoral reforms gave a greater share of the vote to various minuscule opposition parties and minor gains to the PAN. Yet in the 1988 elections, official figures suggested that the PRI lost nearly 20 percentage points from the preceding election in 1982.[26] This was the first time the PRI's official figures conceded the loss of a two-thirds majority in the Congress, the level required to make constitutional amendments. Nonetheless, Cárdenas denounced the election as a fraud (as did Clouthier) and even claimed that Salinas had, in fact, lost the election.

Whether or not the fraud concealed Salinas's defeat, it is clear that Cárdenas's leftist coalition was the primary beneficiary of the PRI's lost support, as the Mexican left never officially polled more than 6 to 9 percent of the vote. While initial reports suggested that the PAN had lost support to Cárdenas,[27] the PAN basically held its ground. Moreover, assuming that the PRI did worse than government figures recognize, then it effectively stole votes from one or both opposition parties to increase its official share. Indeed, while the FDN complained most loudly about fraud, there are good reasons to believe that the PAN also may have performed better than reported. First, despite the fact that Clouthier was probably the most dynamic and popular PAN candidate ever to have run in Mexico at that time, the PAN only saw a marginal increase in its share of the vote, rising from 16 percent in 1982 to 17 percent in 1988. Second, it is particularly unusual that the PAN did so poorly in its traditional bases of support, particularly in northern states, such as Baja California, Chihuahua, and Nuevo León (see Appendix 4). Indeed, in prosperous, industrial, and traditionally *panista* Baja California, the PAN placed third after the PRI and the FDN, yet one year later, in 1989, rallied to oust the PRI from the state government (see Appendix 4).

There are two equally plausible explanations for this trend. On the one hand, focusing on the strategic calculations of PAN supporters, it is possible that many conservatives actually voted for the PRI in order to prevent a leftist victory. On the other hand, taking a less charitable view of the PRI, it may be that the PRI simply allocated votes from PAN strongholds to itself. In either case, recognition of the potential hazard this new competitive scenario held for the PAN led to a dramatic shift in its relationship with the regime. Borrowing from the language of game theorists, this was a shift from the pure zero sum nature of party competition in the 1980s to the more complex dynamics of three player games. When a zero sum game—in which one player's loss is the other player's gain—is restricted to two players, game theorists refer to this as a game of pure competition. Cooperation in such circumstances is highly undesirable because it directly undercuts either player's interests. Yet, games that involve three or more persons are never "purely" competitive; even if the game is "zero sum," there is always the possibility that two players will work at like purposes to the detriment of the third player. In Mexico, this seems to have been the factor that most dramatically changed the relationship between the PAN and the PRI.

Once the Party of the Democratic Revolution (Partido de la Revolución Democrática, PRD) came onto the scene, the strategic dynamics of the game changed, and the PAN was able to use this situation to its advantage by cooperating with the PRI to push through legislation that each party found beneficial to its interests. It is noteworthy that the PAN could have tipped the balance in the other direction by opting to support Cárdenas's efforts to disqualify Salinas's victory. While Clouthier favored this option to any collaboration with the PRI, conservatives within the party leadership were more resistant to any collaboration with the left.

Hence, in the aftermath of the 1988 elections, the PAN cooperated with the PRI to recognize Salinas's fraudulent victory and even to pass constitutional reforms that decreed "governability" powers to the largest party in subsequent elections. In apparent reward for PAN collaboration, the PRI accepted legislation to increase electoral transparency and create new spaces in the legislature for opposition parties, such as further expanding the number of seats available for proportional representation in the Chamber of Deputies and adding new such seats to the Senate. After 1988, the PRI even seemed to take a more tolerant position toward PAN victories at the subnational level. Indeed, the PAN's ability to achieve recognition of its candidates after 1988 generated considerable controversy and accusations of secret negotiations with the PRI, in a so-called concertation (*concertación*) of PRI–PAN interests.

In light of PAN denials of concertation and the fact that Cuauhtémoc Cárdenas also met secretly with Carlos Salinas in the aftermath of the 1988 election, it is difficult to be certain to what extent the PAN's success of the 1990s was an explicitly negotiated pact or simply the de facto result of the PRI's efforts to punish Cárdenas and prevent the new left from growing too powerful. Still, at the very least, it seems reasonable to interpret the Salinas administration's tolerance for PAN success in terms of the new strategic context, as the PAN was now the lesser of two evils in the eyes of a PRI faced with a serious challenge on the left. With PAN's new, more pragmatic focus on advancing its electoral fortunes, the party was now in a position to take advantage of the opportunity.

The Rise of the PAN: Party-Building and New Strategies for Success

From 1990 to 2000, the PAN experienced a veritable flood of electoral victories at the local level, accumulating over 600 municipal governments, four times the number of local victories it had won in the previous fifty years (see Figure 4.1). By 1989, the PAN had already governed a record number of municipal governments for any opposition party; between the party's first mayoral victory in 1946 and those won in 1989, the PAN achieved a total of 146 victories at the municipal level. Yet, this paled in comparison to the party's accumulation of local victories over the next decade, when this num-

Figure 4.1 PAN Municipal Administrations, 1947–2000

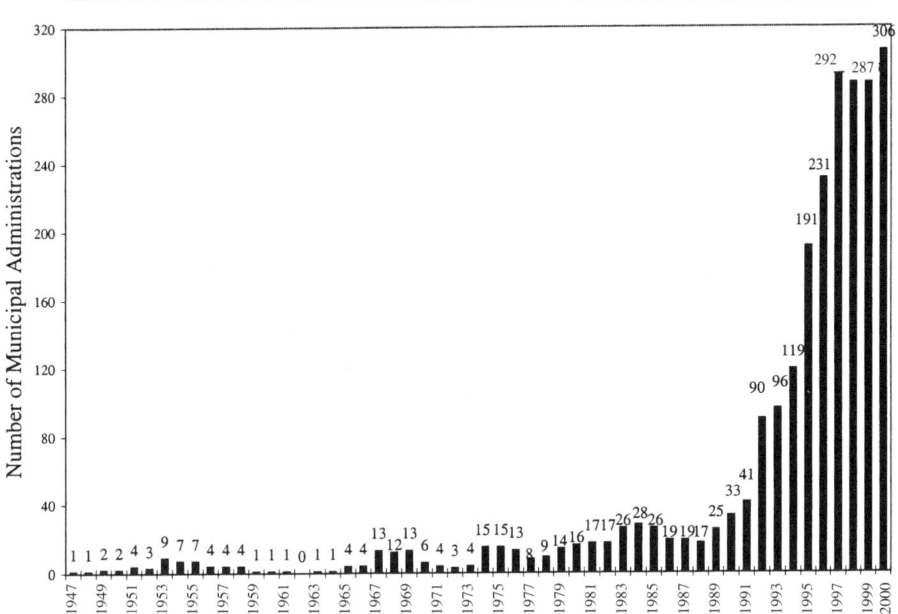

Source: Data obtained from Instituto Federal Electoral.

ber increased to more than 500 administrations in over 335 different municipalities throughout the nation. By 1997, the party boasted 292 municipal governments and had suffered only a slight decline to 287 by the end of 1998. In addition to these mayoral victories, the number of PAN *regidores* (city council members) placed in office rose from 669 in 1987 to 2,529 in 1996.[28]

In contrast to the PRD's strategy of trying to dismantle the regime by launching strong challenges at the highest level, former Federal Electoral Institute Counselor Alejandro Lujambio described the PAN's electoral strategy as one of "democracy through federalism," a bottom-up strategy from local to state and national governments.[29] Generally speaking, the PAN's electoral gains came through gradually stronger bids from the bottom upward, with the party leapfrogging from municipal victories to gains at the federal deputy and state levels that peaked in the mid-1990s. As the PAN fought for, negotiated, and took advantage of reforms to open the political system further during this period, the party's slow and painful trickle of victories during the preceding forty years gave way to a great blue tidal wave of successes by the mid-1990s. The nature of the PAN's progression at the municipal level is made clear by the growth in the absolute number of municipalities from a handful in the 1980s to more than three hundred by 2000 (see Figure 4.1). Yet, since the party never controlled more than a fraction—just over 10 percent—of Mexico's 2,400 municipal governments, none of these figures do justice to the magnitude of the PAN's electoral successes of the 1990s. What must be noted, therefore, is that among the relatively small number of municipalities controlled by the PAN during this period were the majority of Mexico's most important and most populous cities.[30]

Indeed, PAN victories in large municipalities have always accounted for the better part of the population it governed; in 1997, the PAN controlled 32 municipalities, each with populations of more than 100,000 inhabitants. The total of 10,683,441 inhabitants in such cities represented 77.32 percent of the total population governed by the PAN.[31] In contrast, the PAN governed 35 municipalities, each with fewer than 10,000 inhabitants; the combined total of 159,626 inhabitants in these municipalities represented just 1.15 percent of the population governed. Overall, the effect of PAN's success in large municipalities proved extremely important in establishing its electoral base throughout the republic. In fact, by 1998, the PAN governed nearly one-quarter of the national population, that is, more than 27.6 million inhabitants, counting municipal governments alone, not state governments.[32] Moreover, not only was PAN becoming very successful at winning elections and gaining recognition for its municipal victories, the party demonstrated repeated successes in a number of key cases at the municipal level, notably, major cities like Ciudad Júarez, Guadalajara, León, Mérida, Mexicali, Monterrey, Querétaro, Tijuana, and Toluca.

Again, the PAN's mounting electoral strength at the municipal level provided a springboard for its accumulation of victories in direct legislative elections and gubernatorial races. Indeed, its victories in district elections were typically concentrated in and around the urban tide pools of PAN electoral strength. Nationally, such pockets of support enabled steady growth in the PAN's number of federal deputyships, with modest but measurable increases in direct district elections and stronger growth in deputies assigned by proportional representation. Meanwhile, the PAN's gradual accumulation of municipal and district-level victories formed an important base for the party to move on to break through electoral barriers at the state level.

From 1989 to 2003, the PAN placed a total of twenty of its candidates as governors (see Appendix 2). Fifteen PAN gubernatorial candidates were elected in six states in the north and center of Mexico, in addition to four appointed as interim governors and three candidates elected through alliances with other parties.[33] Interestingly, several pathbreaking PAN governors emerged from the case studies of regional repression discussed in the previous chapter, including Ernesto Ruffo Appel (Baja California, 1989–1995); Carlos Medina Plascencia (Guanajauto, 1991–1995); Vicente Fox (Guanajuato, 1995–2000), and Patricio Patrón Laviada (Yucatán, 2001–2007). The PAN's mayoral and gubernatorial successes appear to have had additional benefits for the party, including coattail effects for the party's state deputy candidates. The 1990s saw a significant increase in the number of PAN candidates elected to state legislatures, either through direct electoral contests in single-member districts or as candidates on proportional representation lists, with the number of local deputies rising from 51 in 1985 to 299 by 2000.[34] Likewise, PAN's gains in the national legislature were notable, increasing from 32 to 207 federal deputies and adding 46 senators during the same fifteen-year period (see Table 4.1).

The PAN built upon its electoral successes by strengthening the party's organization. Whereas the party traditionally had been dependent on spontaneous social mobilization as a means of securing electoral victories, by the late 1980s and through the 1990s, the PAN began to operate as a full-time professional party that increasingly sustained its activities between elections. While far from being fully institutionalized, the PAN made important progress toward the development of its party bureaucracy. In key localities, full-time organizational staff made it possible for the party to provide training and events between elections as a means of indoctrinating and training activists and potential candidates. New organizational resources made possible through public funding had a dramatic impact on PAN campaigns and represented a dramatic shift from the past. The PAN had initially rejected public funding when it was introduced in the reforms of the 1970s; at the time, PAN President González Hinojosa argued that public subsidies "would establish a certain economic

Table 4.1 PAN Government Officials Elected to Executive and Legislative Posts, 1985–2000

	PAN Senators	PAN Federal Deputies	PAN State Legislators	PAN Governors	PAN Mayors	PAN City Council Members	Population Governed by the PAN (%)
2000	46	207	299	9	329	4,046	41.46
1999			220	4	287	3,231	34.84
1998			287	4	287	3,231	32.6
1997	31	121	296	4	305	3,414	38.52
1996			267	4	249	2,527	24.4
1995			240	4	218	2,527	24.7
1994	25	119	176	3	128	1,864	15.5
1993			143	3	99	1,600	n.a.
1992			129	2	98	1,338	12.6
1991	1	89	116	1	49	1,209	10.1
1990			122	1	35	826	5.1
1989			115	1	29	705	3.5
1988	0	101	95	0	17	680	0.8
1987			60	0	17	669	n.a.
1985	0	32	51	0	26	200	n.a.

Sources: Data for 1987–2000 obtained from María Elena Álvarez de Vicencio, *Alternativa democrática: Ideología y fuerza del Partido Acción Nacional* (Mexico City: EPESSA, 2001), pp. 160–162. Additional federal legislative data obtained from Francisco Reveles Vázquez (1993, 1996).

Note: n.a. = not available.

dependence of parties on the government."[35] However, the decision to accept public funds under PAN President Luis H. Álvarez led to a marked increase in the quality and quantity of PAN propaganda and electoral materials. In cases where the PAN's local organization attracted new support and activism in the wake of electoral success, increased financial resources could be applied to further its organizational development.

Also, at the local and national levels, the party benefited from a more rigorous application of training programs to prepare candidates and militants for electoral action. The PAN had traditionally engaged in a variety of training programs, but it was not until 1979 that the party's first institute for studies and training was initiated. The Institute of Political Studies and Training (Instituto de Estudios y Capacitación Política) was founded by Carlos Castillo Peraza and operated as a voluntary, supportive network of experienced and educated activists who promoted PAN philosophy and principles by giving lectures around the country.[36]

Over the course of the 1980s, the Institute of Political Studies and Training began to administer training programs with a greater emphasis on electoral mobilization and the defense of the vote through nonviolent tactics. The influence of this emphasis was clear in the party's campaigns in the mid-1980s, as

PAN activists engaged in peaceful demonstrations and hunger strikes to protest electoral fraud. With the incorporation of the Institute's functions into the formal organization of the party and the eventual acceptance of public funding, the PAN began to extend its efforts at training and educating the party's candidates for elected office.

The party has little quantitative data to illustrate the improvements in its candidate preparation, though there are some significant anecdotal examples of candidates' increased preparation. The best and most obvious example may have been the preparation of PAN candidate Diego Fernández de Cevallos for the nation's first live, televised debate in the presidential election in 1994. Fernández's campaign team spent several weeks studying debate tactics used in the United States, England, and France. They prepared voluminously for the event, gathering materials and figures to be used in the debate. Fernández arrived at the studio with boxes of information and notes prepared on a broad range of topics. Cárdenas and his team were obviously underprepared in comparison; the veteran presidential candidate arrived without notes or cards of any kind and stumbled through questions with loosely formulated rhetoric. PRI candidate Ernesto Zedillo was slightly more prepared, having brought along a packet of index cards laden with notes. During the debate, PAN candidate Fernández made repeated reference to his own materials, frequently waving thick wads of documents at his competitors as if to support his arguments with the sheer visible weight of the evidence in hand. Viewers responded very favorably to Fernández's performance, with the PAN candidate emerging as the clear victor in subsequent polls.

Over the course of the late 1980s and 1990s, the PAN began to develop special courses for campaign training and leadership, resulting in better preparation of candidates and activists for the trials of electoral campaigning, defense and monitoring of the vote, and nonviolent postelectoral protest.[37] As a result of this systematic effort, the PAN became better prepared than any party in Mexico to deal with the phenomenon of truly competitive elections. Again, these new norms of organizational efficiency and results-based campaigning probably would not have occurred without the injection of new activists from the private sector and the middle classes. Bringing with them strong educational backgrounds, experience and contacts in business and finance, and familiarity with computer programs and other modern technologies, these new activists redefined and reinvigorated the party.

Changes in the PAN in the 1980s and 1990s enabled the party to perform an increasing number of functions more fully and efficiently than in the past. In large measure, it was greater financial resources that gave the party opportunities to extend its organizational presence at the state and local levels. Although public funding had been available to the party since the late 1970s, the general sentiment within the PAN had been that accepting such funding would place the party at the mercy of the PRI regime and thereby jeopardize its integrity.[38] Under the direction of PAN President Álvarez (1987–1993), however, the party's national leadership reconsidered the issue of public funding for its activities.[39] Though many of the PAN's national counselors remained uncertain about whether to accept public funding made available in 1977 through the LFOPPE, Álvarez pushed for reforms (which were later enacted by the PRI government) that would make public financing more transparent, thereby ensuring that accepting such monies did not make the recipient dependent on the regime.[40]

Access to substantially expanded financial resources dramatically altered the PAN's situation. Along with increased access to daily conveniences like office equipment, new funding meant that the PAN was able to acquire real estate on which to locate local and state-level offices. Public funding also supported the PAN's organizational development by permitting the hiring of full-time employees, and in some cases it even provided salaries for party leaders. With a professional staff, the party now had the capacity to oversee daily affairs, recruit and mobilize militants, and launch counterattacks against the PRI. And because they now had salaried positions, PAN leaders could give their full attention to the party's needs.

Expanding human, material, and financial resources facilitated—indeed, necessitated—organizational specialization. In line with changes at the national level, the PAN developed the administrative capabilities of its local organizations to oversee electoral activities, support the professional development of individuals placed in public office, manage information systems, and so on. As these management functions were professionalized, many day-to-day activities were decentralized through the creation of task-specific committees and subcommittees. The division of labor into smaller units helped the party encourage neighborhood-level participation, and this, in turn, simplified the assignment of electoral activities and other tasks. New activists brought innovative ideas, often drawn from their private-sector backgrounds. Using their professional experience, they introduced modern methods—from increased reliance on advertising to computers and innovative forms of communications—that transformed the organization's everyday operations.[41]

Through the 1990s, the PAN experienced gradual, upward momentum. Still, even as the PRI's only competitor, PAN candidates really had no chance at winning the presidency in any of the elections prior to 1988. However, the PAN's subnational gains appear to have had an important effect on its presidential performance in the subsequent election (see Appendix 3). In 1994, arguably the cleanest federal elections to have occurred by that time, the PAN managed to boost its share from 17 percent to nearly 26 percent of the vote (an increase of over 40 percent). Such an increase demonstrated not only that the emergence of three-way competition at the national level now placed the presidency within any party's grasp, but further indicated that the party's rapid accumulation of subnational victories in the 1990s was favorable to its overall national performance.

Winning Elections and Losing the Party

Much to the lament of politicians and other dreamers, past rates of increase do not necessarily indicate future performance. Indeed, the PAN's record after the mid-1990s has been considerably more mixed than in previous years. Despite the impressive advances described above, PAN's relatively weak performance in the series of state and federal elections in 1997 raised important questions about the party's future electoral prospects. Though 1997 was a banner year for the PAN in some regards, the party's successes failed to match early predictions of the party leadership and political commentators. Months prior to the election, national-level party leaders were not only confident that they would capture the Federal District (Distrito Federal, D.F.) but seemed totally convinced that the PAN would single-handedly introduce the phenomenon of divided government to Mexico by becoming the majority party in the Federal Chamber of Deputies. With the disastrous performance of the party's campaign in Mexico City and the party's failure to maintain even second place in the Chamber of Deputies, these high ambitions were shattered.[42] While gubernatorial victories that same year in Aguascalientes and Querétaro helped to soften the blow, the loss of Chihuahua in 1998 left the PAN two steps forward and one step back. Finally, the sudden and increasing success of the PRD beginning in 1997—assuming second place in the Chamber of Deputies and capturing the D.F. and three governorships by 1999—made the PAN's electoral performance seem all the more dismal. In short, the PAN's electoral performance in 1997 generated considerable uncertainty about its ability to take on the ultimate challenge of overwhelming the PRI in the presidential elections of the year 2000.

The PAN's stalled growth in 1997 was more than an aberration. It reflected the reemergence of the same kinds of internal factional divisions that threatened to destroy the party in the 1970s. A watershed moment for the party came in 1996 with the selection of a new national leadership. The two main candidates in that contest symbolized very different orientations for the party's organizational development and revealed regional rivalries within the party. The contest pitted former Baja California Governor Ernesto Ruffo against PAN National Secretary Felipe Calderón. The process and aftermath of that internal election provides an important illustration of the endogenous factors that drive organizational development.

Ruffo's highly successful gubernatorial term (1989–1995)—the first opposition governorship since the birth of the PRI—had made Ruffo an instant legend in Mexico. Ruffo had previously served as PAN mayor of the port city of

Ensenada, located approximately 60 miles south of Tijuana. Like other entrepreneurs who entered the PAN in the 1980s through their participation in COPARMEX, Ruffo had favorable views of the party and helped bring new life to it: "Since I was a child, I remember that the PAN's political campaigns never won, there was very little and very poor publicity, but it always caught my attention that they were always there."[43] As mayor, Ruffo's struggles against Baja California Governor Xicoténcatl Leyva Mortera helped show the worst face of the PRI and generated widespread public support for the PAN. In his first formal meeting with Ruffo, Leyva attempted to pressure the mayor-elect into defecting from the PAN at gunpoint: "As I was in the process of sitting down, [Leyva] drew a 45 magnum pistol from behind his back and put it on the table . . . but the barrel was pointed right at me. . . . He sat down and crossed his legs. I still can't forget the boots he had on."[44] Given Ruffo's firm refusal to capitulate, Leyva turned to other tactics, directly targeting Ensenada for a variety of abuses.

Ruffo's struggles to obtain the bare fiscal necessities of municipal administration from Leyva's government became widely known.[45] Indeed, largely as a result of the popularity he gained in these conflicts, Ruffo scored his historic gubernatorial victory on the outskirts of the PRI's political empire.[46] Thus, in the contest for the PAN nomination, Ruffo represented the possibilities of a newly decentralized regime that literally bordered on democracy. His campaign slogan in 1989—"Yes, it can be done!" (*¡sí se puede!*)—reflected the can-do attitude of the legions of "new *panistas*" who joined the party and waged successful campaigns in northern states like Baja California, Chihuahua, Guanajuato, and Nuevo León (see Figure 4.2). The PAN's successful

Figure 4.2 PAN Membership Growth by Region, 1989–1999

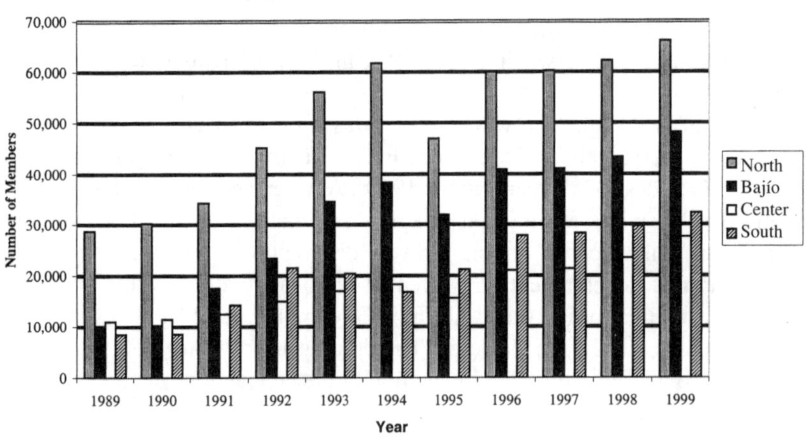

Sources: Regional categories assigned by author. Data for 1989–1994 are from Reveles Vázquez, 1996, p. 30. The source for 1995–2000 is the CEN Registro de Miembros. The PAN publication, Basic Information: Partido Acción Nacional (1994), was also used.

performances in these areas boosted membership significantly in northern states in the late 1980s and early 1990s (see Appendix 5). Ruffo personified these new elements in the party.

Calderón, a bright and serious intellectual, had no successful electoral experience, in contrast with Ruffo. But he had served faithfully within the party's national leadership structures and represented a throwback to the more venerable traditions within the PAN. Calderón was the son of party stalwart Luis Calderón Vega; his family had figured prominently in the party's national leadership for many years. Longtime Panistas could remember the days when young Felipe played in the PAN's Mexico City offices. In short, Calderón literally grew up inside the party. Moreover, Calderón ran under a slogan with clear implications for the PAN's future development: "Winning elections, without losing the party." For those who supported Calderón, the influence of "new Panistas" (Neopanistas), outsiders who lacked loyalty to the party's philosophy and traditions, was becoming a growing problem. In the contest between these two men, Ruffo was clearly the more charismatic and representative of the PAN's new trajectory. New, northern members already represented the vast majority of the party's membership base by 1995, and in the 1980s they enjoyed the support of national party leaders who favored the more proactive vision of Conchello, namely, Pablo Emilio Madero (1984–1987) and Luis H. Álvarez (1987–1993). So it seems counterintuitive that Calderón would emerge victorious in the contest for the party's leadership.

Nonetheless, Calderón defeated Ruffo handily, thanks to two important factors. First, the PAN had experienced a form of brain drain with the migration of its *neopanista* talent from the party organization to elected office and positions within public administration during the 1990s. Hence, while Neopanistas had injected new life into the party and even dominated important leadership positions in the PAN by the early 1990s, they did not sustain their foothold in the internal hierarchy of the party. The result was paradoxical: the more successful the Neopanistas were at gaining elected offices, the less immediately engaged they were within the party organization that placed them in power. The contest between party insider Calderón and the electorally successful Ruffo was, in this sense, a symbolic illustration of two very distinct career trajectories emerging in the PAN. It was also the logical extension of the PAN's internal divisions of the 1970s, with Calderón a literal descendent of González Luna's supporters and Ruffo the very embodiment of Conchello's vision of the party.

Second, the party's restrictive internal procedures for membership and leadership selection carefully insulated the organization against rapid shifts in membership, thereby protecting longtime party stalwarts who were left behind in the party's hierarchy. Formal membership affiliation with the PAN required an individual to be nominated by two current members of the organization, involved a process of internal review, required the payment of party dues, and demanded active and sustained participation in the organization. In short, being a member of the PAN was like being in a close-knit club, rather than part of a modern, mass-based party. Meanwhile, PAN party statutes maintained that the party's national leaders were ostensibly chosen by representatives of the general membership in the party's National Assembly (Asemblea Nacional), which also voted on the party's platform, proportional representation lists, and general plan of action. The Assembly approved a list of 250 national counselors compiled by a committee that drew from nominees proposed by the Assembly and the national executive leadership. In addition to these elected counselors, the National Council (Consejo Nacional) included a number of ex officio members drawn from the past national leadership and high-ranking officials. The National Council helped to select and advise the party's president, but its members did not direct or provide input for the PAN's day-to-day decisions or policies.

For most of its existence, the PAN's National Executive Committee (CEN) was typically composed of anywhere from twenty to forty members. Two-thirds were drawn from a list nominated by the party's president. One-third of the CEN was drawn from a list nominated by the National Council. It is especially important to note the role of the CEN in influencing and setting the agenda in the selection of the National Council. The CEN had a designated number of nominees and also controlled the actual formulation of the list of counselor nominees; therefore, it had significant influence on determining the body that approved its policies, which would select the CEN's successors. In short, these selection mechanisms contributed to a degree of central control that limited the prospects of rapid or major shifts in direction for the organization. The party's leadership structures perpetuated an incestuous relationship. As the "family" candidate, Calderón was able to defeat Ruffo because he had a clear advantage with those party members who really counted: the national counselors. While Ruffo presented a strong challenge, Calderón was the favorite, with 159 votes to Ruffo's 107. In contrast to clashes of the 1970s, however, Ruffo and his supporters took a conciliatory route and ceded victory to their opponent.

Under CEN President Calderón, the PAN made strategic decisions that favored activists who were loyal to party leaders and principles and isolated the party's more pragmatic elements. For example, regulations on party membership were tightened, in an attempt to attract only individuals who were known and trusted by existing members of the organization and who understood and accepted the party's political philosophy. First, this meant preserving and expanding existing requirements for individuals who aspired to become active members of the PAN with full privileges and voting rights. Expanding on these requirements, Calderon's administration introduced new programs for training and evaluation of would-be members. Second, beginning in 1997, the CEN introduced a new category of nonvoting, affiliated party supporters (*adherentes*), effectively creating a separate tier of second-class citizens within the PAN without full privileges of participation. Affiliates were ineligible to run or vote for leadership positions and candidacies for elected office. The classification was ostensibly a trial period with minimal obligations. Yet, in order to become card-carrying members of the party, affiliates were required to meet the above requirements over a six-month period before becoming eligible for membership. As illustrated in Figure 4.3, very few activists who became involved as affiliates from 1997 to 2000 made the conversion to become full-fledged Panistas.

A related factor that restricted the party's growth was that control over membership affiliation for all state committees had recently been centralized to the CEN's national registry of members. Each prospective *militante's* (member's) application was initially processed at the local level and then passed on to the party's Mexico City offices for final review and issuance of credentials. This level of centralized control was useful to ensure quality control of the party's membership roles. Indeed, the sizable dip in registered party membership in 1995–1996 under PAN President Castillo Peraza was actually the result of a massive reaffiliation process—in which all active PAN members were required to resubmit their membership applications—in order to ensure the veracity of party membership; hundreds of dead or inactive members were removed from the rolls. Despite the advantages of centralization, many local leaders and militants expressed frustration that it slowed the

Figure 4.3 PAN Members and Adherents, 1989–2000

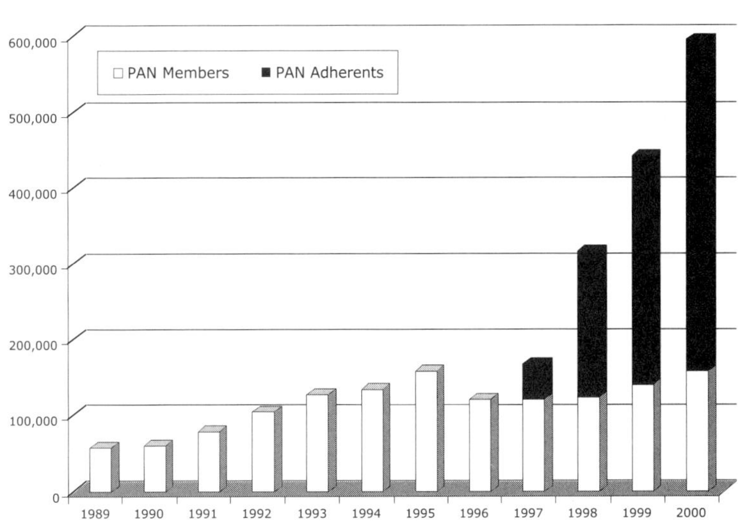

Source: Data obtained by author from *PAN Registro de Miembros.*

process of affiliation and participation as full members (that is, the right to vote in internal elections, to hold leadership positions, to run for elected office, and so on).

All of these innovations were meant to provide filters to improve the quality of incoming members. Most important, the creation of the new category of adherents enabled party leaders to manage rapidly growing support for the party *without* allowing newcomers to influence the organization's internal affairs directly. Given the rigorous entry requirements and long delays in membership processing, many potential members opted not to seek full membership rights in the party. Hence, the PAN's most significant growth was in the category of de facto second-class citizens, which effectively allowed the party leadership to preserve its influence without direct interference from the masses. This careful crafting of party membership restrictions clearly vindicated the arguments of nineteenth-century sociologist Robert Michels, who warned of the "iron law of oligarchy" in party structures. Rather than embracing mass-oriented democracy, the PAN sought to protect itself from it.

To its credit, one result of this shift in policy on membership is that the PAN's registry of activists is without doubt the most nationally accurate and well accounted among any of Mexico's parties.[47] However, in 2000, it was also one of the smallest of any major party in Mexico. Furthermore, the tightening of membership controls and the centralization of membership procedures under Calderón brought the party's booming rate of growth to a standstill, particularly from 1997 to 1998, when the CEN decided to place a temporary moratorium on all new memberships.[48] Even after 2000, the PAN was slow to recapture its previous momentum in organizational growth. Following Fox's victory, the party's membership base remained relatively small in relation to the votes attracted in elections and the population governed. Not surprisingly, the party has been criticized for having weak links to civil society. In many of the PAN's urban strongholds, such as Guadalajara, León, Mérida, Monterrey, and Tijuana, often only a few hundred active party members were responsible for selecting the candidate who would eventually govern over 1 million people. Certainly, this is considerably different from the PRI's traditional, "one-fingered" (*dedazo*) mechanism of selection, but it fell short of the level of civic participation that PAN doctrine ostensibly advocated.

In addition to restrictions on membership, the PAN party leadership's tactics produced critical strategic errors in the 1997 elections. First, the CEN deliberately refused the PAN's full allotment of public funding in the midterm congressional elections. The PAN stood alone in its high-minded sacrifice, and many defeated PAN congressional candidates later complained that this decision had undercut their 1997 electoral campaigns and the overall development of the party.[49] This brought intense criticisms from candidates and local and regional leaders, especially those not closely affiliated with the party leadership, who claimed that they received less assistance than PAN candidates who were allied to the CEN. To make matters worse, candidates favored by the CEN—particularly Carlos Castillo Peraza—delivered a lackluster performance. Second, the CEN centralized the campaign operations for all congressional candidates, providing nationally produced advertisements and campaign paraphernalia so that they would stay "on message." This essentially was the CEN's attempt to maintain control of the PAN's "brand name," but it limited the state and local organizations' flexibility to tailor their campaign messages to their respective audiences.

Hence, the PAN's internal decision-making structures had a significant impact on the party's professional development and application of resources. Its initial refusal of public funding effectively stunted the party's development until the late 1980s, and the decision to refuse part of the public funds available in 1997 proved self-defeating. In the end, both the PAN's organizational development and electoral trajectory suffered from the "slow growth" orientation of the late 1990s. In the 1997 midterm elections, the party sank to third place in the lower house of the legislature, behind the PRI and the PRD, for the first time in the history of its participation in federal elections. Also troubling for some PAN leaders was the impact on the rate of PAN municipal victories, which leveled off abruptly in 1997 and floundered until 2000. In 1998, under Calderón's leadership, the PAN continued to suffer setbacks, notably the loss of the state of Chihuahua after its first PAN gubernatorial administration.

Thus, in the contest between the PAN's competing coalitions, party leaders together with the internal decision-making mechanisms that protected them made critical decisions that stalled the party's organizational development and hindered its electoral performance. Several scholars have described these tensions as conflicts between the party's old and new members. Such a characterization would seem to apply, for example, to the conflict between the national leadership and the members of the Democratic and Doctrinaire Forum (Foro Democrático y Doctrinario, *foristas*), a group of longtime party militants who defected from the PAN in 1993, claiming that the leadership was leading the party away from its basic principles.[50] In reality, however, the *foristas* represented a very small portion of the party's members; only a few hundred withdrew at the national level, and the number of militants who left the party at the local level was negligible.[51] The *foristas*' exit hardly threatened to tear the organization apart in the manner of the PAN's 1976 internal conflict. Nor did it eliminate factional divisions within the party.

Indeed, as illustrated in Chapter 3, the claim that major schisms within the party were and are between old-timers and newcomers dramatically oversimplifies the problem. Although there have been factional divisions within the PAN over fairly major issues, these splits do not appear to be purely generational in character. Rather, factional rifts within the PAN mainly reflect power struggles among individuals and groups with significantly different political philosophies and allegiances competing for candidacies and leadership positions. These multigenerational divisions in some ways reflected the divergent perspectives and connections of the party's founding fathers, the stoic financier Manuel Gómez Morin and the more spiritual Efrain González Luna. Yet, for all subsequent generations, these divisions were played out within the party's leadership structures. As the PAN's experience illustrates, groups within a party organization may benefit from or even manipulate membership roles and internal procedures in the context of internal struggles for organizational control. As the 1990s progressed, for example, the party leadership's efforts to assert control over the organization at a time of increasing electoral gains was an explicit bid by one sector of the PAN to avoid "losing the party." In the process, however, these same leaders created a situation that would lead to their own circumvention, as new groups aligned to support Vicente Fox's bid for the party's nomination in the 2000 presidential elections.

Fox and Friends: Circumventing the Party

In the tradition of the PAN's other northern "barbarians"—individuals such as Conchello, Clouthier, and Ruffo—Vicente Fox heralded from the north-central periphery and entered politics after establishing his career in the private sector. While his early interest in politics brought him close to entering the PRI (in 1984 Fox unsuccessfully lobbied PRI Governor Enrique Velasco Ibarra of Guanajuato to nominate him for a candidacy to the federal legislature), in 1987, Fox became one of hundreds of entrepreneurs and impresarios who joined the PAN and advocated aggressive electoral strategies to oust the PRI.[52] Fox rose to national and international attention in the late 1990s as the unopposed candidate for the PAN nomination and the strongest contender to defeat the PRI in 2000. Given that Fox represented a significant deviation from the orientation of the dominant party leadership of the PAN—firmly entrenched thanks to the internal procedures noted above—how was this individual able to emerge as the face of the party in the 2000 elections? As discussed below, Fox's essential coronation as the PAN candidate was the result of years of strategic positioning and careful organization. Most important, Fox's bid for the PAN nomination and the presidency was one that deliberately circumvented the party's internal processes and the leadership that would have otherwise sought to prevent his candidacy.

In his renegade campaign for the presidency, Fox broke many of the norms of both PAN and Mexican competition. Fox's very early declarations—barely a year after Zedillo's election—that he would run for president placed him far ahead of any other contender, which gave him strategic advantages and exposed him to potential attacks. As governor of Guanajuato, Fox deliberately employed one of the greatest tools of modern presidents, "going public," as a means of generating a national and international reputation. Moreover, Fox and his associates institutionalized their activities in the form of a political organization that closely resembled American-style political action committees (PACs), the Friends of Fox organization (Amigos de Fox). In short, Fox's campaign revolutionized Mexican politics and dramatically altered the dynamics of political competition within his party and in the general election. Understanding how and why Fox's campaign achieved such innovation and success requires a closer look at his longer term trajectory and relationship to the PAN party leadership.

Fox first publicly announced his ambition to seek the presidency in the early 1990s, primarily because of his animosity toward the Salinas administration. The massive fraud that transpired during Carlos Salinas de Gortari's election to the presidency had nearly cheated Fox of a legislative position when he and two other PAN candidates, Elías Villegas and José Pedro Gama Medina, ran for the three federal deputy seats of the city of León, Guanajuato. When León's voters arrived at the polls that Sunday morning, they found hundreds of "pregnant" urns (*urnas embarazadas*), ballot boxes brimming with pre-marked ballots for the ruling party.[53] Local PAN leader Antonio Obregón Padilla lamented that the PRI had disappointed them; the PAN was expecting a "cyber-fraud" (*fraude cibernético*) but instead saw nothing but old tricks: "We expected a fraud, but more refined . . . and they came at us with 'vote tacos,' removal of observers, nonacceptance of voters . . . just old ridiculous things."[54] Outraged voters took matters into their own hands, burning the illegal ballots in the streets or delivering them to the media. In a tremendous display of civic activism, León's citizens themselves took charge of the remainder of the electoral process to assure that their votes were respected.[55] The very next day, the state's electoral commission determined that the PAN federal deputy candidates carried all three federal districts in León.[56] When Fox took his place as a federal deputy in the lower house of the Mexican Congress, he joined other PAN legislators in criticizing Salinas for the massive fraud perpetrated during the elections. In a typical display of boisterousness, Fox actually adorned himself with crumpled, fraudulent ballots—including two ballots on the side of his head as mock Salinas-sized "ears"—and paraded around the Chamber of Deputies portraying himself as the usurper president. This marked the beginning of a series of direct attacks Fox made against Salinas over the coming years, which naturally did little to endear Fox to the president. Not surprisingly, Fox later blamed Salinas directly for blocking his 1991 gubernatorial bid. In that election, also riddled with massive fraud, PRI candidate Ramón Aguirre declared himself victor in the governor's race the very night the polls closed.

In light of the massive fraud, the national and state PAN leadership proclaimed they would "give their all for Guanajuato" and that the PAN would be willing to sacrifice its state party registration in order to defend the vote for

Fox. Yet national-level negotiations between the PAN and *Los Pinos*[57] failed to achieve recognition of Fox's alleged victory and instead produced a compromise that satisfied the PAN, if not Fox. Subsequent to these discussions, Ramón Aguirre resigned, by order of Carlos Salinas, and PAN mayor of León, Carlos Medina Plascencia, was named interim governor. Whereas Medina was a relatively new member of the party (he joined the PAN in 1986) and from the north, Medina was strongly associated with the humanist and "socially responsible" orientations of key national party leaders. Medina was also a more acceptable alternative to Salinas than Fox, as Mayor Medina frequently praised Salinas's hallmark antipoverty program, PRONASOL, for the benefits it brought to Mexico's underprivileged classes. Fox, on the other hand, was incessant in his public criticism of Salinas and his neoliberalism and neopopulism; with regard to NAFTA, for example, Fox outrageously proclaimed that Salinas had tricked Mexicans "like Hitler tricked the Jews."[58]

Although clearly unhappy with the results of the "scandalous fraud of 1991," Fox was cordial to PAN President Luis H. Álvarez and other party leaders when they met in León in the aftermath of the election. While some PAN observers contend that Fox withdrew from politics in an embittered protest against PAN party leaders for not supporting him in 1991, this was not the case.[59] In fact, Fox's formal resignation from politics actually came in 1993 and was more related to subsequent actions by new national party leaders related to the 1994 presidential election, as indicated below. Hence, at least under Álvarez, Fox remained loyal to the PAN leadership and subverted his pride for the good of the party.

However, Fox grew increasingly dissatisfied with both the Salinas administration and the PAN's national leadership under Álvarez's immediate successors, Carlos Castillo Peraza and Felipe Calderón. On the one hand, Fox was frustrated by delays in state-level negotiations over the timing of special elections in Guanajuato, which were to have taken place in 1993. However, PRI leaders in the state legislature delayed the convocation of elections by refusing to cooperate in negotiating the reforms, allegedly due to Salinas's insistence that Fox be prevented from a chance to run for governor until the end of his presidential term. In the end, gubernatorial elections were ultimately delayed until 1995, meaning that Fox could not take office until after Salinas's term ended.

On the other hand, Fox was disappointed by the party leadership when he prepared to pursue his interest in running for president in 1994, which he first declared in 1992 in the aftermath of Guanajuato's annulled gubernatorial elections. Fox's hopes were dashed by national-level negotiations between the PRI and the PAN over reforms to Article 82 of the 1917 Constitution. This article originally required both parents of a presidential candidate to be Mexico-born citizens. Fox (whose mother was born in Spain) and his supporters argued for revision of Article 82 on the grounds that, by relegating him to second-class citizenship, it violated Fox's human rights. Fox asserted that if Salinas truly wanted to open the presidential field to more candidates, he would support the reform. Fox's calls for reform of Article 82 won the support of "half–Mexican" PRI aspirants as well. The PAN leadership initially responded to the idea of a Fox presidential candidacy by publicly supporting constitutional reform. In the final negotiations, however, the reforms passed only on condition that they go into effect *after* the 1994 elections, making Fox ineligible until the year 2000.

A wounded Fox declared that he would be too old to run for president by 2000. He was particularly disappointed in the national PAN leadership's "betrayal" at the bargaining table, which was headed by the PAN's most effective negotiator and coordinator of the party's legislative delegation in the Chamber of Deputies, Diego Fernández de Cevallos. When asked whether delaying the implementation of this constitutional reform meant that the PAN would lose its best candidate, Fernández de Cevallos stated that he did not consider Fox the best—or the only—PAN candidate for 1994. Indeed, with Fox out of the picture, Fernández de Cevallos was able to grab the PAN's presidential nomination for himself, although he denied any such political calculations on his part. Soon after, Fox responded with a very public withdrawal from politics, despite the leadership's appeals for him to remain active in the party. Fox targeted his anger toward President Salinas, with a long and bitter tirade against what he characterized as Mexico's road to destruction:

> As long as Salinas is here, count me out. . . . Vicente Fox will no longer lend himself to raising the hopes of the citizenry, mobilizing them and taking them toward that holocaust, toward that death trap to which Salinas is taking us. I abstain from participating because there are no longer any real conditions for democracy, for electoral transparency, for respect for human rights and political rights. . . . Fox will not . . . participate so long as Salinas is president. With other [presidents] one knew what to look out for. They were not democratic, and we fought to change this, but with Salinas it is deception. He is Machiavellian and pretends to be democratic.[60]

Fox did return briefly to the political arena in 1994 to rally PAN members to defend claimed municipal victories in Guanajuato. However, true to his pledge to wait out the Salinas administration, he did not announce his return to politics until January 1995, by which time he was already wildly popular in Guanajuato. He went on to win the state's governorship when the long-delayed special gubernatorial election was finally held later that year.[61]

Upon winning the governorship in July 1995, Fox went to work almost immediately at preparing his campaign for the presidency in 2000. Fox worked actively to cultivate his own support base within the party in the state of Guanajuato, particularly in the PAN stronghold of León. Yet, his efforts to gain control over the leadership of PAN's state organization did not translate into success in placing his allies in mayoral candidacies or proportional representation seats in the state legislature. Nor did Fox's ability to influence the party leadership at the state and local levels translate into an ability to promote his supporters in national-level positions. In 1997, for example, the national PAN leadership rejected candidates nominated by Guanajuato's state and local leadership in favor of local candidates closer to PAN President Felipe Calderón. Frustrated with the party route to building his party base and perceiving resistance from the national leadership, Fox pursued three deliberate extra-party strategies that ultimately ensured his success in obtaining the nomination and winning the presidency.

First, Fox dedicated at least half his term as governor of Guanajuato to cultivating a national and international presence, as well as a large base of extra-party support, clearly targeted to advancing his presidential ambitions. This was the case despite his early claims in 1995 that he no longer had interest in seeking a higher political office, stating on different occasions: "I will be Governor full-time," "I have a commitment to the people of Guanajuato," and "I know you won't believe me, but I don't want to be President of the Republic."[62] Fox's actions betrayed his words. Domestically, Fox used his position as governor to gain the attention of the national press and to travel extensively to other states, often campaigning in support of like-minded members of the PAN. He also made numerous international trips to Asia, Europe, other Latin American countries, and the United States—allegedly to promote Guanajuato's export industries—which yielded both domestic and international political benefits. While traveling abroad, Fox's audiences included influential foreign business leaders and politicians, Mexico-born voters living abroad (eligible since 1996 for dual nationality and considered a potential pivotal voting bloc in 2000), academic analysts, and foreign journalists, many of whom were charmed by Fox's charisma and denim-and-boots cowboy demeanor.

Fox's strategy of going public and capitalizing on the diplomatic powers of executive government were important factors in promoting his name recognition not only to Mexican voters, but also to domestic and foreign elites who could prove to be potential allies in his quest for electoral victory. Yet, the strategy did cause Fox some problems back at home, where local cartoons portrayed him as a speedy "Road Runner" who stopped for nothing.[63] Hence, when Fox formally announced his candidacy on July 2, 1997—exactly three years before his 2000 victory—the response from Fox's PRI opponents in the state legislature was to pass the only piece of legislation the governor ever vetoed: the Law of Responsibilities for State and Municipal Public Servants. The vetoed initiative would have restricted the movements of mayors and the governor to their own jurisdiction and were clearly aimed at limiting Fox's ability to engage in proselytism. Unfettered by the PRI's gambit, Fox's activities became less and less focused on the affairs of state over the course of his governorship and more and more on the demands of his presidential campaign. Fox finally stepped down and was replaced by Lieutenant Governor Ramón Martin Huerta on August 7, 1999, just over four years into his term.

A second extra-party strategy was initiated at the outset of his campaign in 1997, when Fox's supporters began to organize Friends of Fox. Friends of Fox essentially functioned as a U.S.-style political action committee, in that it could amass large sums of campaign contributions without being constrained by national election regulations. Hence, long before the legal period for campaigning began, Friends of Fox began maneuvering in support of Fox's candidacy by raising funds, distributing trademark booster pins and other pro–Fox materials, and producing a series of televised spot announcements.

Third, Fox was willing to look beyond the narrow conservative bases of the PAN to seek support for his candidacy and, indeed, was willing to support any candidate who would defeat the PRI in 2000. This inclination was made evident by his participation in the San Angel Group (Grupo San Angel), a diverse group of elites that began meeting in Mexico City's southern San Angel district to discuss and promote Mexico's democratic transition. Organized by left-leaning academic Jorge Castañeda, the San Angel Group brought together intellectuals and politicians who shared the goal of unseating the ruling party.[64] Fox's participation in this diverse group clearly distinguished his approach to that of the PAN's national leadership, which had opted to collaborate with the PRI to the detriment of the PRD and generally opposed the strategy of formal electoral alliances with other parties. In short, Fox's circumvention of his own party through candidate-centered public appeals, extramural sources of private funding, and cross-party alliances were the secrets of his success.

Hence, by 1998, when the PAN's national leadership began to discuss selection of the party's 2000 presidential candidate, they were faced with a difficult dilemma. Party leaders from the CEN met in Querétaro that summer to discuss possible selection mechanisms that might block a Fox candidacy but realized that they were at a strategic disadvantage and had few viable alternatives to Fox. Moreover, they realized that the PAN was under external competitive pressures to choose a more open and democratic method of nominating its presidential candidate. The PRD's open candidate selection process demoted the PAN to the position of second most-democratic party in Mexico. The PRI was also beginning to discuss similar internal reforms, and it began to appear that the ruling party might develop more democratic selection procedures than the PAN's.

Under these circumstances, PAN leaders remained unsure whether to open the party to greater participation by nonactivists (as the PRD had done), limit participation to existing members, or maintain the existing selection method, by which a select group of delegates to the National Assembly selected the presidential candidate. Opening the nomination procedures to the masses would have been sure to hand Fox the candidacy, while restricting the nomination process would have made the PAN's nomination the least democratic in Mexico. Worst of all, from the perspective of certain party leaders, even restricting the nomination process to include only the National Council was not certain to prevent a Fox candidacy, given his growing support among leaders in that body. For example, the success of Fox's allies running for governor in Querétaro and Nuevo León in 1998 provided inroads into the national leadership, as governors were automatic members of PAN's National Council.

At the same time, key elements of the national leadership were discredited or disabled during this period. The PAN's loss of the Chihuahua state government and the stagnation of municipal victories under CEN President Felipe Calderón refuted the bright young party insider's efforts to win elections without losing the party. Carlos Castillo Peraza's disastrous performance in the 1997 Federal District election led him to leave the party. His defeat was at least partly the result of national-level attacks on local PAN governments that made the party appear far more conservative than the average Mexico City resident: censorship in the cities of Aguascalientes, Puebla, and Monterrey; the defamation of a national hero in Michoacán; and false rumors of both a city-wide curfew (*toque de queda*) and the prohibition of miniskirts in Guadalajara. Yet it was also partly the result of his own mistakes, such as ill-received jokes that the PAN opposed the use of condoms because they would clog the Mexico City sewer system. Meanwhile, although Diego Fernández de Cevallos remained a prominent figure in the party after his unsuccessful 1994 bid for the presidency, he seemed unwilling to take on further candidacies; some speculated that there were skeletons in his closet. In the end, it is likely that these trends strengthened the hand of the "northern barbarians" and complemented Fox's extra-party strategies to obtain the nomination.

Given limited options to prevent Fox from winning the nomination and the party's recent setbacks, the PAN leadership postponed taking a decision on nomination procedures until after the selection of a new party president in March 1999. In that contest, CEN insider Luis Felipe Bravo Mena trounced Ricardo García Cervantes, a young, lesser-known senator from Baja California. In an apparent compromise, Bravo Mena drew the support of both the national leadership and Fox and many of his supporters, and his margin of victory was the largest of any PAN national president in two decades. The decision reached under Bravo Mena's party leadership with regard to presidential nomination procedures was a compromise. Voting for the party's candidacy would be open to all party members and to "affiliated" supporters, the new category created under former PAN President Calderón.

From the national leadership's perspective, this method of selection protected the PAN by keeping decisionmaking within the party, but it also tacitly acknowledged the inevitability of a Fox nomination. However, the PAN was still thrust into the awkward position of having a relatively "undemocratic" nomination. That is, the fact that Fox ran unopposed made the party's nomination no more than a rubber stamp, undermining the party's efforts to appear internally democratic, relative to the more open proceedings of the PRD and PRI (discussed in more detail in Chapter 5). In effect, the constraints that the PAN's internal institutional arrangements and leadership structures placed upon Fox forced him to seek leverage outside the organization, and his success in building extra-party support in turn undermined these same arrangements and structures.

Some political observers suggested that what the PAN needed in the 1980s and 1990s was a stronger party organization that would be able to withstand "intrusion" by newcomers. For example, Mizrahi (2003) makes the case for greater strengthening of the PAN's organizational apparatus so that the party will not need to rely on outsiders. However, if anything, the PAN's experience shows that the excessive rigidity of the party organization—indeed, the "strength" of leaders in the party hierarchy—was its very weakness. As the PAN's history suggests, organizational rigidity contributes to oligarchy and internal strife, while consensus building is the key to organizational success. Thus, I argue that true strength comes from greater organizational flexibility, based on representation of interests and the ability to incorporate diverse elements through consensus building. This is where the PAN succeeded through visionary leadership in its early years, as well as in the late 1970s and early 1980s. However, PAN leadership was not always so visionary; unfortunately, weighed down by its centralized, hierarchical structures, the party faltered at critical points in its evolution in the mid-1970s and late 1990s.

In the 1990s, members of the CEN's efforts to limit the influence of their competitors within the organization, illustrated by their deliberate efforts to block Fox's candidacy, effectively undermined the linkages between the party and its candidate in the 2000 elections. In other words, rather than maintaining control of the party's institutional integrity, when CEN members forced Fox to circumvent the party, they, in effect, ushered in a new style of candidate-centered politics. This brought some significantly negative consequences for the PAN's institutional development. First, Friends of Fox and its separate membership base was the primary vehicle for Fox's candidacy, and after the election it continued to be largely autonomous from the party. Although this may have made it easier for independent voters and militants from other parties to support candidate Fox, the group's existence undermined an important opportunity to further the PAN's organizational development. Furthermore, weak party affiliation contributed to split-ticket voting in the July 2000 elections. Although the PAN won the presidency, it did not win a majority in either chamber of the federal legislature—and actually lost representation in the 2003 mid-term elections—which greatly complicated executive-legislative interactions during Fox's six-year administration (2000–2006). In the end, Fox's long road to the PAN's presidential nomination and the presidency illustrates the importance of factional competition and internal institutions in driving party organizational development and performance, as well as the enormous consequences for the rest of the political system. The PAN's strategies reflected the short-sighted, centralized decisions of an aloof and insulated central leadership. This internal centralism generated frustration at the subnational level. Candidates and campaign managers, feeling the pinch of the PAN's self-imposed budgetary restrictions, complained that they were at a disadvantage vis-à-vis their competitors. In addition, the barriers created by the national leadership for members' active participation in the party, combined with the highly centralized procedures for controlling membership, limited the party's ability to grow at the local level. As a result, it was difficult for the PAN to take full advantage of upswings in electoral support. In addition, and perhaps more consequential for the party's long-term development, this approach produced significant friction between the party leadership and vocal proponents of party-building and an innovative electoral strategy. Popular state and local leaders who advocated greater flexibility on membership growth, candidate selection, and cooperation with other opposition parties were ignored or rebuked by the leadership.

Reasserting Conchello's Vision

While Conchello lost the battle over the PAN's leadership selection and presidential nomination processes in 1975–1976, he and his supporters effectively won the war for the direction of the party's ideology and developmental strategy in the 1980s and 1990s. However, this direction—and the PAN's internal balance of power—was not certain. Internal divisions and significant growing pains that developed over the course of these two decades ultimately produced important internal schisms and ultimately resulted in a momentous change for the party and for the course of Mexican politics. These tensions reflected the growing pains that resulted from the PAN's electoral success in the 1980s and 1990s. The PAN's experience during this period suggests that successful party-building does not depend entirely on economic conditions, the opening of political institutions, civil society's responses, or competing parties' organizational characteristics. The PAN's party-building efforts also reflected the interplay between shifting membership bases and interest coalitions within the organization, on the one hand, and the established leadership and decision-making structures, on the other. Such internal factors also had an important impact on the party's performance in other spheres of activity and on the Mexican political system as a whole.

The PAN's story conveys a lesson that has important implications for the analysis and promotion of democracy. At least with respect to parties, one cannot simply assume that electoral democratization will lead to more democratic political institutions. Likewise, the role that parties can play in democratizing other institutions depends heavily on the extent to which they are able to fortify themselves as organizations. Fox's emergence as the PAN candidate was the result of complex internal dynamics of the party over the course of nearly two generations and was aided by new patterns of electoral progress achieved at the subnational level. Fox's electoral strategies and his 2000 victory, therefore, clearly reflected the importance of the PAN's internal processes and organizational weaknesses and presaged the coming of a new, decentered regime. Both came with significant consequences for the course of Mexican elections and the emerging era of democratic governance.

Notes

1. Address to the PAN's National Council, March 9, 1996. Calderón Hinojosa, 2002, p. 14.
2. Interview with Vicente Fox in Guanajuato (June 23, 1997).
3. Mizrahi, 1993.
4. Interview with one of Ruffo's PAN successors, former Ensenada Mayor Oscar Sánchez del Palacio in Ensenada (December 6, 1996).
5. Hernández Vicencio, 2001.
6. Chand, 2001, pp. 113–115.
7. Ibid., pp. 113–115.
8. Ibid., pp. 113–115.
9. Arriola, 1994, p. 74.
10. Arriola, 1994, p. 90.
11. Arriola, 1994, p. 74.
12. Clouthier del Rincón, 1988, pp. 11, 68.
13. Interview with Luis H. Álvarez in Mexico City (May 27, 1997). See also Clouthier del Rincón, 1988, p. 5.
14. Ibid., p. 18.
15. Entrevista del Periodista Ricardo Rocha al Ing. Manuel J. Clouthier, Candidato del PAN a la Presidencia de la República, México D.F., 29 de noviembre de 1987, cited in Clouthier del Rincón, 1988.
16. Clouthier del Rincón, 1988, p. 19.
17. Ibid., p. 27.
18. Ibid., p. 75.
19. Ibid., pp. 49, 71, 83.
20. Interview with City Council member Leticia Villegas in León (May 6, 1997) and an anonymous interview with PAN member in León (April 23, 1997).
21. Clouthier del Rincón, 1988, p. 62.
22. Ibid., pp. 4, 61.
23. Ibid., p. 5.
24. Ibid., p. 25.
25. Prior to the 2000 elections, in a private reunion with reporters and political analysts at the offices of the newspaper *Frontera* (in Tijuana), Manuel Bartlett denied the charges that the "crash of the system" interfered with the ballot count. Rather, he

claimed, the computer system that crashed was merely an auxiliary unit that was not meant to provide the final tally. However, later revelations by former President de la Madrid suggested that there was a clear and deliberate manipulation of the presidential vote in 1988. Thompson, "Former Mexican President Reveals '88 Presidential Election Was Rigged," *The New York Times*, March 9, 2004.

26. Baer, 1988, pp. 1–3.

27. Ibid., p. 16.

28. These data were compiled from internal documents collected by Aminadab Rafael Pérez Franco for the Secretaría de Estudios of the PAN in 1996 and from "Basic Information: Partido Acción Nacional" (Mexico City, June 1996), pamphlet insert.

29. Lujambio, 2002.

30. By 1997, the PAN controlled 15 out of 32 state capitals, including Aguascalientes, Cuernavaca, Culiacán, Guadalajara, Hermosillo, Mérida, Mexicali, Monterrey, Morelia, Oaxaca, Puebla, Querétaro, Saltillo, San Luis Potosí, and Tuxtla Gutiérrez. Moreover, including state capitals, the PAN simultaneously governed 15 of the 20 most populous municipalities in Mexico. Mexico City is not considered to be a municipality and is, therefore, not included among the top twenty.

31. Pérez Franco, 1997.

32. If we incorporate the five PAN state governments, the figure rises to 32.6 million people, Mexico's total population. Figures obtained from internal PAN documents and from a pamphlet entitled *¿Qué es el Partido Acción Nacional?* (Mexico City: EPESSA, 1999).

33. Two members of the PAN—Carlos Medina Plascencia in Guanajuato in 1991 and Alejandro González Alcocer in Baja California in 1998—were appointed as governor under unusual circumstances. Medina was selected by President Salinas to serve as interim-governor. González was selected through negotiations in the state legislature with input from President Zedillo and PAN President Felipe Calderón after the death of sitting PAN Governor Terán Terán.

34. Partido Acción Nacional, 1996.

35. Vives Segl, 2002, p. 70.

36. In 1987, a reorganization of the CEN under then President Luis H. Álvarez absorbed the Institute of Political Studies and Training and divided it into the Secretary of Studies (Secretaría de Estudios) and the Secretary of Training (Secretaría de Capacitación), a format later transferred to all state-level organizations.

37. Interview with Carlos Castillo Peraza in Mexico City (July 16, 1998).

38. Under the LFOPPE, PAN accepted free but limited television and radio access, tax-exempt status, and franking privileges for postage and telephone expenses from the federal government, but it refused funds for organizational support.

39. Interview with Luis H. Álvarez in Mexico City (May 27, 1997).

40. The new distribution formula was based on campaign costs, the number of party candidates, and the number of votes cast for a party. Author interviews with Senator Luis H. Álvarez, Mexico City (May 1997) and with CEN Director of Studies Gustavo Vicencio, Mexico City (April 1997).

41. Some longtime party militants also produced innovations. For example, Carlos Castillo Peraza, in his capacity as a plurinominal federal deputy, helped revive Mérida's *panista* organization.

42. In fact, the PAN placed second in terms of relative vote share, but that did not translate into a second-place position in the number of seats in the legislature.

43. Author interview with Ernesto Ruffo Appel in Tijuana (October 27, 1998).

44. Author interview with Ernesto Ruffo Appel in Tijuana (October 27, 1998). See also Amezcua and Pardinas, 1997, p. 40.

45. Leyva's real problems most likely began when he supported Manuel Bartlett over Salinas in the internal maneuvering for the PRI nomination in 1988. Perhaps even more damning was the PRI's loss in Baja California during the 1988 presidential elections to opposition candidate Cuauhtémoc Cárdenas. Leyva was the second governor to be removed by Salinas, who oversaw the resignation and replacement of 17 governors in 14 of Mexico's 31 states. Ibid., pp. 24–27.

46. Cases in which there is a reasonable doubt that the PRI actually won the election include Baja California (1959), Guanajuato (1991), and Yucatán (1969). See Alemán Alemán, 1993; Cicero MacKinney, 1987; Mabry, 1973a.

47. This is also due to the fact that Castillo Peraza had initiated a massive reaffiliation to determine the actual state of membership in 1994, which decreased membership roles in the North and Center but brought a slight increase in the South (including Castillo Peraza's home state of Yucatán).

48. One of the great concerns voiced by slow-growth advocates in the party was that outsiders with little loyalty to the party gained too much influence over candidate selection and too much access to candidacies in the 1990s.

49. Author interview with CEN member Ana Rosa Payán Cervera (July 1997). Many PAN members were convinced they would win both the Federal District and a congressional majority in 1997.

50. The *foristas* alleged undue and antidemocratic cooperation with the government, business's growing influence in party life, and intolerance toward diverse groups and opinions within the party.

51. More important, despite the *foristas'* rhetoric and appeals to PAN traditionalism, the conflict was hardly a schism between old and new elements in the party. Both sides drew equally from the PAN's older militants; for example, Luis H. Álvarez, then president of the CEN, was not a *neopanista*. Many leaders of the Foro (notably Pablo E. Madero) had themselves generated resentment among traditional party members in internal conflicts during the 1970s. Author interviews with Luis H. Álvarez, Mexico City (May 1997); Nabor Centeno Castro, León (May 1997); and Miguel Gutiérrez Machado, Mérida (July 1997).

52. Regarding his *acercamiento* (rapprochement) with the PRI, Fox later admitted, "I was very close to the governor, to the system, but now I have chosen to join in making a change." Quoted from January 12, 1988, *A.M.* interview with Vicente Fox in David A. Shirk and Luis Miguel Rionda, "The Fox Administration: Who's in Charge and What Does It Mean for Mexico?" Paper delivered at the 2001 meeting of the Latin American Studies Association International Conference in Washington, D.C.

53. The alleged mastermind behind the ballot-stuffing was Angel Buendía, a delegate sent by the PRI's national leadership to coordinate the campaign two months prior to the elections. For more detail on the fraud of 1988 in León, see "Por falta de dirigencia perdió en León el PRI: Alfonso Sánchez," *A.M.*, July 12, 1988: A1. Also, see inset, "Suma de Irregularidades," *A.M.*, July 12, 1988: A1.

54. "Sacó el PRI sus trucos más viejos: Obregon," *A.M.*, July 7, 1998: A2.

55. Even so, other types of irregularities abounded, such as voters with legal voting credentials found they were not listed on official rolls, local heads of polling booths hid election materials in their homes, and polling stations were moved without warning.

56. The PAN triumphed across the board in León, even in the presidential race. In all other parts of the state, Salinas was declared the official winner.

57. Los Pinos (The Pines) is the name of the presidential residence. These negotiations were conducted with President Salinas and others in his administration.

58. "Se retira Fox de política," *A.M.*, September 30, 1993: 1B.

59. Loaeza (1999) incorrectly characterizes Fox's separation from the party. Loaeza, 1999, pp. 503–504.

60 "Se retira Fox de política," *A.M.*, September 30, 1993: 1B.

61. Shirk, 1999.

62. Rionda, "Vicente Fox: ¿mito o realidad?" *Dossier político*, June 23, 1996.

63. When Fox was first interviewed by the author in Guanajuato, the meeting literally took place "on the road," as the governor's sport utility vehicle raced from one speaking engagement to another. The author was dropped off outside a restaurant, miles from their starting point.

64. This effort to build a broad, nonideological coalition was reminiscent of Chile's anti–Pinochet plebiscite movement, except that it pursued an elite rather than a mass-based approach. Members of the group came from the right; the left (Cuauhtémoc Cárdenas); and the middle (notably, Adolfo Aguilar Zinser, a former spokesman for Cárdenas' 1994 presidential campaign who, as an Independent federal deputy, later headed the investigation of the corrupt food distribution agency Conasupo). Though he did not participate in Grupo San Angel, it might be appropriate to place Gilberto Rincón Gallardo, one of Fox's opponents from the presidential campaign, in this camp.

5

The 2000 Presidential Election and a New Era of Mexican Politics

History is change.
—Pope John Paul II, 1990[1]

While traditional studies of political parties tend to focus on the external factors that shape their incentives, this telling of the PAN's story has instead centered on the ways in which collective action among strategic actors in the context of a party's internal rules, procedures, and forms of organization contribute to the party's own development and behavior in other arenas. In other words, this is a story that focuses on institutional development from the inside out. Yet, the story of the PAN also helps to illustrate how a party's internal affairs can have important implications outside the party. Indeed, throughout this story, the PAN's development as a party, the strategic choices made by its leaders, and its engagement of key sectors of society all had decisive impacts on the course of Mexico's democratization. Whether referring to the party's internal debates over its strategy toward the PRI regime, the critical internal crisis of 1976, or the decision to incorporate business elites in the 1980s, choices and events inside the PAN have spilled over to influence Mexican politics in fundamental ways. Hence, a party's internal context is not only an important determinant of its own development and behavior, but also has effects that reverberate beyond the party.

Perhaps nowhere were the spillover effects of internal party developments more noticeable or consequential than in the contest for the presidency in Mexico's 2000 elections. The internal dynamics that contributed to Vicente Fox's highly autonomous candidacy and innovative, candidate-centered tactics for self-promotion had important effects on the campaign for the Mexican presidency, the outcome of the 2000 elections, and the kinds of governance challenges that Fox would later face as president. Fox's victory was achieved through innovative strategies for effective political competition in Mexico: his own personal political action committee to finance his campaign; a media-driven, candidate-centered campaign; nonpartisan appeals; and a reliance on Fox's status, visibility, and mobility as governor to build his electoral and political bases of support. Hence, as much as the rise of Vicente Fox was shaped by PAN party leaders seeking to "save the party," it induced the coming of a new era of politics that has dramatically altered the traditional role of political parties in Mexican campaigns and elections.

The Campaign for the 2000 Presidential Election

The race for the presidency in the 2000 Mexican elections was unlike any other in the nation's history. This election was unique not only because the final result swept out the ruling party after seventy-one years, but because of the way the campaign for the presidency was conducted. Never before had there been such emphasis on the process of selection in determining the kinds of candidates running for the Mexican presidency. Rarely, if ever, before had the voters and the kinds of appeals made by the candidates been so important. Never before had the organization of an electoral campaign been so effectively managed by a candidate of the opposition, especially with regard to ensuring turnout among its supporters on the day of the election. Never before had the campaign strategies and interactions of the major candidates—particularly the use of negative attacks—been so intense and critical to the ultimate outcome of the election.

Clearly, the 2000 presidential election was not only about Mexico's transition to democracy, but also about the emergence of a distinct model of democratic competition that brings with it significant dilemmas in multiple arenas of political interaction. In the 2000 election, the candidates, driven primarily by Fox's lead, relied on the incorporation of "Americanized" strategies and methods. That is, in ways unlike any previous contest for the Mexican presidency, this campaign resembled those typically observed in "advanced" democratic countries, most notably the United States. Thus, in some ways, the Fox phenomenon seemed to present a contagion from the north; that is, a weakening of the traditional role of programmatic political parties in the electorate, such as examples widely observed and studied in the United States in the late twentieth century.[2] In studies of other countries affected by these trends, David L. Swanson and Paolo Mancini describe this transformation as a process of "Americanization," which involves "the export and local adaptation of particular campaign techniques, and . . . modernization, the more general and fundamental process of change that . . . leads to adoption of these techniques in different national contexts."[3] Broadly conceptualized, the term "Americanization" incorporates a variety of other modern trends, including the increased control of information (especially that information thought necessary to make sound decisions) by political "experts." The role of the media in "framing" issues and the transformation of citizenship to "spectatorship" diminish the direct personal involvement of citizens in political activities and campaigns.[4]

Understanding how this new context affected the course of the 2000 election requires attention to a number of key aspects of campaigns in modern democracies. First, almost any modern campaign begins long before the open contest among rival candidates nominated by different parties. The formal and informal factors that shape the process of nomination are, therefore, critical determinants of the kind of candidates and, ultimately, the kind of leaders who will prevail in an election. Vicente Fox's campaign for the presidency began at least three years prior to his formal nomination by the PAN on September 12, 1999, and was made possible by careful maneuvers designed to overcome potential opposition from the party leadership. Fox was so successful in establishing his position within the party that he ran unopposed by any challengers, a first in the history of PAN's nominations for the presidency.

The making of the other major candidates—PRD candidate Cuauhtémoc Cárdenas Solórzano and PRI candidate Francisco Labastida Ochoa—also involved the processes of jockeying for position and vying for national-level visibility. In the summer and fall of 1999, respectively, both the PRD and the PRI held open primary elections to determine their presidential candidates for the 2000 elections.[5] In many ways, the races within these two parties were shaped by the early emergence of Fox as the PAN's candidate and responded to campaign strategies that were well under way. Unlike Fox, Labastida faced significant challenges from other major players in the PRI, but he temporarily enjoyed a significant boost of popular approval and credibility because of the PRI's unprecedented display of open democratic procedures in the party's primary. However, the resources expended and the divisions that emerged in the "pre-campaign" process had significant costs for Labastida. Similarly, though following Fox's lead by preempting competitors in his party, Cárdenas's strategy for capturing the nomination in the PRD's primary seems to have ultimately undermined not only his party's democratic procedures but his campaign as well.

The 2000 presidential election was also defined by the kinds of appeals the candidates made to voters: how they presented themselves, their platforms, and their relationships to the electorate. As in metaphors used to describe campaigns in the United States and elsewhere, candidates in the 2000 Mexican elections had a product to market to voters under one of three brand names or party labels (PRI, PAN, or PRD). The intensity of the marketing effort in 2000 hinged on one critical fact—the voters really counted. Thus, the candidate and campaign that were best able to appeal to and mobilize voters ultimately achieved success. The kinds of appeals made by the major candidates for the presidency in the 2000 election are considered at length in this chapter, with particular attention to Fox's ability to frame the election as a choice between a long-needed change and an intolerable status quo.

The kind of campaign organization that the candidates had at their disposal was a third major factor in the 2000 election. The PRI had long relied on a style of organization that resembled the U.S. political machines of days past, when electoral fraud, voter intimidation, and vote buying were widespread practices that had corrupted the democratic process. Yet, PRI governments of recent decades had either sold or bargained away many of the resources that had long enabled such practices in Mexico. Moreover, while the PRI and PRD recovered from the fractious primary elections that had yielded their candidates, they were confronted with the electoral juggernaut that the Fox campaign organization had become. Fox's ability to draw on experienced marketers, a diverse coalition of prominent supporters, U.S. campaign consultants, and the massive "para-party" organization of Amigos de Fox helps to explain his ability to appeal to a wide spectrum of voters.

Additionally, as in U.S. campaigns, the strategic interaction of the candidates in the media—particularly on television—was a critical determinant of success in this election. While the 1994 presidential election had introduced the first formal televised debate among major candidates, the campaign six years later was distinguished by two major debates. These debates effectively captured and even helped shape the dynamics of the campaign. The first debate, on April 25, 2000, involved all the candidates, including Porfirio Muñoz Ledo of the Authentic Party of the Mexican Revolution (Partido Auténtico de la Revolución Mexicana, PARM); Gilberto Rincón Gallardo of the Social Democratic Party (Partido Democracia Social, PDS); and Manuel Camacho Solís of the Central Democratic Party (Partido Centro Democrático, PCD). Both Fox and Labastida were successful in framing that first debate as a contest between two alternatives: PRI or PAN. Indeed, because PARM, PDS, and PCD typically received less than 2 percent each in public opinion polls, the two remaining debates involved only Fox, Labastida, and Cárdenas. Several important "Americanized" trends prevailed in these debates; particularly, the extensive use of emotive appeals at the expense of substantive policy debate and frequent negative attacks by all three candidates.

PRI and PRD Primaries in the 2000 Presidential Elections

The 2000 Mexican presidential campaign was greatly extended by the preemptory candidacy by Fox. As discussed in Chapter 4, Fox successfully prevented competition for the PAN nomination by maneuvering very early to attract financing, supporters, and a national and international reputation as the best choice for Mexico in 2000. Hence, Fox's early emergence as the PAN's candidate stood in stark contrast with the PRI and the PRD nominations processes with significant consequences. Indeed, the challenges faced by Fox's rivals from the outset played an important part in determining the outcome in the general election and help in this analysis to underscore both the influence of internal party dynamics in shaping outcomes and Mexico's new political reality, in which such factors will play an increasingly prominent role.

The Fantastic Four: The Battle for the PRI Candidacy

What was most striking about the PRI nominations process in the 2000 presidential election was the degree to which it adhered to democratic methods of internal selection. This was astonishing because, throughout its existence, the ruling party's nomination process had depended entirely on presidential discretion in the designation of his successor. This informal power of appointment was widely known as the *dedazo*, roughly translated as the "finger-tap," because it referred to the metaphorical pointing of the president's finger.[6] As Jeffrey A. Weldon (1999) suggests, the selection process was probably the root of presidential power in Mexico, because the sitting president could deliver the ultimate prize for party loyalty and good behavior: the presidency itself.[7] This guaranteed the unequivocal fidelity of would-be aspirants and their clientelistic networks of followers (*camarillas*) within the party. In other words, the selection of a successor was a president's ace-in-the-hole, and contenders for the prize were anxious to curry the sitting president's favor. Thus, the president was cautious about the unveiling (*destape*) of his eventual replacement, recognizing that once a successor was revealed, he himself would become a lame duck, and his one-time supporters would be clamoring to curry favor with his successor. PRI party loyalty, as strong as it was, was simply the manifestation of a rational respect for the power of the presidency, whoever held the position. In the end, that power was not vested in the person of the president but in the office itself.

The *dedazo* was an instrument with other important effects. Throughout the history of the PRI Party, the president served as the ultimate arbiter of the multiple interests and sectors within the party. Over time, the balanced treatment of these different elements in the process of succession helped to ensure harmony and power sharing within the revolutionary family. Indeed, some scholars have even suggested that successive presidential administrations alternately shifted their favor from one wing to another within the PRI in the manner of a swinging pendulum.[8] Each president served as the pivot of that pendulum, using the process of succession to direct the prize carefully from one group to another. Indeed, the pendulum's failure to swing from the technocratic, neoliberal wing back to the party's leftist-nationalist elements in the late 1980s may help to explain the exit of the PRI elements that eventually formed the PRD and contributed to the continued decline of the PRI.

By the 1990s, the president's power-bestowing digit had already overextended itself and—many believed—required amputation. Carlos Salinas had chosen not one, but *two* successors, due to the assassination of his first choice, former PRI President Luis Donaldo Colosio. Colosio had been lauded for his profile as a reformer within the party, though he was selected by the traditional practices of the PRI and was a close follower of Salinas. Whether he would have proved the messiah of a kinder, gentler, and more democratic PRI was left unanswered by an assassin's bullet in the border city of Tijuana-Baja California on March 23, 1994. With the circumstances of Colosio's death clouded in doubt, Salinas was forced to find a replacement. In the end, he selected Ernesto Zedillo, Salinas's former secretary of Education and Colosio's campaign manager.

The selection of Zedillo brought to power—probably for the first time in modern Mexican history—a man with little or no evident desire to hold the position and few connections or followers within the ruling party. Because the circumstances of Zedillo's selection were unique, they made him completely unpredictable. Would his lack of ambition and his political weaknesses turn him into a tool of the party's most hard-line elements, or would he choose to distance himself from the party altogether? Throughout his presidency, even Zedillo himself did not seem to know the answer to this question. On the one hand, he declared that he would break precedent and maintain a healthy distance from the PRI. On the other, over the course of his term, Zedillo appeared to violate this pledge repeatedly by collaborating closely with hard-line elements and PRI party leaders. The PRI presidential nominations process for the 2000 elections was, thus, an important test of the extent to which Zedillo was willing to cut off his own most powerful presidential appendage. In the end, Zedillo opted for internal party democracy and urged the PRI to come up with the best candidate for the task.

Thus, what stands out most about the PRI nomination for the 2000 election was the apparent opening of the selection process, not only to the party's mass bases but to society at large. It was Mexico's first truly open primary. Arguably, Zedillo's apparent disinterest in power-broker politics may have had more to do with the circumstances that led to his selection than to a deeply rooted personal dedication to democratic ideals. Yet, the amputation of the "big finger" also demonstrates the different context in which the PRI found itself at the end of the 1990s. The PRI no longer had the organizational capacity to rely on a spoils-based system, where state-fueled economic growth and generous political patronage provided corrupt politicians with functional or performance legitimacy. Moreover, the PRI, faced on both the right and the left with significant challenges from parties that employed relatively democratic internal procedures, also needed to modify its practices in order to remain competitive. One reason why PAN and PRD candidates were winning at the state and local levels was that democratic nominations proceedings generated popular candidates with local appeal. In contrast, traditional PRI practice often involved top-down imposition of candidates who had few supporters and little charisma. Many, therefore, believed that the PRI's best hope to win was to hold a competitive presidential primary in 2000.

Ironically, while the primary indeed proved the PRI's most open and democratic contest in history, accusations of antidemocratic practices were also the loudest, and perhaps the most damaging, in the PRI primary. Once Zedillo renounced the privilege to select his successor, surrendering his powerful prerogative, there was no reason for would-be candidates to maintain a show of discipline and respect for him. As a result, the PRI's primary was marked by an intensely competitive campaign. The PRI's four main contenders included Interior Secretary Francisco Labastida, former Tabasco Governor Roberto Madrazo, former Puebla Governor Manuel Bartlett, and former PRI President Humberto Roque Villanueva. This group was referred to (charitably) during the 2000 primary as the "Fantastic Four," in reference to the Marvel comic book popular in the United States. The contest among them was an all-out brawl with little of the party discipline seen in the past.

Even the most obscure of the four characters, former PRI President Roque Villanueva—perhaps symbolizing the role of the comic book heroine, "Invisible Woman," to the PRI's version of the Fantastic Four—lambasted the ruling party's traditional tactics and its "official candidate." In Matamoros, Roque openly asserted that the PRI needed to move beyond such practices as the "carting" (*acarreos*) of voters to the polls and the use of electoral fraud; he also criticized the official line that seemed to favor Labastida, who had recently been identified as the choice of several PRI governors.[9] Meanwhile, if Villanueva acted as the invisible contender, Manuel Bartlett may well have played the role of the Fantastic Four's cantankerous, gritty troglodyte known as "The Thing." Bartlett, the *pri-nosaurio,* or party hard-liner, who allegedly rigged the computer outage during the 1988 elections, entered the primary with a harsh and skeptical vision of the process. Evidently unable to withhold his own criticism for the good of the team, Bartlett warned ominously of "the risk that the party will fracture and disappear" and complained openly that the primary had been "so unfair and irregular, that the November 7 [primary] elections should be the first and the last" to be held by the PRI.[10]

Former governor of Tabasco, Roberto Madrazo, with his fiery personality, may well have been born to play the role of the "Human Torch" in the PRI's version of the Fantastic Four. Madrazo was far and away the most vocal and proficient in his application of explosive negative campaign techniques against Labastida, with help from U.S. consultants Douglas E. Schoen and former Clinton adviser James Carville.[11] In his attacks, Madrazo accused Labastida of being a "perfect failure," who could be no match for a strong candidate like Vicente Fox. In addition, Madrazo tried to portray Labastida as a Mexico City insider whose self-purported claims of nearly forty years in government without dirtying his hands were hardly something to brag about. The common Mexican's hands, Madrazo argued, "are dirty with the sweat of work."[12]

In trying to peg Labastida as a representative of the old-style traditions of Mexican politics, Madrazo even accused Labastida of being the favored candidate of former President Carlos Salinas, perhaps the most reviled symbol of PRI corruption in recent memory. Madrazo and his team also consistently asserted that the primary was patently unfair and tainted with corruption. One of Madrazo's simplest but most effective campaign slogans—a highly irreverent criticism of the process, the "official" candidate, and even the president—crudely proclaimed: "Screw the system!" Consistently trying to cultivate his image as a reformer, rebel, upstart, and man of the people, Madrazo almost appeared on the verge of bolting the PRI. Rumors spread that he had talked to former PRI members who had defected to the PRD about the prospect of running as the candidate of another party.[13]

Like both Bartlett and Roque, Madrazo's most damning criticisms involved the assertion that Zedillo's "big finger" was firmly attached and pointed directly at Labastida. Indeed, one of Madrazo's key campaign slogans capitalized on the fact that his last name was also a colloquialism for "a firm blow": roughly translated, Madrazo's primary campaign slogan urged PRI voters to "Crush the Finger-Tap" ("Dale un Madrazo al Dedazo"). For the Madrazo campaign, this was precisely the kind of antagonistic appeal that helped get the attention of voters and capitalize on discontent with the system.[14] Yet Madrazo's accusations that Labastida was the "official candidate" presented an odd paradox: if Zedillo had been following the traditional practice of selection, it would have been political suicide for Madrazo to complain about it so publicly. Moreover, if the president did prefer a specific nominee, this was not evidenced by public declarations or other clear demonstrations of support. Also, ironically, Madrazo himself was widely regarded as one of the PRI's most hard-line politicians. His election as governor of Tabasco in 1994 had been clouded with accusations of fraud and by revelations that his campaign—purported to have reached the equivalent of U.S.$70 million (with the help of illegal contributions from fugitive banker Carlos Cabal Peniche, among others)—had far surpassed the $1 million limit. The worst accusations against Madrazo linked him not only to Salinas, but also to other southern politicians of ill repute: Victor Cervera Pacheco (the "Kingfish" of Yucatán) and Mario Villanueva (the former governor of Quintana Roo who had fled the country on accusations of corruption and ties to narcotrafficking).

Whether Labastida was indeed the preferred candidate of President Zedillo, Madrazo's aggressive attacks were born out of intense competition for the nomination. In retrospect, as much as Labastida seems to have had the advantage, the outcome of the PRI primary was far from certain. Polling organizations came up with fairly different predictions during the months just prior to the primary: Indemerc Louis Harris (the Mexican affiliate of Louis Harris &Associates Inc.) conducted a survey in September 1999, and Pearson conducted an October poll for Labastida's campaign.[15] While the Pearson poll predicted a relatively large Labastida victory, the slightly earlier Harris poll suggested that Madrazo had the advantage (see Table 5.1).

In the end, the November 7, 1999, primary proved Pearson to be more accurate (see Table 5.2). Winning 272 of 300 or over 90 percent of electoral districts, Labastida proved far and away the definitive choice of the PRI in a primary with a reported turnout of 9.72 million voters at 64,900 polling stations, manned by 400,000 poll workers across the country. As intended, the use of winner-take-all districts created the appearance of a complete shut-out of the weaker candidates, thereby strengthening the apparent legitimacy of the party's candidate. Labastida reportedly received 5.33 million votes, Madrazo placed far behind with 2.76 million, and a total of 1.63 million votes were divided among Bartlett, Roque Villanueva, and nullified ballots.[16]

Most members of the opposition reacted to the PRI primary by urging their members to abstain from voting to avoid giving legitimacy to the process.[17] Yet, the legitimacy of the primary came under question soon after the final results were posted, as pollsters like Daniel Lund of Mori de Mexico and Alejandro Moreno of Reforma found discrepancies in the level of turnout reported by the PRI and possible evidence of ballot stuffing in some states.[18] Estimates of turnout ranged between 6 million and 10 million voters, but aside

Table 5.1 PRI Nomination Polling Data

	Harris/Azteca Poll (September 1999)	Pearson Poll (October 1999)
Francisco Labastida	29.1%	47%
Roberto Madrazo	37.7%	37%
Manuel Bartlett	14.8%	6%
Humberto Roque	10.0%	4%
Undecided	9.4%	6%

Sources: "Front-Runners Francisco Labastida and Roberto Madrazo Steal Spotlight in Governing Party's Debate," SourceMex, http://ssdc.ucsd.edu/news/smex, September 15, 1999; "Encuesta: alcanzan priístas a Fox," *El Universal,* October 4, 1999.

Table 5.2 PRI Open Primary Results for "Fantastic Four"

Candidate	Votes
Francisco Labastida	5,337,545
Roberto Madrazo	2,766,866
Manuel Bartlett	579,434
Humberto Roque	422,069

Source: www.pri.org.mx (accessed November 11, 1999).

from the actual turnout and distribution of the votes, the most important outcome of the primary was that it did not cause a rupture of the PRI. Madrazo, with uncharacteristic discipline, accepted the final results with little protest. At last, the PRI had its candidate.

In part, Labastida's victory may have reflected the relatively measured response of his campaign, no doubt partially influenced by his U.S. campaign consultants. In U.S. campaigns, taking the high road is often the most successful and appropriate behavior. Despite a few harsh jibes—in one analogy Labastida's campaign team claimed that Madrazo was to democracy what Hitler was to human rights—most of Labastida's mud slinging was in "self-defense" and consisted of accusing Madrazo of telling a "long series of lies."[19] Labastida—a veritable Mr. Fantastic, the elastic Marvel comic book leader of the Fantastic Four—simply allowed most of Madrazo's attacks to bounce back. Labastida's decision to wear kid gloves throughout the campaign was probably a forward-thinking strategy: if he were to win, Labastida would need to draw on the support of those who were attacking him. Both before and after the primary took place, Labastida made repeated public invitations to Madrazo for the two to chat over "coffee, tea, lunch or dinner."[20] Immediately after capturing the nomination, Labastida openly appealed to the other candidates to mend the wounds of the past through an effort that he referred to unglamorously as Operation Scar (Operación Cicatriz).

In the short run, Labastida and the PRI appear to have received a significant boost of support from the party's first primary. In the year before Labastida received the nomination, polls gave the PRI only 37 percent among voters, but even just prior to the November 7 primary, the PRI had climbed nearly 10 percentage points in opinion polls.[21] In the weeks that followed his success, Labastida continued to enjoy a very comfortable lead against the opposition. In the final analysis of the PRI's performance in the 2000 elections, however, the intense competition of the primary also brought about serious liabilities.

Competitors for the nomination spent considerable energy and resources and often engaged in fierce attacks that aired the PRI's dirty laundry in public and provided opposing parties with ammunition for the real campaign. Indeed, previously unimaginable criticisms were launched in the PRI primary: Manuel Bartlett claimed that both Madrazo and Labastida had violated the spending limits for the primary contest, Madrazo even attacked PRI National President José Antonio González Fernández because of his alleged favoritism toward Labastida.[22] Christina Alcayaga, one of Labastida's Mexico campaign coordinators, lamented that the "primary has been a cultural struggle for us. There are going to be winners and losers, and it's going to leave wounds."[23] Indeed, highly competitive primaries tend to exhaust a party and its candidate physically, emotionally, and financially in ways that an uncontested nominee does not have to suffer.

Another problem with primaries is that they require candidates to target their appeals to party militants and not to the electorate at large. Party militants are often more likely to prefer a candidate who emphasizes the policy platform and ideological themes that attract them to the party, rather than more moderate positions that would appeal to the less politicized or more centrist voters who may be critical to success in the general election. However, the PRI's contest was an open procedure, and the appeals made by the candidates were not strictly partisan. Indeed, the PRI's problem turned out to be that the party was not really appealing to "party ideologues" who could then rally to support the candidate because they shared some broader goals or identification. In effect, the organizational consequence of an open primary may be to reduce the connection between the candidate and erstwhile core supporters in the party.

Thus, Labastida was forced into an unlikely position for a PRI candidate. He was forced to employ resources that might have otherwise been directed against the opposition, including his own stamina as a candidate. He was forced to compete in a very public setting, drawing attention to alleged weaknesses and liabilities pointed out by members of his own party every time he defended himself. In the end, it is not surprising that PRI voters found it difficult to mobilize in support of Labastida in the general election.[24] Moreover, the democratic, if somewhat fractious nature of the PRI primary points to a tremendous irony in the 2000 race for the presidency: the nominations proceedings for both the PAN and the PRD were almost completely devoid of any competition. That is, both of the major opposition presidential candidates ran unopposed because they effectively circumvented regular party procedures in order to ensure their own nominations.

The Preemptive Candidate of the PRD

The PRD primary was polemical for two reasons. On the one hand, the party had barely overcome the scandals that arose during its leadership renovation on March 14, 1999, when allegations of improper procedures tainted the marginal victory of Amalia García over Jesús Ortega. Though García eventually emerged as the victor in a recasting of the ballots, continued allegations that she was the preferred candidate of Cuauhtémoc Cárdenas further undermined the credibility of the party's internal democratic processes and perpetuated an image of the PRD as a party dominated by a single personality. On the other hand, though he was widely considered his own party's strongest candidate, Cárdenas chose not wait to compete in the PRD's contest for the nomination and instead accepted the outside nomination of the Labor Party (Partido del Trabajo, PT). Though he saw this as a bid to speed up the nominations process à la Fox, Cárdenas's preemptive maneuvers created friction with other would-be candidates and some second-generation party leaders, who felt he was practically obliging the PRD to accept his candidacy (as indeed he was).

At root in both dilemmas was a fundamental crisis of institutional development. That personalities run strong in party organizations is not unusual in Mexico or elsewhere. While in many respects both the PRI and the PAN were highly institutionalized parties, both were created by men, Calles and Gómez Morin, who single-handedly guided the parties' early organizational formation according to their own visions, as different as they were. Observers of party organizations throughout Latin America have frequently pointed to the way that personalities and personalism are dominant in many parties throughout the region; this was perhaps epitomized by Argentina's Peronist Judicialista Party, which institutionalized itself around the mythology of Juan Perón. Recent history illustrates that party organizations, especially fledgling parties, in the United States often fail to overcome the problem of personalism. The Reform Party spawned by Ross Perot's 1992 independent presidential candidacy experienced highly publicized growing pains, as the organization attempted to wean itself from dependence on its flamboyant founder. The emergence of a competing group of personalities and leaders dedicated to strengthening the Reform Party's organization and its electoral performance led to conflict and the departure of some prominent members—most notably the party's first governor, Jesse Ventura of Minnesota—from the party, which essentially crippled the organization.

Similarly, by the mid-1990s, tension had developed within the PRD because of the tremendous influence of Cárdenas within the organization. Cárdenas and his close collaborators had created and assiduously cultivated the PRD in an effort to institutionalize the electoral alliance and political movement spawned by his 1988 bid for the presidency. Given that many believed Cárdenas was robbed of his rightful victory in that election, the party naturally backed its founder in a second bid to claim the presidency six years later. However, with the approach of the 2000 elections, the so-called colonels—the middle-level and second-generation leaders who had emerged within the organization—began to contemplate the long-term institutional development of the PRD and the possibility of life after Cárdenas.[25]

Thus, the 1999 internal elections to select the new party president were in part a referendum on the role of Cárdenas and on the future role of a new generation of leaders in the organization. In this sense, the fact that the process was riddled with technical, organizational, and credibility problems was a major calamity for the PRD and for Cárdenas's 2000 candidacy. The internal elections were held on Sunday, March 14, 1999, but took over a week to resolve because of technical difficulties and public wrangling between the top two candidates, who were locked in a dead heat amid accusations of serious irregularities. There were major technical problems recognized by the PRD's General Electoral Services Committee (Comité General de Servicios Electorales, CGSE), which acknowledged the inadequacy of its preliminary result assessment mechanism and recognized significant problems in monitoring the polls in certain states (e.g., on election night, the PRD announced that it did not have complete data on the polling places in Oaxaca). Additionally, there were shifting margins of victory in a public tug-of-war between García and Ortega.[26]

Interestingly, all of the major contenders reported results that seemed to show a "definitive" victory in their favor: at one point on election night, both García and Ortega claimed margins of victory of over seven points within half an hour of each other. Even worse, there were serious accusations of fraud and old-style PRI shenanigans. Both major candidates obtained unusually high percentages of the vote (around 80 percent) in a handful of states—Jalisco, Puebla, Zacatecas, and Sonora—where a large number of voters had recently become affiliated with the PRD, a possible indication that they were followers of PRI leaders who had recently defected from the ruling party.[27] The contentious results were annulled, and the conflict was ultimately resolved through a recasting of the votes on June 25, 1999. In this second balloting, the results gave Amalia García an ample victory, though the voter turnout was significantly reduced.

In large measure, the original May 14, 1999, internal elections were a casualty of the PRD's national referendum on the Fobaproa held seven months earlier. (The Fobaproa was a major bank bailout scandal in Mexico, roughly equivalent to the U.S. Savings and Loan scandal of the 1980s.) In that referendum, organized in just four weeks, the party established 18,500 polling places nationwide with a budget of 10 million pesos. In contrast, the internal elections had more than two months to prepare and were only able to establish approximately 6,000 polling places because of a more limited 5 million peso budget. Also, the internal selection process was swamped: 3 million voters participated in internal elections, compared with the 600,000 who had turned out for the Fobaproa referendum. "The Fobaproa [referendum] broke the PRD. We still have financial problems because of the spending on the famous referendum," Porfirio Muñoz Ledo said on the day of the internal elections.[28] In addition, the fact that allegations of fraud took place in places where the party had recently absorbed prominent PRI defectors added to the PRD's reputation as a wastebasket for the ruling party.

In light of the issues at stake and the scandals that emerged in the party's internal elections, the prospect of an open primary for the election of the PRD's 2000 presidential candidate presented special concerns. First, the credibility of the internal procedures of the PRD had come into question, which could potentially prove a significant liability for a party that had staked its position in Mexican politics on opposing the legitimacy of the PRI. This was somewhat resolved by the extent to which party leaders and the candidates effectively cooperated in shoring up the selection process and patching up the wounds that developed initially in the March internal elections. Second, the role of Cárdenas in the conflict—lending his support to Amalia García during the internal campaign and the postelection wrangling—gave credence to critics' allegations that Cárdenas remained the strong man (*el caudillo*) of the PRD. This image might have been diminished if Cárdenas had faced significant competition in the party's primary and would have been completely dispelled if, however unlikely, he had lost the nomination to a rival candidate.

Both scenarios were undermined on May 29, 1999, when the Labor Party (PT) announced its decision to support Cuauhtémoc Cárdenas—who had accepted the offer one day prior to the announcement—as its candidate for the presidency in 2000. The PRD had been in negotiations about a possible electoral alliance with the Labor Party, the Social Alliance (Alianza Social), and the Nationalist Society and Union for Democracy (Sociedad Nacionalista y Convergencia por la Democracia) in the two weeks preceding this announcement, but the Labor Party took matters into its own hands by extending an invitation to Cárdenas on May 26. Having won only 2.58 percent of the vote in 1994 and an even smaller percentage in 1997, the PT was in danger of losing its registration and was particularly anxious to make a deal that would help increase its electoral presence. The prospect of an alliance with the PRD was especially favorable to the Labor Party, which had benefited greatly from the electoral spoils of such agreements in the past.[29] Though the possibility of an opposition-wide alliance—including the PAN—was still on the table, the Labor Party was growing impatient, as the candidates of the ruling party and Fox continued to gain ground toward obtaining the nominations of their respective parties. The Labor Party's leading politician, Senator Alberto Anaya, was explicit about the motives of his party: "Politics cannot be waited for, they have to be provoked. . . . [W]e don't want to be left behind the PRI and the PAN."[30]

While Cárdenas's many fans may have been elated at this news, the Labor Party's announcement and Cárdenas's decision to accept were a bit more provocative than some sectors of the PRD would have liked. Porfirio Muñoz Ledo, who had already announced his intention to seek the PRD's nomination, accused Cárdenas of violating PRD statutes.[31] However damaging Fox's strategy may have been to his relationship with the PAN, Cárdenas's decision to seek outside support was a more serious liability both for his relationship with his party and for his overall prospects as a candidate. Like Fox, Cárdenas appears to have alienated certain groups within the PRD that were trying to move away from the personalism of Cárdenismo and closer to a more self-sustaining, institutionalized party organization. But unlike Fox's preemptive bid for the nomination, Cárdenas's strategy actually caused one of the founding members of the PRD—bombastic former priísta Porfirio Muñoz Ledo—to bolt the party. A few months after Cárdenas accepted the Labor Party's nomination, Muñoz Ledo decided to accept the presidential nomination from the Authentic Party of the Mexican Revolution (PARM), after expressing frustration on several occasions with Cárdenas's imperious behavior.

Muñoz Ledo's exit was important for a number of reasons. First, if the new generation of leaders vying for power in the internal structure of the PRD was known as the colonels, the party's most notable generals were Cuauhtémoc Cárdenas and Porfirio Muñoz Ledo. Thanks to the intellectual inspiration of then Spanish ambassador from Mexico, Rodolfo González Guevara, both men were partners in the formation of the internal "Democratic Current" that advocated a critical perspective within the ruling party and opposed Salinas's designation as the party's candidate in 1988. Muñoz Ledo and Cárdenas both left the PRI together in the same year and worked together to promote the left-wing coalition that ultimately supported Cárdenas's candidacy.

Having served the PRI for many years at the national and international levels—even as the Mexican ambassador to the United Nations—Muñoz Ledo was an artful and well-seasoned politician. A fiery orator who pulled no punches, he had competed skillfully with Cárdenas for past candidacies, even besting Cárdenas in a fierce debate at the Mexico City Polyforum in the race for the party's nomination for the 1997 Mexico City mayoral election. Muñoz Ledo's alienation was, therefore, both a practical loss for the PRD and extremely symbolic. Moreover, while Muñoz Ledo's decision to leave the party was not particularly damaging to the PRD in numerical terms—polls rarely gave him more than 2 percent of any probable vote—the fact that he became one of Cárdenas's most dogged critics in the campaign was probably much more significant.

Indeed, the exit of Muñoz Ledo presented a negative image of Cárdenas as a bully within his own party. In an interview with the *New York Times*, Muñoz Ledo complained, "Cardenas is stuck in backwardness and dogmatism. . . . He betrayed his friends who believe in a modern leftist party."[32] Muñoz Ledo himself engaged in the art of betrayal against the Labor Party when he ceded his support to Fox. In the end, Muñoz Ledo's exit increased the ranks of Fox's coalition of supporters and thereby contributed to the image that Fox was working hard to develop: a candidate of transition who was tolerant of diverse political ideologies. Though Muñoz Ledo had repeatedly claimed he would make no such endorsement, Fox was a long-time acquaintance with whom Muñoz Ledo appeared to share considerable mutual respect. Indeed, though he had run against Fox in Guanajuato's 1991 gubernatorial contest, Muñoz Ledo ultimately supported the PAN candidate's claims of victory against the PRI in that election.

In the end, Cárdenas's strategy for ensuring his nomination bore important differences from that used by Fox and seems to have done more harm than necessary. On the one hand, Cárdenas's maneuvers had potentially negative effects for the development of the party's already circumspect norms and institutions for internal selection. This alienated other leaders in the party apparatus, including both the middle-level leaders who were dedicated to the process of institutionalization and one of the most significant figures in the party since its foundation. On the other hand, the use of the Labor Party to circumvent the PRD's selection mechanisms created another significant limitation for his campaign. While Fox had secured his nomination by building Amigos de Fox into a highly financed, megaorganization with a substantial mass base, Cárdenas established no such superstructure to supplement or replace the functions of his party. In short, he snubbed his own party without lining up an adequate alternative vehicle to propel his candidacy.

Marketing the Candidates: What Kinds of Appeals?

Voters mattered in the year 2000. This simple fact had not always been true in previous elections. In the past, many voters' lack of education, resources, and access to the mechanisms of justice meant that they could be easily manipulated, cajoled, or even paid to vote for the PRI. Voter rolls were often so erroneous that the ballots of dead people and fictional characters were counted among those of the living, and because of the PRI government's control of the electoral process, sometimes these fraudulent votes were counted twice. The political opposition's weakness was attenuated by its inability to monitor the polls to prevent fraud by the ruling party. In legislative elections, malapportionment, that is, unequal population distributions in electoral districts, compromised the principle of political equality—one person, one vote—and gave disproportionate levels of representation to PRI supporters in less populated, rural areas. In short, in the past, the PRI's electoral victories had often really been more of a rubber stamp than a political mandate to govern. In this regard, the 2000 Mexican presidential elections were quite different. The openness and competitiveness of Mexican elections was made possible by electoral laws and oversight mechanisms that had been tried, tested, and gradually improved over the course of the 1990s. By the year 2000, the prospect of a massive fraud or manipulation of the vote was smaller than at any point since the 1930s.

The fact that votes mattered meant that the kinds of campaigns waged by the major candidates had to appeal to voters. Though simple, this was a somewhat novel concept for the ruling party and for the opposition. In the past, the PRI could get by with tiresome revolutionary rhetoric that had nothing to do with its policies or the political reality of voters. Likewise, opposition candidates who had no real chance of winning also had little incentive to tailor their appeals in order to gain majority support. In the year 2000, both the PRI and the opposition had to target their messages to voters in ways that related to the interests, concerns, and identities of everyday Mexicans. Because voters mattered more so than in any previous presidential elections, success hinged on the candidates' abilities to appeal to voters and the kinds of messages employed in the process of the campaign.

In the United States and elsewhere, campaign messages are often developed through simple phrases or incidents that capture the essence of complex ideas and issues most important to voters. While many critics lament voters' collective lack of sophisticated analysis and in-depth political knowledge, there is a certain logic and efficiency to the way voters consume political information. The calculus of the reasoning voter is simply this: given a choice over a number of infinitely complex options, heuristic simplifications help to simplify the decision-making process.[33] A heuristic way of understanding involves a conceptual frame of reference—such as an analogy, an association, a metaphor, or a stereotype—that can be used to evaluate information. For example, voters often use the party identification of the candidate as a major "cue" that indicates, at least to voters who believe that there are significant differences between the parties, where a candidate is likely to stand on certain issues.

Whatever shortcuts voters may use, they do so because they have other interests and obligations besides politics. They have to pay attention to their jobs, families, medical problems, education, recreational activities, traffic congestion, and an endless assortment of other matters that are important to them. As much as politics is relevant to each of these, greater political activity and political awareness do not often provide immediate solutions to the problems of everyday life. Hence, many voters do not feel that they have the time, resources, or inclination to be fully engaged in the political system. Rather, many voters therefore try to understand as much as possible with as little time, effort, and information as possible.

A significant liability of this rational informational calculus is that the slogans and images that stick in voters' minds may misrepresent actual facts and lead to inaccurate conclusions. Still, informational shortcuts often confirm reasonable opinions held by voters and may even lead politicians to target their messages in a more efficient manner. In the 2000 Mexican elections, all of the candidates recognized the importance of developing efficient messages in order to affect the calculus of voters. For example, Fox understood the importance of vilifying the PRI, while identifying himself as the most viable candidate of the opposition. Likewise, given Fox's strategy, Labastida understood the importance of distancing himself from the traditional image of the PRI, while discouraging voters from opting to take the road less traveled. Caught in the middle, Cárdenas understood the importance of boosting his position in the race, even if that meant attacking a fellow member of the opposition. To some extent, the three candidates all employed similar strategies to market their different personalities and programs. All three candidates produced self-promoting narrative accounts of their political experiences and agendas for Mexico. Fox first published his book *To Los Pinos* in 1998, which was followed by Cárdenas's *Words of Cárdenas* in 1999, and Labastida's ironically titled *The People Make Change* in 2000. But, in the end, these three candidates had different degrees of success in conveying their messages to the public; the variance came down to the main issues that really matter to voters and how credibly each of the candidates could stake his positions on those issues.

Labastida: A New PRI, Closer to You

To all appearances, Labastida actually emerged as the candidate of a new kind of PRI: a PRI that was no longer dependent on the whims of the president, that employed democratic procedures to deliver the most popular candidate possible, and that tolerated divergent voices and self-criticism. Moreover, the ideas that the PRI actually had changed and that the PRI could and would continue to change became fundamental selling points of the Labastida campaign. Therefore, the failure of the Labastida campaign must be understood partly as a result of its inability to polish the PRI's tarnished image as a corrupt, archaic structure incapable of resolving the long-standing problems that plagued the daily reality of millions of Mexicans.

This reality, that Labastida was unable to change the PRI's image, is worthy of mention. Many observers of the 2000 elections noted the irony of such intense opposition against the ruling party, given a relatively strong economy. Indeed, Mexico had made a remarkable recovery from the 1994 economic crisis and maintained a seemingly stable economic forecast for the foreseeable future. However, for many Mexicans, that recovery did not yield demonstrable results. While approximately 57 percent of the population remained above the poverty line—according to INEGI and CEPAL categorizations—the percentage of Mexico's population living in "extreme poverty" rose from 16 percent in 1992 to 28 percent in 1999, with the rest struggling to remain in the unattractive category of "intermediate poverty."[34] The poorest of the poor, Mexico's indigenous population, remained in abominable conditions: three-fourths had not finished primary education, and nearly half of indigenous children under the age of five were malnourished.[35] Yet, their plight had been ignored for centuries and actually helped perpetuate PRI power by creating a rural Mexican underclass that could be taken advantage of, bought, and lied to by unscrupulous members of more privileged classes.

Where, then, was the cause for discontent in the year 2000? Macroeconomic indicators provide some indication. While unemployment had been reduced to nearly 3 percent (from its twenty-year peak of 6.2 percent in 1994), average real wages in Mexico had declined by nearly 20 percent from 1980 to 1994, and this figure continued to decline another 20 percent below 1980 levels toward the end of the 1990s. Of course, those at the bottom end of the spectrum had it much worse; by 1998, the real minimum wage had lost over two-thirds of its buying power over two decades. By the time of Zedillo's state of the union address in 1999, SEDESOL figures revealed that the number of Mexicans living in poverty had grown to 26 million people, nearly double the 14 million at the start of his administration.

Labastida's campaign employed two major slogans that aimed precisely at addressing these issues. The campaign started with the slogan, "For a New PRI, Closer to You" (*Para un nuevo PRI, más cerca de tí*), bringing attention to the tremendous change already achieved in the ruling party. So fervently did Labastida seek to promote an image of change and renovation that he was not shy about drawing attention to past mistakes. During the first televised debate of the general campaign, he said, "Vicente, you make so many promises, you remind me of the old PRI."[36] He added, "I have the character to make big changes so we can leave behind this period of belt-tightening. . . . I represent the real change."[37] Later, Labastida drew on a slogan that recognized the need to channel the resources of the government to address longstanding social problems: "Let Power Serve the People" (*Que el poder sirva a la gente*). Both slogans were marketing the idea of political change. Both slogans capitalized on Labastida's well-earned image as the party's first democratically elected candidate. Both slogans promised something that a majority of voters apparently desired, given the growing support for democratic reforms and a greater variety of political alternatives in recent years.

Yet, the problem with both of these slogans was that they promised change from the candidate of a party that had remained in power for seventy-one years, just two years shy of the average life span of a typical Mexican. While the Labastida team understood the importance of selling the ideas that the PRI had changed or could change in a positive way and that the party was becoming closer to the people, this message unwittingly communicated the idea that there was something *very wrong with the PRI* in the first place and that it was distanced from the voters. In addition, the noble idea that "power should serve the people" implicitly acknowledged decades of impunity and neglect by the PRI and its government officials, including Labastida himself. Borrowing from the rhetoric of change famously employed in the 1992 U.S. presidential election by James Carville—one of Labastida's own campaign consultants—Fox observed, "Mr. Labastida is talking to us about change, and he's been inside the PRI for 37 years. . . . He was secretary of interior, secretary of agriculture, he was a state governor, and we didn't see change. It was all just more of the same."[38]

Hence, as much as the PRI primary distinguished Labastida from previous candidates of the ruling party, he was still a man of the system. Indeed, Labastida's first major post was as secretary of Energy, Mining and State-Owned Industries in 1982, an unenviable post to accept after oil prices had plummeted and the debts Mexico accumulated in anticipation of oil revenues became subject to dramatically increased international interest rates. In addition to negotiations over oil prices, Labastida oversaw the sale of hundreds of government-owned businesses, including banks, hotels, and restaurants, to reduce overhead and obtain much needed government revenues. In 1986, Labastida left his cabinet position to accept the PRI's nomination for the governorship of Sinaloa.

The 1986 election for governor pitted him against the wealthy and charismatic Sinaloan businessman, Manuel J. Clouthier—the man who single-handedly inspired Fox and hundreds of others like him to join the PAN in the mid-1980s. After his defeat in the contentious gubernatorial elections, Clouthier went on organizing in Sinaloa, working to mobilize voters against fraud in the state's midterm elections in 1989. During his October preparations for that election, Clouthier was killed in a mysterious car accident. Clouthier's death was made all the more suspicious by an attempt by another car to run his daughter Tatiana off the very same highway while she was similarly involved in antifraud mobilization in the 1991 gubernatorial elections. For Fox and others who suspected that Labastida had something to do with Clouthier's death, the 2000 race was no doubt seen as an opportunity to settle a long-standing vendetta against a former governor whom they deemed corrupt and benefiting from power gained illegitimately.

In his own description of his term as governor, Labastida stressed his integrity. Labastida made much of the difficulties he faced against the powerful narco-crime syndicates of Sinaloa.[39] Two close associates in his administration, a bodyguard and the head of Sinaloa's state police, were killed in conflicts with alleged drug traffickers and their supposed federal collaborators. Ultimately, Labastida claimed, it was these deaths and threats on his own life that led him to accept a position as Mexico's ambassador to Portugal. Still, Labastida's claim that he had been a crusader for justice was an issue of considerable speculation during the 2000 campaign. Described by Fox as the "cradle of narcopolitics," Sinaloa, along with Durango and Chihuahua, the other nodes of the "critical triangle" of Mexican drug production since the 1950s, was one of the states most heavily infested with narcotics production and trafficking, particularly the growing of marijuana and opium poppy.[40] Labastida's critics asserted that, contrary to his claims, he was deeply involved with Sinaloa's narcotraffickers and that he prematurely left the governorship for Portugal precisely because his illicit dealings produced enemies in one or another of the contending narco-organizations. Supporting these allegations, in a 1998 assessment of Labastida's appointment to Zedillo's cabinet, a CIA report leaked to the *Washington Post* revealed that "Labastida has denied receiving payoffs but has acknowledged privately that he had to reach unspecified agreements with traffickers and turn a blind eye to some of their activities."[41] Hence, any evidence that Governor Labastida had fought courageously against one group of narcotraffickers may have simply covered up his activities assisting another.

In the end, whether real or exaggerated, the inconsistencies between Labastida's image and his message were ripe for exploitation by Fox and his campaign staff. Although the allegations may have been totally false, Labastida's candidacy in the general election, as in the primary, was dogged by questions about his integrity as a candidate and as the representative of a new kind of PRI, one that would use power to serve the people.[42] In the general election, Labastida's efforts to persuade voters with his policy vision were undermined by the electorate's fixation on other issues, namely issues of change. Hence, Labastida lost the 2000 presidential election because he failed to inspire his own supporters and because he was unable to sell the image of himself—a twenty-seven-year veteran of the political hierarchy—as the champion of a "new PRI." Despite the best efforts of capable political strategists, Labastida ultimately represented "more of the same" and only drew attention to the ruling party's weaknesses, past mistakes, and perpetual efforts to mask continuity as change.

Fox: ¡México, Ya!

Even more so than his opponents, what Fox represented as a candidate was defined primarily by the messages and images developed during his campaign, rather than by his party affiliation. As a candidate from the private sector, Fox capitalized on his image as a self-made man, capable of managing the operations of one of the most recognizable companies in the world. Still, this image ignored important details. While Fox did indeed demonstrate merit and business acumen during his career, he and his family also benefited from long-standing privileges, thanks to large land holdings obtained before the 1910 Revolution. The land had been accumulated by Fox's grandfather, who fled to Spain with his family during the worst years of the Mexican Revolution. These land holdings were preserved in the family name by breaking them into smaller plots that would not be subject to land-reform initiatives. Hence, the idea of Fox as a representative of everyman was greatly exaggerated. Yet, Fox was highly successful in developing and capitalizing on this image to reinforce the central messages of his campaign.

First, Fox's physical appearance and personal characteristics played heavily into his image as a candidate. Tall and mustachioed, Fox's "look" played on traditional Mexican images of masculinity. This represented an important transformation of Fox as a person and politician; by his own account, his appearance had not always been an asset. In his youth, Fox's lanky frame made him feel physically and socially awkward, and for many years he had covered his face with a beard that softened and grayed his appearance. During his second race for the governorship in Guanajuato, Fox began to undergo a makeover, particularly when he reluctantly shaved his beard under pressure from members of his campaign committee. Fox could capitalize on his status as a sex symbol more so than other candidates, if only because of the fact that he remained "available." Like Labastida, Fox's marriage had crumbled while he held the governorship of his state; unlike Labastida, who remarried María Teresa Uriarte soon after, Fox remained a bachelor. Thus, despite persistent rumors that he maintained a clandestine relationship with his director of Communications and campaign press secretary, Marta Sahagún, Fox's macho image may have been enhanced because of his single status. For macho men of all ages (or those who imagined they were), the image of Fox as a "free man" may well have inspired both admiration and secret envy.[43]

In addition, Fox's physical appearance and personal image as a candidate was also greatly affected by his political fashion sense. During his career with Coca-Cola, the company culture of commitment to brand loyalty was such that Fox never wore the company colors of the enemy: blue was for Pepsi; red was for Coke. As a member of the PAN and as governor of Guanjuato, Fox seemed to obey a similar oath of loyalty to his party colors, donning a seemingly endless supply of denim duds and chambray shirts at practically every public appearance. Fox's penchant for blue apparel, however, was about the extent of his party-based appeals and, in some ways, illustrated the limits of his connections to the PAN. Despite the traditional importance of the Mexican family in the Catholic Church, Fox was divorced. Despite his privileged background and connection to business, Fox dressed and talked in a familiar manner with which the ordinary people in Mexico could more closely identify.

Most important, Fox was all about F-O-X, the three letters boldly emblazoned on his belt buckle. Fox made tremendous efforts to market himself like a product: maximizing recognition of his face, his name, and his slogans, rather than familiarizing voters with the details of his policy agenda and party doctrine. Moreover, Fox's commitment to a casual look—rarely appearing in public in a jacket and tie, even at formal functions where such attire predominated—brought criticisms that Fox was not sufficiently stately to assume the office of the presidency. Nevertheless, the casual look also played well into Fox's image as a common man; indeed, it was literally his blue-collar image that strengthened Fox's appeal to classes not traditionally affiliated with his party. This candidate-centered appeal was, therefore, at least symbolically part of Fox's effort to build a broad coalition for change.

Significantly, as Fox developed as a public speaker, the deep inflections of his voice and blunt, unrefined public declarations further cultivated his image as a masculine figure. His early political communication skills, by Fox's own admission, were quite limited. As a candidate for the national legislature in the 1988 election, Fox stammered and stuttered through his first public speeches to tiny, disinterested audiences in Guanajuato.[44] Still, Fox developed his skills with time, perhaps drawing on his adolescent experiences as his classmates' verbal antagonist. Devising clever nicknames for his fellow students was a favorite pastime and remained a consistent aspect of Fox's personality throughout the campaign, as he liberally applied amusing monikers to members of his campaign staff and reporters alike. However, Fox reserved his sharpest quips for his opponents, as when he questioned Labastida's manliness by pronouncing his opponent's name as "La Vestida" ("The Cross Dresser"). Moreover, by drawing heavily on a vernacular common in the Mexican countryside from which Fox hailed, he was able to promote his image as a man of the people, who was averse to the pretentious airs and flowery language of traditional politicians.

Also clever at cultivating name brand recognition, Fox worked to make his name an important part of the images and messages of the campaign. The letter of his first name became a symbol of everything that the campaign was about: V for Vicente, V for Victory. The image of Fox standing with his index and middle fingers in the air became a dominant marketing tool in the campaign. Additionally, this emblem was cleverly associated with the campaign's emphasis on change by combining the V symbol of Fox's hand as the Y in the Spanish word "*Ya*," meaning "Now" or "Enough." This symbol was recreated in the form of giant foam hands—popular among fans at sporting events—with outstretched index and middle fingers. These foam hands were waved ubiquitously at Fox's public rallies, and on one occasion, Fox creatively added yet another image to the campaign by pulling back the foam index finger to expose only the middle finger in his version of Madrazo's slogan: "Screw the System!"[45]

In short, consistent in message and image, Fox represented all that Labastida aspired to but failed to become: Fox represented change. Fox's personal image was an important part of this message. Fox seemed different from other politicians in both his manner and appearance. He appeared to be untainted by connections to the system with which so many Mexicans had become disenchanted. Arguably, there were important inconsistencies in Fox's image and personal reality. Despite his loutish antics and low-country vocabulary, his professional experience in the boardrooms of one of the world's most important multinational companies belied a certain level of skill and refinement. Perhaps most important, his family's privileged status—dating to before the Revolution—raised questions for some about how much of a change Fox himself represented. Still, on the whole, Fox presented the image of change convincingly. He used personal style, clever symbolism, and strategic posturing in ways that effectively presented him as an alternative to the status quo and did so in ways that convinced voters he was the best possible option to defeat the ruling party's candidate.

Reinventing Cárdenas: Evolution of a Venerable Leftist

Given his particular life circumstances and multiple experiences as a presidential contender, Cárdenas's image was more layered and complex than those of his competitors. To some, he was still undoubtedly the modern incarnation of "Tata" Lázaro, Mexico's answer to FDR. To others, he was the man who stood up against the system to fight Salinas and the neoliberal agenda, only to be robbed of his rightful victory in the 1988 elections. And to some young people, who encountered him at the polls for the first time in the 1997 Mexico City elections, Cárdenas emerged as a soulful, socially conscious guru in contrast with the unappealing candidates of the PRI and the PAN. However, despite the diverse images he evoked, Cárdenas's persona and messages in the 2000 contest ultimately seem to have failed to overcome past limitations or to address the issues most relevant to voters in this election.

The origins of Cárdenas's image can be traced directly to his lineage as the son of Lázaro Cárdenas, one of Mexico's most popular presidents. In her comprehensive treatment of the development of Cuauhtémoc Cárdenas's presidential candidacy in the 1988 elections and the eventual emergence of the PRD, Kate Bruhn (1997) describes "the transference of a powerful emotional loyalty from Lázaro to Cuauhtémoc Cárdenas." According to Bruhn, many Mexicans revered Lázaro Cárdenas with a "quasi religious devotion," in remembrance of the social policies he initiated to help the landless, the laborers, and the poor in the 1930s. While he benefited from this personal connection to Mexico's great leap forward, Cuauhtémoc Cárdenas's image was tainted by extremely negative coverage in the Mexican media, especially during the years immediately following his break with the PRI in 1988. Thereafter, Cárdenas was frequently portrayed as a volatile agitator, with photographs and news clips capturing images of unflattering and angry poses: these made him appear to be a power-hungry buffoon or a raging radical. However, if this was a vendetta by the Salinas administration against its 1988 rival, Cárdenas's supporters paid the heaviest price. That is, while media portrayals of Cárdenas made him into a monster, over 300 members of the PRD were killed or "disappeared" from 1989 to 1994. To explain the plight of the PRD, Bruhn (1997) invoked the image of David, the biblical hero who defeated Goliath, the champion of the Philistines: "Unlike David, Cárdenas did not fell his opponent with the first blow. One can only imagine what an enraged and bruised Goliath might have done to David if David had missed."[46]

Yet, Cárdenas and his party survived the stormy, repressive years of the Salinas administration. In his 1997 campaign for the mayorship of Mexico City, Cárdenas successfully emerged from the onslaught of the Salinas-era smear campaign as a kinder, gentler candidate. Then, Cárdenas traded dour frowns for modest smiles, appealing to voters as the respectable choice in a field of unappealing candidates. At the same time, freed from outright oppression, the PRD began to prosper in 1997, strengthening its organization and fortifying the party's mass bases by mobilizing grassroots community organizations called the Sun Brigades (Brigadas del Sol), in reference to the party's logo of a rising sun.

However, the renewed popularity of Cárdenas that came with the 1997 election was fleeting, as his stewardship of the Mexico City government quickly came under fire and the PRD began to suffer from its own growing pains. First, winning the Mexico City government was like a booby prize. While the PRI had all of the support and resources of the federal government at its command when it controlled Mexico City, the incoming PRD government did not. In 1997, Mexico City was still recovering from economic and social problems stemming from the post–Salinas peso devaluation and economic crisis. High levels of crime, as well as the public's perceptions of lack of personal security due to the crime concentrated in Mexico City, were among the most pressing challenges faced by the new administration. Cárdenas was able to do little to overcome these problems and was troubled by conflicts with and within the legislative assembly. Meanwhile, Cárdenas himself became increasingly involved in internal conflicts emerging within the PRD at the national level and later ended his term prematurely to start his campaign for the presidency. Upon his departure from office, Cárdenas's successor, Rosario Robles, began to achieve progress in managing these problems. Later she was discredited in bribery scandals related to the PRD's administration of Mexico City.

Nonetheless, Cárdenas appeared to start the 2000 campaign with significant advantages. Long forgotten were the angry images conjured by a hostile media, and there seemed to be few negative effects resulting from his lackluster performance as governor of Mexico City. Cárdenas hoped to project the same kind of upbeat image in this campaign that had been so successful in 1997. During the campaign debates, Cárdenas declared, "I am a happy man, without bitterness or rancor. I am engaged in this struggle and, just as I am a man of principles and conviction, you will always see me like that."[47] In short, Cárdenas wanted to be seen differently, as a new man who was well positioned to win the day in the 2000 elections. Unfortunately for Cárdenas, the actual development of his image and messages seemed to make him appear envious of Fox and unusually favorable toward the ruling party, perceptions that ultimately undermined his candidacy.

Despite the formal slogans and political appeals of Cárdenas's campaign, his rhetoric and behavior during the race appeared more personally and ideologically opposed to Fox than to Labastida. On the surface, it seemed to many of his detractors that Cárdenas's refusal to bow out and cede the advantage to Fox was out of personal envy and mulishness. Yet, Cárdenas consistently framed his opposition to Fox in ideological terms, keeping true in rhetoric and form to his father's legacy and vision of the state as the protector of the nation. Moreover, Cárdenas deliberately adopted a very different approach to the campaign compared with Fox. The champion of Mexican nationalism, Cárdenas seemed to be the candidate least comfortable with the advent of "Americanized" campaigning: at the outset, he declared that his campaign would not be "frivolous like in the United States, but rather it [would] go into deeper issues."[48] The fact that this strategy was ineffective, in so far as Cárdenas's presidential aspirations were concerned, has much to do with the problem of the candidates interactions, electoral strategy, and the dynamics of party competition in Mexico's new politics.

Strategies of Engagement: What Kind of Interaction?

The extent to which the marketing of ideas and individual qualities to voters was critical in this election is striking. In past presidential elections in Mexico, voters essentially did not matter; therefore, candidates seldom used campaigns as vehicles of communication and persuasion. Not so in 2000. Indeed, the campaigns became an essential part of the election and—as the candidates jockeyed for positions that would maintain the favor of the electorate—a means of reflecting and channeling the demands of voters into the political arena. Because voters mattered and would ultimately determine the outcome like never before, the campaigns comprised the beginnings of accountability at the national level in Mexican politics.

Similarly, the ways that the three main candidates engaged each other in the competition for the presidency also served as critical determinants of the outcome of the 2000 race. It is difficult to ignore how tellingly Fox's candidacy and the nature of his relationship with the PAN shaped the campaign and facilitated his victory. The interactions between and among each of the three major candidates in this election illustrates the complicated dynamics of three-party competition in Mexico and the particular issues and images that can successfully be marketed to Mexican voters. On the whole, the tactics used in the campaign, particularly the proliferation and intensity of negative campaigning in various media, had a notably Americanized flavor.

The Making and Unmaking of the Opposition Alliance

In the summer of 1999, many analysts were optimistic about the prospect of an opposition alliance to topple the ruling party. There were signs of apparent disposition on the part of the PAN and the PRD. The two parties' major candidates, Fox and Cárdenas, seemed eager to lead a large front against the PRI, and both appeared confident that they would emerge as the best choice to do so. And on the surface, this option seemed a no-brainer: combined totals of the PAN and the PRD in most elections easily amounted to a simple majority—greater than 50 percent of the vote. By July 1999, it appeared that where there was a will, there was almost certainly a way. Still, the very idea of a left-right alliance was difficult to imagine just a few years earlier.

The birth of the PRD in 1989 had radically reshaped the Mexican party system. While the PAN had found itself in bitter opposition to the regime during the state and local elections of 1985, the aftermath of the 1988 presidential election had created new opportunities for cooperation between the PAN and the ruling PRI. Meanwhile, because the PRD suffered tremendously as a result of this bargain and because of the extreme conservatism of some *panistas*, there was no love between Mexico's left and right for most of the 1990s. Then, in 1997, the PRD outperformed the PAN not only in the first open election for the Mexico City government, but also knocked the PAN from its historic position as the second largest force in the lower chamber of the legislature. Thus, as strong as Fox's campaign apparatus had become by 1999, the PRD had already recouped much of the ground lost in the years preceding the new left's impressive debut in 1988.

An alliance between the PRD and the PAN was, thus, considered a way to avoid splitting the electorate between two viable opposition parties and a strategy that would ensure an end to the PRI regime. The state and local elections of early July 1999 were seen as an important proving ground for a PAN–PRI electoral alliance at the national level. In that election, two states, Nayarit and Mexico state, seemed to represent the possible scenarios almost perfectly. In the former, a single candidate, a PRI defector, emerged as the candidate of a coalition of opposition parties that included both the PAN and the PRD. In the latter, the PAN appeared to have the upper hand over the PRD in a tough race against the PRI. The final results of the July 4 election favored the coalition candidate in Nayarit, but the PRI triumphed over a divided opposition in Mexico state. This seemed to deliver a clear message: though divided they lost, together the PAN and the PRD could trump the PRI even in a tough race.

More than a question of ideology, the choice came down to a question of how badly the opposition parties—and voters—wanted to remove the PRI. Indeed, at least until 2000, Mexican voters' views merely spread across a simple left-right political spectrum. Mexican politics appears to manifest a left-right dimension: liberals and conservatives are divided primarily over their view of the role of the state and over the application of progressive or traditional values in society. However, in Mexico, the existence of a single hegemonic political party for seven decades imposed an additional dimension to political issues and decisions: voters were either for the system or they were against it. Indeed, in a study of political attitudes in Mexico in the 1990s, scholars Jorge I. Domínguez and James A. McCann suggested that the pro and antisystem cleavage was the supreme cleavage that determined voter behavior in Mexican elections.[49] In other words, when deciding whether and how to vote in elections, Mexicans first thought about their perceptions of the system. If they were in favor of the system, they voted for the status quo by supporting the PRI. If they were opposed to the system, they were likely to vote strategically—even voting against their preferred party or candidate—by supporting the strongest opponent to the ruling party.

This background places Cárdenas's decision to take an ideological stance and become a vocal critic of Fox in context. Cárdenas was so personally or ideologically opposed to Fox's candidacy that he was willing to risk a continuation of the status quo, while Fox was faced with the challenge of ensuring that the election was framed around "system" issues. As Alejandro Moreno observes:

> What mattered was the credibility and visibility of an opposition message centered on the PRI regime and the need for change. Voters may have been effectively coordinated around that single idea. As in the 1992 "it's the economy, stupid!" motto [summarizing] the American election's underlying meaning, many Mexicans who supported Fox seemed to be driven by a similar reasoning: "it's the PRI, stupid!"[50]

Meanwhile, Cárdenas was more focused on attacking Fox than on attacking the PRI: "I don't think he represents the real and deep change that Mexico needs," Cárdenas insisted.[51] But in Cárdenas's insistence that he himself represented the "real and deep" alternative that Mexico presumably needed came a certain dilemma. He was not even close to gaining majority support in any major poll registered during the campaign. So his attacks on Fox suggested an apparent willingness to subject Mexico to six more years of PRI rule to prevent any change through a Fox victory. Thus, rather than focusing on Labastida—the representative of the ruling party and (according to most polls) the front-runner in the race—Cárdenas targeted his campaign messages and attacks toward Fox. For example, the PRD candidate took great pains to characterize Fox as the threat to one of the most prominent legacies of Cárdenas's father, the nationalized oil corporation, Petroleum of Mexico (Petróleos Mexicanos, PEMEX). Indeed, very early in his campaign, Fox had ventured as close as any politician in recent memory to saying that he would denationalize PEMEX: "We must agree that Mexican oil, without a doubt, belongs to the Mexican people. But this does not mean that it belongs to the federal government."[52] Given such statements, Cárdenas appeared to be more concerned about his own ideological objectives or his pride than about the prospect of a democratic transition, given that it would be artificial and shallow in his own view.

In the end, both Cárdenas and Fox were able to see themselves as the candidates of a broader alliance in 2000, though not together. On the one hand, Cárdenas's preemptive maneuvering inside his own party established him as both the PT and PRD candidate. On the other hand, when the prospect of a PAN–PRD coalition fell through, Fox and the PAN successfully negotiated an electoral coalition with the Mexican Green Party, a relatively new force in Mexican politics. Despite its rather weak credentials as an environmental party—the PVEM's founder and president was apparently unaware that polar bears and penguins reside on opposite poles of the planet—the PVEM provided Fox with a coalition partner and enabled him to bill his candidacy as a part of an "alliance for change" (Alianza Para el Cambio).[53]

Negative Campaigning

One of the prevailing characteristics of modern campaigns in the United States and elsewhere is the use of negative campaigning. To be sure, personal attacks, mudslinging, and other forms of negative campaigning are not in and of themselves a new element in politics. What is new in politics is the prevalence and effectiveness of campaign messages—particularly negative campaign messages—in a technologically sophisticated environment where information travels with instant, almost universal coverage. In the past, negative information published in print media or declared in campaign speeches traveled relatively slowly and to a smaller number of people. If the opponent's charges were false, the victim of an attack had plenty of time to respond and correct people's perceptions; if true, their impact was small and perhaps likely to be forgotten because the message was not consistently reinforced.

In the modern, televised world, a thirty-second negative advertisement can impact voters instantly and repeatedly for days or even weeks before its victim can respond effectively. In campaigns, as in daily life, first impressions can be powerful and lasting, making it all the more difficult for a victim to rebut false allegations or to address factual information properly. Negative campaigning was an especially important feature of the 2000 Mexican presidential elections, as so many of the messages and lasting images of the campaigns came from the negative attacks employed by the candidates.[54] No candidate took the high road. No candidate emerged unscathed. Both Cárdenas and Labastida attempted to undermine Fox's candidacy with accusations that he would privatize PEMEX. Though somewhat cautious not to alienate Cárdenas or his supporters, Fox worked consistently to create an impression of Labastida as inferior and dishonest, calling him a "little man, petty bureaucrat, liar and fraud" (*hombrecillo, pequeño burócrata, mentiroso y embustero*).[55] Accusations flew in virtually all directions that the candidates, their families, or members of their party had benefited from the controversial Fobaproa bank bailout scandal. Likewise, third-party attacks on the candidates were also prevalent in the 2000 Mexican elections. PRD legislator Félix Salgado Macedonio proclaimed publicly that Fox should join Cárdenas's Alliance for Mexico: "because he is not going to win; he is the son of foreigners, the son of Malinche, of betrayal, and of shame."[56] That Salgado evoked the name of Malinche—Hernán Cortés's indigenous translator and lover who is perceived as a betrayer of the native people—was a supreme insult and unlikely to convince Fox to support Cárdenas.

Throughout the campaign, Fox's attacks against Labastida were perhaps the most noteworthy because not only were they extremely personal in nature in the style of U.S. campaigns, but also highly effective. Consistently emphasizing both Labastida's personal shortcomings and the corruption of the system, Fox chided Labastida for acting like a "sissy" and described the PRI as a party of "bloodsuckers, leeches and black adders."[57] Fox's negative attacks were particularly effective because they had a particularly Mexican flavor. Notably, the use of *machismo*—the traditional concept of manliness in Mexico and other Latin societies—played a key role in such attacks. Indeed, as hard as Fox worked to cultivate an image of himself as a capable, charismatic "real man," he appeared to have worked even harder to portray Labastida as weak, effeminate, and even homosexual. In the contest of gendered superiority, making oneself look like more of a man often involves ridicule and derision to make others appear less so. Indeed, the character assassination did not necessarily have to be true or even make sense—Fox once derided Labastida by calling him "a faggot tied to his wife's apron strings"—to be effective.[58]

The most devastating attack, however, came from Labastida's own undoing. In the first of the two nationally televised debates, Labastida complained of Fox's unrelenting attacks and use of obscene gestures in references to him: "He has called me shorty, gay, 'The Transvestite,' whipped. . . . It doesn't offend me. He offends Mexican families with these words."[59] Labastida's attempt to gain voter sympathy by decrying Fox's negative attacks was ineffective in at least three ways. First, by raising the issue, Labastida repeated and drew greater attention to the negative attacks, some of which might not have been noticed previously by many voters. Second, Labastida's tone and evident frustration—even the unfortunately high-pitched, nasal, and "unmanly" quality of his voice—communicated an image of weakness that was potentially detrimental in a contest where "masculinity" was a prevalent issue. Third, and worst of all, it gave Fox an opportunity to deliver an immediate and devastating reply: "My dear Mr. Labastida, perhaps I can stop using obscenities, but you [and yours] can never stop being scheming, bad, and corrupt rulers. You can never be rid of that."[60]

In the end, negative attacks such as these had strong effects in both directions, affecting voters' perceptions of both the attacker and the person attacked; but such attacks ultimately hurt Labastida more than they did Fox. Fox's negative attacks against Labastida had counterproductive effects, because both Fox's and Labastida's poll ratings tended to decline in the weeks when his campaign went the most negative. Nevertheless, the effectiveness of Fox's negative attacks appeared to have given him the election. Indeed, in the first major panel study of Mexican voting behavior, researchers found that turnout in the 2000 elections was significantly reduced as a result of citizens' disengagement and disillusionment resulting from negativity during the campaign. That is, negative campaigns have a powerful effect on elections not because they attract more voters to a candidate but because they discourage voters from showing up at the polls. If done well, negative attacks succeed primarily in demobilizing the supporters of one's opponents. While all three candidates went negative, it was Fox who used negativity earliest, who launched the most negative attacks, and who did so most effectively.

Debating the Debates

One of the most important dynamics of interaction among the three candidates during the campaign came in March 2000, as they prepared for the second and final televised debate. Because of Fox's success in the first debate, each candidate had important reasons for preferring not to engage in a second debate. Fox, who benefited greatly from the first debate, merely stood the risk of appearing less successful in the second debate. Similarly, if he was truly ahead in the race, as internal polls consistently led his team to believe, then appearing in a debate would have simply given Labastida and Cárdenas a chance to jeopardize his standing. Meanwhile, Cárdenas and especially Labastida—who came off as the loser in the first debate—had obvious reasons to be cautious about returning Fox to the limelight and exposing themselves to further humiliation. As a result, during the weeks before the second scheduled debate, the three candidates and their campaign teams waged intense negotiations over the conditions and format for the debate. The debate over the debates culminated on Tuesday, May 23, during a live, televised meeting of the three candidates. In the aftermath of that confrontation, which would be referred to as Black Tuesday, many predicted that Fox had totally extinguished any hope of winning the presidency.

The day began with continued confusion over the prospects of a debate, which, after much negotiation, had finally been scheduled for Friday, May 26. Yet on Tuesday morning, Fox gave Mexico's two main television stations conflicting accounts: informing Televisa that he remained uncertain as to whether he would participate in Friday's debate and telling TV Azteca that he would focus on other campaign activities instead. Despite these declarations, Fox arrived at Cárdenas's campaign headquarters that afternoon with the explosive announcement that both Televisa and TV Azteca were prepared to televise the debates that very evening at 9:00 P.M. However, he was immediately contradicted by Joaquín Vargas, the head of the National Chamber of Radio and Television Industries (Cámara Nacional de la Indústria de Radio y Televisión, CIRT), who claimed that CIRT would require at least 48 hours' notice to prepare for the debate. They were soon joined by Labastida, who voiced his agreement with Cárdenas, that both were prepared to move forward with the debate on Friday. But Fox insisted that the debate be held "today," claiming that he had evidence from both television stations that they were indeed ready to move ahead immediately. His opponents were not convinced:

> "We would like to see that declaration in writing," said Cárdenas.
> "Fine, we will confirm it in writing," replied Fox. "I have a letter which says that they are available for today on channels nine and seven."
> "We want to see the letter," responded Cárdenas.
> "We'll arrange it right away," said Fox.
> "Well, why don't you arrange it, and then we'll talk," said Cárdenas.[61]

Both Vargas and Labastida sat in silent disapproval during the exchange. Cárdenas, taking a serious tone and pose, was visibly irritated. Fox's campaign staff hurriedly phoned TV Azteca to request a written letter of confirmation from the company president. Meanwhile, Fox eyed Cárdenas:

> "Agreed or not?" Fox asked.
> "Well, where is the letter, in your campaign headquarters?" Cárdenas asked impatiently.
> "It will just take a second, I'll get it taken care of it right away," replied Fox. "Are we agreed?"

At this point, Labastida declared his insistence that—letter or no letter—he would not debate that day. The situation being created was extremely uncomfortable. Neither of Fox's opponents wanted to appear unwilling to debate, yet they had fallen into an ambush and were unprepared to accept Fox's unexpected proposal. Fox had demonstrated his confidence and capability in the previous debate, when both candidates were prepared and questions were structured. With good reason, neither candidate was enthusiastic about the prospect of facing Fox unprepared and on his own terms. The atmosphere under the white canvas tarp in Cárdenas's headquarters, with lights and cameras pointed at the three recalcitrant candidates, was extraordinarily tense. Soon, after consultations with his campaign team, Fox made a new declaration. The letter would arrive by fax at 6:30 P.M. They waited.

At 6:30 a fax arrived stating that the letter was being completed and would arrive soon. Fox's resolve appeared to weaken, as he declared, "If there is no agreement to complete the debate today, we will do it Thursday and be done with it."

> "I'm disposed to do it today, if it is technically possible," Cárdenas replied quickly.
> "I remind you both that the CIRT asks for 48 hours," Labastida asserted.

Finally, the letter arrived by fax. Yet when Fox took it, he announced that the transmission was incomplete, and had left off the second half of the letter. "It seems that the fax doesn't work here. It shut off and isn't working," he said. Still, he held the partial fax and—apparently reading out loud—proclaimed that there was a willingness to have the debate from 9:00 P.M. to 10:30 P.M. that evening. Unsatisfied, Cárdenas stood his ground: "We do not have the necessary conditions, we will do it Friday."

"The debate is today," Fox insisted. "Today, today, today!" The PAN candidate now began to complain that Cárdenas and Labastida had formed a secret alliance and were conspiring against him. He lamented that doing the debate today "would have been so simple but they didn't want to." However, Fox appeared to be shedding crocodile tears when contradictory accounts suggested that he had lied. That evening, one of the television stations clarified its position by announcing: "Televisa had never offered time for a debate to any presidential candidate or political party, not to Cuauhtémoc Cárdenas, to Vicente Fox, or to Francisco Labastida." After rebuking attempts by any candidate to involve the media in the debate, Televisa broadcaster Joaquín López Dóriga held up a piece of paper: "this is the letter that was sent, and it does not have . . . a second part."[62]

In the end, in the debate over the debates, Fox appeared to many as obnoxious, irresponsible, and deceitful. However, his obstinacy ultimately paid off in a number of ways. First, though unable to secure a U.S.-style media question-and-answer format, the PAN candidate was able to negotiate a more flexible format with substantial give-and-take among the candidates during the Friday, May 26, debate. After his opening remarks—an apology and recognition that even his mother always thought he was too stubborn—Fox insisted that his behavior reflected the "firmness and character" that were needed to confront the PRI. He also took the opportunity to confront his critics on various policy issues, insisting that he would promote a secular government and would protect PEMEX from privatization. He made direct appeals to Cárdenas, asking him not to divide the vote by running a failed third-party campaign. Reaching out to Cárdenas and other opponents, he announced his intention of forming "a government of transition, a government of harmony and national understanding, plural, and all-inclusive." By Monday, polls suggested that the debate had helped Fox, with approximately 42 percent of respondents backing the PAN candidate and 45 percent supporting Labastida.

Second, thanks to both the "Black Tuesday" incident and the actual content and format for the debate, Labastida and Cárdenas seemed like allies working together to combat Fox. Finally, Fox was able to turn his outrageous behavior into a campaign theme that was completely consistent with his central message of change. That is, after "Black Tuesday," Fox was able to use the slogans "Now!" and "Today!" interchangeably to reinforce the same idea. In televised advertisements, the iterated chant of "México, Now!" became the simple drumbeat of "Today, today, today. . . ." In short, Fox's gambit appeared successful and created a whole new set of marketing opportunities.

Why Fox Won the 2000 Election

The 2000 presidential campaign was the most heavily and professionally polled election in Mexican history, but most analysts consistently failed to predict Fox's victory over Labastida. Pollsters came up with a number of explanations for their miscalculations. Some lamented the failure to accurately interpret the intentions of undecided voters, though it is not even clear that such predictions could be reliable. Others raised the possibility that voters simply changed their minds during the final two weeks before the election to vote strategically for the opposition, but this is difficult to confirm because polls were prohibited by federal electoral regulations during that period.[63] *Reforma* pollster Alejandro Moreno provided perhaps the best and simplest explanation. His findings suggested that polls leading to the 2000 elections failed to predict who would turn out to vote. On the one hand, pollsters depended too heavily on measures of whether respondents had voted in the past; younger, first-time voters who tended to support Fox were, therefore, undercounted. On the other hand, pollsters failed to give sufficient weight to respondents' self-professed probability of voting and level of interest in the campaign.[64]

Thus, understanding why Fox won requires some analysis of two questions: what kinds of voters were drawn to the different candidates, and which ones were more likely to turn out to vote? Probably for different reasons, Fox seems to have most effectively drawn the support of younger and urban voters, while Labastida had a distinct advantage among older voters, the uneducated, and housewives (who may also have been more likely to fall into both categories due to larger numbers of educated Mexican women in the workforce today). In theory, the PRI should have won, given that its traditional share of the electorate was larger and turned out more consistently than voters who supported Fox's PAN/PVEM coalition in the 2000 election.

Fox benefited from higher turnout among his supporters for a number of reasons made evident by this discussion. First, Fox benefited from the support of voters with higher levels of political education, interest, and participation, while the PRI was more dependent on its traditional bases (see Tables 5.3 and 5.4). These traditional PRI supporters may have turned out less strongly in this election than in the past, in part because of the ruling-party machine's declining access to resources. It is worthwhile to reiterate that the number of states controlled by PRI machines dropped from twenty-nine in 1994 to twenty-four by 2000, and nearly all of Mexico's top twenty major cities (including the capital) had fallen to the opposition. While certain key states still had strong patronage-based machines, particularly in the South, this was much less the case nationwide than in the past. Hence, patronage-seeking PRI supporters, traditionally drawn to the ballot box by the promise of PRI largesse, were likely to have had fewer incentives to come to the polls.

Table 5.3 2000 Mexican Presidential Election Results

	Number of Votes	Percent of Total
Vicente Fox Quesada (PAN–PVEM)	15,988,740	42.52%
Francisco Labastida Ochoa (PRI)	13,576,385	36.10%
Cuauhtémoc Cárdenas Solórzano (PRD–PT)	6,259,048	16.64%
Gilberto Rincón Gallardo (DS)	592,075	1.57%
Manuel Camacho Solís (PCD)	208,261	0.55%
Porfirio Muñoz Ledo (PARM)	157,119	0.42%
Total[a]	36,781,628	97.80%

Source: Instituto Federal Electoral, www.ife.org.mx (accessed November 5, 2002).
Note: a. Does not include all votes cast (e.g., improperly cast ballots, write-in candidates, etc.).

Alternatively, this may have been yet another important indication of the weakness of the PRI machine and, ironically, the growing integrity of Mexico's electoral processes. That is, rates of political participation were unconvincingly high under the PRI, as they may have reflected both the use of fraud and the contrived mobilization of the electorate through patronage politics. Electoral reforms and efforts of civic activists to protect the vote over the course of the 1990s were instrumental in ensuring that official vote tallies reflected actual levels of support, rather than inflated numbers contrived for the benefit of the ruling party. Certainly, electoral fraud was still possible in certain PRI strongholds even during the 2000 elections, but it was far less prevalent in this election than in any other. Hence, the decline in PRI support

Table 5.4 Exit Poll from the 2000 Presidential Election

	Labastida	Fox	Cárdenas
Total Vote	35.8	42.7	16.5
Men	35.8	42.7	16.5
Women	40.0	43.0	14.0
Ages 18–24	32.0	50.0	17.0
Ages 60+	42.0	35.0	22.0
No Schooling	46.0	30.0	21.0
College Degree	22.0	60.0	15.0
Public-Sector Workers	37.0	41.0	19.0
Private Sector	31.0	53.0	15.0
Students	19.0	59.0	17.0
Housewives	43.0	41.0	15.0
Voted "for a change"	15.0	66.0	18.0
Voted "for the candidate"	50.0	28.0	18.0
Voted "for loyalty to the party"	9.0	8.0	12.0

Source: Global Exchange, www.globalexchange.org/countries/mexico/dem/campaign.html.pf (accessed June 11, 2001).

and the overall decline in official levels of voter turnout in the 2000 election may have also reflected the growing transparency and legitimacy of elections in Mexico.

Still, both of these explanations tell only part of the story of why Fox managed to mobilize more support at the polls and reduce support for the PRI, because they leave out the importance of events and tactics used during the campaign. Fox definitely succeeded in framing the election as a battle for change and presented himself as the best option to ensure that change. With snappy campaign rhetoric, popularized by some of the best advertising and strategizing that money could buy, Fox portrayed the 2000 election as a choice between the PRI regime and democratic change. Yet Fox's campaign was also designed to reduce the number of people making that decision who would support the regime. Using a campaign with few ideological or programmatic stances, Fox focused instead on villainizing the regime and its candidate. This strategy helped gain support from swing voters and served to demobilize disheartened PRI voters, who found it difficult to turn out for a candidate, a party, and a system that had been so disparaged by the Fox campaign.[65]

Furthermore, because Fox so deliberately and successfully divorced his candidacy from his party, he may have received additional support from an unusual source: strategic voters on the left. That is, support from pragmatic voters on the left may have contributed to the divergence between predicted outcomes and actual results. Even with Cárdenas in the race, many left-leaning voters probably saw the election as Fox deliberately tried to frame it: a choice between change and the PRI. If so, such leftists cast their votes for Fox as a strategic option—not the sincere expression of their desired preference—in order to prevent yet another PRI victory. Evidence to support this theory can be found in the example of voters in Mexico City, where a majority of voters supported Fox for president but elected the candidate of another party (PRD candidate Manuel López Obrador) to govern the capital. As a result, Fox's impressive 44 percent of the vote did not translate into similarly strong support for PAN legislative candidates; though they received a significant boost from Fox's coattails, PAN federal deputy candidates still trailed Fox by six points with 38 percent of the vote.

A final and related point is that Fox's victory was a surprise because support for Fox greatly exceeded any previously achieved by a PAN candidate. In this sense, Fox's victory was very much his own, rather than a victory for his party. That is, while Fox drew on a long tradition of PAN participation in presidential elections, his campaign clearly focused on the candidate and his campaign message rather than on the party and its programmatic goals. From the very beginning, Fox's campaign was a renegade operation that divorced itself from the PAN, invested heavily in media-savvy campaign strategies, and sought mass support from all ideological directions. Throughout the campaign, Fox drew considerable criticism for his tactics and his lack of consistent positions. Yet, Fox was clearly the most successful of the three major candidates—not only in the sense that he won the election, but also in the way that he conducted his campaign and employed new strategies for winning. Fox's impressive margin of victory over both the PRI and the PAN (in the legislature) illustrated the extent to which his triumph was more a victory for the candidate than his party.

Mexico's New Campaign Politics

In the end, there were many factors in the making of the 2000 elections. Over the course of the three preceding decades, there had been a gradual erosion of the ruling party and changes in the nature of traditional institutions that had supported the PRI-dominant system. The formation and consolidation of the autonomous Federal Electoral Institute was the single most important institutional development affecting the conduct of national elections in the 1990s. The role of the media was of tremendous importance in ensuring a more level playing field than in the past. The Mexican citizenry was also significantly different from fifty years or even two decades earlier; it was a mobilized and engaged citizenry, capable of saying "no" to fraud, bribes, and trickery. The influences of international media, electoral observers, and large numbers of Mexicans who lived abroad were also significant in creating pressure for respecting democratic procedures.

Interestingly, two of the most outstanding elements of the selection process, the promotion of the candidates and their messages and the interactions among the three contenders, bore stark resemblances to modern, U.S.-style campaigns. These proved to be cause for alarm in some quarters, as there are certainly important drawbacks to Americanized democratic processes, especially when they are fueled by electronic media and newfound sources of campaign finance and organization. Successful PRD mayoral candidate Andrés Manuel López Obrador lamented during the 2000 elections, "Combine money, television and the large number of Mexican voters who are nearly illiterate, and you could elect a cow as president."[66] Indeed, while Americanized elections have yet to place a cow in office, many critics of U.S. politics both at home and abroad might agree with characterizations of some U.S. politicians as "bovine." In any case, Fox was completely upfront about the simplicity of his strategy: "We are going more and more the route of the United States. . . . Have charisma and look good on TV, and you can become president."[67]

Fox did not hesitate to draw attention to the way that Americanized tactics could be used to manipulate voters. A familiar technique employed in U.S. campaigns is to draw on anecdotes about the plight of individuals who exemplify a larger problem that the candidate hopes to resolve. To emphasize his commitment to resolving public safety problems and the inability of opposition governments to do so, Labastida used the first debate to tell the story of an elderly woman who complained to him about crime in a PAN-governed state. Fox was quick to use the opportunity ironically to decry the "Americanization" of the campaign: "Mr. Labastida comes with these pretty stories that his [U.S.] advisor James Carville gives him. This is very American, to speak of these little stories that never really happened. This is the only thing that Labastida is learning, to follow the signals of Mr. Carville."[68]

The irony, of course, is that more than any other candidate it was Fox himself who introduced and practiced these new tactics most successfully in the 2000 election. It is important to reiterate that Fox's Americanized approach to the 2000 election began long beforehand and was shaped in important ways by the challenges he faced inside and outside his party. Recognizing that PAN party leaders were intent on protecting their control of the organization from the influence of the party's new pragmatic wing, Fox and his supporters created their own organizational apparatus, campaigned heavily outside the party and across ideological lines, and focused on running a candidate-centered, media-savvy campaign that largely ignored the PAN's programmatic agenda. This approach not only enabled Fox to overwhelm all potential opposition within his party, but also armed him well for the battle against the PRI. Entering the general election, Fox's campaign had more financial resources, more effective messages, and broader appeal than any other previous PAN campaign for the presidency. Most important, these strategies ultimately helped win Fox the presidency. Whether they could help him achieve the changes he promised for Mexico during his presidency was another matter.

Notes

1. Quoted from Salinas, 2002, p. 272.
2. Green and Shea, 1999; Heard, 1962; Hrebenar, et al., 1999; Johnson-Cartee and Copeland, 1997; Joslyn, 1984; Keefe, 1998; Levine, 1992; Popkin, 1991; Sundquist, 1990; Wattenberg, 1990.
3. Swanson and Mancini (1996) argue that modernization consists of (but is not limited to) "steadily increasing social complexity" and, as a result, the transformation of politics to one of interest group liberalism that they believe is best captured by Dahl's model of the polyarchy. "In this arena, the mass media system undertakes socialization functions which previously were performed by the political parties," pp. 6–9.
4. Ibid., pp. 12–15.
5. In fact, the PRD proceedings did not constitute a fully "open" primary, because would-be voters were required to join the party in order to support a nominee. However, eligibility to participate in the nominations process was extremely flexible and open, even allowing individuals to sign up as party members immediately prior to casting their votes.

6. Castañeda, 2000; Garrido, 1989; Nava Polina, et al., 2000; Weldon, 1999.

7. Weldon, 1999.

8. Cornelius and Craig, 1991.

9. "Descarta Roberto Madrazo Pintado acudir a Los Pinos," *El Universal,* October 27, 1999: 6.

10. Medellín, "La elección interna será la primera y la última: MBD," *El Universal*, October 21, 1999, sec. Nación: 8.

11. Both Madrazo and Bartlett had pressured early on, with television spots and mass appeals, to bargain for terms that were favorable to them, rather than the extended U.S.-style regional primary and party convention advocated by Zedillo. According to Federico Estevez, a nationwide primary election on a single day would have provided the greatest possibility for local fraud by the organizations of regional bosses like Madrazo, Bartlett, and their allies; Zedillo ostensibly opposed this and saw the U.S. system—in which parties conduct a series of state-level primaries when candidates gradually accumulate delegates who ultimately cast their votes at the national convention—as a way to ensure stopgaps and protections against fraud and a victory by the wrong kind of candidate. Yet because the participation of Madrazo and Bartlett was necessary to ensure a real democratic challenge for the nomination, the PRI ultimately opted for a single vote, though it used three hundred winner-take-all districts rather than a nationwide vote that could be inflated by candidates in their regions of strength. Personal communication with researcher Federico Estevez of the Instituto Tecnológico Autónomo de México.

12. Smith, "Mexico's PRI Holds First Presidential Debate," *The Los Angeles Times*, September 9, 1999.

13. Zárate Vite, "'Hay algo' en relación con Roberto Madrazo, afirma Monreal Avila," *El Universal*, October 8, 1999, sec. Nación: 10.

14. According to one of Madrazo's key campaign strategists: "Our strategy was to make a lot of noise with the first ad and to position Roberto as a rebel with a cause in the PRI, and it has worked beautifully." SourceMex (August, 18, 1999).

15. Moore and Ward Anderson, "'Fantastic Four' Take to the Air; Mexican Ruling Party Sets Precedent with TV Debate in Presidential Race," *The Washington Post*, September 9, 1999.

16. Dillon, "Mexican Pollsters Challenge Size of Turnout in the Primary," *New York Times*, November 17, 1999.

17. In informal interviews, some PAN supporters later claimed to have voted in the primary in an attempt to boost support for Labastida, whom they saw as a lesser threat to Fox than Madrazo.

18. Dillon, "Mexican Pollsters Challenge Size of Turnout in the Primary," *New York Times*, November 17, 1999.

19. Dillon and Preston, "As Mexican Primary Vote Nears, Angry Recriminations," *New York Times*, November 7, 1999: 1:3.

20. Guarneros, "Llama Labastida a la unidad," *El Universal*, October 7, 1999, sec. Nación: 6.

21. Hayward, "Desestima Labastida calificativo de 'oficial,'" *El Universal/San Antonio Express News*, October 26, 1999, sec. Nación: 9.

22. Aguirre, "Madrazo y Labastida rompen reglas: MBD," *El Universal*, October 5, 1999, sec. Nación: 6.

23. Dillon and Preston, "As Mexican Primary Vote Nears, Angry Recriminations," *New York Times*, November 7, 1999: 1:3.

24. Lawson and Klesner, 2004.

25. "La crisis de los coroneles," *La Jornada*, March 3, 1999.

26. Ibid. The two other candidates, Rosalbina Garavito and Mario Saucedo, shared less than one-third of the vote.

27. Ibid. Each of these states yielded approximately 22,000 votes. Nearly 60 percent of all voters in the internal election were concentrated in the states of México, Michoacán, Mexico City, Tabasco, Veracruz, Jalisco, Oaxaca, Chiapas, Guerrero, and Puebla. Mexico City and the state of Mexico held the largest concentrations of voters, totaling approximately 160,000 or one-third of the electorate.

28. Ibid.

29. Such alliances had been successful in the 1998 state elections in Tlaxcala, in which a PRD–PT–PVEM coalition behind former *priísta* Alfonso Sánchez Anaya won with 46.5 percent of the vote over the PRI's 44.26 percent. This success was repeated in Baja California Sur the same year when the same three parties obtained 52 percent. Klesner, 1999.

30. Aguirre M., "El PT tiene candidato," *La Jornada*, May 30, 1999.

31. Ibid. Article 92 of the PRD's statutes called for sanctions against members of the party that "confirm a coalition with any governmental interest or with other parties independently of the party leadership."

32. Preston, "At Hopeful Moment, Feud Tears at Mexico's Left," *New York Times*, July 15, 1999.

33. Popkin, 1991.

34. Aguayo Quezada, 2000, p. 199.

35. Ibid., p. 71.

36. Smith, "PRI Candidate, Top Rival Clash in Presidential Debate," *The Los Angeles Times*, April 26, 2000.

37. Dillon, "TV Debate Energizes Challenger in Mexico," *New York Times*, April 27, 2000.

38. Ibid. Interestingly, during Bill Clinton's 1992 run against Republican incumbent President George Bush, the slogans, "Change versus more of the same. The economy, stupid. Don't forget health care" were posted in the Democrat's campaign headquarters.

39. Labastida Ochoa, 2000.

40. Celia Toro, 1995.

41. Waller, "The Narcostate Next Door," *Insight on the News*, December 27, 1999: 20.

42. Lawson and Klesner, 2004.

43. However, in as much as Fox's macho image may have attempted to draw the support of women, it is not clear that he succeeded in doing so: housewives were among the few exit poll categories in which Labastida ultimately bested Fox—43 percent to 41 percent—on election day. Smith, "Fox Rode the Gusting Winds of Change, Says Times/Reforma Survey," *The Los Angeles Times*, July 3, 2000.

44. Fox, 1999.

45. Moore, "Getting Down and Dirty in Mexico," *The Washington Post*, April 16, 2000.

46. Bruhn, 1997.

47. "Candidatos presidenciales debaten 26 May," *Reforma*, May 26, 2000.

48. Ramírez, "Nueva imagen de Cárdenas, sin la sonrisa ganadora del 97," *El Universal*, October 9, 1999, sec. Nación: 8.

49. Domínguez and McCann, 1996.

50. Moreno, 2000b.

51. Berman, "Mexico's Third Way," Analysis, *New York Times*, July 2, 2000.

52. Eisen, "Mexico Presidential Candidates Tread Lightly on Subject of Need to Reform Oil Industry," *Oil Daily*, August 25, 1999.

53. In May 2004, in discussing the controversial decision of PVEM Federal Deputy Jorge Kahwagi to use his vacation time to participate in a reality television show titled "Big Brother VIP," PVEM President Jorge Emilio González Martínez remarked that "if someone wants to go to Alaska to swim with the penguins, they can do it." Penguins are autochthonous to Antarctica, but there are no penguins in Alaska. More serious problems with the PVEM came to light in 2003, when allegations of corruption were leveled at several high level PVEM officials, including González Martinez (dubbed "el niño verde"). "Kahwagi saldrá el domingo de BB: Emilio González," El Universal online, May 18, 2004 (accessed May 18, 2004). For a detailed account of PVEM corruption, see Gaya, Catalina, "Enemigos de la ecología," in *Cambio,* March 6, 2004: 10–14.

54. Moreno, 2003.

55. Zárate, et al., "Sospecha FLO de viajes de Fox a EU," *El Universal*, May 6, 2000, sec. Primera: 1.

56. Author's translation: "Porque él no va a ganar; es hijo de extranjeros, es un hijo de la Malinche, de la traición y de la vergüenza." Gómez, "Rechazan que Cárdenas cambie su imagen 'seria,'" *El Universal*, April 13, 2000, sec. Nación: 10.

57. Moore, "Getting Down and Dirty in Mexico," *The Washington Post*, April 16, 2000.

58. Hernandez Navarro, "Mexico's Gringo-ized Vote," *Nation*, July 3, 2000: 6, 7.

59. Labastida complained, "Me ha llamado chaparrito, mariquita, La Vestida, mandilón," to which Fox replied, "A mí tal vez se me quite lo majadero, pero a ustedes lo mañoso y lo corrupto no se les va a quitar nunca." Moore, "Rivals Trade Barbs in Mexican Debate," *The Washington Post*, April 26, 2000.

60. Dillon, "Mexico's Candidates Hold First Presidential Debate," *New York Times*, April 26, 2000; Moore, "Rivals Trade Barbs in Mexican Debate," *The Washington Post*, April 26, 2000.

61. Cervantes, "Rehúye Fox acuerdo para debate," *El Universal*, May 24, 2000, sec. Primera: 1.

62. Ibid.

63. Beltrán, "¿Por qué fallaron las encuestas?" *Revista Nexos*, August 2000; Llamas, "El voto estratégico en la jornada electoral del 2 de julio," *Revista Mexicana de Comunicación,* 2001. Accessed on April 1, 2004. www.mexicanadecomunicacion.com.mx/Tables/RMC/rmc77/voto.html.

64. Moreno, "Encuestas y resultados: un electorado imprevisible," *Enfoque,* August 13, 2000.

65. Moreno, 2003, p. 249.

66. Dillon, "TV Debate Energizes Challenger in Mexico," *New York Times*, April 27, 2000.

67. Moore, "In Selling of Candidates, Mexico Tries U.S. Way," *The Washington Post*, November 5, 1999: A25.

68. Smith, "PRI Candidate, Top Rival Clash in Presidential Debate," *The Los Angeles Times*, April 26, 2000.

6

The PAN in Power and the Challenges of Democratic Governance

> *I am not interested in being President of the Republic, I am not interested in being candidate for President. Mine is another vocation. However, it is my absolute and total responsibility, on my life if necessary, to launch the final battle to remove the PRI from Los Pinos and achieve a true democratization for the country. Once this is achieved, I will go back home. Politics is not where I should be.*
>
> —Vicente Fox Quesada, 1997[1]

On December 1, 2000, Mexico inaugurated Vicente Fox Quesada as its first president from outside the PRI since 1929, in the first peaceful transfer between opposing forces in Mexico's history. Fox's campaign pledges promised to bring political reform, administrative efficiency, anticorruption measures, indigenous rights, prosperity, and—most important—"change" to Mexico. Enthusiastic about this promising and different future, the nation emerged exuberant and relieved from the 2000 presidential election and the end of PRI hegemony. Yet, change does not come easily. From the time that the PAN began to accumulate electoral victories at the state and local levels in the 1980s and 1990s, successful opposition candidates like Fox, indeed Fox himself, faced special challenges and an incredibly steep learning curve after decades of single-party rule. As Mexico's first opposition president, Fox had numerous challenges ahead in learning to manage Mexico's federal bureaucracies, intragovernmental relations, and international relations.

The first years of the Fox presidency held some important parallels to the experiences of PAN governments at the subnational level, particularly to Fox's own experience as governor of the state of Guanajuato. The patterns of political recruitment, the tense nature of executive-legislative relations, the weak political linkages with society, and the questionable effectiveness of Fox's policies and political reforms closely resembled those seen in his state government and in many ways were consistent with other PAN administrations at the subnational level. Moreover, for better or worse, these patterns also may have much to do with the essential doctrine of the PAN, as articulated by the philosophies of its founders and enhanced over the course of the party's development. Above all, the accomplishments through the better part of the Fox administration fell far short of promises he made during his campaign for the presidency—and even further from the expectations created by his dazzling rise to power.

Most important, the challenges Fox faced and his approaches to dealing with them were affected by the manner in which he came to power and the distant nature of his relationship with the PAN. As a candidate, Fox had depended more on a carefully crafted media image than on the support of PAN's party leaders, organizational infrastructure, and (limited) mass membership base. In government, the lack of a strong party organization, combined with PAN's weak position in the legislature, gave Fox little leverage to promote his policy and reform agendas. This, in turn, contributed to the Fox administration's tendency to rely on the president's public image and popularity, following the pattern he set both as governor of Guanajuato and candidate for president. In short, in many ways, the new era of democratic change that Fox himself helped bring to Mexico revealed itself to be more problematic and challenging than many had expected.

The Challenges of PAN "Opposition Governance"

Despite a tremendous difference in scale, the challenges President Fox faced from the outset of his administration were actually quite similar to those confronted by opposition governments that emerged at the state and local levels over the preceding two decades. The one major difference was that, unlike opposition governments at the subnational level, Fox confronted no political adversaries at higher levels of administration. This was an important advantage for Fox, because state and local opposition governments often experienced or at least complained about unfair treatment from higher levels of public administration, particularly in the distribution of resources. While opposing partisan relations between levels of government constituted the defining characteristic of "opposition governance" in Mexico, the term is used only very loosely here to point out the novelty of a national government derived from the opposition. As the opposition party best able to secure electoral victories at the state and local levels, the PAN's leadership had accumulated some significant experience by the time Fox took power. Indeed, over the 1990s, some striking similarities began to emerge in the PAN's elected officials' approaches to governance, which contributed to the party's continued success in key cases such as Ciudad Júarez, Guadalajara, León, Mérida, Mexicali, Monterrey, and Tijuana.

Scholarly analysis of such governments in the 1980s and 1990s provided some useful insights into the types of policies and reforms most important to the PAN.[2] Works on this subject first addressed PAN governments as the novelties that they were—given decades of near total fusion of party and government under the PRI—and focused on the initial challenges faced by opposition governments. Typically, the first steps of new PAN state and local governments reflected the concerns that brought them to power. That is, when PAN governments initially came to power in the 1980s and 1990s, it was often as a result of citizens' frustrations with specific cases of corruption in the outgoing PRI administration, as well as a general desire to promote change in the political system. Practicing "good government" was, therefore, a top priority for early PAN administrations at both the state and local levels. Rather than duplicating PRI practices, the PAN developed innovative approaches to public administration that emphasized an end to wasteful and illegitimate uses of government resources, merit-based political recruitment, civic participation in government decisions and projects, and effective management and enhancement of fiscal revenues. Above all, PAN governments emphasized transparency and efficiency in the day-to-day management of the government and worked carefully to document their achievements to this end.

It is important to note that the first PAN administrations to take power after decades of PRI control of the state or municipal government also had to deal with difficult problems of transition. PAN government functionaries complained of various forms of sabotage committed by outgoing PRI administrations to prevent a smooth transfer of power. The first day on the job for Tijuana's first PAN mayor, Carlos Montejo, was filled with symbolism. When Montejo arrived at his office, he found the seat of government literally broken: a defective swivel chair sat in the middle of an office with empty filing cabinets and a floor littered with papers.[3] As revealed repeatedly in interviews with first-time PAN mayors, this was not uncommon. Outgoing PRI functionaries often sacked or destroyed official records, office materials, and equipment, often withholding information on the day-to-day operation of city and state agencies. As a result, the incoming PAN administrations often had to start from scratch and devise their own methods to run the local government machinery. New PAN administrations used these situations to their advantage by developing innovative practices and raising standards for professional conduct among government employees.

Meanwhile, due to decades of political centralization, the PAN's state and local administrations were forced to deal with the limited financial capacity and restricted political authority of subnational government, particularly at the municipal level. On the one hand, PAN governments focused intensely on fiscal initiatives designed to improve revenue generation, including tax reform and more efficient administrative management of government finances. Taxpayer rolls were updated and, in many cases, new tax assessments were applied after many years of remaining at the same level. Inefficient and sometimes selectively lenient methods of tax collection under the PRI were cast aside, and, in cases where the PAN gained control of the state government (such as Baja California), tax rates were actually raised to compensate for the weak condition of state and municipal finances. Hence, the irony of the PAN's rise to power was that, despite the party's conservative orientation, it often tended to promote greater tax collection in an effort to support greater governmental capacity.

On the other hand, PAN state and local governments also struggled to assert their constitutionally mandated powers and increase federal revenue sharing at the state and local levels. For example, upon taking power in 1989, the administration of Governor Ernesto Ruffo Appel pressured the federal government for a more equitable distribution of federal revenue, an unprecedented act in a system where governors refrained from making waves to remain in favor with the all-powerful president. Through Ruffo's dogged efforts to bring attention to disparities in federal revenue sharing, government transfers to Baja California increased by more than 18 percent in real terms from 1989 to the end of his term in 1994 (from 447.9 million pesos to 529.61 million pesos).[4] Three years later, the advent of the first opposition-dominated Chamber of Deputies (1997–2000) brought new reforms that modified the distribution of transfers, according to a federally determined formula, circumscribing the level of discretion in revenue flows to the state and local level. These "new federalism" reforms improved the prospects for long-term planning in public administration, increased the transparency of state revenue sharing and fiscal contributions to municipalities, and reinforced the functions of municipalities, as enumerated in the original Article 115 reforms enacted by President de la Madrid in 1983.

On the whole, the PAN's early opposition governments faced an assortment of challenges related to their political orientation to the system. Four aspects of PAN governance at the subnational level are of particular relevance to evaluating the particular features of the Fox administration: (1) political recruitment, (2) executive-legislative relations, (3) state-society relations, and (4) policy formation and political reform. First, virtually all incoming governments from long-excluded opposition groups in Mexico faced significant challenges with regard to administrative start-up. A particularly important issue for any new opposition administration was that of *political recruitment*, which, in turn, shaped other aspects of PAN governance. Driven by a desire and mandate for change, incoming opposition parties typically seek to undue the administrative practices of the past by rooting out the rascals in the government bureaucracy and introducing new methods for political recruitment, often drawing on members of their own campaign teams and political parties. In Mexico, the historical fusion of the ruling party with the governing apparatus presented two challenges to PAN governance: There were few outside the PRI government who knew how to manage its apparatus; however, excessive linkages between the PRI and the government made it necessary for the PAN to rethink the nature of party-government and state-society relations to ensure a break with the past.

Political scientists who advocate responsible party government assert that elected officials should represent the interests and platforms of the party that placed them in office. Direct involvement of partisans in the making of public policy is seen as one way to ensure this. Yet, new governments of the opposition do not have sufficient human capital and/or prior experience to fill all the administrative positions at their command adequately. Moreover, strict allocation of government positions to members of a single party may have negative implications, because democratically elected officials are theoretically obligated to govern for the whole of society, not just their supporters. PAN mayors and governors often struggled with the problem of identifying qualified, trustworthy government personnel, as well as to what extent they should draw upon members of their own party, other political organizations, the private sector, and society at large.

A second and often related problem for PAN governors and, to a lesser extent, for mayors was how to manage *executive-legislative relations*, both with regard to their own party and to the legislature as a whole. Again, the PAN faced particularly soul-searching questions about party-government relations because it had railed for decades against the party-as-government model of the PRI, but had not established a clear alternative for how to manage the desires and expectations of the party in relation to its elected officials. The electoral formula used in Mexican municipalities, which had used at-large elections and selected city council members by proportional representation since reforms passed in 1983, generally ensured that most mayors had at least a plural majority of support in sessions of the city council (*cabildo*). This formula reduced the difficulties of divided government at the local level. However, at the state level, this was distinctly not the case. Indeed, most first-time PAN state governments arrived in power without a majority of their own deputies in the legislature. Hence, new PAN governors typically wrestled with the difficult challenge of divided government, a problem that PRI governors of the past never had to face.

At the national level, party-government relations under Fox were similarly complicated by the fact that no party—and no electoral coalition—held an absolute majority in either house of the Chamber of Deputies. This presented a situation significantly more complex than mere gridlock between the executive branch and the majority faction of the legislature, as it meant that shifting coalitions could be formed to advance different and changing agendas. In other words, this complex situation offered the slim possibility that Fox might forge coalitions between his own party members and those from one of the other major parties in the Congress, depending on the issue at hand.

In fact, in some cases—notably that of indigenous reform—Fox actually depended on the opposition to pass legislation that he supported when the PAN did not. Thus, one of the most interesting dynamics of the new Mexican politics is the multitude of scenarios and considerations in party-government relations.

Third, opposition governments in Mexico in the 1980s and 1990s often attempted to bring new kinds of interactions between the government and the governed, essentially redefining *state-society relations* in Mexico. The PRI was able to maintain power for seventy-one years, in part, through a very successful model of political incorporation—corporatism—that organized and coordinated key sectors of society. For new opposition governments, including Fox's, developing alternative modes for state-societal relations presented difficult challenges. Naturally, there were obvious reasons why the new government might wish to work to dismantle existing PRI networks, breaking away from the corporatist model. Nevertheless, the traditional organization of interests and the practice of corporatism presented strong incentives to continue following the model; also, few viable alternatives existed for promoting civic involvement in public affairs. Meanwhile, the nature of Fox's electoral campaign—with an emphasis on marketing the candidate as a product for public consumption—and his tenuous relations with the legislature, including his own party, naturally leaned toward a political style of "going public" to generate political support rather than promoting a deeper relationship with civil society. The latter would have involved intensive organization and mass incorporation.

Fourth, PAN state and local governments often started out with a *policy and reform agenda* that emphasized administrative reorganization and greater transparency in an attempt to eliminate unwanted practices, such as electoral fraud, corruption, and administrative inefficiency. In the later stages, particularly after the start-up challenges of opposition governance had been met, many PAN governments attempted to make improvements in public works and services and eventually devoted greater attention to community building and social development over the course of multiple administrations. In this sense, PAN state and local governments seem to have approached policy development in a sequential fashion. That is, they first focused on getting the reins of administrative control firmly in their grasp and later steered government toward improved public works and new social policies that reflected their programmatic political and ideological agendas.

Indeed, some PAN state and local governments even turned to problems related to social development, community building, and other moral or aesthetic concerns (such as city beautification and museums). To the extent that PAN governments were able to define their relationship with civil society, there were two broad trends. First, PAN administrations made important strides in building a new kind of state-society relationship, based on direct civic participation, new forms of community outreach, and public-private partnerships. To be fair, civic participation was, in fact, something that could be seen early on in PAN administrations, particularly as they confronted some of the "start-up" challenges of opposition governance. Notably, citizens frequently came out to support PAN administration during key conflicts with the PRI and its supporters. For example, in Ensenada, Baja California, and León, Guanajuato, the first PAN mayors of these two cities were faced with sanitation strikes caused by PRI supporters and instigated by malevolent PRI governors. In both cases, the mayors, other municipal government employees, and citizen volunteers rolled up their sleeves and removed piles of garbage from city streets for several weeks. Citizens also became more responsive to the municipal government in terms of meeting their basic tax obligations, thanks at least in part to a newfound faith in public administration.

PAN administrations also developed innovations such as the much-touted Citizen Wednesday (Miércoles Ciudadano) program, which was started in León by Luis Quiroz, the PAN's third mayor in Guanajuato's largest city.[5] This program encouraged citizens to make their particular needs and concerns known to the local government through weekly one-on-one sessions with the heads of municipal departments for public lighting, paving, drainage, water, public safety, and social welfare.[6] The program proved to be wildly successful and soon became the principal point of access between citizens and the government in León and was quickly adopted by other PAN governments throughout Mexico, thanks in part to the efforts of the PAN-affiliated Association of Mexican Municipalities (Asociación de Municipios Mexicanos, A.C.).[7] Mayors and representatives from other PAN municipalities began to visit León to evaluate the program and consider strategies for implementing it elsewhere.[8]

The Citizen Wednesday program also provided the Quiroz administration with a formidable tool to evaluate the needs of the city. By keeping track of the types of needs and complaints voiced by citizens, as well as general information about the individual citizens themselves, the local government could use geographic information systems (GIS) and databases to identify the types of problems specific to particular time periods and areas of the city, drawing on powerful visual tools, such as sophisticated maps and graphs, for analysis and multimedia presentations. For example, in León, the program was most frequently visited by residents of the center city because of their relative proximity to City Hall; those living in the outskirts of the city had more difficulty participating in the program. This meant that the application of the program slightly benefited middle-class residents, who tended to attend the program to address middle-class concerns (e.g., parking issues and payment of property taxes). At the same time, residents of poorer, more marginalized neighborhoods could still be easily identified by the types of concerns that they raised, which were primarily focused on basic necessities (e.g., housing and provision of water services).[9] In short, the innovations of PAN governments in public outreach and community participation at the subnational level provided innovative and successful models for practical implementation.

A second major aspect of the PAN's approach to social issues in the 1990s was a noticeable tendency toward moral conservatism in key cases. As much as the PAN was taken to task by critics for failing to take on issues of community building and not developing links to civil society, PAN governments were also fiercely criticized when they attempted to address social issues related to moral conduct: as in the distribution of alcohol permits, regulation of prostitution and adult entertainment, enforcement of legal prohibitions on abortion, and the censure of art in public places.[10] In this sense, the PAN was damned when it did and when it did not take a stand on social issues. In their own defense, many PAN governments pointed out that they were simply enforcing laws that PRI governments of the past deliberately overlooked. Still, in choosing to do so, PAN governments gradually began to demonstrate a political orientation distinctly different from their PRI predecessors.

Moralism was especially notable in Fox's home city of León, Guanajuato, and other parts of the Bajío, Mexico's Bible Belt.[11] León's PAN municipal government generated national attention for its efforts to prohibit "table dancing," a provocative form of commercial sex entertainment in which nude women dance on the tables and laps of customers.[12] Local PAN officials explained that, among other things, table dancing can be dangerous to the women because the men get too close to them. In their defense, PAN functionaries claimed, "there have to be limits . . . [in order to preserve] the good customs of our society. . . . [T]hese days young people can go astray due to a lack of moral principles."[13] One official noted that "decent customs" might include "going for a walk in the plaza or going to mass on Sunday, among other wholesome activities"; for such *panistas*, table dancing was as indecent a practice as "urinating in the public square."[14] Besides, they argued, nude dancing was still allowed; only interactive table dancing was prohibited: "[People think] we are prudes (*mochos*), but no."[15] Still, table dancing was not the only target of moral vigilance. PAN local governments in Aguascalientes, Monterrey, and León were accused of censorship when the City Museum attempted to censure art exhibits.[16] Also, the PAN's first municipal administration in Yucatán decided to clean up the annual carnival celebrations in the capital city of Mérida; topless Cuban dancers were now to be banned on the mainland. Likewise, the PAN began to monitor theaters and public events in that city to ensure morality and good customs.[17]

It is important to note that the moralistic overtures of PAN governments typically played well to local audiences. In contrast to the reactions of outrage seen at the national level, above all in Mexico City, the moral intervention of PAN local governments often did not generate as much controversy in local communities, especially in areas where the church had strong influence.

According to former PAN Party President Carlos Castillo Peraza, these stories did not negatively affect the PAN in these places because "the people governed by the PAN knew they were false."[18] However, when such instances captured the attention of the national media, they became a liability for the party's national image, even where exaggerated or portrayed incorrectly. The most famous case of exaggeration was in Guadalajara, where the PAN mayor was accused of prohibiting miniskirts and imposing a draconian curfew in 1997. The miniskirt controversy was the result of a confrontation between a municipal government official—not the mayor—who asked a subordinate to alter her manner of dress; the offending article of clothing was not a miniskirt but a blouse, and the request was not part of an administration- or city-wide policy enacted by the PAN government.[19] The supposed curfew was, in fact, an exaggeration of statements made by the mayor, in which he suggested that citizens might try to stay home after dark due to rising indices of crime that plagued the city and the country following the peso crisis. PAN leaders claimed that media attacks such as these were due to the resentment of reporters who no longer enjoyed bribes from PRI mayors and governors.[20]

Still, the PAN's moralistic image made it difficult for the party to make inroads outside of its traditional strongholds and ultimately colored perceptions of the Fox administration upon taking office. Indeed, many of Fox's detractors raised the specter of the PAN's religious conservatism and worried that his administration would take Mexico to the right. Fox's own behavior appeared to support their fears. Fox became the first president since the Revolution to visit the shrine of the Virgin of Guadalupe prior to his inauguration and made no secret of his religious practices. Also, the record of conservatives in Fox's home state—and of PAN governments throughout Mexico—seemed to confirm the party's religious and moral orientation. For example, following Fox's election to the presidency, PAN state legislators in Guanajuato attempted to pass a reform to the State Penal Code that would have punished abortion even in cases of rape.[21] This gave way to an intense debate that went beyond state borders and was only resolved when interim Governor Ramón Martín Huerta vetoed the initiative.[22] During his tenure as governor and in his first years as president, however, Fox tended to take more ideologically neutral positions and did not express strong opinions of extreme conservatism.

On the whole, PAN governments behaved consistently with the core philosophical tenets of the party that are the legacy of the practical Manuel Gómez Morin and the more spiritual Efraín González Luna. The practices of good government—efficiency and transparency—associated with PAN governments were astonishingly similar to those of late-nineteenth- and early-twentieth-century Progressive reformers in the United States.[23] Similarly, the PAN's story was one in which urban professional elites rose to challenge the hegemony of patronage-based machines by promoting institutional reforms and good government. Hence, in the 1980s and 1990s, PAN governments did not just do PRI-style government better; rather, they assumed new roles that the PRI could not or would not have assumed. In this sense, PAN governments lived up to the vision of the party projected by founder Manuel Gómez Morin. Meanwhile, the PAN's social orientation followed the vein of Efraín González Luna, both by "helping others to help themselves" and by asserting moral values into the public sphere. Thus, the PAN was similar to straitlaced reformers in the United States who railed against vice and substance abuse from the 1880s through the 1920s.

In the end, the historical tensions between the PAN's two sometimes divergent ideological currents tended to manifest themselves in the governments the party brought to power in the 1980s and 1990s. However, it was the party's more pragmatic current that predominated in the Fox administration's patterns of political recruitment, executive-legislative relations, state-society relations, and agendas for reform and policy implementation. For those doctrinaire elements of the party who feared that pragmatism would undermine the PAN's ideological integrity and program for governance, the Fox administration was a magnification of these trends at the national level.

Political Recruitment Under Fox

Political recruitment and elite politics has been a subject of interest to Mexico scholars for many years. Scholarly works on this topic have ranged from studies of the revolutionary origins of PRI regime elites to more recent analyses on political recruitment among opposition governments.[24] Early scholarship on elites in twentieth-century Mexico focused especially on how the 1910 Revolution reshaped Mexico's political hierarchy. Much of this work followed the vein of studies into power, elites, and comparative governance that were popular in the 1960s and 1970s.[25] Elite studies on Mexico were particularly focused on debates about the nature and extent of the 1910 Revolution. More specifically, scholars wanted to know: was the Revolution a social revolution, a bourgeois revolution, or not a revolution at all? Studies of elite incorporation into the new regime, therefore, focused on the degree to which the middle class was represented by Mexico's national political elite. From early studies, such as Peter H. Smith's *Labyrinths of Power: Political Recruitment in Twentieth-Century Mexico* (1979), to more recent studies drawing on more sophisticated and comprehensive data sets, notably Roderic A. Camp's *Mexico's Mandarins: Crafting a Power Elite for the Twenty-First Century* (2002), the general finding was that Mexico's political elites were the inheritors of a "bourgeois movement that sought to modernize, not overthrow, the country's capitalist system."[26] Significantly, that process of economic "modernization" through Revolution brought with it a sharp and increasing divide between Mexico's economic elites and those who governed.

These observations provide an important point of reference for evaluating Mexico's recent political alternation. Throughout much of the post-Revolutionary history of the PRI regime, businesspeople traditionally abstained from entering the public sector, and politicians generally refrained from entering the private sector.[27] In many cases, businesspeople saw politics as a dishonest profession and preferred to let others dirty their hands. That is not to say that business interests were neglected by political elites or vice versa. On the contrary, there were enormous benefits to be reaped by close association between money and power. Mexico's wealthiest and most prominent business elites were intimately allied with PRI governments and often exerted an indirect but important influence on politics. Still, at least in terms of recruitment and career development, business and politics were very separate worlds. Thus, for the most part, politics was largely left to experienced politicians (*políticos*) and bureaucrats.

Historically, political experience meant involvement in the internal hierarchy of the PRI organization, typically through a faction (*camarilla*), consisting of personal connections to superiors and subordinates.[28] *Políticos* had considerable experience in overseeing electoral competition, mass mobilization, and other strategies for maintaining regime support. In what some referred to as a system of party-government symbiosis, PRI *políticos* provided the organic linkages that bound the regime to a dissonant array of middle-class elites, big-business interests, workers, and peasants.[29] Most *políticos* were schooled in the nation's public universities (particularly, the UNAM), in the trenches of PRI electoral campaigns, and as public appointees of their successful patrons in the clientelistic chains of PRI incorporation. Moreover, they were best able to progress through these networks when they were linked by familial and geographic ties to Mexico's power structure.

Technocrats (*técnicos* or *tecnócratas*) rose to prominence in Mexico during the economic crises of the 1970s and 1980s. Reminiscent of Porfirian *científicos*, modern-day Mexican technocrats typically drew on their postgraduate training overseas to advocate policies, economic formulas, and concepts they had observed in practice in modern industrial nations.[30] As Camp (1995) points out, most Mexican leaders born prior to 1950 who studied abroad did so in Europe. However, the new generation of technocrats increasingly studied in the most revered universities of the United States; for example, those educated at the Instituto Tecnológico Autónomo de México (ITAM) frequently found their way to Yale University (thanks to the guidance of ITAM's economic guru and Yale graduate, Leopoldo Solís).[31] In the 1980s and 1990s, given the need for experts capable of dealing with a series of economic crises, such technocrats became increasingly predominant in their influence over public policy and even supplanted *políticos* as candidates for public office.

Like his immediate predecessor, President Ernesto Zedillo Ponce de León was drawn from the technocratic model. Zedillo and half of his appointed cabinet went to the United States for their graduate studies, with Zedillo obtaining a Ph.D. at Yale. Another third of Zedillo's cabinet did graduate work in England. In all, four-fifths of Zedillo's cabinet had some postgraduate training abroad. Despite these rich experiences, Zedillo and his crew were largely inexperienced and unrepresentative of the PRI's traditional *políticos*. Zedillo, like three-fourths of his cabinet, had never run for public office before becoming the PRI's presidential candidate. Indeed, Zedillo had been an "accidental candidate," with no political experience and poor links to the PRI.[32]

Once president, he made early indications that he would seek to break the traditional linkages between the PRI and the presidency by maintaining a healthy distance (*sana distancia*) between the two. This appears to have been easier said than done, because through much of his six-year term (*sexenio*) and even in the open primary for his successor, Zedillo was frequently criticized for reverting to the traditional model of *presidencialismo* (extreme presidentialism) by devoting much of his attention to internal party affairs. However, in the final analysis, Zedillo's relationship with the PRI—and ultimately the process of democratization in Mexico—seems to have been more complex. Lacking any firm ties to his party, Zedillo appeared to be relatively tolerant toward the political opposition, allowing continued gains at the state and local levels and even allowing the PRI to lose its majority in the lower house of Congress. Yet, at the same time, as the opposition picked away at the weakest elements of the regime, Zedillo's strongest pillars of support seemed increasingly to come from among the ruling party's most hard-line elements.

Zedillo's initial appointees seemed to draw heavily from the technocratic side, despite the incorporation of the late Luis Donaldo Colosio's supporters (including Liévano Sáenz and Santiago Oñate Laborde) and the few appointees Zedillo drew from the PRI's traditional core (such as Ignacio Pichardo Pagaza and Silvia Hernández Enríquez).[33] Zedillo also marginally increased the representation of women (from two under Salinas to three). More significant, though, was the appointment of two members of the political opposition to key positions, namely, Julia Carabias of the Unified Socialist Party of Mexico (Partido Socialista Unificado de México, PSUM) as environmental secretary and Antonio Lozano of the PAN as attorney general. Still, despite this token bid at pluralism to signal political openness and win outside support, Zedillo's government was solidly *priísta*. In fact, in retrospect (after the humiliation of Lozano in the course of delicate investigations of political assassinations and corruption), pluralism appears to have been, in part, a clever strategy to scapegoat and humiliate the opposition. Still, there was some continuity in elite trends within the Zedillo administration. First, the predominance of appointees educated at public universities was consistent with general trends among PRI governments. Like 82 percent of his cabinet appointees, Zedillo had received his undergraduate education at one of Mexico's public universities, the National Polytechnical Institute (Instituto Polytécnico Nacional, IPN).[34] A second traditional characteristic of his administration was the political and geographic "centralism" of his appointees. While Zedillo's roots were found in the northern state of Baja California, nearly seven out of ten members of his cabinet originated from Mexico City.[35]

New Patterns of Political Recruitment in the Opposition

As noted in previous chapters, the same economic crises to which PRI technocrats responded in the 1980s gave rise to other patterns of elite mobilization and integration in Mexico over the same decade. As growth declined, debt multiplied, and inflation soared in the early 1980s, Mexico's once aloof impresarios and entrepreneurs like Fox grew more political, joining and becoming active in the ranks of the PAN. Most important, they began to run for public office and win, bringing with them new perspectives and practices to public administration in Mexico.[36] Since such governments were typically characterized by an emphasis on principles of good government—openness in the administration of public resources, rational allocation of public resources, and maximizing the common good rather than particularistic benefits—PAN governments generally attempted to recruit individuals with high levels of credibility, practical managerial experience, and a vision of the PAN's constituency as coterminous with society itself.

Naturally, the extent to which PAN governments have been successful in delivering on these objectives is a subject for debate. One concrete reality is that PAN governments often lacked sufficiently qualified personnel to fill key positions with members of their own party and were inclined or left with no choice but to incorporate members of the PRI and elements from the private sector in key positions. Another is that—successful or not in achieving their goals—the number of such PAN governments at the local and state level multiplied rapidly over the course of the 1980s and 1990s. Thus, hundreds of municipal governments and a handful of state governments provided on-the-job training for an new generation of public officials and contributed to new trends in elite recruitment and public administration.

In the state of Guanajuato, for example, Governor Vicente Fox (1995–1999) started his term with what he called a super- or mega-team (*equipazo*), an elite group allegedly selected through a rigorous evaluation process. Fox noted that PAN members were not happy with this approach: "From the beginning [they came] looking for jobs and with the idea that once the PAN arrived in power, the *panistas* would all enter to form part of the government. I differ totally on this . . . here [in Guanajuato] we chose a professional team, where we looked for the best people without attention to what party they came from."[37] Fox felt that the party needed to release its candidates, like parents: "[Y]ou should hug them, feed them, give them principles, and let them go on to govern."[38]

Even so, the selection process and the credentials of Fox's team were not necessarily as novel or as super as advertised. While Fox claimed to have carefully studied more than 450 résumés and recommendations from society, many of the members of Fox's team were drawn from his close circle of friends or the previous administration.[39] Over time, the composition of the state government's cabinet gradually became somewhat polemical, as appointees were eventually linked to extreme conservative views. This was especially the case for Fox's State Secretary of Education, Fernando Rivera Barroso, who was brought into the national spotlight with the debut of a controversial pamphlet, *How Guanajuato Teaches* (*Así educa Guanajuato*), that, among other things, pondered "the art of punishment."[40] Interestingly, Fox's presidential administration would take a similar approach to recruitment and would experience similar criticisms at the national level. Long-term and recent trends in political recruitment raise several important questions about what kinds of changes will be brought by political alternation. First, how did the composition of Fox's administration in 2000 illustrate a shift in the relationship between party and government from that found under the PRI? Second, to what extent did Fox, himself a prominent, successful member of Mexico's business community, incorporate business elites into his administration, thereby breaking a post-Revolutionary divide? And to what extent did Fox's new administration differ in its reliance on technocrats to fill key positions on economic policy? Third, given the different regional bases of the opposition in Mexico, did the new Fox administration bring a greater regional diversity to the executive branch? Fourth, with respect to educational background, how did patterns of recruitment change from the previous PRI governments? While significant changes followed in the first years of Fox's administration, analyzing his initial appointments offers useful comparisons to the preceding administration and instructive insights into the patterns of political recruitment under Mexico's first opposition president.[41]

El Gabinetazo: Recruitment Patterns Under President Fox

Upon his inauguration, Fox named fifty-two appointees to his cabinet and high-level government offices which, as in Guanajuato, he colorfully described as his mega-team or El Gabinetazo. Immediately following the July 2 election, Fox had announced that he would embark on an expedition to seek out the most qualified individuals to join his government, regardless of party affiliation and without favoritism (*amiguismos*). The main qualifications for this super-team were to be a world-class managerial style and a love of Mexico. To find the highest quality functionaries, Fox hired professional headhunting organizations like Korn/Ferry International, Spencer Stuart y Asociados, Smith Search, and Amrop Internacional.[42] Whether it lived up to Fox's characterizations, the results of this much vaunted expedition yielded a very different kind of cabinet from those of the past.

First, one of the most notable features of Fox's new government was the lack of representation of his own party in high-level government positions. The number of card-carrying members of the PAN appointed to the Fox administration was quite low, particularly in comparative perspective. During the previous seven decades of PRI rule, party and government were indistinguishable for all practical purposes; generally, all federal officials in PRI governments were either members of the ruling party or simply assumed to be so. Fox's decision to staff 75 percent of his top appointees with officials having no formal party affiliation—as well as 8 percent from parties other than the PAN—represented a massive shift in the composition of Mexican government. Only about one-fifth (19 percent) of Fox's original fifty-two top appointees were drawn from the National Action Party (see Figure 6.1). Roughly the same proportion of appointees were incorporated as members of his cabinet, with four appointees (18 percent) formally affiliated with the PAN.

The main point is that a significantly limited proportion of Fox's appointments—approximately one in four—were given to card-carrying members of the PAN, and only four had presence at the cabinet level. It is worthwhile to note that PAN appointees were entrusted with positions that were key to promoting longtime PAN objectives such as transparency (Comptroller Secretary Francisco Barrio), efficiency (head of the President's Office of Governmental Innovation Ramon Muñoz), and democratic governance (Interior Secretary Santiago Creel).[43]

First, Francisco Barrio, from Chihuahua, was appointed as secretary of Control and Administrative Development, charged primarily with combating corruption. Like Fox, Francisco Barrio Terrazas entered the PAN during the

Figure 6.1 Party Representation Among Top Fifty-Two Fox Appointees

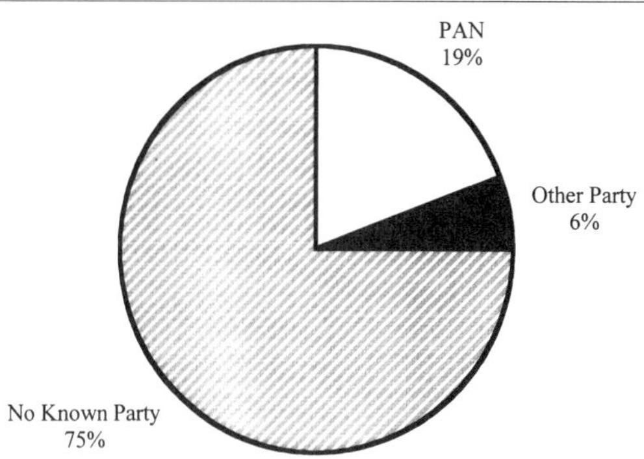

Source: www.presidencia.gob.mx (accessed August 15, 2001).

1980s, lost a gubernatorial election clouded by controversy and accusations of fraud, and went on to run for the governorship a second time and win. Second, Ramón Muñoz served as a close political adviser to Fox in Guanajuato and during the campaign. Very familiar with U.S. initiatives to improve efficiency in government, notably the reinventing government model of the Clinton-Gore administration, Muñoz also brought plenty of practical local experience from his earlier position as an official in the PAN municipal government in León. Most important, Muñoz was a dyed-in-the-wool *panista*, who—like Fox and many other PAN leaders from the Bajío—was educated in Jesuit institutions and had once considered the priesthood. In this sense, Muñoz was in many ways a walking fusion of the PAN's pragmatic and religious sides.

Third, for one of the most significant positions in his new government, the secretary of the Interior, Fox appointed *panista* Santiago Creel. Creel worked as an attorney at a prestigious Mexican law firm and as a journalist and publisher (founding the magazine *Este País*). Creel's family had a history of involvement in the PAN, though he remained politically unaffiliated through the mid-1990s, even serving as a nonpartisan citizen adviser to the Federal Electoral Institute's General Council (1994–1996). Later, he ran and won as a PAN candidate for the federal legislature in 1997 but was not formally installed as a member until 1999. Thereafter, Creel distinguished himself by boosting the PAN's performance as its candidate in the Federal District in the 2000 elections, with considerable help from rising support for Fox in the last weeks of the presidential campaign. Creel's presence in the Fox government was initially seen as a boost to the PAN, particularly with the incorporation of notable party members like José Luis Durán Reveles and Juan Molinar Horcasitas in undersecretary positions.[44] However, the incorporation of other subsecretaries who had no linkages to the party, such as María Amparo Casar, an academic who had been skeptical of candidate Fox, provided counterbalance inside the Interior Ministry.[45]

Meanwhile, despite Fox's self-proclaimed interest in reaching out to other parties to generate a broad-based and inclusive government of transition, his ability to build a government coalition was limited. It is interesting to note that Fox appears to have made no effort to incorporate members of the Mexican Green Party (Partido Verde Ecologista de México, PVEM), the only other party to join his Alliance for Change coalition. This revealed that the Fox's electoral alliance was little more than that: two parties supporting the same candidate but without prior agreements reflecting the programmatic interests of the coalition partners. As a result, PVEM members were not appointed to top-level positions that might have been obviously appropriate for their party, like the Secretariat of Environment or even the Energy Secretariat; eventually, the PVEM withdrew its support from the coalition and began to side with the PRI. Meanwhile, though a significant number of PRI (and former PRI) appointments were ultimately made by Fox, the PRI's leaders opted to focus on internal damage control and refused to integrate high-profile members of their party—like Elba Esther Gordillo, leader of the PRI's popular sector—into the Fox administration. Likewise, the leftist PRD refused to allow its members to accept any formal positions in the new government, despite Fox's efforts to persuade Cárdenas of the need for a united front.[46]

If not his party, coalition partner, or the other major parties, then from what sources did Fox draw his appointments? Here again, the recruitment process in the Fox administration followed the pattern set in his Guanajuato state government. After casting favoritism aside and supposedly reviewing hundreds of résumés in the head-hunting process, Fox's *gabinetazo* drew heavily from his own inner circle in Guanajuato and his personal ties to the business sector. Indeed, fifteen (28 percent) of Fox's top fifty-two appointees had worked in some significant capacity in the Fox campaign, and five appointees—one-third of those with prior experience in PAN governments—were drawn directly from his gubernatorial administration in Guanajuato. Fox justified these appointments on the grounds of their experience, but other factors seemed to come into play. For example, Fox appointed Jaime Cristóbal Jaquez as National Water commissioner on the basis of his "broad experience as the director of companies linked to the utilization, use, processing and care of water."[47] However, Jaquez's broad experience in this area was accumulated during his twelve years working for Coca-Cola's Mexican Soft-Drink and Mineral Water Division. While water may be a critical ingredient in the production of sodas, it was not plainly obvious that soft-drink manufacturers had any particular aptitude for administering a nation's water supply. In short, such appointments suggest that the objectivity of the head-hunting process for the Fox administration was at least somewhat exaggerated.

Indeed, the case of Jaquez illustrates an important trend in the Fox administration; from the outset, the extent of private-sector involvement in government positions was far greater than under any president since the birth of the PRI. Given his background as a hardworking executive for Coca-Cola—where he worked his way from a local sales route to the top of its Latin American operations—this tendency was hardly surprising. Indeed, much of Fox's administration shared similar private-sector experience but had comparatively little experience in government (see Figure 6.2).

While over half of Fox's top appointees had some previous experience in the public sector, nearly as many (46 percent) had private-sector experience. However, despite the difference in private- versus public-sector experience, there was significant continuity from the Zedillo to the Fox administration with regard to the concentration and orientation of economists in the administration. While 36 percent of Zedillo's cabinet had degrees in economics or business administration, the same percentage of Fox's appointees to cabinet positions had similar degrees, including two degrees in accounting. Moreover, Fox's selection of Zedillo's former teacher and intellectual mentor, Francisco Gil Díaz

Figure 6.2 Prior Experience of Top Fifty-Two Fox Administration Appointees

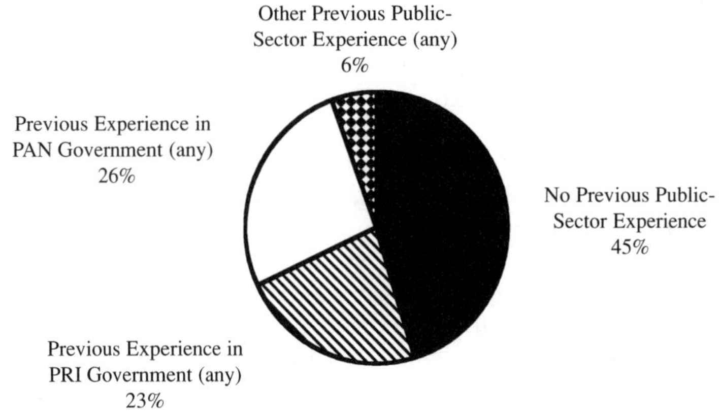

Source: www.presidencia.gob.mx.

as secretary of the Treasury and Public Credit, suggested the continuation of neoliberal policies emphasizing deregulation and open-market competition from recent PRI administrations.[48] Hence, despite or perhaps consistent with a shift toward greater private-sector involvement in the Fox government, there was very little change in the apparent direction of Fox's economic policy.

In contrast, one of the more notable aspects of the Fox administration was the regional origin of his top appointees. Only 40 percent of the original fifty-two top appointees of the Fox team came from Mexico City, while over half originated (by birth) from other regions and the United States (see Table 6.1).[49] Interestingly, the regions represented outside of Mexico City were

Table 6.1 Region of Origin of Fifty-Two Top Fox Administration Appointees

Region of Origin	Number	Percentage
Mexico City	21	40
North	12	23
Center/Bajío	12	23
South	1	2
Foreign Born (U.S.)	3	6
Other/Unknown	3	6

Source: www.presidencia.gob.mx.

more consistent with where electoral support for the PAN was strongest in the 1990s, the north and center.[50] In this sense, Fox's political recruitment mapped onto the two internal currents found historically within the PAN; that is, its traditional appeal to northern business interests and its appeal to religious sectors in central regions like the Bajío Bible Belt.

Meanwhile, the appointment of three foreign-born officials (including former Baja California Governor Ernesto Ruffo) was another interesting aspect of the Fox team, particularly in light of the possible role of Mexican migrants in the United States in the 2000 and future elections. This constituency was considered of strategic interest during the Fox campaign in 2000 because, though not eligible to cast absentee ballots, many Mexican migrants encouraged their families back home to participate in the 2000 elections. Likewise, given the prospect of possible absentee voting in 2006, it is not surprising that Fox created a special office to promote the interests of Mexicans abroad, initially headed by Juan Hernández, a Fox campaign team member and Chicano son of immigrants to the United States.

Finally, another major difference between Fox's appointments and those in past PRI administrations could be seen in the pattern of private versus public education. PRI governments established a long tradition of recruitment from Mexico's public universities. Fox's government demonstrated a significant shift away from this pattern. In high-level positions in the administration, over half of Fox's appointees received their undergraduate education in private universities in Mexico and abroad (see Table 6.2). Conversely, including national and regional public universities as well as the Mexican military academies, less than 40 percent were educated in state-sponsored undergraduate institutions in Mexico City or other states. Mainly due to the participation of U.S.-born individuals in the Fox government, the administration also included a significant number of appointees educated at foreign undergraduate institutions.[51]

When looking only to the cabinet level, the educational profile of Fox's government appeared much more like that of his predecessor. For example,

Table 6.2 Undergraduate Educational Institutions of Fifty-Two Top Fox Administration Appointees

Type of Institution	Number	Percentage
Private Institutions	23	44
Public Institutions	16	31
Foreign Private Institutions	5	10
Heroic Military/Naval College/Superior War College	4	8
Other (data not available)	4	8

Source: www.presidencia.gob.mx.

sixteen appointees (73 percent) of Fox's cabinet had degrees from public universities (either at the national or state level), while six (27 percent) had degrees from private universities (including Fox's alma mater, the Jesuit-run Universidad Iberoamericana). This represented a modest shift toward private institutions compared with the Zedillo cabinet, which drew 82 percent of its appointees from public institutions and 18 percent from private institutions. However, once again, there was a significant difference in the geographic locations of the public institutions that educated Fox's cabinet members. That is, in another indication of the "decentralized" origins of officials in the Fox government, a larger proportion of the cabinet was educated in the provinces rather than coming solely from public institutions in Mexico City.[52]

Assessing Recruitment Patterns Under Fox

The use of mostly nonpartisan criteria to select appointees to public office under Fox was totally unprecedented in Mexico. Indeed, at least on the surface, Fox's team appeared to be one of the most politically diverse administrations Mexico had ever seen, with representatives from the private sector and different political parties. Drawing from the general patterns found above, the appointments Fox made during his administration might be roughly divided into four key groups (*grupos*): the Grupo PAN, Grupo San Angel, the Grupo Monterrey, and the Grupo Guanajuato.

First, Fox appointed members of his own party into key positions, albeit to a much lesser extent typical under PRI governments of the past. The relative absence of PAN partisans in the Fox administration was closely related to the nature of Fox's circumvention of the party, which contributed to tensions in the president's relationship with his party while in government. Second, harking back to his involvement with a rainbow coalition of anti-PRI activists and intellectuals known as the San Angel Group, Fox also reached out to include some colorful characters in high-level positions in his administration. Jorge Castañeda, founder of the San Angel Group and flamboyant leftist academic, was placed in the influential position of foreign minister. Adolfo Aguilar Zinser, who also participated in the group, was named as head of the newly created position of National Security Adviser. Fox even threw a bone to two former challengers on the left, including Porfirio Muñoz Ledo and Gilberto Rincón Gallardo. Ironically, these individuals received positions within the Fox government, while newfound allies in the PAN–PVEM alliance were excluded from positions. Third, there appeared to be an important connection between the Fox administration and the industrially developed northern city of Monterrey. This connection was seen primarily in the region of origin, education (ITESM and its campuses throughout Mexico), and some of the business connections of Fox appointees. The later appointment of Nuevo León Governor Fernando Canales Clariond as Mexico's Economic secretary strengthened this association. Finally, perhaps the most influential group in his administration followed President Fox from his home state of Guanajuato to the presidential residence at Los Pinos, quite literally in one case. Key members of this group included members of his gubernatorial administration as well as close advisers from his campaign.[53]

Above all, Fox's continued distancing of himself from the party, his failure to draw on experienced PAN partisans until late in his administration, and his emphasis of style over substance all limited the extent to which successful experiences and lessons of PAN municipal and state governments were reflected in the challenges of his presidency. In particular, the extent to which he depended on his core gubernatorial and campaign team at the national level, rather than elements from his party, also presented a significant liability. Indeed, elements of the PAN were understandably frustrated with Fox's decision to virtually exclude the party from his administration, which at least initially complicated Fox's relationship with both the PAN and the Mexican legislature as a whole.

Executive-Legislative Relations Under Fox

Fox's administration was characterized by two major trends in the area of executive-legislative relations: (1) a weak relationship between Fox and his party and (2) the continuation of opposition domination in the legislature. PAN members were significantly underrepresented among Fox's high-level Fox appointees, whose experience came from nontraditional (45 percent), PRI (23 percent), and other (6 percent) sources. In part, its lack of representation in Fox's government was consistent with the PAN's traditional abhorrence of the PRI's inbred model of party as government and Fox's campaign promises to seek a plural government of transition. The PAN had long insisted that the unholy overlap of party-as-government was an inherent cause of government corruption, impunity, and stagnation. Yet, the lack of PAN representation in Fox's government was also related to the highly independent, candidate-centered nature of Fox's campaign in 2000. During his campaign, Fox made repeated references to the idea of his government as one of transition, in which multiple political perspectives would be incorporated in the construction of a new, democratic regime. In this sense, Fox implicitly rejected the idea of his administration as a government of the PAN.

This lack of party representation in Fox's government caused immediate frustration in the PAN, particularly among its legislators. At the meeting of PAN legislators in Puerto Vallarta in August 2001, President Fox was deluged with complaints from PAN federal deputies for including non-*panista* functionaries in the midlevel and state delegations of the federal government. Fox was greeted with shouts of "today, today, today!" (*¡hoy, hoy, hoy!*), when he assured them that he was working on this problem, and shouts of "no, no, no," when he said that no qualified *panista* had been left out who fit the profile for and aspired to an appointment in his government. Fox smiled and said, "Send me the list, send me the names, and we will look into it shortly." PAN Deputy Teresa Gómez Mont, for example, asked, "Where is the program of the PAN?" and expressed frustration that the Fox administration was filled with middle-level government officials from the previous administration who were "corrupt people and political bosses" (*corruptos y caciques*). Some *panistas* were concerned about the lessons of Eastern Europe, notably the comment of Vaclav Havel that "temporary inexperience is better than permanent sabotage."[54] Fox tried to reassure the legislators, by saying that "the great doctrine and project of our party forms the philosophy and project of my government. We work to push them forward and put them in practice every day, as quickly as the current political situation allows."[55] Over the course of his term, Fox made minor adjustments to his cabinet that increased PAN representation but generally attempted to maintain the integrity of his initial team. In addition, Fox's deliberate efforts to meet regularly with party president Luis Felipe Bravo Mena and the party's legislative leaders, Senator Diego Fernández de Cevallos and Federal Deputy Felipe Calderón, helped to smooth party-government tensions over time.

Still, while Fox was gradually able to heal the wounds within his own party, the PAN remained outnumbered in both houses of the Congress. This situation of divided executive-legislative government presented an enormous obstacle. This was a sea change from executive-legislative relationships of the ancien regime. Traditionally, overwhelming PRI majorities—and nonthreatening levels of representation for all other parties—meant that the Mexican Congress functioned primarily as a rubber stamp for presidential initiatives and secondarily as a political menagerie to create an artificial sense of democratic pluralism. This made the democratic notion of checks and balances between the executive and the legislature a truly foreign concept in Mexico. The executive dominance of the legislature first began to change when the PRI lost its two-thirds majority in the Chamber of Deputies in 1988, which forced President Salinas to seek opposition support for constitutional amendments but still enabled the PRI to pass regular legislation with a simple majority. From 1991 to 1994, the PRI briefly regained its qualified majority and lost it again in 1994. It was under President Zedillo, however, that the PRI lost its absolute majority in the Chamber, with its share of seats in the legislature dipping to 47.6 percent in 1997.[56] With a combined PRI-PRD opposition majority in both the Chamber and the Senate, Fox inherited a significantly weaker presidency relative to the legislature than Mexico had ever seen. Hence, the probability of executive-legislative deadlock for Fox seemed high (see Table 6.3).

Indeed, in the first year of the new administration, many anticipated that the Fox government would be completely paralyzed by the opposition-

Table 6.3 Seats in Mexican Chamber of Deputies, 1991–2003

Party	1991	1994	1997	2000	2003
PRI	320	299	236	211	224
PAN	89	119	121	206	151
PRD	41	65	126	50	97
PVEM	—	—	6	17	17
PT	—	9	7	7	6
PSN	—	—	—	3	—
PAS	—	—	—	2	—

Sources: Figures for 1991–1997 obtained from Yolanda Meyenberg Leycegui, in "La Cámara de Diputados y la oposición en México," in Germán Pérez and Antonia Martínez (eds.) *La Cámara de Diputados en México* (Mexico City: Cámara de Diputados de la H. Congreso de la Unión, LVII Legislatura, 2000). Figures for 2000 obtained from Enrique Davis-Mazlum, "A Balance of Power Emerges in Mexico," La Prensa San Diego, September 1, 2000. Figures for 2003 obtained from Mexican Chamber of Deputies website www.camaradediputados.gob.mx/, accessed on August 4, 2004.

dominated Congress. In fact, key initiatives were clearly blocked or delayed with apparently strategic, partisan motivations from the opposition. In particular, early difficulties faced by the Fox administration—notably in its efforts to pass major fiscal and energy-sector reforms—seemed to illustrate the hopelessness of the situation. The Congress's rejection of constitutionally mandated travel requests by the president in the second year of his term contributed to the image of a politically hostile Congress.[57] Meanwhile, Fox's repeated exercise of the presidential veto during his term—a total of five times during the first half of his administration—was unprecedented in the preceding thirty years of Mexican politics and illustrated his own efforts to counter the opposition-dominated Congress.[58] In short, the situation of divided government seemed to have created a bleak legislative context.

On the other hand, despite the worst predictions of many pundits, the Fox administration demonstrated remarkable success in handling the situation of divided government. This was not apparent from portrayals in the Mexican and international media, which tended to focus on Fox's failure to pass key presidential initiatives successfully due to congressional opposition. However, closer analysis of legislative trends belied the dire predictions and assessments of many political analysts. Most analysts ignored the fact that, through the first half of his term and into the second, the vast majority of the president's legislative initiatives were successful. In part, this reflects the quantity and not the quality or nature of the bills passed, as many of the president's successful bills might be considered of minor importance; for example, each year the legislature granted authorization for eight to twelve presidential requests for international travel. Critics tended to focus more on the relatively small number of initiatives that did not pass through the opposition-dominated legislature (such as the few instances that Congress refused to authorize presidential travel).

Yet, the opposition-dominated Congress passed groundbreaking, even controversial legislation proposed by the president, such as the Federal Law for Transparency and Access to Public Government Information (to ensure political transparency and access to public records); the Science and Technology Law (to increase the coordination of information among government agencies and improve the transparency of government grant-making in the sciences); Federal Law to Prevent and Eliminate Discrimination (bolstering protections provided in the 2001 indigenous rights amendments by assuring protection from "discrimination based on ethnic or national origin, sex, age, disability, social or economic condition, health, pregnancy, language, religion, opinions, sexual preference, or marital status"); Federal Tax Code reforms (including key sections originally included in the failed 2001 fiscal reform package); Amendments to the Federal Criminal Code (to protect child victims of sexual exploitation); and the Law of Promotions and Commendations of the Mexican Army and Air Force.[59] Meanwhile, though the PRI introduced significantly more legislation than both the PAN and the PRD under Fox, both minority parties were able to achieve passage of a significant number of their legislative initiatives in the Congress. Indeed, none of the three major parties was shut out of the legislative process in either House.[60]

Thus, despite the worst predictions (and some notable early setbacks), the Fox administration was unexpectedly productive in passing its initiatives through the legislature. This was not entirely surprising, considering the possibility of shifting alliances. As noted in Chapter 4, three-way competition among political parties is not a zero-sum game: the possibility of shifting alliances to support different legislative initiatives means that no party is necessarily destined to lose. Hence, despite important setbacks on some key initiatives, neither Fox nor the PAN was consistently prevented from passing legislation in the opposition-dominated legislature, because either the PRI or the PRD could serve as a potential partner. In the end, the notion that the Congress was deadlocked by divided government was significantly exaggerated in the media and in public opinion. As a result, the public's general perception of the Fox administration was that he was unable to live up to expectations because of these challenges.

Hence, the real problem for the Fox administration was not the president's ability to advance his programmatic agenda through the legislature; instead, the most serious problem was the challenge of managing relations between the state and civil society in a new Mexican political context. As the president's party was no longer an arm of the state, Fox could have tried to draw more effectively on the strategies for state-society relations found among successful subnational governments of the PAN. In this sense, Fox's greatest liabilities were his failure to draw on the many resources of the PAN and his proclivity to be more interested in the art of the constant campaign than in the hard slog of governance.

Going Public: New State and Society Relations Under Fox

For Fox's critics, the start of his administration on December 1, 2000, confirmed their worst fears about his personal style.[61] Prior to his inauguration that morning, Fox made public appearances at the Shrine of the Virgin of Guadalupe and at a breakfast with children in a poverty-stricken barrio in Mexico City. Fox's detractors portrayed these visits as proof of the new PAN president's right-wing, moral agenda and his overly populist tendencies, respectively. Moreover, Fox's informalities during the inauguration ceremonies sparked criticism even from members of his own party, particularly the PAN's 1994 presidential candidate and incoming leader of the PAN in the Senate, Diego Fernández de Cevallos. Fernández openly reprimanded President Fox for breaking custom with informal greetings to his family before the legislative body, for injecting appeals to indigenous communities and underprivileged groups into the formal text of the oath of office, and even for the fashion faux pas of wearing a brown (not traditional black) suit.

Still, Vicente Fox brought with him a versatile wardrobe and wore many different outfits that day, revealing a more complex approach than his critics credited him with. Indeed, there is perhaps no better metaphor than fashion to understand Fox's personal and political style. The day of his inauguration, Fox went from church clothes, to street-smart denim, to inaugural suit and tie with remarkable speed and ease. Later that evening, the new president pulled off his tie and descended to the center square of the world's largest city to celebrate with crowds. Soon after, Fox donned formal wear and headed back to an exclusive dinner with luminaries from around the world. In the weeks and months that followed, Fox went on to don the traditional garb of indigenous people in southern Mexico, tour his ranch in cowboy boots with the United States' newly inaugurated Texan president, and implore the world to mediate the negative impacts of globalization while wearing a designer suit at the World Economic Forum in Davos, Switzerland. The consummate man of many hats, Fox brought to the office of Mexico's presidency the savvy ability to market himself in many ways to many different people.

Here again, Fox's personal style as president was similar to the one he used as governor in Guanajuato, an image he later perfected as a candidate. The first six months of Fox's state government began as a genuine honeymoon period, which gave the administration substantial time to plan its work for the coming term. During this period, Fox enjoyed tremendous media coverage of his activities and took advantage of the opportunities to "sell" his message to the public. So actively did Fox pursue the spotlight in his efforts at "going public" in Guanajuato, that he was characterized as "an eager-to-please protagonist drawn to the footlights and microphones wherever they present themselves. . . . Fox was rapidly transformed in a brand name, a trademark, in the way that he once sold Coca-Cola, he now uses marketing for Guanajuato as the land of opportunity."[62]

Governor Fox's media honeymoon declined as inconsistencies emerged between rhetoric and reality. The media and political analysts pointed to the errors, omissions, and exaggerations of the Fox administration. Six months into the new PAN governorship, some critics and informed citizens had already grown concerned by the lack of an overall governmental plan, the lack of an ambitious plan for public works, a return to patterns of public indebtedness to private banks, the continued bureaucratization of state agencies, and the neglect of local government needs expressed by PRI mayors. Fox, no longer the darling of the media, appeared bothered by the sudden change in his status. Nonetheless, in part due to his constant efforts of self-promotion during his quest for the presidency, Fox remained enormously popular throughout the state.

Similarly, as president, Fox experienced severe criticisms for the yawning gap between promises and his actual accomplishments in office. Regardless of some significant accomplishments (noted in the previous section), critics and the public expressed fairly negative perceptions of Fox's progress on key initiatives and campaign promises. Nonetheless, Fox himself enjoyed high approval ratings throughout his term. Fox's popularity might reflect the public's perception of a personal association between Fox and Mexico's democratic transition; it also seemed to reflect a new approach to managing relations between state and society in the new Mexican political context, at least as managed by President Fox. That is, Fox tended to behave in office as if still on the campaign trail and to emphasize an image of success rather than focusing on developing careful and detailed plans for governance. In short, making the transition from governor and candidate to president required an entirely different set of skills and experiences that Fox did not seem to have. Yet, the administration's lack of any significant attempt to draw on the PAN and the lessons it could have offered from state and local experiences limited the overall policy accomplishments of the Fox administration.

Fifteen Minutes of Change: Public Policy and Political Reform Under Fox

Fox came to the presidency with great confidence, if not a bit of hubris, regarding the policies and reforms that would be accomplished by his administration. Perhaps most memorably, Fox famously boasted during his campaign that he would resolve the thorny situation of the Chiapas indigenous insurrection in "fifteen minutes." In addition, Fox claimed that his government would accomplish gross domestic product (GDP) growth rates of over 7 percent annually, greater investment in Mexico's human resources, prosperity for small and medium businesses, modernization of the agricultural and energy sectors, a corridor of infrastructure investments stretching from Mexico's South to Panama, resolution of the dire situation in Mexican public security, as well as political reforms to ensure the consolidation of Mexican democracy. During and after the campaign, many critics viewed Fox's claims as underanalyzed, arrogant, and foolish. Yet it was the vague promise of "change," rather than specific policy objectives enumerated during the campaign, that enabled Fox to defeat the PRI.

Indeed, the Fox administration brought a dramatic change from the Mexico of the past, where the PRI's all powerful president was the personification of a symbiotic fusion of party and government, where consistent legislative majorities ensured the longevity of the PRI machine, and where political support was won not through general public appeals but through particularistic distribution of government resources through a vast, serpentine labyrinth of power. Moreover, this change was apparent from Fox's inauguration into office, not just over the first months, but indeed within the first "fifteen minutes." That is, from the outset, Fox was a weak president with limited representation of his party in government and in the legislature, tense relations with the legislature, and a media-centered personal style primarily focused on maintaining high approval ratings. What, then, did this change mean for the implementation of the many policies and political reforms Fox promised during his long campaign for the Mexican presidency?

Here again, some insights can be gained from looking to Fox's prior experience in government as governor of Guanajuato. In Guanajuato, despite an equally dramatic shift from past PRI governments, an enormous gulf between public expectations and actual policy implementation was the result of exaggerated claims, political impasses, and a stunning lack of planning in that first Fox administration. At the national level, Fox's approach to policy and political challenges was similar to that seen during his gubernatorial term in Guanajuato. As in Guanajuato, the development of President Fox's policy agenda took much longer than expected (the National Plan for Development was delayed by several months) and tended to employ vague generalities rather than clearly articulated solutions. Meanwhile, the situation Fox inherited was full of concrete and difficult challenges that would not be resolved by quick fixes. At the top of the list were Mexico's long-standing macroeconomic problems, the armed conflict in Chiapas, the need to boost federal revenues, energy-sector reform, poverty alleviation, reforming the administration of justice, and generating new constitutional reforms to ensure effective democratic governance. Soon after taking office, Fox also hoped to engage his newly anointed U.S. counterpart, George W. Bush, who was finally named the victor in a hotly contested election. By the midpoint of his term, Fox's accomplishments across the board were mixed at best, vividly illustrating both the challenges and merits of democratic governance.

Precursors to Change: Political Reform and Policy Implementation in Guanajuato

Consideration of Fox's antecedents in Guanajuato and the challenges of political reform and policy implementation during the Fox presidency offers useful insights on Mexico's new political context and the dilemmas confronting Fox, the PAN, and presidential administrations for the future. Vicente Fox took office as Mexico's first democratically elected PAN governor in the state of Guanajuato in December 1995, receiving the office from interim-Governor Carlos Medina Plascencia, the former PAN mayor of León who was appointed by Carlos Salinas in 1991. The transfer of power from one *panista* to another presumably meant that the new governor could begin his administration with relatively low start-up costs. Nonetheless, it took several months for Fox to compile his agenda and policy formulations. When Fox finally presented his formal *Plan of Government, 1996–2000* political observers were disappointed.[63]

The five main challenges that Fox's plan outlined were criticized as obvious and underanalyzed, while the proposed solutions were also seen as "unclear" and "excessively disconnected." Some local analysts suggested that Fox had all the necessary attributes to be an excellent candidate but lacked the skills required for good public administration: a long-term strategic vision, careful attention to detail, a conciliatory disposition, and sensitivity to society.[64] For example, in Governor Fox's education policy, the programs that stood out included "Scholarship 1000" (Beka 1000) and Window to the World (Una Ventana al Mundo).[65] The latter program promised to bring at least one computer to each of Guanajuato's 5,500 primary schools but ran up against budgetary and infrastructural limitations faced throughout the state; the majority of the state's schools for basic education were understaffed and located in poor and rural areas; many lacked basic facilities (decent chalkboards, lecterns, desks, typewriters, and filing cabinets), were given little to no administrative assistance, and could not take advantage of the program.[66]

Governor Fox's economic and social policies also drew criticism. When campaigning for the governorship of Guanajuato, Fox identified the state's unemployment crisis to be the most urgent priority for his new government. However, soon after taking over the governorship, Fox proclaimed that the problem had radically abated and—despite the highly rural character of the state—instead drew attention to the low indices of unemployment in Guanajuato's urban centers. To support these claims, Fox drew on statistics generated by a new state information agency called INFO, which contradicted many of the figures of the National Institute of Geographical Statistics and Information (Instituto Nacional de Estadística Geografía e Informática, INEGI), particularly with reference to indices of poverty.[67]

Meanwhile, state officials' grand visions of reinventing government under Governor Fox yielded an extensive paragovernmental structure consisting of offices and agencies created by executive decree. Many of these agencies proved redundant or superfluous. One example of the replication of government services could be found in the Coordinating Office for Regional Development in Guanajuato (Coordinación para el Desarrollo Regional del Estado de Guanajuato, CODEREG). CODEREG partially duplicated the functions of Guanajuato's Secretariats of Finance and of Economic Development and also served as an intermediary between the state and local governments (in apparent contradiction to Article 115 of the Federal Constitution).[68]

Some of Fox's programs were created with the original idea that they would be turned over to civil society or private-sector operation, but they never were. Such was the case, for example, of the Lucas Alamán Center for Economic Growth (Centro Lucas Alamán para el Crecimiento Económico, CILACE), the Center for Human Development, and the Guanajuato Santa Fe Micro-Credit Company (Microcréditos Santa Fe de Guanajuato, A.C.). Critics charged that the governor's plans for social policy made only very loose, commonsense references to the problem of poverty in the state and lacked a clear policy for helping vulnerable groups, such as migrants and the urban poor.[69] Worst of all, the entire program for social policy was delayed until two years into the Fox administration; it was announced in June 1997, just one month before Fox officially launched his campaign for the PAN's presidential nomination.

Overall, Fox's state government illustrated a persistent tendency to emphasize style over substance. Highly innovative and attractive-sounding programs were marketed to the public with a certain level of hyperbole about their actual accomplishments, possibly even rivaling the propaganda of past PRI administrations. Most important, Fox's projected image of successful, inventive management of his state's problems worked. Fox was widely popular as governor and was also very well received in other parts of Mexico and the international arena on the basis of this image. In this sense, Fox's governorship was characterized by a highly successful marketing campaign, related largely to his near constant devotion to his quest for the presidency. Once Fox became president, his approach to the development and implementation of public policy was noticeably similar to that seen in Guanajuato. While innovative and often provocative, this tendency contributed to both exaggerated expectations and poor follow-through for his administration's programs.

The EZLN and Indigenous Rights Reform

One of the first major items Fox faced as president had little connection to his experience in Guanajuato. The indigenous conflict whose resolution he contemplated so casually during the campaign had no precedents from his experience as governor. Thus, in advocating a reinitiation of government talks with the Zapatistas, Fox drew on the experience of senior *panista* leader Luis H. Alvarez, whom he appointed as head of the Commission for Concordance and Peace. In response to the new opportunities presented by the Fox administration, the Zapatistas engineered a "march" on Mexico City, touring several cities by bus—with numerous speeches by the popular "Sub-Commander Marcos"—before finally arriving in the capital to present their concerns. Despite Fox's best efforts, however, the Zapatista Army of National Liberation (Ejército Zapatista de Liberación Nacional, EZLN) refused to provide him with a photo-op and instead insisted on appearing before the Senate. It was here that the Fox administration met its first significant snag in the Congress. While Fox favored a rapid and amicable resolution of the Chiapas conflict, key segments of his party were not in agreement. The PAN faction of the Senate, led by Diego Fernández de Cevallos, objected even to the idea that the EZLN should be permitted to address the Senate in the ski masks they used to protect their identities. Indeed, even after the PRD and PRI supported the widely popular movement's right to address the Senate, all PAN senators left the floor in protest. Hence, as the Senate was addressed on national television by EZLN representative "Esther," one of seven commanders of the rebel group, the entire PAN section of the Senate was unoccupied.

In the end, the Congress worked out an amendment to recognize indigenous rights. While this was the first major reform addressing the status of indigenous people in Mexico since the Reforma of the nineteenth century, the EZLN was ultimately unsatisfied with the agreement because it failed to protect local autonomy and otherwise backtracked on key provisions of the San Andreas Accords negotiated in 1996. Mainly, the Zapatistas desired additional protections for indigenous rights to "collective land rights, control of natural resources, access to media in native languages, customary law, and the legal recognition of indigenous 'peoples' (rather than communities) as subjects of domestic law."[70] While the EZLN expressed discontent with the new legislation, the Zapatistas retreated to their positions in Chiapas without laying down their arms.[71] With the conclusion to the Chiapas rebellion still uncertain, Fox moved on to the issue of fiscal reform and his agenda for economic development.

All That Glitters Is Not Gold: Economic Development and Social Policy

Upon taking office as president, Fox was fortunate at least in one very important sense. Every Mexican president from 1970 onward inherited a political or economic crisis of significant proportions. However, to the credit of the Zedillo administration, Fox entered the office in a situation of relative economic tranquillity. Mexico's balance of payments and servicing on foreign debt were in order, thanks to careful macroeconomic management following the 1994 peso crisis. Meanwhile, in addition to Zedillo's conscientious stewardship, Fox benefited from the confidence of investors in Mexico's new business-friendly president. Also, the continuity of economic policy assured by Fox's inclusion of key Zedillo administration officials in the Gabinetazo likewise contributed to the relatively smooth transition and the absence of a major economic crisis.

However, where Fox attempted major economic reforms—such as fiscal reform and energy-sector restructuring—he was blocked by the opposition-dominant legislature and indeed lacked general public support for his proposals. As in the case of PAN state and local governments, improving federal tax revenues was seen as an urgent priority to facilitate the Fox administration's initiatives. In 2001, Fox introduced legislation to bolster the intake of the federal government by raising and broadening the application of the value added tax (VAT). The Fox administration focused primarily on value added taxes, because such taxes are easier to collect and monitor than others; however, the Fox administration also sought to increase income taxes for individuals (personas físicas) to the level of businesses and incorporated entities (personas morales). On the value added tax, Fox failed to secure the necessary support, partly because of the unpopularity of his efforts to broaden the VAT to include food, medicines, books, and other traditionally exempt items. Fox's proposal was unsuccessful due to doubts within his own party, staunch PRI and PRD opposition in the Congress, and a general public outcry against the initiative.

The failure of its fiscal reform proposal dealt a significant blow to the Fox administration and arguably made it much more difficult for the new government to fulfill some major promises made during the campaign. Again, PAN state and local governments were most successful at making improvements in works and services when they were first able to introduce administrative and fiscal measures to increase revenue streams. Without significant increases in federal revenues, for example, the administration found it difficult to pursue some of the strategies Fox proposed for economic development and social policies to alleviate poverty. Still, Fox's policy agenda in these areas had limitations of its own. As in Fox's administration in Guanajuato, it is questionable whether his policies were sufficiently well planned or feasible to meet the lofty objectives and expectations set by his rhetoric as president. That is, as in Guanajuato, several of the innovative programs Fox proposed to promote growth and poverty alleviation at the national level—microcredit assistance to small- and medium-sized businesses, energy sector reform, infrastructure improvements—lacked adequate planning, private sector financing, or political support. Despite this rhetoric, other initiatives proposed by President Fox tended to pour old wine into new bottles by continuing recent PRI programs and approaches to economic policy and poverty alleviation.

First, with regard to the new programs introduced by Fox and the Gabinetazo, there was a striking pattern—disturbingly familiar to those who followed his record in Guanajuato—of flashy but poorly articulated plans. The case of microcredit assistance was one example highly reminiscent of the Santa Fe Micro-Credit program Fox introduced as governor in Guanajuato. The Santa Fe program was designed to help small business out with loans, ranging from approximately $50 to $500, tailored to small businesses and street stands (*changarros*) and was to be financed by joint funding from private investors and the public sector. In short, this program was meant to serve as a shining example of the power of public-private partnerships and the spirit of small-scale capitalism. Unfortunately, despite a board of distinguished businesspeople from throughout the state, the Santa Fe program never obtained the funds initially promised by the private sector, and Fox was forced to rely mainly on government coffers in order to provide credit. Even more problematic, the Santa Fe program failed to establish the necessary mechanisms and training programs to ensure repayment; hence, the program ultimately functioned as a system of direct subsidies, rather than a sustainable credit agency that fostered entrepreneurialism and fiscal responsibility.

At the national level, Fox's much touted plan for a nationwide microcredit financing program titled the National Micro-Credit Financing Program (Programa Nacional de Financiamiento al Microempresario, PRONAFIM), sought to involve nongovernmental organizations (NGOs) in the process of distributing government loans as microcredits. Unfortunately, as in Guanajuato, PRONAFIM did not begin with adequate levels of funding (only 200 million pesos for 40,000 borrowers) or means of distribution (because few organizations met government registration requirements).[72] In other words, in attempting to avoid the mistakes made in Guanajuato, the Fox government made lending criteria so strict that loan eligibility was too difficult for the many high-risk people who needed loans.[73]

Other new policies Fox proposed at the national level were significantly delayed or failed to advance beyond the "proclamation stage."[74] Most notable, in this regard, was Fox's extremely ambitious program for a regional development project in southern Mexico, the poorest region of the country: the Puebla-Panama Plan (Plan Puebla-Panamá, PPP). This project sought to create a corridor of infrastructure development from southern Mexico throughout Central America through international financing of highways, ports, and airports. While praised by the IMF, this program met almost immediately with significant challenges. Local political opposition—notably from the EZLN—questioned the core objectives of the program, as the modernization program would undoubtedly destabilize life for millions of indigenous people. This, in turn, complicated the task of obtaining international support from sources that encouraged local participation in projects. Additionally, without adequate government funding to jump-start the $20 billion initiative originally proposed by Fox, the administration was forced to reduce the scale and scope of the project dramatically. Some critics even questioned the market potential for trade between Mexico and Central America, due to "the low volume of trade" between them.[75] Naturally, such criticisms overlooked the possibility that low trade is itself often a symptom of inadequate infrastructure, because improvements would increase the potential gains from trade.[76] Still, the potential for competition from businesses in Central America with lower costs of labor and production, which currently lack adequate infrastructure to be fully competitive, might have been initially destabilizing for Mexican businesses.

One example of mixed success in innovation was a public-private partnership investment program entitled "With You, Hands to Work" (Contigo, Manos a la Obra), administered through the Ministry of Development (Secretaría de Desarrollo Social, SEDESOL). Through the "Hands to Work" program, Fox promised to promote investments by international foundations, private businesses, wealthier municipalities, and universities in hundreds of poor communities throughout Mexico; indeed, the program received support from high-profile backers like CEMEX, Microsoft, and the Monterrey Technological Institute (Instituto Technológico de Estudios Superiores de Monterrey, ITESM). Still, both government and nongovernmental funding for the program fell short of expectations.[77]

Meanwhile, to a significant degree, the economic and social policies of the Fox administration continued the policies of the previous administration and indeed followed the tendency of recent PRI governments to employ market-driven solutions to social problems.[78] Interestingly, one major PRI initiative that did not follow this market-based approach but that Fox reluctantly continued and expanded, was the PROGRESA program initiated by the Zedillo administration. Through this program, poor families received material benefits—nutritional supplements, food stipends, primary health care, and educational stipends—as incentives to keep their children (especially girls) in school; hence, the program had a long-term view to the problem of poverty but also provided relief for short-term needs. However, the use of direct subsidies to combat poverty ran against the Fox administration's philosophical orientation, which advocated market-based approaches to economic and social policy.[79] The Fox administration was also skeptical about PROGRESA due to perceptions of political manipulation of social policy under both Salinas and Zedillo. Yet, the program had a sizable constituency of nearly 13 million beneficiaries, more than 14 percent of all Mexicans. Also, international lenders, such as the IMF and the World Bank, enthusiastically supported the program because of its "considerable success in targeting poor families and improving certain indicators of well-being." Hence, the program was continued, with a substantial boost from the IMF, albeit under the new name of Oportunidades.[80]

In short, while Fox enjoyed surprising success in passing key initiatives in the Congress, his administration's effectiveness with regard to policy implementation fell significantly short of expectations. The Fox administration's limited accomplishments can only be attributed partially to the situation of divided government and the legislature's resulting refusal to increase federal revenues through much needed fiscal reforms. Still, Fox's characteristic failure to move beyond platitudes and slogans to develop detailed plans for policy implementation was his administration's greatest weakness with regard to limited accomplishments in the key issue areas of economic development and poverty alleviation.

Remaking Mexican Politics: Rule of Law and Constitutional Reform

Despite the real or perceived limitations of its actual accomplishments, the Fox administration, after its first three years, sought to achieve some tangible and long-lasting results that would effectively transform the political system, notably in the related areas of rule of law and democratic governance. At the time Fox took office, security issues stood among the top priorities of Mexicans, who were still reeling from rising indices of crime and corruption in the aftermath of the 1994–1995 economic crisis. Upon entering office, Fox addressed these situations with two of his most important early reforms: the creation of a Secretariat of Public Security (Secretaría de Seguridad Pública) and a new coordinating office on national security. The Public Security Secretary, Alejandro Gertz, succeeded in re-creating the Federal Preventive Police (Policía Federal Preventiva, PFP), and also began to restructure the National System of Public Security (Sistema Nacional de Seguridad Pública, SNSP). This system, initiated under President Zedillo, incorporated all federal and subnational law enforcement and security agencies under the coordination of the Ministry of Public Security.

In addition, Fox opted to continue a trend toward militarization of domestic security that began in the 1980s. Notably, Fox appointed a former military general, Rafael Macedo de la Concha, as Mexico's chief prosecutor; skeptics noted that there was no such thing as a "former" general in Mexico and warned that the agency would develop excessive ties to the military. Indeed, under de la Concha, the attorney general's office integrated military personnel into high-ranking positions and exhibited a tendency to draw on the military.[81] Indeed, when the Fox administration created a new national police force in the form of the Federal Investigative Agency (Agencia Federal de Investigaciones, AFI), a cognate to the U.S. Federal Bureau of Investigation, to replace and augment the functions of the former Federal Judicial Police (Policía Judicial Federal), staffing for this new agency drew heavily on military personnel.

Despite criticisms that Fox was simply continuing PRI policies that he had criticized during the presidential campaign, he made some significant accomplishments in the first few years of his term. Fox made progress in the disruption of narcotrafficking networks, major crackdowns on corruption, and initiatives to promote transparency in regarding human rights violations. Notably, in early 2002, the Mexican and U.S. officials accomplished a long-standing goal—the disruption of the Tijuana cartel—with the killing of Ramón Arrellano-Felix by local officials in a shoot-out in Mazatlán, Sinaloa, and the arrest of Benjamin Arrellano-Felix by elite counternarcotics units in the city and state of Puebla. Also, the sacking of forty-six allegedly dishonest customs administrators nationwide sent a message that the administration hoped to prevent corruption and organized crime in government.

Naturally, many challenges remained. Ongoing problems of narcotrafficking, human rights violations, and corruption continued to undermine the rule of law in Mexico. At every level and across every aspect of the administration of justice in Mexico—crime prevention, criminal investigation and arrest, prosecution, sentencing, incarceration, and reintegration to society—experts identified major problems of institutional design, training and professional standards, transparency, and accountability. As a result, a deep sense of distrust among Mexican citizens further undermined the justice system, contributing to the nonreporting of crimes and an unwillingness to strengthen the hand of police in response to crime.[82] Across the board, these problems necessitated a major systemic overhaul and a dramatic transformation of citizen perceptions, neither of which could be accomplished within Fox's term.

Hence, in the second half of Fox's term, the attorney general's office announced a set of constitutional amendments and laws intended to overhaul the administration of justice in Mexico. The proposals, presented by Attorney General Macedo with President Fox at a conference on "Innovation in Security and Justice," outlined major structural and procedural changes. The most potentially significant structural reform in the package was a proposal to give "greater autonomy" to the Office of the Attorney General, with the intention of insulating the nation's chief prosecutor from political manipulation and other undo influence. In addition, the attorney general's office proposed the unification of all federal police forces under its authority. Notably, the proposal would unify the secretary of Public Safety's newly created PFP with the attorney general's new AFI unit.

The Fox administration's concerns about ensuring the independence of the attorney general's office stemmed from problems encountered by the PAN during the Zedillo administration. On taking office, President Zedillo took the historic step of appointing PAN member Antonio Lozano Gracia as attorney general, largely to lend credibility to the investigation of the March 1994 assassination of PRI presidential candidate Luis Donaldo Colosio. Lozano, a young, accomplished lawyer, was the first active member of the PAN to serve in any PRI government. Lozano's ability to conduct his investigation was impeded by resistance to and within the Office of the Attorney General. PAN leaders and Lozano himself believed that these impediments were due to interference from corrupt elements in the ruling party that sought to prevent any resolution of the Colosio case. Lozano eventually resigned in frustration, and subsequent prosecutors similarly failed to resolve the case. PAN leaders interviewed later admitted the party's strategic error in accepting the position, given its lack of independent investigative authority.[83] The reform of the attorney general's office proposed under Fox was, therefore, at least partly motivated by a desire to increase its effectiveness in the investigation of controversial cases.

There were at least two major schools of thought on the proposed initiatives to restructure Mexico's public security bureaucracy. On the one hand, bureaucratic centralization is a frequent response to complex problems. Gains in efficiency often result when bureaucracies with similar and even overlapping jurisdictions are brought together into the same organization, thanks to more effective coordination and information sharing. On the other hand, diffusion of authority and the perpetuation of overlapping jurisdictions can also provide benefits, by fostering bureaucratic competition and reciprocal oversight among different agencies. The logic of this second position supported the decision not to unify all federal agencies in the U.S. government's response to terror threats.

Through the attorney general's proposals, the administration clearly sided with the former, centralization perspective. Yet, given the increasing militarization of the attorney general's office and federal police forces, structural reforms that would unify the forces held potentially serious negative consequences. Since these structural reforms would simultaneously concentrate police powers in the attorney general's office while decreasing their accountability to the executive, there was significant potential for unchecked corruption and abuse of authority. Indeed, the fact that the Ministry of Public Security had identified cases of high-level corruption in the attorney general's AFI in the first half of the Fox administration raised serious questions about the wisdom of placing the PFP under its control.

In addition to these structural reforms, the Fox administration also contemplated a number of procedural innovations that would dramatically transform the administration of justice. The two most significant reforms contemplated the presumption of innocence until a suspect is proved guilty and the possibility of adversarial oral argumentation in criminal trials. In recent years, large numbers of accused criminals have sat in jail without being sentenced, or worse, were sentenced without proper defense. Indeed, early in the Fox administration, Public Secretary Gertz observed that "the nation's jails are full of minor criminals and of persons that could not pay for a good defensive counsel."[84] New measures to provide stronger legal defense and to presume innocence were aimed at addressing this problem. The presumption of innocence before the law would move Mexico away from Napoleonic legal tradition, which effectively placed the burden of proof on the accused. Likewise, the introduction of adversarial oral argumentation into the legal system contemplated a dramatic shift in Mexican legal practice that would facilitate swifter resolution of criminal trials and greater transparency in trial procedures.

In addition to these major reforms to the judicial system, the Fox administration also presented a comprehensive package of reforms soon after the inaugural session of Mexico's new Congress on March 15, 2004. Mexican political institutions in the twentieth century were developed to resolve or at least respond to a whole set of problems. From the chaos of the Revolution to the transition itself, the development of a single hegemonic party, the exceedingly strong executive power, the centralization of political authority at the federal level, the electoral mechanisms of selection that ensured predictability, and even the opposition political parties of the system were all institutional responses to specific dilemmas. Therefore, the "Reform of the State" that the Fox administration hoped to accomplish really focused on developing new institutions or recasting old ones to address the new political reality of the twenty-first century.

To wit, the Reform of the State package presented by the Fox administration included new legislation and constitutional amendments primarily intended to ensure transparency and accountability in the political system. The reforms were unveiled by Interior Minister Santiago Creel and described as reforms "to make our democracy efficient . . . to construct stable majorities . . . [and] to create a certain degree of order."[85] As first introduced, the reform package sought sweeping changes in the areas of human rights, information management, legislative organization, executive governance, judicial interpretation, interbranch and intergovernmental interaction, and electoral reform. Some of the specific measures introduced by the Fox administration would clearly set limits on whatever party captured the presidency in 2006 and, therefore, provided preventions against abuse.[86]

Other measures were sure to generate significant controversy and debate because they could potentially alter the balance of power, not only in the coming administration but over the longer term. For example, several proposed initiatives would dramatically change the nature of democratic representation, such as reducing the degree of proportional representation, changing the timing of elections, and providing new mechanisms for public referendums. One key question regarding these new governance reforms was whether they would have made a difference if they had been in place during the Fox administration and how they might affect future policy making. In addressing this question, Interior Sub-Secretary Francisco José Paoli Bolio connected the failure of previous initiatives—such as the energy reform—to a lack of consensus that might have been better achieved under the proposed reforms.[87] Yet, this approach to strengthening the president's party focused on creating external institutional mechanisms, rather than building and strengthening the party from within.

There were other potential problems. The reforms would have greatly strengthened the president's veto—by allowing him to approve segments of legislation—thereby reducing the incentives for negotiation and reducing the separation of powers between the executive and legislative branches; partial veto power would effectively convert the president into the chief legislator. Meanwhile, the reforms that posited changes to the nature of democratic representation—raising the threshold for minority party representation, introducing referendums, and harmonizing the timing of elections—seemed unnecessary and potentially harmful. The process of electoral reform in Mexico, culminating in 1996, had already achieved a substantial degree of electoral transparency and competitiveness, as witnessed by Fox's own electoral victory and relatively high levels of competitiveness at the subnational level. However, efforts to alter the system of representation or create new electoral influences could skew the electoral balance of power in highly unpredictable ways. For example, the idea of introducing a national referendum with a relatively low (1 percent) threshold for a public vote would likely yield a wave of poorly conceptualized and highly contested initiatives that would undermine professional legislators and policymakers.

Perhaps the most controversial part of the reform package was a proposal to allow reelection, which flew in the face of a major tenet of the Mexican Revolution. The president's Reform of the State initiative sought to change Articles 59 and 116 of the Mexican Constitution to permit the immediate reelection of both legislative and local offices. While each of the major parties began to support the possibility in the early part of the Fox administration, the PAN was the first to advocate publicly for reelection. The PAN offered several justifications for reelection, mainly derived from lessons learned from the experience of its state and local governments. First and foremost, proponents of reelection saw it as a much needed measure to ensure an electoral connection between politicians and their constituents. Without such a connection, proponents argued, politicians lacked an incentive to be responsive to the citizens they supposedly represented; whether or not citizens approved of a politician's achievements or conduct in office, his or her fate was predetermined. Interestingly, Mexico had made significant advances relative to other Latin American countries in the systematic recording and publication of legislators' votes; yet these efforts to provide transparency were not complemented by opportunities for voters to use this information to pass judgment. Proponents argued that reelection would introduce the possibility for voters to hold accountable those politicians seeking to remain in office.

Second, PAN-elected officials had long argued from experience that reelection would allow for more competent politicians. Traditionally, despite even the PRI's lock on power, continuity in public policies from one administration to the next was quite rare. Prohibitions on reelection meant that all new governors and mayors would come to office with their own agendas, staffs, and projects. At the state level, where governors served six-year terms, this was not as problematic as at the local level, where three-year terms required mayors to leave office just as they were getting familiar with the demands of municipal government. Likewise, Mexico's unusual prohibition on congressional reelection—found in few other national legislatures around the world—contributed to very low levels of experience among legislators; from 1934 to 1997, 86.7 percent of Mexico's legislators served only one three-year term (an additional 11 percent served more than once).[88] Hence, as the PAN accumulated governmental experience in the 1980s and 1990s, its elected officials and even many party leaders became convinced that three-year terms for mayoral, city council, and legislative positions were too short for politicians to gain experience or implement effective programs. With reelection, the accumulation of knowledge and experience would presumably enable public officials to plan and implement better public policy. Likewise, successful politicians would derive advantages from the job security provided by satisfied constituents, so it would be more attractive for them to stay in office.

Despite its apparent advantages, the attempt to introduce reelection had some significant potential sources of resistance. On the one hand, the general public in Mexico remained sceptical and, to a certain extent, ill informed, about its potential advantages. Prior to the unveiling of the president's reform package, a February 2004 Mitofsky poll found that only 16 percent of Mexicans favored reelection. However, this same poll suggested that public support for the initiative might improve with more information about the positive implications of reelection, such as the prospect of more experienced politicians and greater accountability.[89] On the other hand, there was the possibility of resistance from party leaders who traditionally enjoyed substantial power because of their ability to determine the fates of single-term politicians; PRI party leaders were especially advantaged because the party's monopoly made it the only channel for career politicians to move through the political system. Yet, with reelection, individual politicians would potentially hold greater allegiance to their constituents and less to their party organizations.

The timing of the reform package was significant. Presenting the initiative in the second half of Fox's administration had at least two advantages. It left open the possibility that the internal composition of the legislature would shift in Fox's favor after the midterm election. This scenario did not materialize. Waiting until the second half of his administration ostensibly gave Fox time to prepare a more careful and detailed reform package and to negotiate this package with the party leaders. This, unfortunately, also proved unsuccessful. The chief disadvantage of the late introduction of the state reform initiative was that the time left for debate and negotiation was restricted and came exceedingly close to the 2006 presidential election.

At such a late stage, the possibility of reform seemed to depend on expectations about the impending succession. For example, a high level of competitiveness among the PRI, PAN, and PRD might increase each party's incentives to strengthen the presidency, because all three parties would consider their chances equally good to obtain power. Conversely, if any single party appeared to have a clear advantage going into the 2006 election, the other two parties might act preemptively to prevent a stronger president in the next term. In the end, the fate of the president's proposals would depend on the calculations of those with a vested interest in the reform, incumbent elected officials, and their estimation of the strategic possibility of ensuring their continued access to power over the longer term.

U.S.-Mexican Relations, Security, and Immigration

At the outset of the Fox and Bush administrations, there was an ebullient mood about U.S.-Mexican relations, thanks to the two presidents' similar personal styles, conservative political orientations, and mutual appreciation for each other's country. Moreover, there appeared to be a sincere effort on the part of the Bush administration to reach out to Mexico on areas of long-standing tension. Bush's early declarations that drug-trafficking and undocumented immigration stemmed from U.S.-side demands and that both required a joint, bilateral approach was an important recognition of U.S. responsibilities. This seemed to pave the way for closer cooperation and new directions in policy formation. Sure enough, the announcement of significant blows against Mexican narcotrafficking organizations and proposals for major revisions to U.S. immigration policy supported this notion when Presidents Bush and Fox met in Washington, D.C., on September 6, 2001. Both countries seemed poised to embrace changes that would bring about stronger networks for cooperation.

Five days later, terrorist attacks on September 11, 2001, instantaneously shifted U.S. security priorities and significantly undermined the fledgling agenda for U.S.-Mexican collaboration and integration. Though the terrorists had all entered the United States legally, public alarm about the highly porous nature of the U.S.-Mexican border was immediate. In the worst of possible scenarios, some alarmists claimed, well-established networks for the trafficking of human beings and contraband could be used for smuggling terrorists and weapons of mass destruction into the United States. In subsequent months, the United States and Canada would implement a new border security agreement, the so-called Smart Border Agreement, a version of which would also be signed with Mexico on significantly less advantageous terms.

Later, in early 2002, during the international debate over U.S. proposals for aggressive action against Iraqi President Saddam Hussein, tensions heightened between the United States and Mexico. Mexico found itself under pressure because it held one of the UN Security Council votes that could have provided greater legitimacy to the U.S-led effort. Open admonishments addressed to the Fox administration from the U.S. Embassy in Mexico City and from high-profile diplomats like Henry Kissinger raised concerns—although they were unfounded—that Mexico and its citizens living abroad would become victims of a backlash from Washington. Tensions only began to fade after the first year of the U.S.-led war against Iraq. Later, in March 2004, in a sign of thawed relations, the two presidents met again in Texas and began to reopen talks on the possibility of a new immigration accord to facilitate the legal employment of guest workers to the United States from Mexico. However, as both countries headed closer to highly competitive elections in fall 2004 and 2006, respectively, critics tended to see the effort to reform immigration as a Republican political ploy to gain Mexican American votes, rather than part of a comprehensive plan for moving toward greater U.S.-Mexican integration. With strong challenges from the opposition in both countries, it was not clear who would emerge as head of state in either election. Hence, the result of both political contests would be the likely determinant of the course of U.S.-Mexican relations for the remainder of the decade.

Style over Substance: Evaluating the Policy Making and Political Reform Under Fox

To the extent that the Fox administration attempted to introduce groundbreaking policy measures, the pattern was strikingly similar to the one he used in his state government. That is, as in Guanajuato, Fox's initiatives that appeared innovative and promising on the surface were mostly generated by hype, the impressive marketing technique of a successful salesman. Hence, it is quite possible that the central dilemma of the Fox administration in its first years was not its failure to obtain political support for its programs, but rather its failure to produce viable programs worthy of political support. In other words, in the democratic marketplace of ideas, Fox found it much more difficult to convince citizens with flashy, sugarcoated programs than it was to sell them Coca-Cola in the private sector. Fox's tendency toward governance through slogans, combined with his reliance on former PRI functionaries and elements of the private sector, left Fox without a clear and comprehensive program for governance. This suggests that successful policy implementation at the national level would require Fox and future presidents to obtain greater public and political support by providing clear objectives, detailed plans for implementation, and strong evidence that the administration will not only follow through but also produce results. While developing a stronger party apparatus might have helped in the formulation of such a program for governance, Fox's distant relationship with the PAN and its lack of participation in his government was a significant contributing factor to the party's setbacks in the midterm elections of 2003.

Assessing the Fox Administration: Lessons from the 2003 Midterm Elections

The 2003 federal midterm elections were seen by many as a referendum on Fox's promises to bring change to Mexico. If indeed this was the case, it was a long and costly assessment. The campaign for control of the Mexican Congress—as well as six of thirty-two state-level governments and dozens of major cities—lasted 109 days and cost the equivalent of nearly half a billion U.S. dollars in public funds. For all the effort and expense, only 26 million of 65 million eligible voters—a paltry 40 percent—showed up at the polls, setting a new record for abstention in Mexican federal elections (see Figure 6.3). Meanwhile, both of the PAN's major opposition parties, the Institutional Revolutionary Party (PRI) and the Party of the Democratic Revolution (PRD), improved their performances relative to President Fox's National Action Party (PAN). Most pundits promptly proclaimed the election a major defeat for both Fox and the PAN.

Fox's first three years in office were characterized by a divided government and a bureaucracy still run largely by members of the PRI. For this reason, the PAN ran on a slogan asking voters to "take the brakes off change." Nonetheless, in the aftermath of the election, the Congress remained in the hands of the divided opposition, led by a still recovering PRI and a rapidly rising PRD. Four of Mexico's small parties failed to obtain the minimum 2 per-

Figure 6.3 Turnout Among Registered Voters, 1964–2003 (as a percentage)

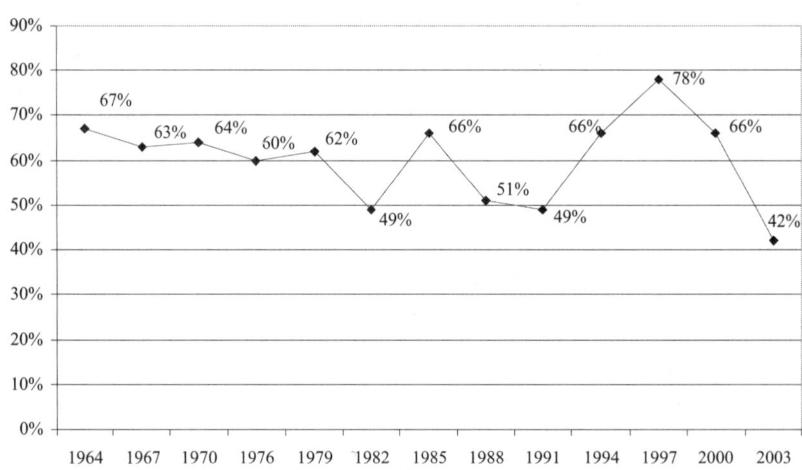

Source: Data presented by Joe Klesner, "Mexico's 2003 Midterm Elections: Implications for the LIX Legislature and Future Party Consolidation," academic conference at the University of Texas–Austin, September 15–16, 2003.

cent of the national vote required to keep their registrations, which will send them to the graveyard of political history. The death of Mexico's Lilliputian parties, which confuse voters and tie up public funds, was perhaps the best news for those hoping to strengthen the mandates of the larger parties. Indeed, in the midterm elections, the PRI gained a total of fourteen new seats, rising from 210 in 2000 to 224 in 2003; the PRD made even greater relative progress, increasing its total number of seats from 52 to 95 (see Table 6.4). The PRI's resilience in the 2003 election was due less to the effectiveness of its national leadership than to the strengthening of its seventeen newly empowered state governors and the local political machines operating in hundreds of municipalities, the fattened children of decentralization. This partly explains why the PRI not only was able to gain new seats in the legislature in 2003, but also to hang on in governorships in Campeche, Colima, and the state of Mexico.

Meanwhile, the PAN lost more than one-quarter of its seats in the Congress, with the actual number of seats dropping from 207 to 153. Still, the PAN remained well ahead of its more mediocre 1997 midterm performance, when it gained only three new seats. In this sense, the PAN's losses, while severe, were partly a correction for the boost the party experienced in the 2000 elections. Indeed, its losses in 2003 suggested that the party's gains in 2000 were the result of the coattail effect related to Fox's victory, which actually fell short of his own share of the vote. In this sense, the 2003 elections proved that the PAN never actually succeeded in building a party organization capable of maintaining the gains made in 2000. The implications for the PAN's near-term electoral prospects and its ability to govern effectively were potentially quite gloomy. Indeed, many critics pointed to the failures, mistakes, and

Table 6.4 Party Representation in the Chamber of Deputies Before and After 2003 Midterm Elections

	58th Legislature (2000–2003)				59th Legislature (2004–2006)			
	District Seats	PR Seats	Total Seats	% of Seats	District Seats	PR Seats	Total Seats	% of Seats
PRI	131	78	210	42.0%	160	64	224	44.8%
PAN	136	71	207	41.4%	82	71	153	30.6%
PRD	26	28	52	10.4%	55	40	95	19.0%
PVEM	6	10	16	3.2%	3	14	17	3.4%
PT	1	6	8	1.6%	0	6	6	1.2%
Others	0	7	7	1.4%	0	5	5	1.0%

Sources: Cámara de Diputados del Congreso de la Unión at www.camaradediputados.gob.mx; Instituto Federal Electoral at www.ife.org.mx; Observatorio Electoral Latinoamericano at www.observatorioelectoral.org (accessed April 10, 2004). Some data presented by Peter Ward at "Mexico's 2003 Midterm Elections: Implications for the LIX Legislature and Future Party Consolidation," September 15–16, 2003. The Mexican Center of the Teresa Lozano Long Institute of Latin American Studies at the University of Texas–Austin.

Note: In 2000, the PCD, PSN, and PAS ran in alliance with the PRD. In 2003, the PSN and PAS lost their registrations due to failure to meet the 2 percent threshold.

setbacks of the Fox administration across multiple policy areas, as well as the politically fractured Congress that prevented implementation of Fox's agenda, as major liabilities for Mexico's political future.

Such critics overlooked two key points. First, sometimes no policy results from democratic decision-making processes. That is, when no clear consensus exists—whether because policies are poorly formulated or not supported by a sufficient majority of the population—the decision not to implement a policy is a valid, even wise result. For better or worse, the Fox administration failed to make a strong case for several key proposals it submitted to Congress and failed to convince the public that the proposed policies presented an improvement from the status quo. Meanwhile, the limitations imposed on the president's ability to pass his agenda are a reflection of the democratic process: producing changes in a democratic system often can be slow, cumbersome, and frustrating.

Second, critics also overlooked the relative success of the Fox administration. Despite the much lamented state of divided government, Congress passed more legislation under Fox than under the previous president and at least partly addressed many of the major issues of concern. While quantity of legislation does not indicate its quality or effectiveness, it is worth noting the breadth and long-term implications of legislation passed, particularly in new and long neglected policy areas, such as indigenous reform and access to public information. The fact that Fox did not come up with the resolution to Mexico's major policy challenges—economic growth, energy sector reform, poverty alleviation, strengthening the rule of law, and others—is not surprising or even necessarily troubling. These challenges could only be met over decades, not years. Still, the fact that Fox misled voters to believe that his administration could accomplish both an end to PRI rule and major policy changes was a disservice to Fox's legacy and to any would-be PAN successor.

Nevertheless, the 2003 elections left each of the three major parties within striking range of the presidency in the next federal elections in 2006. The PRI's legislative gains and consolidation of its state and local power bases left it well positioned to set the agenda in the 2006 election, with the greatest numerical odds of winning. As PRI president, Roberto Madrazo earned much of the credit for the PRI's resurrection. Madrazo personally appointed many of the PRI's candidates for state and local office in 2004. Since many were successful at ousting the PAN, even in traditional urban strongholds like Ciudad Juárez and Tijuana, they will be in a better position to support Madrazo's likely presidential bid in 2006.

Meanwhile, the PAN remained the country's second largest party, with several potential candidates aspiring to follow in Fox's footsteps. Sadly, for would-be PAN nominees, Fox's circumvention of the party in 2000 made it even more likely that party leaders would try to apply a restrictive nomination process in the next election, meaning that the party's candidate would be more representative of the PAN than the general electorate. In fact, the PAN decided to maintain a relatively closed primary (allowing only PAN members and adherents to choose the party's 2006 nominee).

A very public disagreement between Fox and former PAN President Felipe Calderón presaged the tensions that would arise in the pending primary. In June 2004, Fox publicly criticized Calderón for initiating his presidential campaign while still serving in public office; the previous year, Fox had appointed Calderón as head of PEMEX. Discomfited by Fox's reprimand, Calderón promptly resigned to pursue his campaign. Fox's criticism of Calderón was not only ironic, considering his own early campaigning activities for the presidency, but also hinted at the president's possible preference for the candidacy of Interior Secretary Santiago Creel. If the party selected Calderón, it would be a clear move toward a candidate more representative of the party; if it selected Creel, it would vindicate Fox. Much would depend on the extent to which PAN loyalists felt alienated by the Fox administration and new PAN adherents continued to identify with the party despite their second-class status.

Meanwhile, the spectacular performance of the left-leaning PRD had caught many by surprise in the 2003 election. The PRD's gains ground against both the PRI and the PAN, polling roughly one-fifth of the national vote. The PRD's performance was bolstered by the rising popularity of Mexico City Mayor Andrés Manuel López Obrador, also known by the acronym "AMLO." López Obrador, whose second-surname literally means "worker," was well known for his Spartan lifestyle, early-morning daily press briefings, and 1994 electoral showdown with the PRI's Roberto Madrazo in a fraud-riddled gubernatorial election in Tabasco. López Obrador's ambition to seek the presidency was obvious from the outset of his mayoral term (2000–2006).

While pundits likened López Obrador to Brazil's President Luiz Inácio Lula da Silva ("Lula"), López Obrador's similarities to Fox may ultimately prove more apropos. Following, in Fox's footsteps, López Obrador began early in his term as Mexico City mayor to generate popular support through impressive public works and popular social programs. Perhaps even more important, he turned for financial support to Mexico's business community, drawing early backing from Carlos Slim, Mexico's wealthiest businessman. In the absence of party organizations with organic ties to civil society, the average citizen may yet again turn to the candidate best capable of projecting his own image as Mexico's savior. López Obrador's early popular personal appeal as a candidate (akin to that of Fox) trumped voter's attention to key issues in a way that stumped many political pundits. Indeed, indications of high-level corruption in the PRD and his own administration did not deter a significant number of López Obrador's supporters. This, combined with limited options within the PAN, suggested at the time of printing that López Obrador's personal appeal could make him a strong candidate to win the presidency in 2006.

Conclusions

Indications from the first half of Fox's administration are that Fox was more committed to a national project advocating diverse points of view, rather than particular ideological or partisan objectives. His recruitment decisions and early policy directions confirm this commitment. There has been an enormous turnover among and a significant shift in the overall profile of high-ranking public officials. Fox's appointments to public office suggest a shift to a less partisan, more entrepreneurial, more regionally decentralized, and more diversely educated administration. While this may be a credit to Fox's vision of a transition team, it has also left him at odds with his own party and his electoral alliance partner, the PVEM, and generated very public tensions between Fox and his own party in the Congress. Politically, therefore, Fox is more dependent on the pure energy of his personal style and charisma than past presidents and more likely to rely on strategies long employed by poll-savvy modern U.S. presidents. Still, this Americanized style runs the risk of becoming a liability if the president is not skillful in preserving and effectively applying his political capital. Indeed, massaging data and spinning information to reflect more positively on an administration seem much closer to the PRI than to the stated PAN goals of transparency and good government.

This problem may become more severe as it becomes increasingly evident that the Fox administration has not yet developed a clear or detailed direction for public policy. Moreover, the trend is especially troublesome as it appears consistent with Fox's policies and practices as governor of Guanajuato, which generated results that were large on hype and low or at least questionable on substantive results. However, given the magnitude and variety of the tasks at hand, it is not clear that even the best-laid plans of Fox would resolve Mexico's economic underdevelopment, continued poverty and economic disparities, and growing unemployment.[90]

Indeed, it is important to realize that Fox's administration could not solve all of Mexico's problems. However, his term provided an opportunity to lay the groundwork for future advances. By moving toward a new model of efficiency and accountability in public administration, Fox could set a new standard for professionalism in Mexican society. By consolidating democratic competition and governance, Fox could enable future debates on policy that will reflect the preferences and interests of the Mexican people. And by recognizing that long-term solutions are needed to ensure economic development, Fox may be able to establish a pattern of investment in infrastructure and human capital that will enable Mexico to prosper in the twenty-first century. The key, however, is for Fox to breach the divide between rhetoric and reality by putting into practice clear, detailed, and concrete solutions of the kind that brought the PAN so much success during the 1980s and 1990s.

Notes

1. Author interview with Vicente Fox Quesada in Guanajuato (June 23, 1997).

2. Arriola, 1998; Espinoza Valle, 2000; Espinoza Valle, 1998; Mizrahi, 1996; Mizrahi, 2003; Mizrahi, 1992; Rodríguez and Ward, 1994; Rodríguez and Ward, 1995; Rodríguez and Ward, 1992.

3. Interview with Carlos Montejo (Fall 1997).

4. Shirk and Hoffecker, "Mexico in Transition: Power and Revenues Are Shifting—Gradually—to State and Local Governments," *San Diego Union-Tribune*, August 15, 1999.

5. Coll noted that one of their main challenges would be to "clean up" the local government, given that they would inherit "an administration deteriorated and 'sacked' by current functionaries, a public debt of 20 million pesos, and a level of corruption that [has produced] more than 300 aviadores" (a term used to describe government employees who report to work only to pick up their checks; they fly in on payday and then take off). "México se pinta de azul, primero fue Jalisco después Guanajuato y Yucatán," *A.M.*, February 23, 1995: 4B.

6. "Piden Empleos a Quiroz," *A.M.*, May 12, 1995: 1B.

7. Tijuana was a notable exception: "When we reviewed [Miércoles Ciudadano] with our regidores we decided that perhaps this program worked in smaller and medium-sized cities . . . . I think that contact with the citizenry should be made every day, and in a city as big as this, you would take out your desk, and the line of requests would be immense. I believe that the mayor walking around in the streets, well, it looks nice, it's friendly, you know? In the newspapers it's popular. We felt more comfortable attending to the problems [directly] in the municipal delegations, in checking with the delegate and his collaborators to find the solution to these problems and to hold meetings in the delegations." Interview with José Guadalupe Osuna Millán (1998) in Tijuana.

8. The first visitors were Victor Manuel Larios Muñoz of Lagos de Moreno and César L. Coll Carabias of Guadalajara, two of the PAN's newly elected mayors in Jalisco. Coll and Larios visited León's 7th "Citizen Wednesday" and sought the advice of their more experienced fellow panistas to help resolve problems similar to those experienced during the Medina administration.

9. Interestingly, one of the early revelations of the Citizen Wednesday program was the severity of the difficult economic situation resulting from the peso devaluation in the mid-1990s, leading to further initiatives by the Quiroz administration to provide temporary relief during the crisis. Two such programs—Help Yourself By Helping (Ayúdate Ayudando) and In León, We Give Each Other a Hand (En León Nos Damos La Mano)—provided limited New Deal–style relief in exchange for six hours of labor per day to generate small-scale public works projects. The crisis also led the municipal government to promote a more active and better funded Integral Family Development program (Desarrollo Integral de la Familia, DIF), which made special efforts to deal with an increase in the number of street children by establishing the Rescue at the Crossroads (Rescate en el Crucero) program. This program encouraged citizens to buy and hand out coupons that could be redeemed by children at Rescue centers for clothing, food, and other items. Interview with Citizen Wednesday Coordinator LCC Adriana Muñoz López in León (June 7, 1997).

10. Arriola, 1998; Espinoza Valle, 1998; Loaeza, 1999; Montalvo Ortega, 1996; Valencia García, 1998; Valencia García, 2002.

11. There the local government passed a new police code that authorized the municipality to intervene in a variety of "moral deviations," including inciting or

engaging in carnal commerce in a public place; public drinking and smoking in unauthorized zones; speaking or signing obscenities and insults in public; loud noises that offend one's neighbors; causing a panic at public events; causing danger to other persons in public places; showing the genitals in public places or events without the expressed permission of the corresponding authorities; using force, insults, or having a lack of respect toward police authorities; scandalous or disrespectful behavior in sessions of the city council or public offices; two or more persons "engaging in erotic acts without the intent to copulate"; exhibiting pornographic material in shop windows; and forms of begging in public places that put the beggar in danger or physical risk. "Estudian reglamentar 'conducta' de leoneses," *A.M.*, May 5, 1997: 1B.

12. León's Department of Fiscalization and Control (Fiscalización y Control), which regulates vice for the municipality, took a firm stance against such establishments on the grounds that the spectacle presented a "lack of morality and decent customs" and thus was a violation of the Regulations for Commercial Establishments of León. "Prohiben 'table dance,'" *A.M.*, August 8, 1995: 1B.

13. "No atentan contra moral los 'Table Dance,'" *A.M.*, August 10, 1995: 1B.

14. "Moral es . . . ir a misa los domingos," *A.M.*, October 5, 1995: 1B.

15. "Prohiben 'table dance,'" *A.M.*, August 8, 1995: 1B.

16. The Museum's director claimed that the title suggests pornographic work and was deemed inappropriate. The artist objected, claiming that his work had nothing to do with pornography; "I respect and admire the female body, thus my work may have some erotic content, but not pornographic," he argued. In the end, this conflict was given little attention by the local press and community, a reaction that seems similar to other cases of PAN censorship in and around the Bajío, where the PAN later came under attack on charges of moralism in the national press (particularly *La Jornada*). "Censura Museo de la Ciudad nombre de exposición," *A.M.*, February 28, 1997: 1B.

17. Adding to the moral tone of the PAN's first administration in Mérida was the Pope's visit in August 1993, where Mayor Ana Rosa Payán demonstrated her euphoria over the Pontiff's visit with extensive praise and a statue (the "Vicario del Cristo") to mark the "sacred site" on which relations between Mexico and the Church were reestablished. Right down to her final official words as Mayor, Payán invoked the name of the Christian god. "I want to express my greatest hopes for 1994, the year in which we will have to consolidate our anhelos [desires] of liberty, democracy and justice. May God help us." Payán, 1991.

18. Interview with Carlos Castillo Peraza in Mexico City (July 16, 1998).

19. According to Carlos Castillo Peraza, the blouse was worn without a brassiere. Getting to the bottom of this controversy revealed the importance of participant observation and field research and the limits of archival research. Incidentally, author interviews revealed the widespread use of short (above the knee) skirts in PAN offices and at political events, primarily by women. Interview with Carlos Castillo Peraza in Mexico City (July 16, 1998).

20. Interview with Carlos Castillo Peraza in Mexico City (July 16, 1998).

21. The original text read: "Abortion is not punishable . . . when the pregnancy is the result of a rape." Article 228 Guanajuato State Penal Code.

22. This was primarily the result of a response to a state poll that found 53 percent of respondents opposed the reform.

23. No doubt Gómez Morin observed their efforts with tremendous interest during his consulting activities in New York City, around the time Fiorello LaGuardia and other reformers worked to combat the Tammany Hall political machine.

24. O'Shaughnessy, 1977; Putnam, 1976; Riddell, 1974; Smith, 1979.

25. Domhoff and Ballard, 1969; Lipset and Solari, 1967; Mills, 1956.

26. Quoting Smith, 1979, pp. 78–79. See also Camp, 2002; Camp, 1995.

27. Arriola Woog, 1988; Camp, 1989; Chand, 2001; Shadlen, 2000.

28. Cornelius and Craig, 1991; Fagen and Tuohy, 1972; Langston, 1993; Langston, 1994.

29. Suárez Farías, 1991.

30. Centeno, 1997; Centeno, 1990; Lindau, 1992.

31. Camp, 1995.

32. Oppenheimer (1998) provides a riveting journalistic account of the complicated events that brought Zedillo to the PRI candidacy and the presidency. Carlos Salinas de Gortari (2002) provides an interesting alternative version of these events, p. 272.

33. Camp, 1995.

34. In fact, with the exception of military officers, all of these publicly educated cabinet members were graduates of the UNAM.

35. Camp, 1995.

36. Arriola, 1998; Cabrero Mendoza, et al., 1996; Cabrero Mendoza, et al., 1995; Campuzano Montoya, 1995; Hernández Vicencio, 2001; Mizrahi, 1996; Mizrahi, 1993; Mizrahi, 1992; Mizrahi, 1998; Rodríguez and Ward, 1994; Rodríguez and Ward, 1995; Shirk, 1999.

37. Interview with Vicente Fox Quesada in Guanajuato (June 23, 1997).

38. Ibid.

39. At least six members of Fox's administration (Martín, Camarena, Mendoza, Pons, Brehem, and Gadsden) continued in their positions from the previous administration of interim PAN Governor Carlos Medina.

40. Rionda, "El arranque: Fox y su gente," *El Nacional de Guanajuato*, June–December 1995.

41. The most notable personnel shift occurred on the one-year commemoration of his June 2 victory, when President Fox married one of the eight high-level female Foxistas, Martha Sahagún, who then served as his official spokesperson. Thereafter, Sahagún left her position as his spokesperson and was replaced by Francisco Ortiz Ortiz.

42. D'Artigues, 2002.

43. In this sense, Creel's appointment is highly significant. Mexico's Interior Secretariat was long seen as a sinister organization responsible for maintaining political control through electoral fraud and intimidation of members of the opposition. To his cabinet, Fox also appointed Secretary of Agriculture Javier Usabiaga Arroyo, a PAN member from Guanajuato (who also participated in Fox's gubernatorial administration in the same capacity), and Secretary of Social Development Josefina Vásquez Mota, a PAN federal deputy elected in 2000. She became one of three women on Fox's cabinet, among a total of eight initial high-level female appointees in the Fox administration.

44. In July 2002, Molinar was replaced by former PAN legislator Francisco José Paoli Bolio, who took over the ministry's constitutional reform project.

45. Presenting on a panel at a conference on conservative parties in Latin America, sponsored by the Center for U.S.-Mexican Studies of the University of California, San Diego in 1998, Amparo launched severe criticisms of the PAN and expressed her adamant belief that Fox could not possibly win the 2000 election. Author's notes.

46. D'Artigues, 2002.

47. Biographical description available at www.presidencia.gob.mx, accessed September 21, 2001.

48. President Carlos Salinas' Secretary of Programming and Budget, Pedro Aspe, was also Gil Díaz's student and a former mentor to Zedillo.

49. While the entire Fox team was geographically heterogeneous, his cabinet was less so. Indeed, when compared to Zedillo's cabinet, the differences were somewhat less dramatic. While 68 percent of Zedillo's cabinet originated in the Federal District, the same was true for 59 percent of Fox's cabinet.

50. For the purposes of this discussion, northern Mexico includes eleven entities within two states of the U.S. border: Baja California, Baja California Sur, Sonora, Sinaloa, Chihuahua, Durango, Coahuila, Zacatecas, Nuevo León, San Luis Potosí, and Taumalipas. Central Mexico includes the thirteen states of Colima, Nayarit, Jalisco, Aguascalientes, Guanajuato, Querétaro, Hidalgo, Michoacán, Mexico State, Morelos, Puebla, Tlaxcala, and Veracruz. Southern Mexico includes the seven states of Guerrero, Oaxaca, Tabasco, Chiapas, Campeche, Yucatán, and Quintana Roo.

51. It is unclear whether Martha Sahagún's undergraduate degree was completed abroad during her studies in Dublin, Ireland.

52. One final observation related to education and recruitment patterns in the Fox administration relates to the case of Education Secretary Reyes Tamez Guerra. Fox's decision to appoint Tamez Guerra was based on a campaign promise he made to accept the nominee of the National Association of Universities and Institutions of Higher Education (Asociación Nacional de Universidades e Instituciones de Educación Superior, ANUIES).

53. Among them were Ramón Muñoz (Governmental Innovation), Javier Usabiaga Arroyo (Agricultural Secretary), José Luis Reyes Vázquez (Justice and Security Advisor), and Carlos Flores Alcocer (Office of the Presidency for Strategic Planning and Regional Development). Even spokeswoman-turned-bride Martha Sahagún of Michoacán formed a part of this group because of her service in Fox's gubernatorial administration.

54. Interview with PAN consultant Fredo Arías King in Mexico City (June 2, 2001).

55. Also of irritation to many Panistas was that Alfonso Durazo left the ranks of the PRI only recently before joining the government as Fox's own personal secretary. Núñez, "Pide Fox a panistas respaldar su gestión," *Reforma*, August 26, 2001: Section A1.

56. Lujambio, 2000.

57. Weldon, 2002.

58. At the time of printing, President Fox also issued one subsequent veto in the Spring 2004 term. Weldon (Fall 2003) notes that the presidential veto was relatively common from 1917–1969 but was not used from 1970 to 2001.

59. Compiled from the Mexican Congressional Report Series, CSIS Mexico Project. See Weldon, 2002; Weldon, 2003.

60. In 2002, for example, the PAN succeeded in passing amendments and legislation to provide a constitutional basis for congressional legislation on tourism, to clarify procedures for the substitution of legislators who need to leave their term of office, to regulate franchises, and to regulate electronic transactions. Weldon, 2002.

61. The author credits Luis Miguel Rionda for providing much of the background on Guanajuato and particularly those insights gained from collaboration between the two authors on a conference paper on this subject. See Rionda and Shirk, 2001.

62. Rionda, "Vicente Fox: ¿mito o realidad?" *Dossier político*, June 23, 1996.

63. In the past, plans presented by both PRI Governor Rafael Corrales Ayala in 1986 and by PAN interim-Governor Carlos Medina Plascencia during each of his four years in office (1991–1995) were presented in a timely fashion and tended to be extremely detailed. In contrast, critics complained that Fox's plan was more like a "sales brochure" than an actual governmental plan. Ibid.

64. Ibid.

65. Rionda, "Un gobierno en busca de brújula," *El Nacional de Guanajuato*, June 30, 1996.

66. Rionda, "Comentarios a una entrevista a Fox," *El Nacional de Guanajuato*, July 7, 1996.

67. One result was the much publicized conflict that developed between Fox and President Zedillo's then Secretary of Social Development Esteban Moctezuma. Each of the two public figures utilized the indicators and data generated by their respective sources and drew radically different pictures of Guanajuato's political reality.

68. Rionda, "Un gobierno en busca de brújula," *El Nacional de Guanajuato*, June 30, 1996.

69. Rionda argues that the Center for Human Development (Centro para el Desarrollo Humano) was founded as a counterpart to an organization founded in Pakistan by the economist Mahbub ul Haq, an expert on issues of human development. Ibid.

70. Stavenhagon, 2003.

71. The EZLN remained inactive at the time of printing in 2004.

72. In one of the best treatments of this program, Spalding points out that few microcredit programs had the requisite experience in microcredit lending (three years) or a sufficiently high loan recovery rate (93 percent) to qualify, and many savings and loan programs did not have the legal status necessary to participate. Spalding, 2001.

73. Ibid., p. 13.

74. Pardinas, 2004; Spalding, 2001.

75. Pardinas, 2004, pp. 71–72.

76. For example, the lack of port infrastructure in Nicaragua hindered potential linkages between Mexico's footwear industries and leather producers in Central America's poorest countries. Author interview in León, Nicaragua (September 12, 2003) of Leonel Aguilar, a leather producer in Nicaragua who exports to Fox's home state of Guanajuato.

77. Spalding, 2001, p. 33.

78. Spalding observes a "notable shift in the social discourse and formal vision surrounding social policy" in Latin America and distinguishes the distinction between the "old style" interventionist and redistributive social policies of the 1960s–1970s, and the "new style" social policies that emphasized market incentives and individual responsibility as a means for combating poverty in the 1980s and 1990s. Ibid., p. 33.

79. According to Spalding, one of the most significant "on-going challenges for social policy development in a neoliberal age" is that "market-oriented social policy initiatives are often less successful at reaching the most impoverished, [while the] best targeted programs are those not centered on the role of the market." Ibid., p. 16.

80. Pardinas, 2004, pp. 71–72.

81. Arzt, 2003.

82. Remarks of Marcelo Ebrard at the Conference on "Reforming the Administration of Justice in Mexico," May 16, 2003. Center for U.S.-Mexican Studies, University of California–San Diego. Wayne A. Cornelius and David A. Shirk, Conference Report, *Reforming the Administration of Justice in Mexico* available at http://usmex.ucsd.edu/justice.

83. Interview with Felipe Calderón, July 1999.

84. Bergman and Azaola, 2003.

85. Author's notes. Remarks by Santiago Creel at the conference on "State Reform in Mexico" sponsored by the Center for U.S.-Mexican Studies, University of California–San Diego, in collaboration with Mexico's Ministry of the Interior on April 2–3, 2004.

86. For example, a proposal to establish the autonomy of official information sources, namely, the National Institute of Statistics and Geographic Information (Instituto Nacional de Estadística y Información Geográfica, INEGI) and the Federal Institution for Information Access, would reduce the potential for manipulation of information by the reigning executive.

87. Author's notes. Remarks by Francisco José Paoli Bolio at the conference on "State Reform in Mexico" sponsored by the Center for U.S.-Mexican Studies in collaboration with Mexico's Ministry of the Interior on April 2–3, 2004.

88. Carbonell, 2000.

89. At the time of the Mitofsky poll, public support for reelection increased incrementally from 16 percent to 18 percent when respondents were prompted with information about the advantages of reelection. Consulta Mitofsky at www.consulta.com.mx accessed February 17, 2004.

90. Here Fox's ability to direct domestic circumstances will depend heavily on the fate of the U.S. economy, with which Mexico's own has grown inextricably intertwined by nearly two decades of economic liberalization.

7

Mexico's New Politics and the Prospects for Democracy

The influence of the Party, in more than half a century of constant work, has been invaluable for our Country. Its presence in Mexico's political panorama has left its footprint everywhere, fostering the values and concerns that go on helping to forge the civic consciousness.

—María Elena Álvarez de Vicencio, 2001[1]

The 2000 victory of Vicente Fox was heralded worldwide as the coming of democracy to Mexico. While true in many ways, this sweeping observation ignored the struggles that came both before and after this watershed event. Indeed, important as it was, Fox's victory was only the transition from PRI rule, a mere step in Mexico's larger political transformation. The crumbling of PRI authoritarianism and the rise of democracy in Mexico took place not in the course of a single campaign or election, but over the course of decades. The PAN had been a principal player in Mexico's political transformation from the moment of its birth in 1939 and through the long years of struggle against PRI hegemony and repression. In many ways, it was an appropriate vindication that, through its survival and struggle over the course of six turbulent decades, the PAN ultimately became the vehicle for democracy's dramatic debut in 2000.

The path to victory was neither easy nor certain. The PAN's accumulation of electoral support and administrative experience in the cities and states of the Mexican periphery required the party to wrestle with significant organizational challenges and internal transformations that were less obvious to outsiders. In exploring why and how the PAN rose to become a vehicle both for Mexico's transition and its transformation, this book has emphasized these subnational and organizational challenges. Focusing on these aspects of the PAN provides useful insights into the dilemmas of democratization for those who sought to promote it.

Moreover, this emphasis sheds light on important aspects of Mexican politics that traditionally have been ignored. The underlying assumption of much scholarship on Mexico was that its post–Revolutionary political system was a massive monolith, dominated by national-level actors and institutions. The PRI's labyrinthine powers were seemingly as impenetrable for scholars as for opposition groups seeking representation in the political system. Hence, for many years, the nature of Mexico's political system prevented observers from paying much attention to what went on inside its parties, particularly the PRI. Instead, the parties were treated as black boxes in scholarly analyses that focused more on macro-level trends and events that seemed to set the national agenda and perpetuate the status quo. Compared to Mexico's giant—its Goliath—the PRI, the PAN appeared minuscule and irrelevant.

Likewise, Mexico's subnational arena was often treated as a place of peripheral concern. Events on the fringes were often dwarfed in the eyes of political observers, as they were more focused on national and international crises and events that shaped Mexico's macro-political context. The "many Mexicos" that existed at below the radar of national-level politics, geographically and culturally, appeared of marginal importance and impact. Indeed, the profiles of Mexico's national leaders—born and bred in the capital and groomed for power within its national structures—gave little indication to the contrary. All of these factors contributed to a tendency toward system-level analysis and interpretation of Mexico's political past, present, and future.

Yet, the story of Mexico's political transformation, particularly as observed through the experience of the PAN, necessitates some reconsideration of the significance of the internal life of parties and of subnational politics. The PAN's fascinating story clearly illustrates that Mexico is no longer a monolith and probably never was. The PAN's internal institutional life and subnational strategies were of critical importance not only to its own development, but to the transformation of the Mexican political system. Both arenas shaped the strategies and decisions that contributed to the course of regime change and consolidation, and both arenas will be of central importance in shaping Mexico's new political future.

The Life of the Party in Mexico

Political parties can exist without democracy, but democracy cannot exist without parties. Mexico's experience vividly illustrates this truism. Single-party hegemony ultimately gave way to multiparty democracy through the deliberate struggles of determined political actors, mobilized and organized as teams of men and women with shared principles and objectives. That is, Mexican authoritarianism was overcome by what Max Weber called the children of democracy: those who organized and supported actual political parties.

Understanding the role that parties played in Mexico's transformation and will continue to play in shaping democratic development in the future will require careful attention to their internal organization and dynamics.

Much scholarly inquiry into the role of political parties in the mid-twentieth century ventured away from such factors; instead, it focused on the exogenous, systemic variables that shaped party behavior: class structures, the design of electoral institutions, and cultural shifts of ideology and political participation. While these factors are by no means unimportant, they are not sufficient to explain the political development and strategic behavior of political parties. The PAN's experience suggests that the life of a party is also shaped in very significant ways by its internal context, including the strategic interactions, material constraints, institutional design, and even cultural aspects of its organization. In short, the PAN's experience shows the importance of the internal life of parties as they respond to their external environments.

The PAN's internal institutional design and its different, sometimes competing, currents shaped its organizational development and responses to shifting external opportunity structures in fundamental ways. While the party attracted a wide variety of activists and drew on the political philosophies of a rich and diverse pool of distinguished leaders, the two predominant currents within the PAN stemmed directly from recruitment patterns and lines of political thought set by its two main founders, Manuel Gómez Morin and Efraín González Luna. Deprived of opportunities to serve in government, the best, brightest, and most committed members of the party occupied posts within the PAN, which, in turn, contributed to the organization's rich internal life and sound organization. In many ways, the strong role and insulation of party leaders in the PAN helped to ensure the party's long-term survival. As their primary arena of political activity, these leaders worked to develop highly structured and institutionalized internal procedures and organization within the PAN. These structures then shaped the collaboration and competition between party leaders and activists who affiliated with one or the other currents within the organization.

One of the central dilemmas for the PAN and the single issue that generated the most internal tension throughout its different currents was the party's relationship to the political system. The PAN almost constantly wrestled with the issue of whether and how to participate in Mexico's sham democracy, in which the PAN was nearly always destined to lose against the hegemonic PRI. Party leaders were especially divided over the question of how vigorously to protest instances of fraud and whether or how to negotiate acceptable compromises that would satisfy the party's long-term objectives of bringing democracy to Mexico. Within the PAN, party leaders frequently found themselves at odds not necessarily because they disagreed on this goal but because they had different time horizons and senses of urgency. Different perspectives contributed to tensions over the choice between conciliation and conflict in Mexico's divided "loyal" opposition.

The party's more politically assertive elements pushed for electoral participation and also sought to protest instances of fraud and electoral manipulation. The party's more cautious elements, in contrast, saw the value of collaboration with the regime to negotiate key reforms that increased the party's access to power and longer-term change, such as the introduction and expansion of proportional legislative representation and the strengthening of electoral oversight. Ironically, the more the PAN attempted to take advantage of new spaces won through conciliation, the more this brought the party into conflict with the PRI, as witnessed by the bloodshed in electoral conflicts that occurred in León, Tijuana, Mérida, and elsewhere. Such instances of conflict and repression contributed to heightened internal tensions within the PAN.

Indeed, the internal disarray of the 1970s was in many ways a referendum on the party's pragmatic conciliation with the regime in the face of significant instances of repression experienced in state- and local-level contests. In that period, there was a shift from the conciliatory leadership of PAN Party President Adolfo Christlieb, a promoter of the party's Catholic identity, to the more confrontational leadership style of José Angel Conchello, a champion of the party's more secular and business-minded elements. These two orientations came into conflict in the mid-1970s as the PAN sought to capitalize on the regime's diminished legitimacy. The struggle between Conchello and González Morfín rearticulated the twin profiles of the party, as the headstrong businessman from Monterrey clashed with the son of the cerebral and religiously oriented González Luna.

These internal tensions had important spillover effects on the larger Mexican political system, because the PAN's resulting failure to produce a presidential candidate in 1976 caused the PRI to introduce new institutional measures to bolster opposition parties. The introduction of a slightly more generous system of proportional representation increased opportunities for the PAN and for other opposition parties. Moreover, while Conchello lost the battle over the party's presidential nominee in the 1976 election, he ultimately won the war to promote a more assertive electoral strategy for the PAN in the 1980s and 1990s. The party's deliberate efforts to recruit disaffected elements from the private sector, in the vein of Conchello, helped to invigorate the party and contributed to its electoral successes at the local and state levels. Important gains made by these new activists in the 1980s laid a foundation for the party's electoral progress and successful governance in the 1990s. Yet even here, the PAN's strategy of electoral assertiveness ran up against significant resistance from the regime.

For this reason, the regime's political crisis in the wake of the fraudulent 1988 presidential election and PAN party leaders' decision to take advantage of the new strategic dynamics of the Mexican party system presented a critical juncture for both the PAN and for Mexico. That is, the emergence of a new, leftist opposition party reshaped the dynamics of party competition in ways that enabled the PAN to benefit from its electoral assertiveness and its at least tacit conciliation with the regime. The PAN's cooperation with the PRI to ensure Mexico's "governability" during the Salinas administration yielded key political reforms that increased electoral transparency and brought greater recognition of PAN local and even state electoral victories.

Even so, the PAN's progress did not bring an end to the internal tensions over the party's political orientation and strategies. The growth of the party during the 1980s and 1990s brought new tensions among the party's predominant currents. The rise of the PAN's new entrepreneurial elements in the footsteps of Conchello—the likes of Clouthier and Fox—was a serious concern for party leaders such as Carlos Castillo Peraza and Felipe Calderón, who sought to protect their own vision and influence within the party. Ultimately, those tensions led to Fox's deliberate circumvention of the PAN to seek the party's nomination and the presidency through a more independent, candidate-centered campaign.

Many Mexicos: The Subnational Politics of the PAN

The PAN's gradual triumph through state and local victories—whether a deliberate or de facto strategy of democracy through federalism—illustrated the importance of Mexico's subnational arena. During the 1980s, the champions of Conchello's vision of the PAN, the prodigal entrepreneurs who abandoned the party and politics in general during the 1950s and 1960s, returned to the political arena in response to the regime's poor handling of the economy and a variety of political crises.

Significantly, these committed newcomers entered the PAN and rapidly acquired positions as Mexico's mayors, city council members, national and state legislators, and even governors. From the 1980s to the 1990s, the number of PAN municipal governments increased more than tenfold, the party's candidates captured and retained key state governments, and one in three Mexicans became subject to the policies and decisions of PAN administrations.

In many ways, the PAN's experience at the subnational level sheds further light on Lesley Byrd Simpson's (1967) notion that there are "many Mexicos." That is, at the subnational level, the PAN came to represent not only distinct geographic and regional identities, but also the face of a newly emerging, modern Mexico. In other words, the PAN represented many Mexicos—distinguished by geography, regional identity, political culture, and even generations.

With the party's accumulation of electoral successes in the 1980s and 1990s, political observers gradually began to characterize the PAN as a party of the industrially developed North. To be sure, the PAN had a strong organizational presence and important successes in states such as Baja California, Chihuahua, and Nuevo León. Moreover, these states stood at the forefront in pushing Mexican politics toward change, both in the 1910 Revolution and during Mexico's protracted process of democratization. In addition, the PAN developed a substantial presence in Mexico's North, Center, and even the South. Indeed, the party's traditional organizational presence and early electoral successes in the states of Guanajuato and Yucatán, as well as in major cities throughout Mexico, belies more recent characterizations of the PAN as a regional party.

In fact, a more accurate characterization of the PAN is that it is an urban party, one supported by elements of the figurative North that resides in most metropolitan centers. In this sense, the PAN could well be characterized as a latter-day movement for Mexican urban reform, reminiscent of early twentieth-century progressives who toppled the mass-oriented, ethnic political machines in the United States. Similarly, the PAN historically was composed primarily of educated and morally conscientious—their detractors would say sanctimonious—urban professionals and middle-class actors. Indeed, the PAN traditionally drew its strength from more educated, professional, and upwardly mobile citizens than those represented by the PRI. As Mexico's cities grew in size and importance in the later half of the twentieth century, this constituency expanded and proved an important asset for the PAN. In effect, the PAN capitalized on the emergence of a "new" Mexico that grew increasingly urbanized, both figuratively and literally, over the latter part of the twentieth century (see Table 7.1). The rise of Vicente Fox and other political entrepreneurs who flocked to the PAN was, in many ways, the emergence of a truly modern Mexico. Fox, like the PAN, was an expression of a new brand of Mexican federalism, in which politics was increasingly asserted from the bottom up, due to the empowerment of ordinary citizens, city council members, mayors, state legislatures, and governors.

Table 7.1 Rural and Urban Support for 2000 Presidential Candidates in Exit Poll Data

	Rural	Urban
Vicente Fox Quesada	27.9	48.0
Francisco Labastida	49.4	33.4
Cuauhtémoc Cárdenas	21.6	16.1
Gilberto Rincón Gallardo	0.4	1.9
Manuel Camacho	0.7	0.6
Total	100	100

Source: Alianza Cívica, www.alianzacivica.org.mx/, accessed June 11, 2001.

In short, the Mexico of the PAN was not geographically limited to the country's industrially developed North, but extended to the urban and modern elements found everywhere in Mexico, albeit with greater prevalence in the North. In some ways, this aspect of Mexico's political transformation was also part of a trend felt throughout Latin America and the world, thanks to the forces of modernity and globalism. These forces empowered local and regional actors by providing instantaneous transmission of events and ideas, rapid transportation across distances, and the economic integration of the country's center and periphery. However, this is not to suggest that modernity triumphed in Mexico. Sadly, the Mexico of the PAN is not the Mexico of the majority of the country's population. Most Mexicans are poor, undereducated, and often hungry. While the PAN may aspire to change these conditions—not solely for the purpose of expanding its own political constituency—two of the greatest long-term challenges for the party will be (1) the development of a political program that advances the rational and practical agenda of Gómez Morin, the architect of Mexico's financial system, while (2) remaining true to the compassionate, humanistic ideals of men like Christlieb, González Luna, Castillo Peraza, and Calderón. Otherwise, the huge gap between the majority of the people and those who have the ability to make changes will give the party little political purchase in the future.

Most important, in the new political context, all major parties now have a direct stake in the longtime PAN agenda of fortifying Mexican federalism. Strengthening state and local governments, as well as the federal legislature and judiciary, could make politics less of a zero-sum competition to control the presidency. PRI and PRD support for such initiatives would ensure their own access to power and resources in the future. Similarly, granting reelection to legislators and state and local officials would allow the parties to gain more experienced candidates and consolidate existing political spaces. In any case, neither the PRI nor the PRD wants to see the PAN bring back the old rules and become the PRI of the next millennium. Nor is the PAN currently in a position—ideologically or organizationally—to become the new hegemon.

Fox, the PAN, and the New Opposition

The challenges of Mexico's new political context became evident soon after Fox's election. For Fox and the PAN, the internal divisions that contributed to Fox's circumvention of the party had major implications. The composition of his government—made up overwhelmingly of members of his campaign staff and people from outside the PAN—was one significant result of the party's divisions and contributed to further disappointment for PAN members who either coveted spoils or believed that a clean slate was necessary to root out PRI corruption. More important, while Fox's highly independent campaign was successful in ensuring his election, it failed to strengthen the party and transfer residual coattails to his team members running for legislative office. This not only left him short on PAN partisans in the Mexican Congress, but also was aggravated by disagreements between Fox and members of his own party on key policy questions such as tax reform and indigenous rights. Fox's inability to translate his own image and popular appeal to the PAN was confirmed in the July 2003 midterm elections, when the PAN lost legislative seats despite the overwhelming popularity of the president leading up to the election.

The tensions between the PAN and the Fox government were definitely problematic at the outset of his administration, particularly as there appeared to be little consensus on key programs he placed at the front of his agenda, notably indigenous and fiscal reforms. As was common for the party at local and state levels, the PAN seemed confused about how to handle party-government relations at the national level. Indeed, in the early part of Fox's term, the PAN seemed to retain an opposition mentality toward his administration. This gradually began to change. Fox met regularly with party leaders and even made very public overtures of goodwill toward Senator Diego Fernández de Cevallos, who initially emerged as one of Fox's greatest critics and legislative obstacles. A former presidential candidate and longtime rival of Fox, Fernández was one of the PAN's most powerful party leaders during the Fox administration; winning him over—or at least keeping him quiet—was a major accomplishment. In the end, the finite nature of Fox's term as president seemed to be the main factor alleviating party-government relations; there were few reasons for hostility as the party grew more focused on the next election and on insulating the party from the possibility of another renegade nominee.

Meanwhile, both the PRI and the PRD had to adapt to Mexico's new political context. That is, in the wake of Fox's election, both parties faced internal contests for power within their own organizations and adjusted to new subnational trends that would greatly impact their development in the post-2000 context. PRI and PRD party leaders began to adjust to the new political reality by maneuvering within their organizations and consolidating local bases of support, always with an eye to the next presidential elections in 2006.

On the one hand, it became clear early on that the PRI was in a fragile state, and many wondered whether the party would survive without its lock on power. Yet, the PRI not only survived, it actually seemed to thrive in a new context of newly empowered subnational political actors. No longer dependent on the downward flow of resources from an all-powerful president, the PRI state and local machines came into their own and helped deliver significant national-level gains in the 2003 midterm election. Moreover, the contest among national party leaders—notably, Roberto Madrazo and Esther Gurría—played out in terms of their ability to draw on local and regional support within the party. While these contests for power in the PRI will involve many unknowns and surprises, one certainty is that subnational dynamics will be a critical determinant of party politics and its ultimate fate.

On the other hand, the new Mexican political reality seemed more significant for the PRD than for any other party. Until Fox's victory, the 1988 election that gave birth to Mexico's new left was its only real shot at capturing the presidency; indeed, some fervent supporters still believe that PRD founder Cuauhtémoc Cárdenas actually won that election. In Mexico's new political scenario—where party politics and subnational players have a significant new role—the PRD may be poised to expand its popular base of support dramatically and even to compete seriously for the presidency. The improved prospects for success by an independent-minded candidate with limited ties to his or her party leadership, as embodied by Fox, will similarly hold true for future candidates of the PRD. Assuming that the PRD can identify pragmatic candidates capable of winning elected office—or vice versa (that such candidates identify themselves with the PRD)—Mexican politics may well become a contest between real but moderate ideological alternatives.

Once again, observers will need to look to the subnational arena to predict (or at least understand) the possibilities and outcomes of this new context. In the aftermath of Fox's victory, many prematurely looked to national-level figures in his cabinet or the opposition to make early predictions about the 2006 elections. However, those who understood the implications of the new dynamics of Mexican party politics and the importance of the periphery also predicted the probable rise of a new kind of candidate. Like Fox, such a candidate may draw on mass media appeal and locally cultivated experience to outmaneuver political rivals both inside and outside the party. In this sense, Fox opened the door to a new context, wherein promising outsider candidates—competing in increasingly competitive, expensive, and vicious campaigns with highly unpredictable electoral results—are likely to succeed and become par for the course. In this context, Mexico's presidency is now within reach of candidates who, like Fox, successfully cultivated their own personal bases of support though savvy media appeals and by using subnational elected office as a means for obtaining national recognition. Hence, as Mexico moves toward the 2006 elections and beyond, the real question is whether Mexico's parties will learn lessons from the experiences of Fox and the PAN to build stronger connections among such candidates, parties, and government.

Mexico's New Politics: Prospects for Democracy

The Fox administration was faced with one of the most difficult challenges of governmental and political reform in Mexico's history. When the PRI always won, the rules of the game were clear. Now that Mexico has lost that equilibrium, individual politicians and political parties are maneuvering and learning to maneuver on a new, more level playing field. As they adjust to the new context, many of the old rules will need to be reconsidered and revised, as Mexico's citizens, interest groups, parties, and—crucially—the legislative, executive, and judicial branches vie for relatively balanced positions of power and, in so doing, advance the democratic development of the nation.

Despite the challenges Fox faced during his administration, most signs pointed to the positive side of the "change" he had promised during his 2000 campaign. That change was not, perhaps, what many anticipated or hoped for, but it was a change for the better, nonetheless. Change meant orderly adherence to democratic procedure, instead of the massive frauds and post-election devaluation hangovers of the past. Change meant an end to the abuses of political monopoly and acceptance of the challenge of political competition and cooperation. In this sense, change meant gridlock, seen in the United States as the hallmark of the balance of power. Change meant that after 2000, the Mexican president and other politicians would be more accountable for their actions or inactions in public office. Not one of these changes was fully accomplished during the Fox administration; some had been accomplished over decades before, and some were only beginning to manifest themselves in the new political context.

Still, for all its faults, the Fox administration's overall direction seemed to confirm Mexico's continued progress toward consolidating democracy. The real dilemma for Mexico is that democracy, particularly modern democracy, is messy and uncertain. Modern democratic change is driven more by media and money than in the past, when mass incorporating organizations ruled the day through strength in numbers. In the new Mexican politics, as Jorge Castañeda observed, "Newspapers don't matter, and speeches don't matter—nothing matters but TV."[2] While this may be a bit exaggerated, the point can hardly be ignored: mass media—and the money that buys air time and short attention spans—is clearly one of the most important driving forces in modern democracy.

Even in this context, the continuing development and institutionalization of Mexico's political parties, particularly the PAN, will be of vital importance for the future of its democracy. Mexican voters have experienced an almost overnight transition to a new kind of campaign and political environment. Now empowered with effective suffrage, Mexicans—40 percent of whom live in poverty—are confronted with the kinds of slick political advertising, negative campaigns, candidate-centered appeals, and questionable financing methods that rankle and confuse citizens even in so-called advanced democratic systems like the United States. For this reason, paying attention to what happens inside Mexico's parties will be more important than ever.

While responsible, programmatic parties cannot be asked to take full responsibility for educating and mobilizing the masses, parties will continue to determine, at a minimum, what kinds of candidates emerge before the general electorate, where these candidates stand on issues that matter to voters, and how each party's successful candidates will resolve their collective action problems and administrative challenges once in office. In this sense, Mexico's parties will need to adapt to a challenging context, in which their capabilities and influences are not necessarily diminished, just different. That is the nature of Mexico's new politics and the nature of democratic change.

Notes

1. Álvarez de Vicencio, 2001, p. 165.
2. Moore, "Getting Down and Dirty in Mexico," *The Washington Post*, April 16, 2000.

Appendixes

Appendix 1 PAN Party Presidents, 1939–2004

	CEN President
1939–1949	Manuel Gómez Morin
1949–1956	Juan Gutiérrez Lascuráin
1956–1959	Alfonso Ituarte Servín
1959–1962	José González Torres
1962–1968	Adolfo Christlieb Ibarrola
1968–1969	Ignacio Limón Maurer
1969–1972	Manuel González Hinojosa
1972–1975	José Angel Conchello Dávila
1975	Efraín González Morfín
1975	Raúl González Schmall
1975–1978	Manuel González Hinojosa
1978–1984	Abel Vicencio Tovar
1984–1987	Pablo E. Madero Belden
1987–1993	Luis H. Álvarez Álvarez
1993–1996	Carlos Castillo Peraza
1996–1999	Felipe Calderón Hinojosa
1998–2004	Luis Felipe Bravo Mena

Note: CEN is the PAN Party's Comite Ejecutivo Nacional (National Executive Committee).

Appendix 2 PAN Governors, 1989–2010

	State	PAN Governor
1989–1995	Baja California	Ernesto Ruffo Appel
1991–1995	Guanajuato	Carlos Medina Plascencia[a]
1992–1998	Chihuahua	Francisco Barrio Terrazas
1995–2001	Jalisco	Alberto Cárdenas Jiménez
1995–1999	Guanajuato	Vicente Fox Quesada
1995–1998	Baja California	Hector Terán Terán
1997–2003	Nuevo León	Fernando Canales Clariond
1998–2004	Aguascalientes	Felipe González González
1997–2003	Querétaro	Ignacio Loyola Vera
1998–2001	Baja California	Alejandro González Alcocer[a]
1999–2000	Guanajuato	Ramón Martín Huerta[a]
1999–2000	Nayarit	Antonio Echeverría Domínguez[b]
2001–2007	Baja California	Eugenio Elorduy Walther
2000–2006	Guanajuato	Juan Carlos Romero Hicks
2000–2006	Morelos	Sergio Estrada Cajigal[b]
2001–2007	Jalisco	Francisco Ramírez Acuña
2001–2007	Yucatán	Patricio Patrón Laviada
2003–2010	Querétaro	Francisco Garrido Patrón
2003–2010	San Luis Potosí	Marcelo de los Santos Fraga
2003–2010	Chiapas	Pablo Salazar Mendiguchía[b]

Notes: a. Interim governors were not elected by a popular vote.

b. The PAN and other opposition parties (notably, the PRD, the PT, and the PVEM) engaged in successful electoral alliances to oust PRI candidates, as in Nayarit in July 1999, Morelos in 2000, and Chiapas in 2003.

Appendix 3 PAN Vote in Presidential Elections, 1952–2000

	Candidate	Official Vote Totals	Percent of Total Vote
1952	Lic. Efraín González Luna	285,555	7.9
1958	Lic. Luis Héctor Álvarez	705,303	9.5
1964	Lic. José González Torres	1,043,718	11.07
1970	Lic. Efraín González Morfín	1,641,336	11.93
1976	n.a.	n.a.	n.a.
1982	Ing. Pablo Emilio Madero Belden	3,700,045	15.68
1988	Ing. Manuel Clouthier del Rincón	3,267,159	17.07
1994	Lic. Diego Fernández de Cevallos	9,088,765	25.8
2000	Lic. Vicente Fox Quesada	15,989,636	42.5

Sources: Adapted from Franz A. von Sauer, *The Alienated "Loyal" Opposition: Mexico's Partido Acción Nacional* (Albuquerque: Univ. of New Mexico Press, 1974); Silvia Gómez Tagle, *La Frágil Democracia Mexicana: Partidos Políticos y Elecciones* (Mexico City: García y Valadés Editors, 1993); and Instituto Federal Electoral 2000 election results accessed at www.ife.com.mx on November 19, 2003.

Note: The PAN failed to produce a candidate in 1976.

Appendix 4 PAN Regional Performance in Presidential Elections, by State and Percentage of Vote, 1952–2000

	1952	1958	1964	1970	1982	1988	1994	2000
North								
Baja California	9.1%	39.3%	21.4%	25.5%	27.6%	24.4%	36.2%	49.7%
Baja California Sur	0.5%	6.6%	3.1%	5.3%	15.3%	19.0%	32.3%	36.2%
Coahuila	4.6%	5.1%	6.6%	8.8%	25.7%	15.3%	30.6%	48.9%
Durango	10.7%	15.3%	13.6%	13.3%	17.8%	17.0%	27.0%	41.9%
Chiapas	0.7%	2.0%	12.6%	1.1%	2.8%	3.4%	11.7%	26.4%
Nuevo León	9.6%	9.7%	15.6%	15.7%	24.2%	23.7%	39.7%	49.6%
Sinaloa	3.1%	1.9%	1.9%	5.4%	10.6%	32.1%	30.4%	23.8%
Sonora	2.3%	2.7%	1.5%	6.5%	19.8%	20.9%	38.2%	50.8%
Tamaulipas	6.3%	5.2%	3.4%	8.4%	9.8%	9.9%	26.5%	47.4%
San Luis Potosí	5.0%	5.7%	8.7%	9.8%	8.2%	21.2%	25.3%	47.5%
Zacatecas	9.7%	8.3%	20.7%	9.2%	9.7%	10.8%	22.6%	33.5%
Bajío								
Chihuahua	11.9%	35.4%	1.1%	18.3%	25.6%	38.2%	27.5%	48.7%
Guanajuato	20.3%	10.5%	20.4%	19.2%	20.1%	29.9%	29.2%	60.8%
Guerrero	2.9%	1.8%	3.0%	4.3%	4.3%	2.4%	9.4%	18.6%
Hidalgo	0.8%	1.9%	1.6%	2.8%	8.8%	5.8%	17.4%	34.6%
Jalisco	22.2%	11.0%	13.0%	17.0%	25.0%	30.8%	41.8%	53.1%
Edo. de México	2.4%	1.1%	8.3%	15.3%	22.4%	16.3%	25.5%	43.7%
Michaocán	21.5%	12.8%	13.9%	13.1%	11.3%	10.3%	15.1%	28.6%
Central								
Aguascalientes	7.4%	6.6%	8.7%	12.6%	15.8%	28.4%	36.7%	53.9%
Colima	7.4%	10.3%	12.6%	9.2%	4.6%	14.8%	29.7%	48.4%
Distrito Federal	12.1%	20.1%	20.7%	29.4%	23.4%	22.0%	26.6%	43.6%
Morelos	3.8%	4.2%	5.8%	9.7%	10.0%	7.4%	22.6%	45.5%
Nayarit	1.5%	1.3%	7.4%	2.9%	3.4%	5.7%	19.0%	30.1%
Oaxaca	4.5%	4.4%	3.4%	3.4%	6.0%	4.6%	12.9%	26.4%
Puebla	4.8%	4.8%	6.2%	14.4%	9.6%	9.9%	25.9%	42.5%
Querétaro	10.4%	10.5%	8.7%	9.2%	15.4%	19.4%	30.4%	51.9%
Tlaxala	2.4%	1.6%	1.7%	5.7%	10.1%	5.9%	24.0%	35.4%
South								
Campeche	5.8%	12.3%	4.0%	1.9%	6.5%	12.4%	18.3%	40.0%
Chiapas	0.7%	2.0%	12.6%	1.1%	2.8%	3.4%	11.7%	26.4%
Quintana Roo	2.6%	20.1%	3.0%	4.6%	3.6%	9.7%	29.0%	46.2%
Tabasco	2.1%	1.1%	0.6%	1.0%	3.5%	5.3%	7.3%	25.6%
Veracruz	1.7%	2.4%	3.2%	7.2%	3.3%	5.2%	15.7%	39.9%
Yucatán	12.2%	22.6%	14.1%	14.8%	17.7%	31.2%	40.4%	47.1%
% National vote	7.8%	9.4%	11.0%	13.8%	13.8%	15.6%	25.9%	42.5%

Notes: ☐ = Strongest five performances in presidential election year.
No candidate in 1976.

Appendix 5 PAN Membership Growth by Region

State	Region	1989	1990	1991	1992	1993	1994	1995
AGS	Bajío	635	635	35	771	680	683	2,530
BCN	North	1,017	1,014	2,309	3,386	4,318	4,321	3,783
BCS	North	51	65	422	1,122	1,123	1,123	1,768
CAM	South	150	150	150	154	264	312	527
COAH	North	1,498	2,164	2,321	3,477	3,818	3,818	2,433
COL	North	397	443	427	2,022	1,318	1,074	1,919
CHIS	South	412	444	781	1,772	1,965	2,778	2,309
CHIH	North	7,846	7,846	7,846	7,848	13,403	17,496	11,273
DF	Center	4,666	4,798	5,003	5,172	4,942	5,140	3,007
DGO	North	4,159	4,319	3,902	3,902	6,516	7,848	5,308
GTO	Bajío	2,230	2,232	5,215	9,268	9,194	10,259	7,517
GUER	South	1,828	2,019	2,486	2,486	3,523	3,864	3,402
HGO	Bajío	240	282	233	381	853	969	1,450
JAL	Bajío	2,918	2,918	6,725	6,720	11,533	13,049	9,269
MEX	Center	2,356	2,352	2,643	2,979	3,523	4,472	5,792
MICH	South	1,296	1,296	2,094	3,533	2,693	3,033	3,907
MOR	Center	263	287	390	390	540	471	881
NAY	North	372	397	425	396	423	444	1,960
NL	North	1,753	1,753	2,181	3,175	3,807	5,099	6,676
OAX	South	2,347	2,347	2,347	2,887	2,887	2,887	847
PUE	Center	3,356	3,633	3,800	5,712	7,193	7,345	4,979
QTO	Bajío	1,379	1,378	1,602	1,602	2,384	2,600	2,169
QROO	South	n.a.	n.a.	n.a.	n.a.	n.a.	n.a.	727
SLP	Bajío	1,319	1,820	2,318	2,569	7,531	8,365	6,507
SIN	North	8,733	8,732	8,232	10,607	11,170	9,953	4,717
SON	North	1,357	1,672	4,274	6,975	7,308	7,722	4,112
TAB	South	59	60	493	557	513	513	1,834
TAM	North	1,573	1,902	1,959	2,300	2,892	2,895	3,054
TLX	Center	414	469	692	767	789	879	982
VER	South	2,415	2,246	3,248	3,248	3,249	3,420	3,099
YUC	South	n.a.	n.a.	2,693	6,911	5,365	n.a	4,575
ZAC	Bajío	1,138	1,073	1,451	2,100	2,353	2,472	2,530
Total		58,177	60,746	78,697	105,189	128,070	135,304	115,843

Sources: For 1989–1994: Reveles, 1996, p. 30, and PAN, "Basic Information" pamphlet, 1994; for 1995–2000: CEN Registro de Miembros data provided by Oscar Moya and Esperanza García Reyes.

Note: Due to a major adjustment to the PAN's registration roles in 1994 there is a significant change in its membership after that year. Beginning in 1997, the PAN introduced the category of "adherents" (*aderentes*) who have not obtained full membership and privileges. The number of adherents is designated under the years marked with an "A."

Appendix 5 continued

State	1996	1997	1998	1999	2000	1997-A	1998-A	1999-A	2000-A
AGS	2,768	2,768	2,927	3,317	1,973	281	4,794	5,663	7,025
BCN	4,762	4,762	4,762	4,783	4,875	565	1,871	3,403	5,318
BCS	2,177	2,182	2,244	2,564	1,910	100	773	976	1,468
CAM	605	605	621	679	664	296	1,160	2,448	5,845
COAH	2,708	2,709	3,038	3,392	3,439	662	4,536	5,677	9,030
COL	2,983	2,983	2,984	3,163	2,277	44	1,685	2,788	3,745
CHIS	2,963	2,964	3,062	3,233	2,716	2,020	7,602	10,570	17,320
CHIH	12,955	12,975	13,142	13,504	12,711	1,042	5,809	7,295	9,831
DF	3,713	4,012	4,235	4,825	4,841	1,700	13,109	18,447	24,505
DGO	6,075	6,089	6,272	7,005	7,596	2,028	5,406	8,426	14,110
GTO	9,987	10,001	10,351	11,487	9,820	985	5,449	11,369	13,092
GUER	3,745	3,745	3,876	3,939	3,666	1,438	4,862	5,882	9,447
HGO	1,779	1,779	2,030	2,201	2,149	1,609	4,566	7,614	12,113
JAL	10,947	11,089	12,195	14,227	14,597	5,271	13,050	27,417	35,390
MEX	7,515	7,528	8,765	11,460	11,053	2,668	23,877	38,691	48,965
MICH	4,677	4,775	5,213	5,575	5,677	2,428	8,241	15,983	21,823
MOR	1,284	1,285	1,430	1,643	1,374	623	3,709	6,395	9,017
NAY	2,195	2,195	2,266	2,360	2,092	207	2,394	4,252	8,921
NL	9,155	9,160	9,543	10,166	7,991	1,093	5,305	7,665	9,234
OAX	1,289	1,289	1,602	2,234	2,673	3,851	8,120	11,931	30,693
PUE	7,257	7,257	7,690	8,213	6,873	3,156	9,912	13,594	27,510
QTO	2,737	2,737	2,940	3,433	3,203	1,307	3,937	6,717	8,549
QROO	929	929	961	993	874	189	422	682	3,028
SLP	9,291	9,313	9,452	9,949	7,019	967	6,012	17,991	22,202
SIN	6,170	6,337	6,884	7,580	7,140	1,988	6,517	9,840	16,374
SON	5,837	5,842	5,991	6,359	5,034	301	3,312	4,963	8,362
TAB	3,549	3,556	3,563	3,628	1,939	3	1,307	2,086	5,529
TAM	5,005	5,005	5,139	5,355	3,940	963	3,934	5,162	9,234
TLX	1,271	1,271	1,337	1,450	1,293	458	2,663	3,661	5,890
VER	4,103	4,104	4,515	5,472	5,185	3,094	20,623	30,991	42,401
YUC	6,023	6,343	6,358	6,570	5,744	4,234	7,608	9,465	14,885
ZAC	3,382	3,411	3,431	3,549	4,053	515	10,742	12,048	15,070
Total	149,836	151,000	158,819	174,308	156,391	46,086	203,307	320,092	475,926

Acronyms

ACJM	Catholic Association of Mexican Youth (Asociación Católica de la Juventud Mexicana)
AMLO	Andres Manuel López Obrador
CEN	National Executive Committee (Comité Ejecutivo Nacional)
CNC	National Agrarian Worker Confederation (Confederación Nacional Campesina)
CTM	Confederation of Mexican Workers (Confederación de Trabajadores de México)
FDN	National Democratic Front (Frente Democrático Nacional)
IFE	Federal Electoral Institute (Instituto Federal Electoral)
ISI	import substitution industrialization
LFOPPE	Federal Law of Political Organizations and Electoral Processes (Ley Federal de Organizaciones Políticas y Procesos Electorales)
NAFTA	North American Free Trade Agreement
PAN	National Action Party (Partido Acción Nacional)
PARM	Authentic Party of the Mexican Revolution (Partido Auténtico de la Revolución Mexicana)
PAS	Partido Alianza Social
PCD	Partido Centro Democrático
PRD	Party of the Democratic Revolution (Partido de la Revolución Democrática)
PDM	Mexican Democratic Party (Partido Demócrata Mexicano)
PRI	Institutional Revolutionary Party (Partido Revolucionario Institucional)
PRM	Party of the Mexican Revolution (Partido de la Revolución Mexicana)

PRN	National Revolutionary Party (Partido Revolucionario Nacional)
PRONASOL	National Solidarity Program (Programa Nacional de Solidaridad)
PSN	Partido Socialista Nacional
PT	Labor Party (Partido de Trabajo)
PVEM	Mexican Green Ecological Party (Partido Verde Ecologista Mexicano)
UNAM	National Autonomous University of Mexico (Universidad Nacional Autónoma de México)
UNS	National Sinarquist Union (Unión Nacional Sinarquista)

Bibliography

"Admite Cárdenas haberse reunido con CSG." *La Jornada*, April 15, 1999.
Agranoff, R., ed. *The New Style in Election Campaigns*. Boston: Holbrook Press, 1972.
Aguayo Quezada, Sergio, ed. *El Almanaque Mexicano*. Mexico City: Editorial Grijalbo, 2000.
Aguilar Camín, Héctor, and Lorenzo Meyer. *In the Shadow of the Mexican Revolution: Contemporary Mexican History, 1910–1989*. Austin: University of Texas Press, 1993.
Aguirre M., Alberto. "El PT tiene candidato." *La Jornada*, May 30, 1999.
Aguirre, Mayra Nidia. "Madrazo y Labastida rompen reglas: MBD." *El Universal*, October 5, 1999, sec. Nación: 6.
Alcocer V., Jorge. "Recent Electoral Reforms in Mexico: Prospects for Real Multiparty Democracy." In *The Challenge of Institutional Reform in Mexico*, ed. Riordan Roett. Boulder, Colo.: Lynne Rienner Publishers, 1995. 57–75.
Aldrich, John Herbert. *Why Parties? The Origin and Transformation of Political Parties in America*. Chicago: The University of Chicago Press, 1995.
Alemán Alemán, Ricardo. *Guanajuato: Espejismo Electoral*. Mexico City: La Jornada Ediciones, 1993.
Almond, Gabriel A., and Sidney Verba. *The Civic Culture: Political Attitudes and Democracy in Five Nations*. Princeton, N.J.: Princeton University Press, 1963.
Álvarez de Vicencio, María Elena. *Alternativa democrática: Ideología y fuerza del partido acción nacional*. Ed. Partido Acción Nacional. Mexico City: EPESSA, 2001.
Amezcua, Adriana, and Juan E. Pardinas. *Todos los Gobernadores del Presidente: Cuando el Dedo de Uno Aplasta el Voto Popular*. Mexico City: Grijalbo, 1997.
Arriola, Carlos. *¿Cómo gobierna el PAN?* Mexico City: Noriega Editores, 1998.
———. *Ensayos sobre el PAN*. Las Ciencias Sociales. Mexico City: Grupo Editorial Miguel Angel Porrua, 1994.
Arriola Woog, Carlos. *Los empresarios y el estado, 1970–1982*. Las Ciencias Sociales. Mexico City: Miguel Angel Porruá; UNAM, 1988.
Arzt, Sigrid. *La Militarización de la Procuraduría General de la República: Riesgos para la Democracia Mexicana*. La Jolla, Calif.: Center for U.S.-Mexican Studies, 2003.

Baer, M. Delal. *The Mexican Presidential Elections*. Washington, D.C.: Center for Strategic and International Studies, 1988.

Bailey, David C. *¡Víva Crísto Rey! The Cristero Rebellion and the Church-State Conflict in Mexico*. Austin: University of Texas Press, 1974.

Bailey, John, and Arturo Valenzuela. "The Shape of the Future." *Journal of Democracy* 8.4 (1997): 43–57.

Bazdresch, Carlos, and Santiago Levy. "Populism and Economic Policy in Mexico, 1970–1982." In *The Macro-economics of Populism in Latin America*, ed. Rudiger Dornbusch and Sebastian Edwards. Chicago: University of Chicago Press, 1991.

Beer, Samuel Hutchinson. *The Rise and Fall of Party Government in Britain and the United States, 1945–1996*. British Studies. Austin: Harry Ransom Humanities Research Center, University of Texas at Austin, 1997.

Beltrán, Ulises. "¿Por qué fallaron las encuestas?" *Revista Nexos,* August 2000.

Benjamin, Thomas, and Mark Wasserman, eds. *Provinces of the Revolution: Essays on Regional Mexican History, 1910–1929*. Albuquerque: University of New Mexico Press, 1990.

Bennett, Vivienne. "The Evolution of Urban Popular Movements in Mexico Between 1968 and 1988." In *The Making of Social Movements in Latin America: Identity, Strategy, and Democracy*, ed. Arturo Escobar and Sonia E. Alvarez. Boulder, Colo.: Westview Press, 1992. 240–259.

Bennett, W. L. *The Governing Crisis: Media, Money, and Marketing in American Elections*. New York: St. Martin's Press, 1992.

Bergman, Marcelo, and Elena Azaola. "El Sistema Penitenciario Mexicano." In *Reforming the Administration of Justice in Mexico*, ed. Wayne A. Cornelius and David A. Shirk. La Jolla, Calif.: Center for U.S.-Mexican Studies, 2003.

Berman, Paul. "Mexico's Third Way." Analysis. *New York Times,* July 2, 2000.

Blondel, Jean. *Political Parties: A Genuine Case for Discontent?* London: Wildwood House, 1978.

Brandenburg, Frank Ralph. *Mexico: An Experiment in One-Party Democracy*. Philadelphia: University of Pennsylvania, 1956.

Bruhn, Kathleen. *Taking on Goliath: The Emergence of a New Left Party and the Struggle for Democracy in Mexico*. University Park: Pennsylvania State University Press, 1997.

Cabrero Mendoza, Enrique, Rodolfo García del Castillo, and Martha Gutiérrez Mendoza. *La nueva gestión municipal en México: análisis de experiencias innovadoras en gobiernos locales*. México, D.F.: CIDE; M.A. Porrúa Grupo Editorial, 1995.

Cain, B. E., J. A. Ferejohn, et al. *The Personal Vote: Constituency Service and Electoral Independence*. Cambridge, Mass.: Harvard University Press, 1987.

Calderón Hinojosa, Felipe. *Ganar el gobierno sin perder el partido, 1996–1999*. Informes y mensajes de los presidentes del PAN. Ed. Partido Acción Nacional. Vol. 5. Mexico City: Partido Acción Nacional, 2002.

Calderón Vega, Luis. *Los Siete Sabios de México*. Mexico City: National Action Party, 1997.

Camp, Roderic A. *Mexico's Mandarins: Crafting a Power Elite for the Twenty-First Century*. Berkeley: University of California Press, 2002.

Camp, Roderic Ai. *The Zedillo Cabinet: Continuity, Change, or Revolution?* Washington, D.C.: Center for Strategic & International Studies, Americas Program, 1995.

———. *Entrepreneurs and Politics in Twentieth-Century Mexico*. New York: Oxford University Press, 1989.

Campuzano Montoya, Irma. *Baja California en tiempos del PAN*. Serie Disidencias. Mexico: La Jornada Ediciones, 1995.

"Candidatos presidenciales debaten 26 May." *Reforma*, May 26, 2000.

Carbonell, Miguel. "Hacia un Congreso profesional." In *La Cámara de Diputados en México*, ed. Germán Pérez and Antonia Martínez. Mexico City: Cámara de Diputados del H. Congreso de la Unión, LVII Legislatura, 2000.

Castañeda, Jorge. *Perpetuating Power: How Mexican Presidents Were Chosen*. Trans. Padraic Arthur Smithies. New York: The New Press, 2000.

———. *La herencia: arqueología de lasucesión presidencial en México*. Mexico City: Aguilar, Altea, Taurus, Alfaguara, 1999.

Celia Toro, María. "Mexico's War on Drugs." In *Studies on the Impact of the Illegal Drug Trade*, ed. LaMond Tullis. Boulder, Colo.: Lynne Rienner Publishers, 1995.

"Censura Museo de la Ciudad nombre de exposición." *A.M.*, February 28, 1997: 1B.

Centeno, Miguel Angel. *Democracy Within Reason: Technocratic Revolution in Mexico*. 2nd ed. University Park: Pennsylvania State University Press, 1997.

———. *The New Cientificos: Tecnocratic Politics in Mexico, 1970-1990*. Ph.D. diss. Yale University, 1990. Ann Arbor, Mich.: UMI Dissertation Services, 1993.

Cervantes, Jesusa. "Rehúye Fox acuerdo para debate." *El Universal*, May 24, 2000, sec. Primera: 1.

Cervantes Varela, Andrés. *Memorias del PAN (1973–76), Tomox*. Partido Acción Nacional. Mexico City: Partido Acción Nacional, 2002.

———. *El ejemplo de Conchello: Una aproximación a la vida y al ideario de José Ángel Conchello*. México, D.F.: EPESSA, 2000.

Chand, Vikram K. *Mexico's Political Awakening*. Notre Dame, Ind.: University of Notre Dame Press, 2001.

Christlieb Ibarrola, Adolfo. *Baja California: Avanza de la Democracia*. Mexico City: Partido Acción Nacional, 1968.

Cicero MacKinney, Roger. *Correa Racho: Tiempo de la Libertad*. Mérida: Editorial Dante, 1987.

Clouthier del Rincón, Manuel J. *Diálogos con el pueblo*. Mexico City: PAN, 1988.

"Cómo Responde el Pueblo a la Agresión." *La Nación*, June 28, 1959: 13–16.

Cornelius, Wayne A., and Ann L. Craig. *The Mexican Political System in Transition*. La Jolla, Calif.: Center for U.S.-Mexican Studies, University of California, San Diego, 1991.

———. *Politics in Mexico: An Introduction and Overview*. Reprint series, 1. San Diego, Calif.: Center for U.S. Mexican Studies, University of California, San Diego, 1984.

Cornelius, Wayne A., Ann Craig, and Jonathan Fox, eds. *Transforming State-Society Relations in Mexico: The National Solidarity Strategy*. La Jolla: Center for U.S.-Mexican Studies, University of California, San Diego, 1994.

Cornelius, Wayne A., Todd A. Eisenstadt, and Jane Hindley. *Subnational Politics and Democratization in Mexico*. U.S.-Mexico Contemporary Perspectives Series, 13. La Jolla, Calif.: Center for U.S.-Mexican Studies, University of California, San Diego, 1999.

Cornelius, Wayne A., Judith Gentleman, and Peter H. Smith. *Mexico's Alternative Political Futures*. Monograph Series, 30. La Jolla, Calif.: Center for U.S.-Mexican Studies, University of California, San Diego, 1989.

Cornelius, Wayne A., and David A. Shirk. Conference Report. *Reforming the Administration of Justice in Mexico*. May 16, 2003. Center for U.S.-Mexican Studies, University of California, San Diego. Available at http://usmex.ucsd.edu/justice.

Craig, Ann L., and Wayne A. Cornelius, eds. *Political Culture in Mexico: The Civic Culture Revisited*. Newbury Park, Calif.: Sage Publications, 1989.

D'Artigues, Katia. *El Gabinetazo*. Mexico City: Grijalbo, 2002.

"Del Propósito de Francisco I. Madero A. . ." *La Nación,* November 12, 1942: 11–12.

"Descarta Roberto Madrazo Pintado acudir a Los Pinos." *El Universal,* 1999: 6.

DiClerico, Robert E. *Political Parties, Campaigns, and Elections*. Upper Saddle River, N.J.: Prentice Hall, 2000.

Dillon, Sam. "TV Debate Energizes Challenger in Mexico." *New York Times,* April 27, 2000.

———. "Mexico's Candidates Hold First Presidential Debate." *New York Times,* April 26, 2000.

———. "Mexican Pollsters Challenge Size of Turnout in the Primary." *New York Times,* November 17, 1999.

Dillon, Sam, and Julia Preston. "As Mexican Primary Vote Nears, Angry Recriminations." *New York Times,* November 7, 1999: 1:3.

Domhoff, G. William, and Hoyt B. Ballard. *C. Wright Mills and the Power Elite*. Boston: Beacon Press, 1969.

Domínguez, Jorge I., and James A. McCann. *Democratizing Mexico: Public Opinion and Electoral Choices*. Baltimore: Johns Hopkins University Press, 1996.

Domínguez, Jorge I., and Alejandro Poiré. *Toward Mexico's Democratization: Parties, Campaigns, Elections, and Public Opinion*. New York: Routledge, 1999.

Dresser, Denise. *Neopopulist Solutions to Neoliberal Problems: Mexico's National Solidarity Program*. La Jolla, Calif.: Center for U.S. Mexican Studies, 1991.

Duverger, Maurice. *Political Parties: Their Organization and Activity in the Modern State*. New York: John Wiley and Sons, 1966.

Eisen, Peter. "Mexico Presidential Candidates Tread Lightly on Subject of Need to Reform Oil Industry." *Oil Daily,* August 25, 1999.

Eisenstadt, Todd A. *Courting Democracy in Mexico: Party Strategies and Electoral Institutions*. Cambridge; New York: Cambridge University Press, 2004.

"El Partido Oficial Esta Derrotada de Antemano en Baja California." *La Nación,* May 3, 1959: 14–15.

"Encuesta: alcanzan priístas a Fox." *El Universal,* October 4, 1999.

"Entrevista del Periodista Ricardo Rocha al Ing. Manuel J. Clouthier, Candidato del PAN a la Presidencia de la República, México D.F., 29 de noviembre de 1987." In *Dialogos con el pueblo: Los primeros cien dias de campaña*, ed. Partido Acción Nacional. Vol. 1. Mexico City: EPESSA, 1988. 13–31.

Epstein, Leon D. *Political Parties in Western Democracies*. New Brunswick, N.J.: Transaction Books, 1980.

Espinoza Valle, Víctor Alejandro, ed. *Alternancia y Transición Política: ¿Cómo Gobierna la Oposición en México?* Mexico City: Plaza y Valdés, S.A. de C.V., 2000.

———. "Gobiernos de Oposición y Participación Social en Baja California." *Frontera Norte,* 10.20 (1998): 103–20.

"Estudian reglamentar 'conducta' de leoneses." *A.M.,* May 5, 1997: 1B.

"Facinerosos del Gobierno-Partido Asaltan al PAN en Mérida." *La Nación,* December 15, 1969, Numero 1290. 2nd ed. Año 28: 2–3.

Fagen, Richard R., and William S. Tuohy. *Politics and Privilege in a Mexican City*. Stanford Studies in Comparative Politics, 5. Stanford, Calif.: Stanford University Press, 1972.

Fletcher, Frederick J. *Media and Voters in Canadian Election Campaigns*. Toronto, Canada: Dundurn Press, 1991.

Fox, Vicente. *A Los Pinos: recuento autobiográfico y político*. Mexico City: Editorial Oceano de México, S.A. de C.V., 1999.

"Front-Runners Francisco Labastida and Roberto Madrazo Steal Spotlight in Governing Party's Debate." SourceMex, http://ssdc.ucsd.edu/news/smex. September 15, 1999.

García Orosa, Luis Alberto. *Adolfo Christlieb Ibarrola: Adalid de la democracia*. México, D.F.: Epessa; PAN, 1991.

———. "El Pueblo Está Indignado; Orgulloso y Decidido, Vencerá." *La Nación*, December 15, 1969: 18–20.

———. "Por Encima de la Violencia Oficial, Venceremos." *La Nación*, August 16, 1969: 16–18.

———. "Todo Yucatán Lo Grita: ¡Ganó Correa Rachó!" *La Nación*, December 1, 1969: 5–15.

Garrido, Luis Javier. *El Partido de la Revolución Institucionalizada: La formacion del nuevo estado en México (1928–1945)*. 7th ed. Mexico City: Siglo Ventiuno Editores, [1982] 1995.

———. "The Crisis of Presidentialismo." In *Mexico's Alternative Political Futures*, ed. Wayne A. Cornelius, Judith Gentleman, and Peter H. Smith. La Jolla, Calif.: Center for U.S.-Mexican Studies, 1989. 417–434.

Gómez, Juan Cervantes. "Rechazan que Cárdenas cambie su imagen 'seria.'" *El Universal*, April 13, 2000, sec. Nación: 10.

Gómez Morin, Manuel. *Diez años de México: 1939–1949*. Colección Informes de los presidentes de Acción Nacional. Vol. 1. México: Partido Acción Nacional, 1999.

———. Letter to José Vasconcelos. In *Historia del PAN en La Nación by* Luis Bernal. Supplemental no. 1. Mexico City: Partido Acción Nacional, 1991, p. 14.

———. "Proyecto para envio de una circular a médicos, abogados, ingenieros de toda la república." Memo 1.8 (1939): 1–5.

Gómez Morin, Manuel, and Partido Acción Nacional. *Diez años de México: 1939–1949*. Colección Informes de los presidentes de Acción Nacional, 1. México: PAN, 1996.

González Luna, Efraín. *Humanismo Político*. Mexico City: Editorial Jus, 1991.

———. *Los católicos y la política en méxico*. Mexico City: Editorial Jus, 1988.

———. *El hombre y el estado*. Mexico City: Partido Acción Nacional, 1940.

Green, John Clifford, and Daniel M. Shea. *The State of the Parties: The Changing Role of Contemporary American Parties*, 3rd ed. Lanham, Md.: Rowman and Littlefield, 1999.

"Guanajuato." *unomásuno*, September 15, 1990: 1.

Guarneros, Fabiola. "Llama Labastida a la unidad." *El Universal*, October 7, 1999, sec. Nación: 6.

Hansen, Roger D. *The Politics of Mexican Development*. Baltimore: Johns Hopkins University Press, 1974.

Hart, John Mason. *Revolutionary Mexico: The Coming and Process of the Mexican Revolution*. Berkeley: University of California Press, 1987.

Hayward, Susana. "Desestima Labastida calificativo de 'oficial.'" *El Universal/San Antonio Express News*, October 26, 1999, sec. Nación: 9.

Heard, Alexander. *The Costs of Democracy: Financing American Political Campaigns*. Garden City, N.Y.: Doubleday, 1962.

Hellman, Judith Adler. *Mexico in Crisis*. 2nd ed. New York: Holmes and Meier Publishers, 1988.

Hernandez Navarro, Luis. "Mexico's Gringo-ized Vote." *Nation*, July 3, 2000: 6, 7.

Hernández Vicencio, Tania. *La experiencia del PAN: diez años de gobierno en Baja California*. Tijuana, B.C.: Plaza y Valdés Editores, 2001.

Hierro, Jorge, and Allen Sanginés Krause. "El comportamiento del sector público en México." In *El sector público y la crisis de la América Latina*, ed. Felipe Larrain and Marcelo Slowsky. Mexico City: Fondo de Cultura Económica, 1990.

Hodges, Donald, and Ross Gandy. *Mexico Under Siege: Popular Resistance to Presidential Despotism*. London: Zed Books, 2002.

Hrebenar, Ronald J., Matthew Burbank, and Robert C. Benedict. *Political Parties, Interest Groups, and Political Campaigns*. Boulder, Colo.: Westview Press, 1999.

Johnson-Cartee, Karen S., and Gary Copeland. *Inside Political Campaigns: Theory and Practice*. Westport, Conn.: Praeger, 1997.

Joslyn, Richard. *Mass Media and Elections*. Reading, Mass.: Addison-Wesley Pub. Co., 1984.

Katz, Richard S., and Peter Mair. *How Parties Organize: Change and Adaptation in Party Organizations in Western Democracies*. Thousand Oaks, Calif.: Sage Publications, 1994.

Keefe, William J. *Parties, Politics, and Public Policy in America*. 8th ed. Washington, D.C.: CQ Press, 1998.

Key, V. O. *Politics, Parties, and Pressure Groups*. New York: Crowell, 1942.

Kirchheimer, Otto. "The Transformation of the Western European Party Systems." In *Political Parties and Political Development*, ed. Joseph LaPalombara and Myron Weiner. Princeton, N.J.: Princeton University Press, 1966. 177–200.

Klesner, Joseph L. *The 1998 Mexican State Elections: Post-Election Report*. Western Hemisphere Studies Series, vol. 17, study 1. Center for Strategic and International Studies, January 1999.

———. "Modernization, Economic Crisis, and Electoral Alignment in Mexico." *Mexican Studies/Estudios Mexicanos* 9: Summer (1993): 187–224.

Knight, Alan. *The Mexican Revolution*. Cambridge; New York: Cambridge University Press, 1986.

Krauze, Enrique. *Mexico: Biography of Power*. Trans. Hank Heifetz. New York: Harper Perennial, 1997.

"La crisis de los coroneles." *La Jornada,* March 3, 1999.

La France, David. "Many Causes, Movements, Failures, 1910–1913." In *Provinces of the Revolution: Essays on Regional Mexican History, 1910–1929*, ed. Thomas Benjamin and Mark Wasserman. Albuquerque: University of New Mexico Press, 1990. 17–40.

Labastida Ochoa, Francisco. *La gente hace el cambio: que el poder a la gente*. Mexico City: Océano, 2000.

Langston, Joy. An Empirical View of the Political Groups in Mexico: The Camarillas. Working Paper. México, D.F.: Centro de Investigación y Docencia Económica, 1994.

———. *The Camarillas: A Theoretical and Comparative Examination of Why They Exist and Why They Take the Specific Form They Do*. México, D.F.: Centro de Investigación y Docencia Económicas División de Estudios Políticos, 1993a.

———. *Three Exits from the Mexican Institutional Revolutionary Party: Internal Ruptures and Political Stability*. Mexico City: Centro de Investigación y Docencia Económicas, 1993b.

LaPalombara, Joseph, and Myron Weiner. *Political Parties and Political Development*. Studies in Political Development 6. Princeton, N.J.: Princeton University Press, 1966.

Lawson, Chappell H. *Building the Fourth Estate: Democratization and the Rise of a Free Press in Mexico.* Berkeley: University of California Press, 2002.

Lawson, Chappell. *The Elections of 1997: Campaign Effects and Voting Behavior in Mexico.* Pittsburgh: Latin American Studies Association. International Congress, 1998.

Lawson, Chappell, and Joseph L. Klesner. "Political Reform, Electoral Participation, and the Campaign of 2000." In *Mexico's Pivotal Democratic Election: Candidates, Voters, and the Presidential Election of 2000*, ed. Jorge I. Domínguez and Chappell Lawson. Stanford and La Jolla, Calif.: Stanford University Press; Center for U.S.-Mexican Studies, University of California, San Diego, 2004.

Lawson, Kay. *How Political Parties Work: Perspectives from Within.* Westport, Conn.: Praeger, 1994.

———. *Political Parties and Democracy in the United States.* New York: Scribner's, 1968.

Levine, Myron A. *Presidential Campaigns and Elections: Issues, Images, and Partisanship.* Itasca, Ill.: F. E. Peacock, 1992.

Lindau, Juan David. *Los tecnócratas y la élite gobernante mexicana.* México, D.F.: Editorial J. Mortiz, 1992.

Lipset, Seymour Martin, and Stein Rokkan. "Party Systems and Voter Alignments: Cross-National Perspectives." *International Yearbook of Political Behavior Research,* vol. 7. New York: Free Press, 1967.

Lipset, Seymour Martin, and Aldo E. Solari. *Elites in Latin America.* New York: Oxford University Press, 1967.

Llamas, Jorge A. "El voto estratégico en la jornada electoral del 2 de julio." *Revista Mexicana de Comunicación,* no. 77, September–October 2002.

Loaeza, Soledad. *El Partido Acción Nacional, la larga marcha, 1939–1994: oposición leal y partido de protesta.* Sección de obras de política y derecho. 1st ed. México, D.F.: Fondo de Cultura Económica, 1999.

———. "The Emergence and Legitimization of the Modern Right, 1970–1988." In *Mexico's Alternative Political Futures*, ed. Wayne A. Cornelius, Judith Gentleman, and Peter H. Smith. Monograph Series, 30. La Jolla, Calif.: Center for U.S.-Mexican Studies; University of California, San Diego, 1989. 351–360.

Loret de Mola, Carlos. *Confesiones de un Gobernador.* Mexico City: Editorial Grijalbo, S.A., 1978.

Lujambio, Alonso. "Democratization Through Federalism? The National Action Party Strategy, 1939–2000." In *Party Politics and the Struggle for Democracy in Mexico: National and State-Level Analyses of the Partido Acción Nacional*, ed. Kevin J. Middlebrook. La Jolla, Calif.: Center for U.S.-Mexican Studies, University of California, San Diego, 2002. 47–94.

———. *El Poder Compartido: Un Ensayo Sobre la Democratización Mexicana.* Mexico City: Oceano, 2000.

Lustig, Nora. *Mexico: The Remaking of an Economy.* Washington, D.C.: The Brookings Institution, 1992.

Lux, William Robert. *Acción Nacional: Mexico's Opposition Party.* Ph.D. diss. University of Southern California. Ann Arbor, Mich.: UMI Dissertation Services, 1967.

Mabry, Donald J. *The Mexican University and the State: Students Conflicts, 1910–1971.* College Station: Texas A&M University Press, 1982.

———. *Mexico's Acción Nacional: A Catholic Alternative to Revolution.* 1st ed. Syracuse, N.Y.: Syracuse University Press, 1973a.

———. "Manuel Gómez Morin." In *Revolutionaries, Traditionalists, and Dictators in Latin America,* ed. Harold Eugene Davis. New York: Cooper Square Publishers, 1973b. ix, 210.

Maisel, Louis Sandy. *The Parties Respond: Changes in American Parties and Campaigns*. 3rd ed. Boulder, Colo.: Westview Press, 1998.

Medellín, Jorge Alejandro. "La elección interna será la primera y la última: MBD." *El Universal,* October 21, 1999, sec. Nación: 8.

Medina Valdés, Gerardo. "Entrevista." *La Nación,* 1959: 2–3.

———. "Sr. Presidente: su propio honor exige . . . la desaparación de poderes en Baja California." *La Nación,* May 31, 1959: 16–17.

"México se pinta de azul, primero fue Jalisco después Guanajuato y Yucatán." *A.M.,* February 23, 1995: 4B.

Meyer, Jean A. *The Cristero Rebellion: The Mexican People Between Church and State, 1926–1929*. Cambridge, UK: Cambridge University Press, 1976.

Michels, Robert. *Political Parties: A Sociological Study of the Oligarchical Tendencies of Modern Democracy*. New York: Dover Publications, 1959.

Middlebrook, Kevin J. *Party Politics and the Struggle for Democracy in Mexico: National and State-level Analyses of the Partido Acción Nacional*. U.S.-Mexico Contemporary Perspectives Series, 17. La Jolla, Calif.: Center for U.S.-Mexican Studies, University of California, San Diego, 2001.

Middlebrook, Kevin J. *The Paradox of Revolution: Labor, the State, and Authoritarianism in Mexico*. Baltimore: Johns Hopkins University Press, 1995.

Mills, C. Wright. *The Power Elite*. New York: Oxford University Press, 1956.

Mizrahi, Yemile. *From Martyrdom to Power: The Partido Acción Nacional in Mexico*. Notre Dame: University of Notre Dame Press, 2003.

———. *Voto retrospectivo y desempeño gubernamental: las elecciones en el estado de Chihuahua*. Pittsburgh: Latin American Studies Association, 1998.

———. *Administrar o gobernar? el reto del gobierno panista en Chihuahua*. México, D.F.: Centro de Investigación y Docencia Económicas (CIDE), División de Estudios Políticos, 1996.

———. *Rebels Without a Cause? The Politics of Entrepreneurs in Chihuahua*. Mâexico, D.F.: CIDE, 1993.

———. *The Strengths [i.e. Strengths] and Weaknesses of the PAN in Chihuahua*. México, D.F.: Centro de Investigación y Docencia Económicas, 1992.

Moctezuma Barragán, Pablo. *Los orígenes del PAN*. 1st ed. México, D.F.: Ehecatl Ediciones, 1997.

Molinar Horcasitas, Juan. *El tiempo de la legitimidad: elecciones, autoritarismo, y democracia en méxico*. Mexico City: Cal y Arena, 1991.

———. "Escuelas de interpretación del sistema político mexicano." *Revista Mexicana de Sociologia* 55.2 (1993).

Montalvo Ortega, Enrique. *México: en una transición conservadora. El caso de yucatán*. Mexico City: Instituto Nacional de Antropología e Historia and La Jornada Ediciones, 1996.

Moore, Molly. "Getting Down and Dirty in Mexico." *The Washington Post,* April 16, 2000.

———. "Rivals Trade Barbs in Mexican Debate." *The Washington Post,* April 26, 2000.

———. "In Selling of Candidates, Mexico Tries U.S. Way." *The Washington Post,* November 5, 1999: A25.

Moore, Molly, and John Ward Anderson. "'Fantastic Four' Take to the Air; Mexican Ruling Party Sets Precedent with TV Debate in Presidential Race." *The Washington Post,* September 9, 1999.

"Moral es . . . ir a misa los domingos." *A.M.,* October 5, 1995: 1B.

Moreno, Alejandro. "The Effects of Negative Campaigns." In *Mexico's Pivotal Democratic Election: Candidates, Voters, and the Presidential Campaign of 2000,* ed. Jorge I. Domínguez and Chappell Lawson. Stanford; La Jolla, Calif.: Stanford University Press; Center for U.S.-Mexican Studies, University of California, San Diego, 2003.

———. "Encuestas y resultados: un electorado imprevisible." *Enfoque,* August 13, 2000a.

———. "Negative Campaigns and Voting in the 2000 Mexican Elections." *Conference on the Mexican Presidential Election.* Cambridge, Mass.: Weatherhead Center, Harvard University, 2000b.

Müller, Wolfgang C., and Kaare Strom. *Policy, Office, or Votes? How Political Parties in Western Europe Make Hard Decisions.* Cambridge Studies in Comparative Politics. Cambridge, UK; New York: Cambridge University Press, 1999.

Nava Polina, María del Carmen, Jeffrey A. Weldon, and Jorge Yáñez López. "Cambio político, presidencialismo, y producción legislativa en la Cámera de Diputados." In *La Cámera de Diputados en México,* ed. Germán Pérez and Antonia Martínez. México, D.F.: Miguel Angel Porrúa, 2000. 85–103.

Nickson, R. Andrew. *Local Government in Latin America.* Boulder, Colo.: Lynne Rienner Publishers, 1995.

"No atentan contra moral los 'Table Dance.'" *A.M.,* August 10, 1995: 1B.

Núñez, Ernesto. "Pide Fox a panistas respaldar su gestión." *Reforma,* August 26, 2001: Section A: 1.

Oppenheimer, Andrés. *Bordering on Chaos: Guerrillas, Stockbrokers, Politicians, and Mexico's Road to Prosperity.* Boston: Little, Brown and Co., 1998.

Ortega, Carlos G. *Democracia Dirigida con Ametralladoras, Baja California: 1958–1960.* El Paso, Texas: 1961.

O'Shaughnessy, Laura Nuzzi. "Opposition in an Authoritarian Regime: The Incorporation and Institutionalization of the Mexican National Action Party (PAN)." 1977. Ph.D. diss. Indiana University. Ann Arbor, Mich.: UMI Dissertation Services, 1994.

Ostrogorski, M., and Frederick Clarke. *Democracy and the Organization of Political Parties.* New York: Macmillan, 1902.

Panebianco, Angelo. *Political Parties: Organization and Power.* Cambridge Studies in Modern Political Economies. Cambridge, UK; New York: Cambridge University Press, 1988.

Pardinas, Juan. "Fighting Poverty in Mexico: Policy Challenges." In *Mexico Under Fox,* ed. Luis Rubio and Susan Kaufman Purcell. Boulder, Colo.: Lynne Rienner Publishers, 2004.

Partido Acción Nacional. *¿Qué es el Partido Acción Nacional?* Mexico City: EPESSA, 1999.

Partido Acción Nacional. *Basic Information: Partido Acción Nacional.* Mexico City: Partido Acción Nacional, June 1996. English language. Pamphlet insert in *¿Qué es el Partido Acción Nacional?* Mexico City: EPESSA, 1999.

Payán Cervana, Ana Rosa. *1 Informe de Gobierno Municipal.* Mérida: Ayuntamiento de Mérida, Yucatán, 1991.

Pérez Franco, Aminadab Rafael. *Gobiernos Municipales del Partido Acción Nacional, 1947–1999*. Mexico City: Partido Acción Nacional, Committee Ejecutivo Nacional, 1997.

"Piden Empleos a Quiroz." *A.M.*, May 12, 1995: 1B.

Poniatowski, Elena. *La noche de Tlatelolco*. New York: Viking, 1975.

Popkin, Samuel L. *The Reasoning Voter: Communication and Persuasion in Presidential Campaigns*. Chicago: University of Chicago Press, 1991.

"Por falta de dirigencia perdió en León el PRI: Alfonso Sánchez." *A.M.*, July 12, 1988, A1.

Preciado Hernández, Rafael. *Tribuna Parliamentaria: El Caso Electoral de Baja California, Planteamiento de un Jucio Político, El Conflicto Estudiantil*. Ed. Partido Acción Nacional. Mexico: EPESSA, 1969.

Preston, Julia. "At Hopeful Moment, Feud Tears at Mexico's Left." *New York Times*, July 15, 1999.

"Prohiben 'table dance.'" *A.M.*, August 8, 1995: 1B.

Prud'homme, Jean-François. *The National Action Party's (PAN) Organizational Life and Strategic Decisions*. Ed. División de Estudios Políticos. México, D.F.: Centro de Investigación y Docencia y Económicas, 1997.

Putnam, Robert D. *The Comparative Study of Political Elites*. Englewood Cliffs, N.J.: Prentice Hall, 1976.

"Quería mucho esta ciudad." *A.M.*, March 4, 1997.

Ramírez Carrillo, Luis Alfonso. *Sociedad y Población Urbana en Yucatán, 1950–1989*. Cuadernos del CES, 36. Mexico City: El Colegio de México, 1993.

Ramírez, Lucero. "Nueva imagen de Cárdenas, sin la sonrisa ganadora del 97." *El Universal*, October 9, 1999, sec. Nación: 8.

Reveles Vázquez, Francisco. "El proceso de institucionalización organizativa del partido acción nacional (1984–1995)." Doctoral. Universidad Nacional Autonoma de México, 1996.

———. "Sistema organizativo y fracciones internas del partido acción nacional, 1939–1990." Masters. Universidad Nacional Autonoma de México, 1993.

Reyna, José Luis, and Richard S. Weinert. *Authoritarianism in Mexico*. Inter-American Politics Series, 2. Philadelphia: Institute for the Study of Human Issues, 1977.

Riddell, Adaljiza Sosa. "Who Cares Who Governs? A Historical Analysis of Local Governing Elites in Mexicali, Mexico." 1974.

Rionda, Luis Miguel. "Comentarios a una entrevista a Fox." *El Nacional de Guanajuato*, July 7, 1996.

———. "Un gobierno en busca de brújula." *El Nacional de Guanajuato*, June 30, 1996.

———. "Vicente Fox: ¿mito o realidad?" *Dossier político*, June 23, 1996.

———. "Cambio Político en Guanajuato: La Primera Experiencia Bipartidista en México, 1991–1995." Paper presented at the Latin American Studies Association (LASA) Meeting. Washington, D.C., 1995.

———. "El arranque: Fox y su gente." *El Nacional de Guanajuato*, June–December 1995.

Rionda, Luis Miguel, and David Shirk. "PAN Governance: Challenges for Vicente Fox and the National Action Party?" Paper presented at the Latin American Studies Association Meeting. Washington, D.C., 2001.

Rodríguez, Victoria. *Decentralization in Mexico: From Reforma Municipal to Solidaridad to Nuevo Federalismo*. Boulder, Colo.: Westview Press, 1997.

Rodríguez, Victoria Elizabeth, and Peter M. Ward. *Opposition Government in Mexico*. Albuquerque: University of New Mexico Press, 1995.

Rodríguez, Victoria E., and Peter M. Ward. *Political Change in Baja California: Democracy in the Making?* Monograph Series, 40. La Jolla, Calif.: Center for U.S.-Mexican Studies, University of California, San Diego, 1994.

Rodríguez, Victoria Elizabeth, and Peter M. Ward. *Policymaking, Politics, and Urban Governance in Chihuahua: The Experience of Recent Panista Governments.* U.S. Mexican Policy Report, no. 3. Austin: Lyndon B. Johnson School of Public Affairs, University of Texas at Austin; U.S.-Mexican Policy Studies Program, 1992.

"Rosas Magallón, Gobernador Electo." *La Nación,* August 9, 1959: 13–15.

"Sacó el PRI sus trucos más viejos: Obregon." *A.M.*, July 7, 1998, A2.

Salinas, Carlos. *México: The Policy and Politics of Modernization.* Trans. Peter Hearn and Patricia Rosas. Barcelona: Plaza & Janés Editores, 2002.

Sarmiento, Bernardo. "Lo Principal en el Caso de Baja California." *La Nación,* August 9, 1959: 13–15.

Sartori, Giovanni. *Parties and Party Systems: A Framework for Analysis.* Cambridge, UK; New York: Cambridge University Press, 1976.

Scott, Robert Edwin. *Mexican Government in Transition.* Urbana: University of Illinois Press, 1964.

Shadlen, Kenneth C. "Neoliberalism, Corporatism, and Small Business Political Activism in Contemporary Mexico." *Latin American Research Review* 35. 2 (2000): 73–106.

Shirk, David A. "Democratization and Party Organization: The Growing Pains of Mexico's National Action Party." Ph.D. diss. Ann Arbor, Mich.: UMI Dissertation Services, 2000.

———. "Democratization and Local Party-building: The PAN in León, Guanajuato." In *Subnational Politics and Democratization in Mexico*, ed. Wayne A. Cornelius, Jane Hindley, and Todd A. Eisenstadt. La Jolla, Calif.: Center for U.S.-Mexican Studies, University of California, San Diego, 1999.

Shirk, David A., and Leslie Hoffecker. "Mexico in Transition: Power and Revenues Are Shifting—Gradually—to State and Local Governments." *San Diego Union-Tribune,* August 15, 1999.

Simpson, Lesley Byrd. *Many Mexicos.* Berkeley: University of California Press, 1967.

Smith, James F. "Fox Rode the Gusting Winds of Change, Says Times/Reforma Survey." *The Los Angeles Times,* July 3, 2000.

———. "PRI Candidate, Top Rival Clash in Presidential Debate." *The Los Angeles Times,* April 26, 2000.

———. "Mexico's PRI Holds First Presidential Debate." *The Los Angeles Times,* September 9, 1999.

Smith, Peter H. *Labyrinths of Power: Political Recruitment in Twentieth-Century Mexico.* Princeton, N.J.: Princeton University Press, 1979.

SourceMex. http://ladb.unm.edu/sourcemex/.

Spalding, Rose J. *Early Social Policy Initiatives in the Fox Administration.* Washington, D.C.: Paper presented at the Twenty-Third International Conference of the Latin American Studies Association, September 6–8, 2001.

Stansfield, David E. "The PAN: The Search for Ideological and Electoral Space." In *Dismantling the Mexican State?* ed. Rob Aitken, Nikki Craski, Gareth A. Jones, and David E. Stansfield. New York: St. Martin's Press, 1996. 130–151.

State Reform in Mexico: Conference Report. Conference sponsored by the Center for U.S.-Mexican Studies, University of California, San Diego, in collaboration with Mexico's Ministry of the Interior. April 2–3, 2004. Available at http://usmex.ucsd.edu/conferences/gobernacion.html.

Stavenhagon, Rodolfo. "Mexico's Unfinished Symphony: The Zapatista Movement." In *Mexico's Politics and Society in Transition*, ed. Joseph S. Tulchin and Andrew D. Selee. Boulder, Colo.: Lynne Rienner Publishers, 2003.

Suárez Farías, Francisco. *Elite, tecnocracia y movilidad política en México*. Xochimilco, Mexico, D.F.: Universidad Autónoma Metropolitana Unidad Xochimilco, 1991.

"Suma de Irregularidades." *A.M.*, July 12, 1988: A1.

Sundquist, James L. "Strengthening the National Parties." In *Classic Readings in American Politics*, ed. Pietro S. Nivola and David H. Rosenbloom. New York: St. Martin's Press, 1990. 179–200.

Swanson, David L., and Paolo Mancini, eds. *Politics, Media, and Modern Democracy: An International Study of Innovations in Electoral Campaigning and Their Consequences*. Westport, Conn.: Praeger, 1996.

Taylor, Michael C. "Constitutional Crisis: How Reforms to the Legislature Have Doomed Mexico." *Mexican Studies/Estudios Mexicanos* 13:2 (1997): 299–324.

Thompson, Ginger. "Former Mexican President Reveals '88 Presidential Election Was Rigged." *The New York Times*, March 9, 2004.

Tsebelis, George. *Nested Games: Rational Choice in Comparative Politics*. California Series on Social Choice and Political Economy, 18. Berkeley: University of California Press, 1990.

Valderrábano, Azucena. *Historias del poder: el caso de Baja California*. Mexico City: Editorial Grijalbo, 1990.

Valencia García, Guadalupe. "The PAN in Guanajuato: Elections and Political Change in the 1990s." In *Party Politics and the Struggle for Democracy in Mexico: National and State-Level Analyses of the Partido Accion Nacional*, ed. Kevin J. Middlebrook. La Jolla, Calif.: Center for U.S.-Mexican Studies, University of California, San Diego, 2002. 209–259.

———. *Guanajuato: Sociedad, Economía, Política, Cultura*. Biblioteca de las Entidades Federativas. Mexico City: UNAM, 1998.

Vasconcelos, José. *The Cosmic Race: La raza cósmica*. Translated with introduction by Didier T. Jaén. Baltimore: Johns Hopkins University Press, 1997.

Vera Cuspinera, Margarita. *El pensamiento filosófico de Vasconcelos*. Mexico City: Extemporáneos, 1979.

"Verdad y Testimonio de Baja California." *La Nación*, August 16, 1959: 11–17.

Vives Segl, Horacio. *Memorias del PAN, 1977–80*, vol. 11. Mexico City: Partido Acción Nacional, 2002.

Von Sauer, Franz A. *The Alienated "Loyal" Opposition: Mexico's Partido Acción Nacional*. Albuquerque: University of New Mexico Press, 1974.

Waller, J. Michael. "The Narcostate Next Door." *Insight on the News*, December 27, 1999: 20.

Ward, Peter M., and Victoria E. Rodríguez. *New Federalism and State Government in Mexico: "Bringing the States Back In."* With Enrique Cabrero Mendoza. Lyndon B. Johnson School of Public Affairs U.S.-Mexican Policy Studies Program. Policy Report no. 9. Austin: The University of Texas at Austin, 1999.

Wattenberg, Martin P. *The Decline of American Political Parties, 1952–1988*. Cambridge, Mass.: Harvard University Press, 1990.

Weber, Max. *From Max Weber: Essays in Sociology*. Trans. H. H. Gerth. New York: Oxford University Press, 1958.

Weldon, Jeffrey A. *The Fall 2003 Term of the Mexican Congress*. Mexican Congressional Report Series, CSIS Mexico Project. Washington, D.C.: Center for Strategic and International Studies, Fall 2003.

———. *The Spring 2003 Term of the Mexican Congress*. Mexican Congressional Report Series, CSIS Mexico Project. Washington, D.C.: Center for Strategic and International Studies, Spring 2003. Available at www.csis.org/americas/mexico/WeldonSpring2003.pdf.

———. *The Fall 2002 Term of the Mexican Congress*. Mexican Congressional Report Series, CSIS Mexico Project. Washington, D.C.: Center for Strategic and International Studies, Fall 2002.

———. *The Spring 2002 Term of the Mexican Congress*. Mexican Congressional Report Series, CSIS Mexico Project. Washington, D.C.: Center for Strategic and International Studies, Spring 2002.

———. "Executive-Legislative Relations in Mexico in the 1990*s*." In *Dilemmas of Change in Mexican Politics*, ed. Kevin J. Middlebrook. La Jolla, Calif.: Center for U.S.-Mexican Studies, University of California, San Diego, 1999.

Wilkie, James W., and Edna Monzon de Wilkie. *México Visto en el Siglo XX: Entrevistas con Manuel Gómez Morin*. Mexico City: Editorial Jus, 1978.

Wilson, Frank. "The Sources of Party Change: The Social Democratic Parties of Britain, France, Germany, and Spain." In *How Parties Work: Perspectives from Within*, ed. Kay Lawson. Westport: Praeger, 1994.

Womack, John. *Zapata and the Mexican Revolution*. New York: Alfred A. Knopf, 1968.

"Yucatán, un Rebaño Sumiso." *La Nación,* August 16, 1969: 16–18.

Zárate, Arturo, Lucero Ramírez, Jorge Herrera, and José Luis Flores. "Sospecha FLO de viajes de Fox a EU." *El Universal,* May 6, 2000, sec. Primera: 1.

Zárate Vite, Arturo. "'Hay algo' en relación con Roberto Madrazo, afirma Monreal Avila." *El Universal,* October 8, 1999, sec. Nación: 10.

Selected Interviews

Abreu, Xavier. PAN-CDM, Committee Member, Mérida, Yuc. Mérida, Yuc. August 4, 1997.

Alcantara Soria, Juan Miguel. PAN State Legislator, Guanajuato. Guanajuato, Gto. May 15, 1997.

Álvarez, Luis H. PAN Senator. Mexico City. May 27, 1997.

Arce, Carlos. Director of Asociación de Municipios Mexicanos, A.C. (AMMAC). León, Gto. March 21, 1997.

Camarillo, Refugio. PAN Candidate, State Legislature, Guanajuato. León, Gto. May 5, 1997.

Cárdona, Cuauhtémoc. PAN-CEN, Director of Acción Electoral. Mexico City, March 4, 1999.

Castellanos, Hector. PAN-CDM, Party President. Tijuana, B.C. April 19, 1998.

Castillo Peraza, Carlos. Former-PAN President, resigned from party. Mexico City. July 16, 1998.

Centeno Castro, Nabor. Former-CDM President, León, Gto. León, Gto. May 8, 1997.

Cevallos, Rosa "Luna." PAN-CDM, Committee Member, Mérida, Yuc. Mérida, Yuc. August 26, 1997.

Cicero, Roger. PAN State Legislator, Yucatán. Mérida, Yuc. August 7–8, 1997.

Cifuentes, Alberto. PAN Activist, CDM, León, Gto. León, Gto. June 20, 1997.

Corella, Norberto. PAN Senator. Mexico City. July 8, 1998.

Correa Mena, Luis, PAN-CEN, Director Acción Gubernamental, CEN. Mexico City. February 17, 1997.

de la Peña Jimenez O'Farril, Karla. PAN-CEN, Registro de Miembros. Mexico City. April 25, 1997.
Del Palacio, Jesus. PAN-CDM Party President. Ensenada, B.C. September 25, 1996.
Echegaray, Enrique. PAN State Legislator, Assembly President. Ensenada, B.C. October 14, 1996.
Fox Quesada, Vicente. PAN Governor, Guanajuato. Guanajuato, Gto. June 23, 1997.
Fuentes Alcocer, Manuel. PAN-CDM, Committee Member, Mérida, Yucatán. Mérida, Yuc. August 5, 1997.
Góngora Paz, José. Former PAN Member. Mérida, Yuc. August 28, 1997.
González Alcocer, Alejandro, and Rosalva Magallón. PAN-CDM Candidate for Party President, Tijuana. Tijuana, B.C. July 22, 1998.
Gutiérrez Machado, Miguel. PAN CDM, Party President. Mérida, Yuc. July 23, 1997.
Hernández Jaime, Gabriel. PAN CDM, Party President. León, Gto. June 24, 1997.
Jasso Farias, Juan Diego. PAN Adviser, State Legislature. Guanajuato, Gto. May 15, 1997.
Lozano Padilla, José Luis. PAN Member. León, Gto. May 21, 1997.
Martín Huerta, Ramon. PAN State Interior Secretary, Guanajuato. Guanajuato, Gto. May 7, 1997.
Martínez, Mario. PAN Mayoral Adviser. Tijuana, B.C. March 19, 1998.
Martínez, Rafaela. PAN Member. Tijuana, B.C. February 16, 1998.
Martínez Pérez, Eliseo. Former-Mayor, León Gto. León, Gto. May 28, 1997.
Medina Plascencia, Carlos. Former-PAN Governor, Guanajuato. León, Gto. August 27, 1997.
Mena, Sarita. Wife of Luis Correa Racho. Mérida, Yuc. August 7, 1997.
Obregón Padilla, Antonio. PAN Member. León, Gto. April 8, 1997.
Oliva, Juan Manuel. PAN-CDE Party President, Guanajuato. León, Gto. May 26, 1997.
Ortega, Luís. PAN Member. León, Gto. August 9, 1998.
Osuna Jaime, Hector. PAN Candidate for Senator, Baja California. Tijuana, B.C. July 1, 1998.
Patrón, Patricio. Mayor, Mérida, Yucatán. Mérida, Yuc. July 17, 1997.
Payán Cervera, Ana Rosa. PAN-CDE Party President, Yucatán. Mérida, Yuc. July 15, 1997.
Poot Campos, Joaquin. PAN State Legislator. Mérida, Yuc. August 6, 1997.
Quirós, Luís. PAN Mayor, León, Guanajuato. León, Gto. June 3–5, 1997.
Ruffo Appel, Ernesto. Former-PAN Governor, Baja California. Tijuana, B.C. October 27, 1998.
Sanchez, Laura. PAN Member. Tijuana, B.C. January 1999.
Segura Dorantes, Miguel. PAN Federal Deputy. León, Gto. May 3, 1997.
Villegas, Elias. PAN-CDE Committee Member. León, Gto. May 21, 1997.
Závala, Beatrice. PAN Plurinominal Congressional Candidate. Mérida, Yuc. August 19, 1998.

Index

About the Book

Mexico's presidential elections in July 2000 brought victory to National Action Party (PAN) candidate Vicente Fox—and also the hope of democratic change after decades of single-party rule. Tracing the key themes and dynamics of a century of political development in Mexico, David Shirk explores the evolution of the party that ultimately became the vehicle for Fox's success.

Shirk examines the factors that constrained democracy in postrevolutionary Mexico, as well as the protracted democratic transition that occurred over the last few decades. In the process, he shows that Fox's victory was also the triumph of a new Mexican politics in which voters, candidates, money, and media-driven campaigns—not party leaders or machines—drive political competition. Indeed, Fox's ability to bring democratic change to Mexico, Shirk demonstrates, has been fundamentally constrained by the very trends that brought him to power—with enormous implications for Mexico's political present and future.

David A. Shirk is director of the Trans-Border Institute and assistant professor of political science at the University of San Diego.